SOMETHING WONDERFUL RIGHT AWAY

SOMETHING WONDERFUL RIGHT AWAY

JEFFREY SWEET

New Foreword by the Author

LIMELIGHT EDITIONS

First Limelight Edition May 1987

Copyright © 1978 by Jeffrey Sweet
Foreword Copyright © 1986 by Jeffrey Sweet

All rights reserved under international and Pan-American Copyright
Conventions. Published in the United States by Proscenium Publishers
Inc., New York and simultaneously in Canada by Fitzhenry & White-
side, Limited, Toronto.

Library of Congress Cataloging-in-Publication Data
Something wonderful right away.
    Reprint. Originally published: New York :
Avon Books, c1978.
    1. Second City (Theater company) 2. Compass
Players. 3. Entertainers—United States—
Interviews. 4. Improvisation (Acting)
I. Sweet, Jeffrey, 1950– .
PN2277.C42S46 1987   792'.09773'11   86-27319
ISBN 0-87910-073-7

Contents

For My Parents

Foreword to the Limelight Edition

Part of my purpose in writing this book was to draw attention to the profound influence Second City has had on American entertainment. If anything, that influence has grown stronger in the intervening nine years.

At the time this book first saw print, *Saturday Night Live* was in its early days. Many of the members of that show's original and subsequent casts and the writers who supported them were from Second City, among them Dan Aykroyd, John Belushi, Gilda Radner, Bill Murray, Jim Belushi, Brian Doyle-Murray, Mary Gross, Tim Kazurinsky, Robin Duke, Martin Short, Tony Rosato, Rob Riley, and Nate Herman. Soon after, Second City put together its own series, *SCTV* (*"SC"* standing, of course, for the mother theatre), which featured the talents of alumni John Candy, Joe Flaherty, Catherine O'Hara, Eugene Levy, Andrea Martin, Harold Ramis, Martin Short (before joining *Saturday Night Live*) and Dave Thomas. (Rick Moranis appeared on *SCTV* without having appeared regularly on the Second City stage). These two series proved to be enormously successful and many of the people involved in them went on to write, direct, and/or star in other notable productions, among them such films as *National Lampoon's Animal House, Caddyshack, Splash!, The Blues Brothers, 1941, Trading Places, National Lampoon's Summer Vacation, Back to School, About Last Night . . ., ¡Three Amigos!, Meatballs, Stripes, Tootsie, Heartburn, Summer Rental, Volunteers, Strange Brew, Club Paradise,* and the phenomenally successful *Ghostbusters.* In addition, there was a non-stop stream of TV projects both for broadcast and cable outlets.

The fact that much of the talent behind these enterprises came from a common background did not go unnoticed by the entertainment industry. It became common practice for producers to trek to Chicago and Toronto to pan for performing gold, and a resumé boasting Second City experience made attractive performers even more attractive. Among the other alumni whose faces became familiar through television were David Rasche *(Sledge Hammer),* Betty Thomas *(Hill Street Blues),* Shelley Long and George Wendt *(Cheers!),* Miriam Flynn *(Erma),* Steve Kampmann *(The Newhart Show)* and Fred Willard *(Fernwood Tonight).* Many of the projects mentioned above (as well as others) also employed the talents of writers from Second City such as Will Porter, Eugenie Ross-Leming, Tino Insana, and

Mert Rich. In addition, some alumni became prominent in other arenas. The comedy team of John Monteith and Suzanne Rand followed the pattern Nichols and May established more than twenty years before, moving from nightclubs to Broadway, and Aaron Freeman became a popular standup comedian specializing in Chicago politics (his *Star Wars*-style parody of Mayor Harold Washington's battles with the Chicago City Council added the phrase "Council Wars" to the lexicon of Chicago headline writers).

Nor has the pre-*Saturday Night Live* gang whose ranks form the bulk of the *dramatis personnae* of this book been underemployed. Alan Alda's success as star, writer and director on TV's *M*A*S*H* has been augmented by such projects as *The Seduction of Joe Tynan* (playing opposite Barbara Harris), *Same Time, Next Year* and *The Four Seasons.* Valerie Harper is again the star of a TV series, *Valerie.* Paul Mazursky has directed *Down and Out in Beverly Hills* and *Moscow on the Hudson.* Robert Klein was nominated for a Tony for his performance on Broadway in *They're Playing Our Song* and continues to pack concert halls with shows which subsequently are adapted for HBO. David Steinberg makes frequent appearances on *The Tonight Show,* has directed features and writes, produces, and directs for television. Joan Rivers presides over her own talk show. Alan Arkin alternates acting projects (such as *The In-Laws* and *The Defection of Simas Kudirka*) with directing projects (including a hit revival of *Room Service* featuring several Second City friends). Jerry Stiller starred on Broadway in *Hurlyburly,* his wife Anne Meara won an Emmy as a regular on *Archie Bunker's Place,* and the two of them continue to create and perform some of radio's most effective commercials. Melinda Dillon was twice nominated for an Oscar (for *Close Encounters of the Third Kind* and *Absence of Malice*). Richard Libertini did standout work in *The In-Laws* and *All of Me.* Elaine May co-wrote *Heaven Can Wait* and *Tootsie* and, at this writing, is directing Dustin Hoffman and Warren Beatty in *Ishtar.* And Mike Nichols has maintained his extraordinary record as a director and producer for stage and film with such successes as *Silkwood, Hurlyburly, The Real Thing, My One and Only,* and *Social Security.*

Paul Sills, too, has continued to pursue his vision of what the stage can be. In Los Angeles, he built a modest space in East Hollywood and, under the name *Sills and Company,* assembled a company to play the theater games his mother Viola Spolin had begun developing some fifty years before. Among the friends and colleagues from Second City and other improvisational companies who came to play were Lewis Arquette, Shelley Berman, John Brent, Severn Darden, MacIntyre Dixon, Paul Dooley, Miriam Flynn, Gary Goodrow, Gerrit Graham, Valerie Harper, Tino Insana, Mina Kolb, Maggie Roswell, Anne Ryerson, Paul Sand, Richard Schaal, Avery Schreiber, and Sills's daughter Rachel. Several of these came east with Sills in 1986 for a critically-acclaimed five-month run off-Broadway.

Time has also removed faces from the scene. John Belushi died in 1982. Second City set up a scholarship fund in his memory. Howard Alk, one of the original producers of Second City and a player with both that company and the Compass, died in 1984. John Brent died in 1985; Del Close, his partner on the classic "How to Speak Hip" record, participated in a memorial held at the Chicago theatre.

Second City itself has changed leadership. Following a smashing three-day 25th anniversary reunion in December 1984, Bernard Sahlins sold his interest to the producer of the Toronto company, Andrew Alexander. Joyce Sloane was promoted to full co-producer of the Chicago company, where Sahlins has moved from employer to employee, collecting a salary as resident director. At this writing, Alexander and Harold Ramis are hoping to join forces on a Los Angeles Second City which would also serve as a production company for film and television projects.

Whatever the ventures into other media, the heart of Second City has been and will continue to be in what happens onstage when a group of talented young performers use their wit and insight to transform the serious concerns of contemporary life into comedy. If Second City has become a cultural icon, its members have not abandoned the iconoclastic high spirits which were its genesis more than a quarter of a century ago.

Jeffrey Sweet
October, 1986

Preface

This book started with my realization four or five years ago that a large number of the people whose work in theater and film I admired were graduates of one or more of four improvisational theater companies—The Compass Players, The Second City, The Premise, and The Committee. I had a hunch there was a connection between their common background and their accomplishments and decided to try to find out what it was. Why does having performed with an improvisational comedy troupe seem to increase one's chances of artistic and commercial achievement?

The original idea was to interview the ten or twelve best-known alumni about their involvement with these troupes, which would likely produce a short, entertaining book with some laughs, some nostalgia, and, I hoped, some insight into the business of making theater.

The project, happily, began to take its own head, leading me along with it. After the first few interviews, I realized that there was more in the subject than humorous anecdotes and shoptalk. I took a second look at what I was doing and redefined my objectives. This has resulted in a considerably larger book. Regretfully, as the material accumulated and deepened, in order to do it justice it was necessary to narrow the scope and concentrate on only

The Compass and The Second City. I hope to deal with The Premise and The Committee in a future project.

Basically, then, this book is about The Compass Players and The Second City, two troupes of performers who created humorous material improvisationally. It is about the individuals who linked their fortunes with these troupes, and how working with them affected their lives. It is about the community formed by the coming together of these individuals, and the ties which existed and continue to exist among them even after they left for other work. It is about the larger community in which they lived and for which they played. It is about the social forces which helped shape their personal and professional lives and which they transformed into entertainment on the stage.

The text is made up largely of edited transcripts of conversational interviews taped over a period of three and a half years—from February 1974 to July 1977. The interviews are presented roughly in the order in which the subjects made their first significant contributions to either The Compass or The Second City. As the conversations were not taped in the order in which they are presented, on more than one occasion the reader is likely to find in one conversation references to another which was recorded earlier but is printed further on in the book. For example, in Barbara Harris's chapter, I refer to Mike Nichols's comment that, sometimes, when a scene was really terrible at The Compass, the players would literally jump into Lake Michigan. I talked to Nichols before I talked to Harris, but because he arrived at The Compass after she did, his chapter appears after hers.

A few chapters, such as the one on Paul Sills, are the product of two or more sessions separated by days, months, or even a year or more. It should be apparent when this is the case, or when someone in addition to the interview subject was present during a conversation and contributed to it. Thus, Roger Bowen and Eugene Troobnick pop up in the middle of Severn Darden's chapter.

I make no claim to impartiality regarding the people appearing in this book. I would not have chosen to interview any of these specific individuals did I not respect and admire their work. I also wish to emphasize that all were most gracious during our taping sessions and many were generous in helping me uncover rare tapes, photographs, and documents, as well as often opening doors to other people.

Obviously, I cannot agree with everything everyone says in this book. If I did, I would be a certifiable schizophrenic. Much is included, in fact, with which I sharply disagree. However, I have soft-pedaled my own opinions somewhat throughout as I felt my responsibility was to help each interviewee express as clearly and concisely as possible what he or she wished to say about his/her experience with improvisational theater and its effect on subsequent work. Though the individual chapters are not meant to be personality pieces primarily, inevitably, I think, much of these people's personalities shines through. Naturally, the work one chooses and one's attitude toward it will reveal something of one's character.

As might be expected, the community portrayed here is by no means one big harmonious bowl of good will. Undeniably, certain personality clashes developed at The Compass and The Second City, and, to the extent to which I think they are relevant to the work the companies did, I have incorporated mention of them.

Since it was my intention originally to provide a *Rashomon*-like picture of the Compass-Second City community and its history, I regret the omission of certain significant people's perspectives. Viola Spolin and I simply could not figure out a mutually agreeable way of directly representing her in the book. Peter Boyle and I kept missing connections. Zohra Lampert, John Belushi, Howard Alk, and Bill Mathieu are others I would have liked to include. And Elaine May . . . damn, I wish Elaine May were in this book! We had dinner one night, over which she made one intriguing observation after another. Unfortunately, she placed all quite firmly off-the-record. She indicated she would be willing to write answers to written questions, but I gather she never found the time or the inclination to respond to the questions I sent. I think her absence leaves a great gap in this project. Maybe someday. . . .

History

In the summer of 1955, in a storefront next door to a bar in Chicago's Hyde Park, a group of young people opened a theater—a theater unlike any other in Chicago or, for that matter, the rest of the world.

What distinguished this company from other companies was the process by which a production was put together. Traditionally, a theater presents a cast which, under the guidance of a director, brings to life a playwright's script. These young Chicagoans, however, had disposed of the playwright's services. The words they spoke were their own and they changed from night to night. They called themselves The Compass, and the work they did and the way they went about it proved to be a watershed development in the history of the theater.

The Compass was based on a concept producer David Shepherd borrowed from the *commedia dell'arte*, a form of theater which flourished in Renaissance Europe, particularly in Italy. A *commedia* troupe was a company of comic actors who traveled from town to town giving shows. They used no formal script. Instead, the cast worked from a scenario—a handful of pages tacked up backstage on which was outlined the plot of a piece to be performed. The stuff of a typical scenario was highly farcical in nature, filled with mistaken identities, disguises, con games, and slapstick. The actor would check the scenario to familiarize himself with the timing of his entrances and exits and how he would function in the action. But within these boundaries, he had a great deal of freedom. All his dialogue was improvised, so if the audience were responsive, he had the license to stay onstage and extend his bit for as long as he felt comfortable. Conversely, if the audience were cold, he would merely do what the plot required and make a speedy exit.

A *commedia* troupe usually had several scenarios in its repertoire. The cast of characters was roughly the same from one to the next, and the same person would play the same role from one production to another. If an actor played the lecherous miser Pantalone in one scenario, he played him in every scenario.

Commedia productions were not limited to outright buffoonery. They also had a satiric edge, burlesquing the venality, hypocrisy, cowardice, and stupidity of such traditional authority figures as doctors, merchants, and military officers. In their desire to connect with each particular audience, the cast would ad-lib topical references to local figures and issues. The *commedia* was popular theater in the truest sense. (It also had a profound effect on dramatic literature. A comparison of *A Comedy of Errors* and *The Miser* with contemporaneous *commedia* scenarios testifies to the debt Shakespeare and Molière owed this form of theater. In fact, Molière once shared a theater with a *commedia* troupe.)

It was David Shepherd's idea to create a contemporary version of the *commedia,* a popular theater which, working improvisationally from scenarios, would deal in comic terms with present-day society. The scenario plays would be performed in a setting incorporating elements of the political cabaret theaters such as those in which Bertolt Brecht and Kurt Weill had made their marks in Weimar Germany. Shepherd took this hybrid concept of a modern *commedia* in a cabaret to a friend, a young Chicago director named Paul Sills.

Sills had been exposed to the theater from childhood. His mother, Viola Spolin, was employed as a drama supervisor on the Recreational Project with the Works Progress Administration, and, in his teens, he frequently assisted her.

Spolin had developed a unique approach to the theater, deeply influenced by her training as a recreational director under Neva Boyd in Chicago in the mid-1920s. At the heart of Boyd's work was an awareness of the constructive potential of play. Boyd led inner-city and immigrants' children in traditional games to help them adjust to the society in which they lived. Spolin's contribution was to create new games designed to encourage creativity, making play the catalyst for self-expression and self-realization. They were not games in the sense that they were competitive and were won or lost, but were a means of dealing with theater problems in a playful spirit.

Spolin's rationale was that if you put someone onstage (particularly a child, since she worked most frequently with children) and tell him to "act," he will feel inhibited and self-conscious, but if you transform the situation into a game, the actor, in concentrating his energies on playing the game, will lose his self-consciousness and perform naturally and spontaneously. The trick for the director was to phrase the rules of a game in such a way that playing it would solve a theater problem organically and uncoercively, without having to say "Do this" and "Do that." Rather than telling the performer specifically how to behave, Spolin tried to set up circumstances in which he would arrive at the right choice himself. Her belief was that an actor will absorb a lesson more readily if it is learned through his own experience than if it is spelled out by someone else.

For example, one day in rehearsal with teenagers, Spolin found that the actors playing a romantic scene were shy about touching each other. Instead of saying "Take her hand on that line" or "Touch his shoulder before saying that," she invented a game called "Contact." The rule of "Contact" is that for every line he delivers, the actor must make physical contact with the actor to whom the line is addressed in a way consistent with the sense of the scene. With this objective, the young performers soon forgot their shyness and focused their attention on meeting the challenge of the game. In the course of playing, not only were a number of moments discovered which were retained for public performance, but also a good deal of subtext was revealed, helping the performers to better understand their characters and the play as a whole.

Spolin developed many of her games as the need arose while working with the WPA, with which she became associated in 1938. At the same time the job involved her in training and supervising people to run neighborhood-based theater-oriented projects, she ran her own group, which included both children and adults. In the Chicago *Daily News* of May 26, 1939, Howard Vincent O'Brien published the following account of a performance this group gave:

I certainly saw something! There were about 150 people in the cast—Italians, Greeks, Mexicans, Negroes, and I don't know what other racial strains. They were of all ages and of both sexes.

What they were doing was not exactly a "play." It was perhaps what is called in the trade a revue. But its form doesn't matter. The important thing about it was that it was conceived, written and played by the people themselves. It was a strictly amateur affair. It was an effort to express not what somebody might like to see and hear but what the actors and playwrights and directors thought and felt.

Few will ever see this play; and I doubt if any professional critic will even hear of it. Yet for importance I think it is worth about a dozen Broadway successes rolled into one.

The opening blackout, the night I was there, was the interior of a poor man's home. (You knew it was this, not from the scenery—because there wasn't any—but from what the people said.) There was a man, reading the want ads, and telling his wife how hard it was to get a job. Remember, these are not "actors." They didn't even have "lines." Why should they? All they had to do was talk as they did in their home. Looking for a job wasn't an imagined situation for them. It was the grimmest of realities.

Into this scene comes a politician, with $5 and a basket of food. "Come and see me after the election," he says cheerily. "I'll fix you up. You know I'm your friend. Have a cigar."

Just as the man is taking the cigar, his son comes in

and knocks it out of his hand. "Don't take anything from this politician," he says. "We're not selling America for a cigar!"

The captions of a photo essay from the Chicago *Sunday Times* of September 22, 1940, provide further evidence of Spolin's work at the time: "Today's news is tomorrow's play," "No cues and never in need of a rehearsal," and "Because no play is ever written, the next performance of 'Air Raid' might be entirely different."

In 1946, Viola Spolin left Chicago for Los Angeles (where she lives today) and formed the Young Actors Company, a repertory theater of youngsters she guided till 1955, as she continued to evolve new games.

Paul Sills truly grew up with the games. He performed in children's productions directed by his mother and occasionally conducted workshops for her. Still, he had not decided on a career in the theater when he enrolled at the University of Chicago in 1948.

Also at the University of Chicago at roughly the same time as Sills were Roger Bowen, Edward Asner, Zohra Lampert, Fritz Weaver, Mike Nichols, Eugene Troobnick, Sheldon Patinkin, Bill Alton, Anthony (then James) Holland, Tresa Hughes, Andrew Duncan, Severn Darden, and Omar Shapli, seeking degrees in English, history, psychology, and what-have-you. The campus was also the stomping ground of others such as Shepherd and Elaine May, who got involved in university activities and sometimes sat in on classes without ever having gone through the tiresome formality of enrolling.

It might seem curious that a university with no drama school was a hotbed of so much dramatic talent, but a look at the way the University of Chicago was run reveals how congenial an environment it provided for the theatrically inclined. Under the leadership of Robert Maynard Hutchins, chancellor of the U. of C. from 1945 to 1951, the school was, even by today's standards, remarkably liberal: Anyone who could pass the entrance exams could enroll, no matter how young (Patinkin was fifteen when he entered); classroom attendance was not required; and the grade received in a course was dependent on one final (grueling) comprehensive exam given at the end of the year. Since there was no required busywork, the students had time to engage in other pursuits. One popular extracurricular venture was the University Theatre, a group which produced plays on campus.

Sills initially got involved with the University Theatre as an actor. In 1951, he helped found another group called "Tonight at 8:30," with which he made his directorial debut, staging Lorca's *The Shoemaker's Prodigious Wife.* (Mike Nichols and Omar Shapli also directed their first productions with this company.) Then he returned to the University Theatre; the last show he directed on campus was a production of Brecht's *The Caucasian Chalk Circle* in the spring of 1953.

In the meantime, Sills and Shepherd had become friends and, with Eugene Troobnick, decided to start a professional repertory theater. (Bernard Sahlins, another U. of C. alumnus, later took over Troobnick's duties as coproducer.) They called it the Playwrights Theatre Club. Housed in a 125-seat theater they constructed in what had previously been a Chinese restaurant at 1560 North La Salle Street, Playwrights' first production, a restaging of *Chalk Circle,* opened on June 23, 1953. Working for next to nothing (its first year it was a non-Equity company), the troupe produced twenty-four plays within the next two years, audaciously taking on classics and challenging modern plays on two-week rehearsal schedules. In addition to previously produced plays, they presented a few works by members of the company—after all, it *was* called *Playwrights* Theatre Club—such as Sills's *The Coming of Bildad,* Shepherd's *The Fields of Malfi* (a modern adaptation of John Webster's *The Duchess of Malfi*), and Elaine May's version of *Rumpelstiltskin* (part of Playwrights' children's theater program).

Sills was the group's most prolific director, but Shepherd, May, and others also staged plays. A look at the programs for some of the productions gives an indication of the extraordinary talents in germination. For example, the performers in T. S. Eliot's *Murder in the Cathedral* (directed by Marvin Peisner, yet another U. of C. alumnus) included Edward Asner as Thomas Becket, supported by Sills, May, Troobnick, and Lampert. During Playwrights' life, others joined the group, notably Barbara Harris and a

composer-harpist named Tom O'Horgan, who would later
become a director and stage *Hair, Lenny,* and *Jesus Christ,
Superstar* on Broadway. The beginning of the end of Playwrights came in February 1955, when the fire department
closed them out of the 200-seat theater at Dearborn and
Division which they had converted from a photographer's
studio the previous spring. After the closing, various members of the group presented isolated productions in various
locations before the enterprise totally expired in the fall.

David Shepherd had begun to be disenchanted with
Playwrights well before its demise. On May 25, 1954—just
after Playwrights' first anniversary—he wrote in his journal:

> In a year and a half I have helped build a miserable
> self-centered arts club which talks over the heads of
> its bourgeois members at the same time it licks their
> feet for support. . . . In order for theater to be an
> institution, its audience must love and hate it as they
> love and hate the church and the President. Our fables
> must present not Wozzeck but the Chicago draftee, not
> the Azdak but lawyer Jenkins, not Volpone but Alder-
> man Bauler. . . . For a brief moment last fall, Charley
> Jacobs [another U. of C. veteran involved in the op-
> eration of Playwrights] and Paul and I saw that the
> goal of our theater should be a riot in the audience.
> How could we forget it?

Shepherd began formulating plans for a new venture. His
original idea was to put together a troupe which would play
in the stockyards of Chicago or the steel mills of Gary,
Indiana. Intensely committed to the idea of popular theater
in the strictest sense, he hoped his company would perform
before audiences of workers who did not ordinarily see
plays. The work was to be relevant to the concerns of the
"proletariat," reflect their problems, help give them a sense
of class identity, and arouse them to the inequities of the
system. He took his proposal to the stockyards and steel
mills, but the proletariat weren't interested, so Shepherd
started thinking about setting up his brainchild as a cabaret
theater in Chicago.

In an interview in the January 1955 issue of *Chicago,*

Shepherd discussed his hopes for the company he had decided to call The Compass:

> We'll put on a theater that everybody is interested in and we'll write better plays. Actually, these two reforms are the same. We can't do one without the other. The man in the street obviously isn't interested in the present theater. And we won't be able to get writers to break the traditional style unless we have them write for the man in the street. . . .
>
> Our top price will be less than a dollar and the house will drink and smoke during the performance. We'll have to keep our scripts short so we can give two shows a night. We want to break the three-act form. Some people might think this will become either a night club or a poor imitation of the movies. But we think the theater will benefit from this move into new surroundings, that the acting will improve and the plays will become more exciting, more truly theatrical.
>
> We won't use any sets or special lighting or curtains, and the casts will be small. We'll need strong stories with a lot of action in them—songs, fights, games and orations. We'll encourage pantomime and an intensity the stage hasn't known since Ibsen. We know that if we try to present the world on our stage with ten actors and no set, we run the risk of compressing, selecting and bridging too much too fast. But we think poetry is achieved not by saying vague things in an unreal manner but by economy and intensity. Poetry can't appear overnight at The Compass because it's been dead in us a long time, but a certain excitement can—an excitement we still get from speeches, songs, jokes, sales talks and all the other verbal ornaments that the parlor play is too respectable to admit. . . .
>
> As we develop a new kind of play and audience, we may have to develop an entirely new style of acting.

Though he talked about "writers" and "scripts," Shepherd's objective was to form a company which would improvise from scenarios. He turned to Sills and his other Playwrights friends with the idea, but initially they were not interested. Not one to give up, he explained his concept to

Roger Bowen, a graduate student at—where else?—the University of Chicago.

On May 14 and 15, University Theatre presented a bill of one-acts in the Reynolds Club Theater under the familiar heading, "Tonight at 8:30." The bill included productions of *Chee-Chee* by Luigi Pirandello and *Bedtime Story* by Sean O'Casey, but of greater interest were the two companion pieces, a pair of scenario-plays directed by David Shepherd. The runaway success of the program was *Enterprise,* from a scenario by Roger Bowen, and with a cast including Bowen, Leo Stodolsky, Sid Lazard, Larry Zerkel, Ned Gaylin, Jeri Swee, Omar Shapli, Chessie Plesofsky, and Gerald Siegel. Less successful was Shepherd's second effort, *An Exam Play,* which was improvised by Loretta Deron, Elizabeth Mullikan, Duchess Loughron, and Laurie Richardson from their own scenario. Shepherd again approached Sills, possibly with a tape recording of a performance of *Enterprise,* and this time Sills was sufficiently impressed to agree to take a crack at Shepherd's concept.

Viola Spolin was in town to direct Sean O'Casey's *Juno and the Paycock* for Playwrights. Shepherd prevailed upon her to extend her stay and help train a company capable of implementing his ideas. For roughly a month, she and Sills ran workshops, using her theater games to develop improvisational skills. Then she returned home to Los Angeles (in fact, she never saw The Compass Players in performance) and Sills carried on without her.* Out of the seventy or eighty people who participated in these workshops came the pool of twenty or so from which The Compass initially drew.

After scouring Chicago for a location, Shepherd entered into an agreement with Freddie Wranovics, a bartender at Jimmy's, a popular off-campus watering hole. Wranovics

---

* Viola Spolin would return to Chicago in 1959 to run workshops for The Second City actors. She remained there for several years, continuing to devise games in response to the company's needs. In 1963, her book, *Improvisation for the Theater,* was published by the Northwestern University Press. Packed with two hundred theater games, it is generally acknowledged to be a classic theater text and has gone through more than a dozen printings. She still runs workshops today.

was interested in opening a bar of his own, and Shepherd convinced him that his new troupe would attract customers. Consequently, the Hi-Hat, a bar at 1152 East 55 Street (a couple of doors down from Jimmy's), was renamed The Compass, and a hole was knocked out of a side wall, providing access to the storefront next door. There Shepherd and company built a theater consisting of a few rows of tables and chairs accommodating ninety in front of a small stage. The idea was that the audience would either buy drinks at the bar and carry them in for the show or purchase them from performers doubling as waiters.

On July 5, 1955, The Compass Players made their debut with a production called *The Game of Hurt*, directed by Paul Sills from his own scenario, and featuring in its cast Elaine May, David Shepherd, Robert Coughlan, Loretta Chiljian, Sid Lazard, and Roger Bowen.

This was the beginning of a remarkable explosion of creative energy. Every week the group would take on a new scenario, rehearsing through the day and performing nights to packed and enthusiastic houses. Besides Sills, scenarists included other troupe members such as Shepherd, May, Bowen, and Mickey Le Glaire as well as outside contributors from the Hyde Park community. Before performing the scenario, which usually lasted from forty minutes to an hour, the troupe would present one or two short pieces plus a "Living Newspaper"—a form calling for the cast to read excerpts from the day's paper as if it were a play script, taking the parts of news-figures and employing a narrator where necessary. As if all this weren't enough, after the scenario-play the players would solicit the audience for suggestions for scenes which would then be improvised. Most of the first several scenarios were directed by Sills, with Shepherd and May staging the balance.

Captions from a photo essay on The Compass in the September 1955 issue of *Chicago* convey some sense of the troupe's activity at the time:

Five nights a week, Compass has programs beginning at 9 P.M.; weekends there are late shows too. Monday night is folk music; Tuesday is the workshop, when only audience-directed impromptus are done.
... Audience during an impromptu. The subject of

xxiv

the play, roles for the characters and the plot are all
culled by a director from shouted suggestions by the
audience. Example: someone named a theme—eutha-
nasia (a different groundling immediately clamored,
"Make it juvenile delinquency in Asia"); a three-scene
play involving a mercy killing was plotted in about 20
minutes and staged immediately by four men and a
woman.

. . . Shepherd—producer, scenario-writer, actor, waiter—pulls story out of audience. Plots range from
he-she situations to philosophical dilemmas such as
God's debates with Himself before He decided upon
the creation of the world. Stage, behind Shepherd,
consists of colored, moving panels.

. . . In dialog, the only taboo is cliché. Sometimes
uncomfortably realistic, other times spontaneously
witty (Red Riding Hood: "But you don't look like my
grandmother." Wolf: "I've had a change of life."),
occasional lags are bridged by lots of action and pantomime.

. . . Actress with hastily rigged costume gives a
quick-witted interpretation to a role she can vary
whenever a good idea hits her. Actors momentarily
offstage double as waiters, serving drinks from the bar
next door.

. . . The audience is informal, spontaneous, heckling,
comes from all over town though there is a steady
clientele of Hyde Park denizens who arrive on bi-
cycles and sometimes bring box lunches. The entertainment is fast-moving and intermittent, but because it is
largely impromptu it is never twice the same. People
hate to leave, clamor for more, and the actors, who
mean to shut down at midnight, often keep it up for a
couple of extra hours.

. . . Overflow crowd on the sidewalk in front. In the
bar . . . are classical music over a hi-fi set, a bookshelf
of reference works and current reading and a bartender who recites poetry. Patrons can get a brochure
on how to write a play.

. . . Paul Sills, director, says, "Compass, if carried to
its logical conclusion, is a sort of 'do it yourself'
movement. I'd like to see neighborhoods all over the

city form groups like this. It's a search for a community."

As if to reinforce Sills's statement, the *Chicago Maroon,* the University of Chicago newspaper, announced:

Story tellers, actors, singers, musicians, poets, and debaters and other persons who are interested in entertainment and want to help should come and speak to the appropriate personnel at The Compass.

The Compass's success prompted Shepherd to move it in October to larger quarters in the Dock, a Hyde Park nightclub at 6473 South Lake Park, which converted part of its space into a cabaret with room for 140 patrons.

Other developments were simultaneously reshaping The Compass. In the early fall, Sills, accompanied by his then-wife, Barbara Harris, had gone on a Fulbright grant to England, where, in Bristol, he studied Shakespeare and led improvisational workshops; this was followed by a spell of observing East Germany's Berliner Ensemble. To fill his considerable shoes, Shepherd at different junctures in the balance of the company's history brought in other directors: Mark Gordon, Larry Arrick, and Walter Beakel. (After their trip abroad, Sills and Harris returned to work with the troupe again.) Also, some of the regular players had dropped out, and Shepherd responded by importing from New York Bobbi Gordon, Severn Darden, Shelley Berman, and Mike Nichols (who had left the university some time before and, after a short stay with Playwrights, had headed east to study with Lee Strasberg and try to make it as an actor).

Other key changes were shifts in both the performance of the material and the shape of the material itself. In the beginning weeks, The Compass had presented a new production every week. As time passed, the cast found the intense rehearsal schedule a strain and began extending the runs of the scenario-plays. Then the scenario structure began to go by the wayside as the cast was drawn more and more to shorter pieces. (The scenario structure was not abandoned altogether. Throughout the remainder of the Chicago Compass's existence, scenario-plays sprang up from troupe called Third City. It was unable to duplicate the success of its predecessor and closed shortly. Mazursky and Tucker made a few other similar attempts, then shifted their interests to television and film, where they have been very successful, indeed.

The Broadway engagement, which opened at the Royale Theater on September 26, 1961, under the title *From The Second City*, was the first commercial setback The Second City troupe encountered. Max Liebman reportedly was nervous about allowing the company to chance improvisations in front of the critics, so the company performed only set material and received no opportunity to show off the facility for which they had become famous. Also, the proscenium stage of the Royale seemed inappropriately formal for entertainment which had been nurtured in an intimate atmosphere with the audience sitting at tables, drinking cocktails and coffee. The critics' notices were divided pretty evenly between yeas and nays, and the show folded after a modest run. It immediately reopened on January 10, 1962, in the more suitable environment of a Greenwich Village nightclub called the Square East, owned by Charles Rubin. The Second City was to appear there almost continually for the next four and a half years, finally closing in May 1966. Most of the people who worked there were veterans of the Chicago branch. Among the few exceptions were Alan Alda, Paul Dooley, Barbara Dana, and Bob Dishy. Besides Sills, the New York directors included Sheldon Patinkin, Bob Dishy, Alan Myerson, and Larry Arrick. The last two had major ideological disputes with Sills, which were contributing factors to their departures. Myerson left to open an improvisational company of his own called The Committee, which became as much of an institution in San Francisco as The Second City in Chicago, running from April 10, 1963, to October 1973.

Second City was not alone in bringing improvisational theater to New York. Almost a year before the Broadway engagement, Theodore J. Flicker had formed a company called The Premise at 154 Bleecker Street, six blocks away from the Square East. Flicker both directed and appeared with that group, the other performers in the original company being Joan Darling, George Segal, and Thomas Aldredge. It opened its doors on November 22, 1960, and, after an almost catastrophic start, built up a reputation and went on to run, in one form or another, till the winter of 1963–64. During its life, it additionally employed Gene Hackman, Buck Henry, Godfrey Cambridge, Diana Sands, and Al Freeman, Jr., among many others. (Dustin Hoffman also worked there for a time. He was on the kitchen staff and was eager to perform. Joan Darling remembers he gave an impressive audition, but he used language similar to that Lenny Bruce was using at the time. This language was leading to Bruce's arrests on obscenity charges. The Premise, as a result of Flicker's refusal to pay the police any money under the table, was being hassled by the law as it was. The producers were concerned that Hoffman's language might give the police another excuse to harass their theater, so Hoffman was not cast. Ironically, Hoffman later played Bruce in the film version of *Lenny*.)

Second City continued to flourish in Chicago, though Playwrights at Second City did not. The two swapped theaters, so that the improvisational troupe found itself in the bigger house, and Playwrights in the smaller. Still, Playwrights remained a losing proposition, and it died not long after the switch. Second City continued to run at 1846 North Wells until August 1967, when the group moved into its third and current Chicago home, a three-hundred-seat theater built to order at 1616 North Wells Street.

Since the days of the first company, Second City has not lacked for talent. Among those who have appeared subsequently under its banner are Zohra Lampert, Anthony Holland, Del Close, John Brent, Hamilton Camp, Joan Rivers, Bill Alton, Avery Schreiber, Jack Burns, Larry Hankin, Richard Libertini, Melinda Dillon, Richard Schaal, MacIntyre Dixon, David Steinberg, Robert Klein, Fred Willard, J. J. Barry, Judy Graubart, Peter Boyle, Martin Harvey Friedberg, Burt Heyman, and John Belushi. In addition to Sills, Patinkin, and Myerson, Michael Miller, Joe O'Flaherty, and Cyril Simon have directed, the past several years being codirected by Del Close and Bernard Sahlins.

In addition to the engagements in the cities already mentioned, Second City has paid calls to a number of others. There were three trips to London, in 1962 (when a trade was made with Peter Cook's troupe, The Establishment), in 1963, and in 1965. Toronto was a frequent host of transient companies, one of which included Valerie Harper and Linda Lavin; a resident company, reflecting the Canadian perspective, opened in Toronto in 1973 and, after an initial struggle, was transferred by Andrew Alexander to play in his cabaret complex, the Firehall, where an excellent ensemble is doing booming business. After the first New York run, Second City made two more attempts in Manhattan, one in 1968 and one in 1973, and both disappointing. In 1965, a company made a ten-week tour for the Theatre Guild, visiting Detroit, Cincinnati, Philadelphia, Cleveland, Boston, Pittsburgh, St. Louis, and New Haven; *The Oxford-Cambridge Revue* held the fort in Chicago during this expedition. In 1975, a company took up residence in a dinner theater in Pasadena for a successful nine-month engagement. And The Second City Touring Company, which was formed to give players experience before matriculating to the resident company, frequently plays dates around the country.*

Thus, what started in 1955 as backroom entertainment for an in-group on Chicago's South Side developed into a major theatrical movement. It not only made possible the establishment of a number of troupes that have entertained audiences on an international scale for more than two decades, but it has also been instrumental in encouraging and shaping the development of dozens of this generation's most gifted entertainers.

This is not what David Shepherd had in mind when he formulated his plan for a "theater for the proletariat," but, then, our beginnings rarely know our ends.

---

* From time to time, Second City has ventured into other media with varying success. *The Monitors*, a satiric science-fiction feature movie coproduced with Bell & Howell in 1968, was an unmitigated fiasco. On the other hand, a series of comic documentaries produced for Granada Television in England under the title *Second City Reports* was very well received, as were most of the troupe's appearances on American television.

Also worth noting was another Second City attempt to sponsor legitimate theater. In 1967, The Second City Repertory Theatre at the Harper—a theater in the Hyde Park area of Chicago—presented two plays, Norman Mailer's *The Deer Park* (directed by Sheldon Patinkin) and Chekhov's *The Cherry Orchard* (directed by Paul Sills). These productions and the theater alike died quickly.

Introductory Notes

While working on this book, I took an assignment to interview Louis L'Amour for *Gallery,* a magazine. I hardly expected that a meeting with the popular author of Westerns would give me new insight into the spirit of theater, but during the course of our conversation he told me that, after returning to their village from a battle, Indian warriors would give a kind of performance for their community, proudly relating the heroic exploits of their expedition. L'Amour stressed that the pride was not the pride of individual warriors boasting of their accomplishments. Rather, the pride was that of the community. The individual's accomplishments were viewed as the community's accomplishments. The glory for some heroic deed was not one person's alone but was the shared glory of the tribe.

Hearing this, I recognized that within this tribal custom lay strong clues to the roots of the theater. I came to the personal realization that the origin of theater is in the communal sharing of experience between a group of peers. The actor is ideally one of the community—no higher or lower in status than anyone in his audience—and he and his fellow actors perform stories expressing the concerns of the community.

Most theater today is far away from that ideal. Now the

actor is no longer a peer of his audience but, rather, is apart from it, a member of a magical elite for the privilege of whose company one pays the price of a ticket.

My conversation with L'Amour made me suddenly appreciate how pure and elemental are the ideals which motivated and continue to motivate David Shepherd and Paul Sills's work. And these ideals were determining factors in the way The Compass Players and The Second City were conceived.

Inevitably, much of the work performed on the stages of both fell short of or even contradicted these ideals, but there have been heady moments when improvisational theater met their challenge. The image which most immediately comes to mind was provided by J. J. Barry: the entire opening night audience (including critics) spontaneously rising in unison to join the cast in singing "A Plague on Both Your Houses" while the battles between police and protestors concurrent with the 1968 Democratic Convention were being fought in the neighborhood of the theater. I also remember Severn Darden telling me of the reaction he got from the patrons whenever he strolled among them in the lobby during intermission. "They would say, 'Isn't that one of the actors?' in much the same tone as they might have said, 'Isn't that the man who parked our car?' It was a very nice, comfortable feeling." The democratic spirit is rarely felt in the theater, but it is felt in improvisational theater more often than elsewhere.

Both Shepherd and Sills have tried to extend this democratic impulse, attempting to break down the distinction between audience and performers by making the audience performers. Sills, with Viola Spolin, ran The Game Theatre, where they taught the audience to play Spolin's theater games and so create their own theater. Shepherd is currently involved in trying to form teams of improvisational players from a wide spectrum of social backgrounds. Part of his and Sills's intention is to make people understand that theater is not necessarily a tyranny of the elite, that it does not exist solely for the edification of the small percentage of the public patronizing the commercial stage.

"I think that if you don't have theater, you're deprived," says Shepherd. Shepherd and Sills see theater as a spiritual necessity for a community. The Compass Players and The

Second City were their responses to this need. They have moved on to other responses since, but The Second City continues to function.

Don De Pollo, as Alexi Bolshoi, realizes that the members of his ballet troupe have defected *en masse* to the West and that his superiors in Mother Russia will hold him responsible, then opens the secret compartment of his ring, drinks the poison it contains, and, as pianist Fred Kaz plays a few final bars of *Swan Lake,* expires. Blackout.

Applause. Lights come up as Kaz plays bouncy music and the cast—Ann Ryerson, George Wendt, Jim Sherman, Miriam Flynn, Eric Boardman, and De Pollo—introduce themselves and take their bows. More applause (and some whistles). After a minute, Miriam steps forward.

MIRIAM: Thank you very much. I have an announcement to make and that is that we do improvise here at The Second City after our shows Tuesday through Thursday and Sunday nights and after our second show on Saturday night. That is how we come up with the scenes here at The Second City, based on suggestions from our audience. The improvisations are always free, so if you find yourself in the neighborhood, come on in and join the gang that's already here. We also have a very fine touring company here at The Second City. They perform here on Monday night and improvise after our second show on Friday night. Also, we have a children's show, *Land of the Stage,* on Sunday afternoon. We call it "Sunday, Sunday, the little bastards' funday." (*Audience laughs.*) It's directed by Josephine Forsberg and it's a fine show for the whole family.

And now, we come to the part where you come in. As I said, all of our material for our regular shows is developed from improvisations, and, in order to improvise, we need suggestions from you. So we're going to name some categories, and if there's something you'd like us to deal with, just shout it out. (*Jim Sherman comes downstage with a large pad of paper and a pen and pulls up a chair. He looks expectantly at the audience.*) All right, I have the first category. What I want from you are activities. Anything two or more people might do together you'd like to see on our stage. (*The audience laughs dirty. Miriam looks shocked, hastens to explain:*) Within reason, of course. (*The au-*

dience is quiet, offers no suggestions.) Come on now—
activities.

DON: We'll call on you by name, if we have to. (*Audience laughs. Still no suggestions.*) OK, I warned you:
Sid. . . . (*Audience laughs.*)

MAN IN AUDIENCE (*after a second*): Parachuting!

MIRIAM: All right, parachuting. Any others?

The audience gets into the spirit, tossing out other activities. Another cast member comes forward, asks for suggestions for locations. Another asks for people—either real people in the news or occupations. Another asks for fantasy headlines. (Someone shouts "Daley retires!" to a huge laugh.) Another asks for fears. All the while, Jim scrawls away.

Finally, all the suggestions have been taken. Everyone has left the stage but Jim, who continues writing for another few seconds. Then he looks up and rises from his seat.

JIM: OK, we're going to go backstage with these now . . . and burn them. (*Audience laughs.*) No, hopefully we'll come up with some scenes based on your suggestions. Also, we're getting ready to open a new show, so we may do some work-in-progress. We'll be back in a few minutes, so stick around and talk to your friends. If you don't have any friends, there are some numbers next to the pay phone in the lobby.

Jim heads offstage. The houselights come up. Some of the audience collect their wraps and leave. More stay.

Backstage, the pad with the suggestions has been hung on the wall and the cast, with producer-director Bernie Sahlins, begins to brainstorm ideas for scenes. "For 'parachuting,' what do you say two guys who have bailed out of a plane, and they're talking and all these weird things fly by?" "Like what?" "The Wicked Witch of the West— like that." "Oh, right."

"For 'Daley retires,' what about his retirement dinner?" "Who would be at that?" "Hartigan." "Right, I'll play him." "How about a Mafioso type? I could give him a farewell kiss of death." "OK, and. . . ."

A running order for the set begins to take shape, consisting of new ideas, scenes in progress, and old scenes which can be adapted to suit one suggestion or another.

Introductory Notes

Each scene in the set will be introduced, so introduction assignments are also made. When the list of scenes and introductions has been agreed upon, Cynthia Cavalenes, the stage manager, prints it up and makes photocopies which she gives to the pianist and the director, hangs up backstage, and takes with her up to the light booth.

At about eleven o'clock, the houselights dim and the adventure begins. For most of the next forty-five minues, the cast improvises. Though the basic ideas for some of the scenes have been hashed out in quick backstage exchanges, and other scenes may be well on their way conceptually, for all intents and purposes the cast and the audience are discovering the material simultaneously.

Tonight, things are going well. Tonight, watching them improvise is like watching an expert surfer. The surfer's incredible balance keeping him constantly poised on the crest of a wave; the cast, working from instinct rooted in hours of workshops and past improv sets, riding the crest of the moment. When they are on top, it is a sight to see. There is a thrill in watching them, a thrill born of the precariousness of their position and the ever-present threat that a misjudgment may send them hurtling into a wipeout. At their best, both improviser and surfer seem to possess a kind of grace, creating the illusion of ease in the face of constant peril.

In workshop, Del Close, the codirector at The Second City, has drawn an analogy between improvising and a sporting event. In both improvisation and sport, what grips the audience is the fact that the outcome is truly in doubt. The players in both have, through arduous training, developed skills with which to deal with the unpredictable; but these skills cannot tame the unpredictable, they can only give the players a better chance of not being routed by it. And, in both, the audience's enthusiasm is a major part of the experience. The football crowd cheers a terrific pass, the audience at The Second City applauds the line or bit of business which springs in startled and wide-eyed perfection out of the logic of the situation.

Actually, the audience at The Second City is even more supportive than the average sports audience. The crowd at the ball park or the fight will unhesitatingly boo if even slightly disappointed, but the Second City audience, having a greater investment in the event, is more generous. After all, what is being performed up there came out of the audience's own vocalized concerns. The audience is a collaborator, and so, for its own sake as well as for the cast's, it wants the improvs to succeed. By the act of taking the audience into its confidence, the company has largely broken down the wall dividing participants and observers. There is a sense of shared interest which creates, for a brief but invigorating time, a sense of oneness, an intense experience of community. It is warm and cozy, the air crackles with invention and psychic energy, and *everybody belongs.*

This is a good night I'm talking about.

Oh God, a bad night and the marrow of your bones is heavy with the weight of disaster and you flee the theater hoping to leave the gloom behind you.

But tonight is a very good night, indeed. Not everything works, but the audience is consistently with it, and there is the satisfaction of genuine accomplishment.

The set over, the party reluctantly breaks up. The guests show their appreciation with applause, pick up their coats, and, buzzing with conversation, disperse into the Chicago night.

The audience gone, the cast gathers for Sahlins's impressions of the improvised scenes. Those which seem to have potential for further development are discussed in depth. What did work, what didn't, what could make which work better, perhaps even an idea for a new scene found in the unpromising ashes of one that bombed out. The director's comments are likely to go something like this:

"There is the beginning of something in the roommate scene you did tonight, but I think you made a mistake in going for jokes about your plants rather than exploring the relationship between the two roommates. You introduced an interesting element when you set up that one of them was moving out to get married, but you never dealt with that again. If you try the scene again, pursue that angle. It's more interesting to deal with people than trade quips about rubber plants.

"Now, about the dinner scene. OK, you have a number of characters of different nationalities and you do them well. The problem with the scene the way you did it tonight is that you introduced them all at once. I think that just as a general principle, if you're going to introduce a number of different people in a scene, it's best to introduce them one at a time. Let each of them have a separate beat to establish who they are. For one thing, that lets you get your exposition about the characters out of the way at the top so you can get into the meat of the scene a little quicker."

And so on, with the cast agreeing, voicing objections, tossing out ideas, and generally feeding back. Sometimes, the videotape is run and discussed. (A few years ago, a camera was mounted into the ceiling in front of the stage, and a tape is made of every set. Members of the cast, on their own initiative, also frequently run the tapes with a view to evaluating their work.) Finally, the session is over and the gang breaks for home or further kibitzing in local night-owl hangouts.

And so the process continues. Night after night, new scenes are created, works-in-progress are repeated and, it is hoped, enhanced, and an occasional scene from a past show is revived. After three or four months of this, a sizable amount of material is amassed from which Sahlins and Close select the scenes to be the basis of a new show. Formal rehearsals are called, the material is polished further, a running order is discovered, further adjustments are made during previews, the new show opens, and the cycle begins again. In this manner, The Second City comes up with two or three shows a year. In so doing, The Second City in Chicago has developed more than fifty shows since opening its doors.

The Second City has lived through a lot of history since 1959. With sketches focusing on the ironies and absurdities of contemporary society as its stock-in-trade, it has reflected a good deal of that history. Almost as soon as an issue reared its head in the consciousness of the troupe and its audience, it found some representation on the stage. To listen to the recordings or to watch the tapes or films of past companies is to be confronted with a parade of crazy-mirror images of the past decade and a half: beatniks, squares, cold warriors, ban-the-bombers, fallout-shelter salesmen, bigots, civil rights workers, soldiers, draft-dodgers, Jesus freaks, police, advertising executives, haves, have-nots, and know-nots—a rich assortment of characters displayed for the audience's recognition, sympathy, or censure, and, always, laughter.

Being sketches made on the fly, they rarely approached the depth found in the key, more considered works that emerged from the same times, but they had the raw vitality of the immediate response. The Second City did not have the last word on any subject. Rather, it prided itself on having one of the first words. For instance, it dealt with the moral and social implications of our involvement in Vietnam in 1961, well before that conflict took center stage in the country's attention. If one of the functions of art is to find reason in chaos, then The Second City tended to be a forum for initial assessment of the damages.

That is not to say that The Second City and its sister companies, The Premise and The Committee, were the only sources of this brand of humor, though on the American stage they did have a near-monopoly on it. The late '50s and early '60s saw a remarkable explosion of social satire with the appearance of Lenny Bruce, Mort Sahl, Jules Feiffer, Joseph Heller, and others. Not only were their perspectives similar, but their methods were analogous. To listen to Bruce and Sahl records is to hear two solo improvisational masters in action. Feiffer rarely knew the ending of a strip when he started drawing the beginning, but, in a process analogous to improvisation, followed the pull of the internal logic established in the first panel to its relentlessly funny conclusion. Interviews with Heller indicate he followed a method not unlike Feiffer's in writing *Catch-22*.

The kinship between these satirists and the improvisers was further reinforced by frequent collaboration. Feiffer, for example, made his debut as a playwright at The Second City with a program directed by Paul Sills, and his subsequent plays and films employed the talents of such improvisational alumni as Mike Nichols, Barbara Harris, Alan Alda, Robert Klein, Richard Libertini, Richard Schaal, Bob Balaban, Andrew Duncan, Anthony Holland, Alan Arkin, David Steinberg, Fred Willard, J. J. Barry, Linda Lavin, Paul Dooley, Peter Bonerz, and Cynthia Harris. The film version of Heller's *Catch-22* employed Nichols, Arkin, Balaban, Bonerz, Libertini, Buck Henry, and John Brent.

Introductory Notes

A stage version was directed by Larry Arrick with a cast including Holland and Arkin's son, Adam.

The material utilized at The Second City not only reflected the concerns of the community in which and for which it played, but also reflected (and continues to reflect) the backgrounds of the individuals who performed there. The character of the material has changed considerably between the days of The Compass and what is being played on The Second City stage today, and no small part of this is due to the differences in the actors' personal experience.

The performers in The Compass and the early days of The Second City were largely from the University of Chicago, and what they chose to deal with was colored by their academic background. They came to the stage after pursuing degrees in such fields as literature, the social sciences, and medicine. To a great extent, the later Second City people arrived with experience or training as performers and had not seriously considered non-show-biz careers and so had (and have) comparatively less expertise on non-show-biz subjects. A contrast can be seen in the subjects these two groups chose to parody. Whereas The Compass and early Second City people were more likely to tackle Ibsen, Pirandello, or Hemingway, today's Second City is more apt to take on *Jaws, Let's Make a Deal,* and late-night TV commercials for "greatest hits" collections.

It is also my very subjective impression that there has been a significant shift in the sensibility behind the material. I find the scenes created within the past several years to be much more guarded emotionally than much of the early material. I would not expect to see a scene such as "First Affair" (which is described in the introduction to Barbara Harris's chapter) on that stage today. "First Affair" was a very tender, delicate sketch made memorable by Barbara Harris's deeply affecting vulnerability. In contrast, most of what I've seen recently at The Second City is rooted in what one might describe as a cheery cynicism. Unlike the "people scenes" in which Harris, Arkin, Holland, Alton, and others played characters "straight," The Second City stage today is peopled almost exclusively by clever caricatures. The audience makes no emotional investment in their fates. They are figures created to be laughed at rather than felt for. Why the shift? I have no theory to put forward with confidence. (Are the actors afraid to risk exposing their vulnerability onstage?)

Perhaps one of the reasons for the lack of scenes with "heart" is the fact that the cast is largely unaware that such scenes have been done on The Second City stage in the past. I was startled to discover how little the recent companies knew of the work that had been done earlier. They were aware of the stars among the alumni (pictures of past companies are displayed in the lobby), but, except for the scenes on the two Second City albums released by Mercury Records, they seemed largely unfamiliar with such great early pieces as "First Affair," "Lekythos," "The Exurbanites," *Peep Show for Conventioneers,* and David Steinberg's genie scene. Bernie Sahlins has told me that Second City has a basically antipreservationist attitude about past work. Indeed, were it not for the tapes recorded by WFMT, a local FM station, much of the material would have been lost to time. Sahlins has not encouraged the current cast to listen to these recordings, believing, with some justification, that the focus of their work should be the immediate moment. Perhaps he wishes to discourage imitation of old material. Still, I think it unfortunate that the latter-day companies have not had the benefit of learning from the early casts' considerable accomplishments.

I don't mean to imply that the troupe has deteriorated or become slipshod. It has not. The Second City's main business was and still is to be funny, and I find the recent editions as funny as their vintage predecessors. The point I am trying to make is that The Second City changes. The fact that it continues to evolve is an indication that it hasn't become a frozen commodity but continues to be a vital enterprise. After more than a decade and a half of continuous operation, I think that's quite an accomplishment.

SOMETHING WONDERFUL RIGHT AWAY

1.

David Shepherd

David Shepherd's association with the theater crowd at the University of Chicago began in 1952. Though not enrolled at the university, he became involved with campus theatricals and, through them, met Paul Sills. With Sills and Eugene Troobnick, Shepherd produced Playwrights Theatre Club.

But it is as the founder of The Compass Players in Chicago that he made his most significant contribution to theater. He conceived The Compass, produced it, wrote scenarios for it, and sometimes acted and directed. To put it simply, The Compass and, by extension, The Second City, The Premise, and The Committee came about because of his pursuit of the ideal of a truly popular theater.

After the Chicago Compass closed, Shepherd directed and/or produced a number of other Compass troupes, as well as occasionally supplying The Second City with material.

He continues to experiment with methods designed to involve in theater people from all walks of life. Currently, he is organizing teams of improvisational players in the United States and Canada for the purpose of having them compete in matches. Ultimately, he hopes to have dozens of teams participating in an annual International Improvisational Olympics.

1

SHEPHERD: I remember hearing, when I was fourteen, "The September Song" sung by Walter Huston to a very young blonde, which moved me deeply. I later found out that it was written by Bertolt Brecht's partner, Kurt Weill. I didn't have any idea at the time. I didn't know that I was into an anarchist, leftist, psychedelic culture. I liked "September Song" before I found out it was written by an ex-anarchist, and I liked Coleridge before I knew he was a drug addict.

I majored in English at Harvard, where I acquired an intellectual interest in theater, and I took an M.A. in history of theater at Columbia. All of the other dudes were way ahead of me. They were putting on *Henry V* and they were doing five-hour Ben Jonson plays on campus. And I was just at this primitive level where I was saying, "What we've got to have is a popular theater." I was saying that for, like, ten years. "We've got to have a theater that will work in the Catskills or in a factory or in a school or in a hospital or in a prison!" And everybody thought I was crazy.

I wanted to rejuvenate the theater. My first love was the theater, which I found had been captured by Giraudoux and Shaw and Ionesco, who would come in and turn it into a distorted picture of life. Instead of being about what's happening in the streets of Chicago, it was about love affairs in Nice which took place fifty years ago. And I thought it was obscene for the theater to be dominated by French and English people. I mean, *obscene*. I mean, I'm a Yankee. I'm a W.A.S.P. I want a W.A.S.P. theater, OK? And you can't get it on the East Coast because it's dominated by European culture. So you go to the Midwest, which is what I did.

I met a group of people in Hyde Park who were students who were going to the University of Chicago and putting on shows there. I worked out with "Tonight at 8:30." I did a Shaw play and Paul Sills saw my work and we started to rap about it. We started to rap about a repertory theater, and within nine months it was open.

Q: *Do you remember the first contact you had with improvisation?*

SHEPHERD: I went to see one of Paul's workshops at the University of Chicago. There was no structure, and people

2

were creating constantly. Actually, it turned out the structure was the games. But then I didn't know games. So it was this hidden structure. And Paul was there and just going through his mother's games, which have gotten him through half of his adult life, you know? When in doubt, do a game. His mother taught him how people could relate through improvisation in ways that they did not relate in life. Through closer touching, through fuller expression of feelings, through the fuller use of the resources of things around them. Most people cannot make contact in real life.

That's true of myself, too, you know? I am interested in improvisation because I don't *do it*. I never had it. When I was brought up, I had no encounters with brothers and sisters because I didn't have any. I had no conflict with my mother because I had no mother. I was brought up like a monarch—you know, going to a very fine private school. There was nobody in my family except my father. So I'm interested in embracing a larger community of people which I did not have.

Q: *You were talking about the first games workshop you saw at the University of Chicago....*

SHEPHERD: The students were so good at them that they were able to transform the stage from moment to moment. First it would be a carnival and then it would be a beach at midnight and then it would be trenches in World War II. With hardly any use of lights and with no use of costumes and with a minimum use of props, these ten or twenty kids were able to create a whole afternoon of theater. Out of nothing. Nothing!

Q: *I'd like to get into what the social atmosphere was like in Hyde Park at that time.*

SHEPHERD: Very mixed and very flowing. There were hardhats and intellectuals, steelworkers and students and professors and homosexuals and . . . lots of different people living in low-rent housing before urban renewal hit Hyde Park. And we enjoyed a renaissance of the University of Chicago. The aura through Robert Hutchins. There was a lot of love between people of very different backgrounds. And a lot of these people were in and out of the university, whether they were fifteen years old or forty-year-old paratroop veterans.

Hutchins had set up a very libertarian college in which kids could enter as soon as they could read and write and do math well enough to pass the exams. They could have been twelve years old and going to the University of Chicago, you know? A lot of the people I worked with either lived with U. of C. graduates and staff or were U. of C. graduates and staff. It was a community. An enormous one. When you left it, you might go to Evanston, but you still felt a part of it. And we were there. There was the most conspicuous assertion of civil rights and tenant rights, and people were into community development in Hyde Park like nowhere in Chicago.

Q: *What effect did the McCarthy era have?*

SHEPHERD: Almost no effect. There were very few people who were concerned. I thought it affected my friends in New York much more because I had a lot of blacklisted friends in New York. But in Chicago you felt a kind of piggish strength in the *Tribune* and you felt a liberal candidate might have a hard time, but, during Compass days, it was I who was saying to Mike Nichols, "Let's do something about the Red-baiting," and it was Mike Nichols who was saying, "What does that have to do with my life?" And it was I who was saying, "Look, there's a political climate to this which is stealing over this country, is going to steal our institutions away. Let's check it out. Let's see what's happening." We were never able to address that much. What we were able to address was the tyranny of the middle-class Jewish family. That's what Compass was all about.

Q: *I understand you originally wanted to do Compass in the stockyards.*

SHEPHERD: The stockyards wouldn't have me. I worked in the stockyards in the same area that was organized by Saul Alinsky. It was a very reactionary area. I found no support.

And then I was saying, "I'd like to do a theater in a bar on 63rd Street for the hardhats because those are the people who *need* theater." And my friends were saying, "Bullshit. Our mothers and fathers need it much more than the hardhats on 63rd Street."

This is what Compass came out of—along with my notions of pantomime and what I knew of Robert Breen's

4

chamber theater at Northwestern University. And along with the louvers I designed, which were panels that would turn on pipes, and along with the notion of letting people eat and smoke, which I got from Brecht. If you're going to have a popular theater, you have to let people come and go and smoke and drink—be comfortable and not think of theater as something holy and untouchable.

And get up on the stage and do your number and sing a song if you want, and do it on Monday nights and have folksinging, and relate to what you read, which is the Chicago *Tribune*, the *Sun Times*, the *New Yorker*, or *Popular Mechanics* or whatever people in Hyde Park were reading.

Q: *How did you come up with the idea of working improvisationally from scenarios?*

SHEPHERD: Well, I was forced to go into improvisation because I found that nobody could write the scripts I needed for the theater that was in my head. A theater where everybody would come. I mean *everybody*. Literally everybody. Not only theatergoers, but also non-theatergoers, which meant ninety-five percent of the people who lived in Chicago, whether they're steelworkers or college students who don't have the money to go or the Japanese and black minorities who were sweeping across Hyde Park at the time. Whoever they were, I wanted them in my theater, instead of being in the Lyric movie theater watching Westerns. I wanted them in my theater watching stories about Hyde Park.

It was a church we were running in Hyde Park. I have met girls and boys who were ten years younger than I who said they first woke up in Playwrights Theatre Club or The Compass because it was their first contact with situational morality. And also it was a very heavy attack on their parents going on all the time at The Compass. If you wanted to see your parents under attack, go to Compass. Especially if they're Jewish. It came out of Elaine May's and Paul Sills's and Shelley Berman's love-hate thing with their parents. You know, the permissive Jewish parents. The intellectuals who bring up their children to hate them. When Elaine May would play a Jewish mother or Mike Nichols would play a businessman or when Shelley Berman would play a delicatessen father—these were people who were

5

living out their liberation from their families. They were in analysis and they were using the stage of The Compass to liberate themselves from a whole lot of shit they had fallen into.

Q: *How did you train for Compass?*

SHEPHERD: We had no training except for what Viola was able to do, and then we went on from there. Viola is very good for designing games for teachers who have ten minutes to fill in the classroom. But we had a sixty-minute gap to fill—a "Living Magazine," which lasted about twenty minutes, and then a scenario, which lasted about forty. The scenarios were simply little skeletons for stories based on what was happening in the community. We had no training for doing that.

People would get off the plane and we would throw them onto the stage. We were famous for throwing geniuses onto the stage and letting them swim. That happened to Severn Darden. After his first five hours onstage on Saturday night, we let him go have a drink at the bar. And he was standing there, huffing and puffing and getting back his breath, and somebody ran up to him and said "Sev, you're onstage! You're Dr. Schweitzer!" That was the training. The training was going on in front of the footlights.

Most training is done by teachers talking and the students taking notes. And the teacher says, "This is the theory behind it and this is the history of it and this is how I did it and this is how you will do it." Right? But until the student goes out and does it one time, he hasn't learned anything. I was saying, "I've studied the theory, I know the history, I've done it, now *you* do it *now!*"

When I hired people, I wasn't going on their having academic training you could measure. I was going on something you could not measure, which was a sense of their insight into what was happening in society and the ability to play a whole bunch of parts—old ladies and cops and crooked lawyers and whatever constellation of characters inhabited the social world of our heads.

Now the social world of *our* heads was very different from the social world. It had very few hardhats in it. Our social world included whatever characters Barbara Harris had been studying for years. And she was studying her mother for years. And Elaine May had also been studying

6

under *her* mother for years. They could do their mothers brilliantly. And Elaine May had also been studying Hollywood starlets, and she knew about uptight secretaries. And Severn Darden had been studying German philosophy professors for years. He could do them very well. He did them for days at The Compass. Other people did their things. Whatever they had been studying. It might have been a certain kind of insincerity or braggadocio or. . . . Well, I mean, take the first Nichols and May record, *An Evening with Mike Nichols and Elaine May*. I mean, that's it as far as I'm concerned. There's more crystallized character work on that record than anything else you can listen to.

I was interested in American humor. The kind of things Elaine was writing scenarios about in the first days of Compass. Like blind dates. That's American—blind dates. Used-car salesmen—that's American. We did that one. Veterans coming back from the war—we did that. The conflict between middle-class and working-class values expressed in the bars of Cicero—we did that. The hypocrisy of the ministry—we did that. Every one of those little scenarios was in some way an exploration of the American value system. We did *A Day in the Life of a Cynic*, which was the story of a public relations guy, and we did our tour of Hollywood, and we did our tour of Joe McCarthy—we tried to do just about everything. We did *The Real You*, which Elaine wrote and which was about a confidence-building course. That's very hot stuff now. We did that twenty years ago. We did a pot-smoking scene twenty years ago, before I ever smoked pot.

Sometimes the players would come up with characters and we would find a locus for them. Like, in a later company, Nancy Ponder and Elaine May came up with two spinsters. They were eventually placed in a police station complaining about how all these people were making sexual advances to them. And the cop would just nod. He wouldn't do anything. And they would load him up with all these stories about the sexual advances that had been made by foremen on building sites and the butcher—the way he gave them the liver, you know? It sounds tenuous, but when you saw those two girls do that scene, you'd get

7

a very detailed picture of the sexually frustrated life of single lower-middle-class people forty or fifty years old.

We were way ahead of the times, man, because, if you go to the University of Chicago when you're fifteen, and you bum around the country, and you sleep with various people, you're going to know a lot about what's happening in this country by the time you get to be twenty, twenty-five years old. People like Elaine and Paul Sills and the others, they knew a lot and they were very literate. *Highly* literate. They could talk to the U. of C. alumni. They could talk Kafka, Shakespeare—anything you want. I mean, that was a *smart* company. And the directors were very spaced-out, with a lot of experience, because Larry Arrick had directed his ass off for ten years before he came to work with us, and Paul had really been born on the stage. I had probably less experience than anybody, but I had more crazy ideas to try and work out. So, anyway, that's the way it was—very kind of avant-garde-experienced directors and people with a lot of life experience who were literate.

Q: *You were involved in putting together a number of other Compass companies, weren't you?*

SHEPHERD: There were three companies in St. Louis at various times, and there was a company that played under Larry Arrick very briefly in New York at the Cherry Lane. Lee Kalcheim started a company in Philadelphia, and then there was a company in Hyannisport, and one that opened in Washington under the direction of Ron Weyand. And I did another company in New York at the Upstairs at the Downstairs with George Morrison directing.

Q: *How did you put together these companies?*

SHEPHERD: I would go to New York and put a casting notice in the paper and call up all of my friends and somebody would say, "I would like you to see this person." I was turning down more people who are nowadays stars than I was casting. I turned down Sandy Baron. I turned down Godfrey Cambridge because I didn't have enough room for him in my company. I mean, I went to Hyannisport with only one black—Diana Sands—because I thought there was room for only one black person in a company that was going to play in such a lily-white area. I would have loved to have worked with Godfrey Cambridge.

I remember taking my little old company with Alan

Arkin and Jerry Stiller and Nancy Ponder—this was before
Anne Meara joined us—to a place in Cleveland called the
Alpine Village. The Alpine Village is set up as a kind of
halfway house between the church and the motel where the
bride loses her virginity, and there was an emcee there who
used to make jokes for forty minutes about losing your
virginity. I mean, he was really the main star. That's why
people came there. Because, after the wedding, they could
let their hair down, get a few squeezes from the brides-
maids, and the groom and bride would go off to consum-
mate. And then we came on top of that, dig it? With our
intellectual humor. It was ghastly. The first night they
played, the whole company wanted to come back to New
York. It was nearly the destruction of the company.

Q: *So you think that in order for that gig to have
worked, the material would have had to be more relevant
to that environment.*

SHEPHERD: We would have had to base it on that highly
sexual, institutionalized experience of secretaries getting
married to office boys. That was what was going down at
the Alpine Village and we had no way of responding to
that. We just had our highly tailored, highly rehearsed improvisations about middle-aged spinsters and horror movies.
And then Alan would play the guitar for a few minutes and
that was it.

The problem with Compass was I lost track of the fact
that what I was trying to do was based on the audience, not
the performers. I forgot all about the audience. I should
have been building audiences out there—training audiences
how to improvise and direct and write and get into the act.
But I wasn't. I was really blinded by the success of some of
my friends. I thought that if they were able to make a living
at the industrialization of gags, I should be able to, too. I
thought that some ritual of producing gags would put you
in the Purple Onion for sixteen weeks.

Q: *You've told me that you're no longer interested in
working with professionals; that you're now concerned with
working improvisationally with groups of amateurs.*

SHEPHERD: I don't think there's any reason for not having theater in the living room. I think people should be
doing theater in the living room instead of going out to see
Marcel Marceau for $7.80. I think we can create a style of

interacting for people who are not interacting, who have no release. I think that if you don't have theater, you're deprived. It's as simple as that. Now I'm not proposing that improvisation be used for mental health.

Q: *Then for what? Social health?*

SHEPHERD: I just think that everybody is a creative person and should get to it.

I'm trying to set up social-interaction clubs all over the world using videotape, clubs where people get to meet a lot of other folk who are not created in their own image. Because most clubs are exclusive in the sense that you meet only your brother and sister there. They're set up so that you don't meet anybody different from you. So you end up putting the make on your sister and talking to your brother. Well, I'm trying to set up a club of creative people—thousands and thousands of creative people who interact with each other and do that through videotape and improvisation. I feel it's got to be done. The excitement comes out of interaction between people who are different from each other and they benefit from that. They celebrate common things that are viewed in totally different ways. And that's beautiful.

2.

Paul Sills

Viola Spolin formulated the theories of improvisation for the theater. Paul Sills, her son, has spent the bulk of his career translating theory into practice and, in so doing, has earned a reputation as one of the most important and influential directors in theater.

His professional career began in 1953 as director and coproducer of Playwrights Theatre Company. Joining forces with David Shepherd, in 1955 he launched The Compass Players; then, in 1959, in association with Bernard Sahlins and Howard Alk, he opened The Second City, which he directed for several years.

Feeling the need to explore the possibilities of improvisational theater beyond the revue form, in 1967 he worked with Spolin in The Game Theatre in Chicago. The *modus operandi* of Game Theatre was to have the audience play the theater games for its own entertainment, thus breaking down the distinction between audience and performer. Sills moved from there to involvement with the short-lived Second City Repertory Theatre at the Harper (a theater in Hyde Park), with which he made a rare (and final) appearance as an actor in Norman Mailer's *The Deer Park* and directed a production of *The Cherry Orchard*. He also helped found an experimental theater in Chicago called The Body Politic.

11

Since 1968, Sills has directed his energies toward developing story theater, a form in which performers apply improvisational techniques to the retelling of traditional folk and fairy tales or to the dramatization of history. In addition to his work in Chicago, he has staged story theater productions at Yale, in San Francisco (in what had previously been The Committee's theater), at the Mark Taper Forum in Los Angeles, and in Washington, D.C. A Broadway edition, under the title *Paul Sills's Story Theatre,* proved to be one of the most popular and notable events of the 1970–71 season and led to a *Story Theatre* TV series, which Sills also directed

Paul Sills is not an easy interview. I suspect that, dedicated as he is to an especially impermanent brand of theater—one which lives in the fleeting moment—he is by nature wary of any situation in which spontaneous comment is to be concretized in print. He agreed to meet with me on the condition that he have final approval on quotations attributed to him. With this caveat in mind, I taped an initial session with him and then prepared an edited transcript which I submitted for his approval. He felt it rambled and proceeded to cross out two-thirds of the transcript, eliminating most of what I felt provided insight into the driving forces behind his work.

In the meantime, we had become friendly, and I told him I thought what we had so far wasn't a sufficient representation of his perspective. A year after the first session, we taped a second. I prepared an edited version of this and sent it to him for his approval.

This time, he cut only about one-fourth of the material. This chapter draws on material from both conversations.

A good deal of this book is devoted to various reactions to working with Paul Sills, and quite a bit of it attests to his often upsetting behavior in rehearsal. I cannot confirm or deny these impressions on the basis of my own experience. (The day I attended one of his rehearsals for a project in Chicago called *Sweet Bloody Liberty,* he and his company were in uncommonly good spirits, singing and dancing and tellings jokes and, not incidentally, coming up with exciting things.) I do feel moved, however, to make this personal observation: I don't think I have ever met a person I believed to be quite as impatient with himself. I

12

can well believe this self-impatience might occasionally find expression in flashes of anger. But, if that's how he arrives at his remarkable results, I say why not. (Of course, I've never done a show with him.)

Also, many allegations are made about his inarticulateness in rehearsal. Again, I can make no personal comment on this from my very limited experience of watching him in rehearsal, but I will say that in private conversation I have found him to be marvelously articulate, as I think this chapter will bear out.

Q: *How did you end up at the University of Chicago, a place with no theater department?*

SILLS: Just by a stroke of luck, believe me.

Q: *When you went, did you know that you would be going into theater?*

SILLS: No.

Q: *Did you have any idea what direction you wanted to take?*

SILLS: No, I went to the University of Chicago in order to really comprehend that there *was* such a thing as direction.

Q: *Playwrights was a direct extension of your work at U. of C. Can you tell me a little about it?*

SILLS: We opened with Brecht's *Caucasian Chalk Circle*, followed by *La Ronde* by Schnitzler, then *Wozzeck*, then we would do an original, then we would do *Volpone*. . . . Well, those are all different, so there was no one technique. Our *Wozzeck* was a wonderful production. One of the first productions that had . . . what I've since called the *space* in the theater. So each show was a discovery. We were truly discovering.

Q: *And then you did Compass, which was so radically different from anything that had ever been done in Chicago before.*

SILLS: Or anywhere else. I would like to know where else. This was the first improvisational theater. People say it happened in Zurich back when or something. I don't know. But I think as a theater with a place on the street and a continuous history, it started with The Compass back on 55th Street.

The show usually was about an hour and a half of

13

material. The scenario would have around twelve scenes in it—before that we'd do the "Living Newspaper" as a curtain raiser—and after the scenario play, some special scenes. Which would be a full evening which you could hardly ever duplicate today. We did this every week, a whole new show. For sheer producing, it's never been matched, I think.

The place was small. You couldn't get in. There was never a seat. Never. That was a teeny little room. No admission charged. You couldn't make a nickel. Ninety people at tables and a stage at the end. And there was a picture window you could look in from the street—like a little storefront. And then, next door there was a bar and we'd sell drinks to the people.

Q: *When you started putting together Second City and Compass, what qualities would you look for in the people you'd select?*

SILLS: I worked with who was there. I work with who's near me, who's around, people I know, who's at hand.

Q: *Alan Arkin told me that he thought you had a special genius for putting together companies. Do you have any special approach to that?*

SILLS: Yes. Whoever shows up. (*Laughs.*) Listen, any group at Second City has worked. The company is who is there. You can't exclude anybody who's in it. Special tension has to make it work like a team. I don't form great companies. Just any company is a great company if the people are released to what they can be and do.

Q: *When Second City got started, it got a reputation for very hip, topical humor. Some years later, you were quoted as saying that topical revue material is "asinine."**

SILLS: Oh, I tend to downgrade it, if only because newspapers think that's what it's all about. What's wrong with topical humor? You find topical humor in Ben Jonson, right? We were struggling to hold ourselves alive through give-them-what-they-want principles and, to some extent, maintain our intellectual credits. It was a conscious theater.

Q: *You left Second City to work with The Game Theatre.*

* Charles L. Mee, Jr., "The Celebratory Occasion," *Tulane Drama Review*, Winter 1964, p. 168.

Paul Sills

Was it because of frustration with your work at Second City?

SILLS: I wanted to more seriously go back and work on the theater games which I began to see were something to be explored, studied, thought about, worked on. So I helped set up a place with my mother to do that. We needed a community meeting place, anyway. It was the kind of forum that a community might well adopt, especially our community in Lincoln Park, where the people we lived with were all connected with theater to some extent.

Q: *So Game Theatre was....*

SILLS: An outgrowth of the group, actually.

Q: *An exploration of the community?*

SILLS: And games. Game forms that people could, might play.

Q: *I understand there was no regular company at Game Theatre.*

SILLS: Oh yeah, there was a gang. A crowd hung out there, sure.

Q: *I mean, there were no salaried actors.*

SILLS: No, but these people were there for two or three years. It was a very strong company. Again, that community group.

Q: *How did you arrive at story theater?*

SILLS: There was a narrative technique that was developed by Robert Breen at Northwestern University called chamber theater, and that was a technique very similar to story theater where the actor could speak about his character in the third person. Except they used a narrator. So I just cut out the narrator twenty years later and that was story theater.

Q: *There's been some controversy over whether story theater is really a kind of improvisational theater, arising from the fact that the textual material isn't invented by the performers but is taken from preexistent sources.*

SILLS: I believe it *is* part of improvisational theater. There's basically the same instinct behind it. For me it's the theater for which improvisational theater is the training, if you regard it as a progression.

Q: *One of the things I find so exciting about improvisational theater is that it is the most immediately responsive*

15

kind of theater. It can pick up and deal with a concern of that moment and transform it into a theatrical event.

SILLS: Well, the other theater must, too.

Q: *But the other theater is based on something that was written down in the past, whether it was two weeks ago or four or five hundred years ago.*

SILLS: There is no reason it shouldn't be played in the same sense that improvisational acting is. The acting side of improvisational theater is merely going for reality. Improvisational acting is required if one is to stay in reality. I mean, that's all there is to it. I don't mean that you have to change lines every night, but you can't do it quite the same way every time.

Q: *Because you're a different person every time.*

SILLS: You're a different person, yeah. You see, the work of creation is renewable, renewable, renewable. It *has* to be renewable, I think. So that's what this is all about.

Q: *What do you think it is about this kind of work that develops such good, responsive actors?*

SILLS: That's its secret. (*Laughs.*) When you're talking about free and spontaneous people, you're talking about something that has to happen to them. An organic change has to occur, and improvisation to a certain extent holds the possibility of an organic change for a person. I think the games in Viola's book are special kinds of things. They're not inventions. They're discoveries.

Q: *I understand you worked with her a little on the book.*

SILLS: No, she wrote the book. I helped her the best I could, but all in it is hers.

If a theater game is presented freely and played freely, it has a gift to give. It's a *theater* game. It gives you the gift of an entrance or an exit or a relation on a deeper level than you can ordinarily get.

Q: *It gives you a sense of the richness of your freedom.*

SILLS: Yeah, that's right. Richness, complexity, variety. Actors aren't liberated enough. There are very few free spaces where they can work. Actors' liberation is very important. We've always been, in a sense, preaching it. Improvisational theater stands on that. The actor is an artist. I think improvisational theater and my mother's work are

16

attempts to find that—to go into the possibilities for human development.

It's group work. Groups that play together have a sense of each other that lasts for years. You come into each other's lives. That's why they develop as persons and as actors.

I think theater comes out of the consciousness of the community. If you look at the theater of ancient Greece, it came out of the necessity of the Greek community to handle its spiritual reality in a public form. Theater has always been concerned with this, so why should contemporary theater be any less so? Theater is concerned with reality. Now, reality is not to be defined as what is real for you alone. Reality is shared. And reality of the moment can occur only with spontaneity.

Q: *So if you want to deal with reality, it must come out of something that is shared with others in the spontaneity of the moment, and for that you need theater. To what purpose?*

SILLS: The liberation of the people. The possibility of this country liberating itself. I'm not talking about tearing down building and things like that. I'm talking about personal liberation.

People suffer from fantastic restrictions on their self-understanding or their ability to affect. They're graded, stacked in categories of excellence, measured against all kinds of nonsense standards with the result that their personal selves are locked inside them. The confirmation of their own existence must come to people or else they find it in negative ways such as delinquency or apathy or reactionary behavior, the shrinking of the person from the common good, cynicism, denial, and so on.

I think it's a dark hour and everybody better man the pumps and get in there and get ready because this society has turned out an awful lot of slaves—people who are too afraid to move one way or another—and that could cause a lot of trouble. Samuel Adams said it: "If the spirit of liberty sleeps in the people this will become a nation of tame and contented vassals." That was his prophecy and he wasn't about to let it happen then. I pick up that pride. To me it's very important the people get a little heart and spirit back. Now I can't go up to some guy who's putting in a lot of dead time with his life and say, "Look, you're screwing your own existence." But if the actors hit it, everybody will pick it up.

I think theater is responsible for the image of the human. The concerns of the artists are the concerns of the people. They represent the people, are cast out from the people to do whatever is necessary to save the people's ass. And therefore an artist is responsible to his people. Joyce defined it very clearly at the end of *A Portrait of the Artist as a Young Man:* "I go to encounter for the millionth time the reality of experience and to forge in the smithy of my soul the uncreated conscience of my race." That is part of it.

Q: *But in order for the actor to do this, he must be free.*

SILLS: As I said, actors' liberation is very important. For that you need a free space. A space where work can be freely done, in which a person is free to become. A space in which people share together and, in sharing, free themselves. But you have to have a way to enter into this space, to bring about the possibility of playing together in a reality that wasn't there before creating it together through sharing.

Q: *And that's what happens when you truly play Viola's games.*

SILLS: My mother once did an exercise in a mental institution and got to a "catatonic" person. They were passing along space objects to each other. The "catatonic" had something and he passed it on and the other person knew it was a cat. In other words, what was in the catatonic's head was shared in the space between them. I'm not saying this is a miracle, but it's sort of obvious that something of his self had been transmitted to another. That's what this work is about: the finding of the self in a free space created through mutuality.

All the people who have worked with improvisational theater know that there's a free space they can come back to and they like to come back to. It's something they usually don't get in commercial theater. They'll all say that. It has nothing to do with me. It has to do with that free space. The people who improvise, who make up their own shows in spite of all the suffering attendant on it—and suffering and action are connected, as we're informed by

18

poets and so on—experience a joy that is best expressed by that phrase of Martin Buber's, "The heavenly bread of self-being is passed between man and man."

I'm not interested in improvisational theater *per se*. I'm interested in the establishment of these free spaces where people can do their own work, and I'm interested in the forms which begin to emerge in these free spaces. My concern with form is what leads me on. You could call it "the eternal feminine," like at the end of *Faust*. Finding the forms involves a combination between the spiritual and the earthly. It's an exploration into the unknown, into a world that one can't enter alone. True improvisation is a dialogue between people. Not just on the level of what the scene is about, but also a dialogue from the being—something that has never been said before that now comes up, some statement of reality between people. In a dialogue, something happens to the participants. It's not what I know and what you know; it's something that happens between us that's a discovery. As I say, you can't make this discovery alone. There is always the other.

Q: *What's the audience's part in all this?*

SILLS: As you might guess, I believe the audience-actor relationship is a spatial one; a theatrical situation is one in which a space is created which include everyone.

Q: *One of the most significant contrasts I find between the conventional theater, as exemplified by most commercial theater productions, and improvisational theater is the difference between the actor's relationship to and part in the creation of them. With the traditional theater, you have a role that's already been created by a writer and the director tries to find someone to fit the part, to find the square peg that fits the square hole. . . .*

SILLS: Not in a true company. A director may make a decision as to who plays Vanya and who Astrov, but out of any ordinary company there would be one who tended more toward one role than the other.

Q: *Yes, but you're talking about a preexistent company. What I'm talking about is the way most theater is done now, where you start with a list of characters to cast and hold auditions to find actors to fill those parts.*

SILLS: Most theater is slave-market bullshit.

Q: *That's what I'm talking about. In that kind of theater*

19

the actors are trying to become marketable commodities. But improvisational theater is particularly free. Whereas in the traditional theater you might be a square peg trying out for an octagonal slot, in improvisational theater you create your own square slot.

SILLS: Yes, so improvisational theater can use anyone where he is. So you can take any group of people and get into it, get them going with each other, and then they can entertain a crowd of people who've never seen them before.

Q: *So this all has to do with what you were saying before about people discovering themselves through improvisation, becoming more self-confident.*

SILLS: It's not so much the confidence in the self, it's more the awareness that there is *such a thing* as the self. That the self exists. And, as I said, you can only know you exist in an area of mutuality. That mutuality can exist between an individual and God, but the parallel to that is between man and man. I'm an absolute disciple of Buber, and I don't find a contradiction between Buber and my mother's work. So if you really want to know what to say about the theater, read Buber. A lot of people think they come out of their own heads, that they're self-created. It's not true.

Improvisation has led me to some kind of understanding of the spiritual reality, but I can't express it clearly. I do think that theater and religion and education are very closely connected. Many church people are very aware of the spiritual value of the games. They didn't see it in The Second City because it was clever people entertaining in revue form. But with the kind of group improvisations that happened at The Game Theatre, they become very aware of the spirit's presence. The authentication of the spirit—which has something to do with the church—is vital to the theater and is something that the theater can and must do.

Improvisational theater is also the closest thing you'll find to democracy in the theater. It opens up the possibility of play between the people in the group, and play is an expression of our equality. The crowd I work with regard themselves as equals.

Q: *If everyone is equal, what is your place as director?*

SILLS: Somebody has to help the group become a group. There is a need for a teacher or leader when you're dealing with these forms, and when I'm involved with a group, that's my job.

Q: *In* What Is Cinema?*, André Bazin wrote that the artistic impulse springs from the artist's desire for immortality, to live beyond his death, to achieve some kind of permanence. Yet here you're an artist and the very foundation of your work is in spontaneity and impermanence.*

SILLS: It's a paradox that interests me. The irony is that the art which is most exciting today is impermanent and not meant to last except as an act of love. It's ecologically sound. You don't need to cut down trees to print it up. It just comes out between people. It doesn't want to be written down. It passes in the moment and disappears. Whatever good it does is transmitted like a good deed—like somebody passes on to the next guy a good handshake or a kiss and that opens his heart to helping the next man who is in need. It's that kind of transmission that's crucial in this work.

Something else: Improvisational theater is popular theater, and popular theater is separate from the literary theater.

Q: *Just to clarify terms, I gather when you refer to popular theater, "popular" isn't used as a term to describe a theater piece's reception but its origin.*

SILLS: Right. However popular Neil Simon may be, he is in the literary tradition. Whereas the image of the popular theater is the image of the wagonload of players rolling through the countryside, creating theater pieces out of their sense of forms and language and play—like the *commedia dell'arte* and such. I think the living line of the theater is improvisational theater, that it lies in the possibility of a group of people to construct their own theater independently of a writer. I really don't expect much from the literary theater and haven't for years.

Now, if you're talking about popular theater. I think you have to get back to the primal, which is the stories of the people.

Q: *So that's the connection between improvisational theater and story theater.*

SILLS: Well, I say that story theater and improvisational theater are the same thing. One way of looking at improvisational theater is that it is part of the oral tradition. that it is connected with story-telling, anecdotes, and any form of speaking in the present in front of an audience. Story-telling, like playing a game, is an act of the self. When you truly tell a story, there is self-discovery.

"Snow White" has something to do with the psyche, with the person. Stories are teachings handed down for thousands of years, and what they say is different for every person because every person is different. The stories are a way of helping people grow and grasp the triumph of becoming themselves. And this is why we were able to stage a bunch of children's fairy stories, lug them all over the country, put them on TV, and do them on Broadway without being labeled "children's theater."

Q: *Your comments on the relationship between religion and the theater bring to mind something I heard happened during the riots in Chicago in 1968. The police were rampaging through Old-Town, beating up protestors and others, sometimes following people into their own homes. But there were a number who sought refuge in what had been The Second City beer garden and theater, and the police didn't follow them in. They would chase the people right up to the property line and no farther. It was almost as if something in the collective subconscious of the police and the* protestors *reaffirmed the unity between theater and church so that, in a way, the theater was regarded as if it were a church in the sense that people could, in effect, claim and receive sanctuary there. There's something I find magical about that.*

I understand you were in Chicago at the time working on a story theater interpretation of the American Revolution.

SILLS: In that very sanctuary, the old Second City, in which Story Theatre had just opened. We were rehearsing then, and on the wall outside our theater we had written, "Coming—*The American Revolution!*" I learned a lot about the American Revolution that week. Boston in 1768 must have been something like it was that week in Chicago, what with the troops arriving and the town meetings.

Q: *There was a town meeting that week?*

SILLS: It was the result of the chaos in the street and the authoritarian approach to the citizenry by the oligarchy. The effect all this had on the people of Lincoln Park was very strong. They responded with spirit and we opened the theater to a town meeting to talk about com-

munity-controlled police, or something to prevent the cops
from coming into people's homes and knocking heads off. It
was the only town meeting of a spontaneous nature I've
ever encountered.

We opened *The American Revolution* a month after the
convention, and it was based on the experience of the
people who were in the street. You had people in the
theater who could understand what the Boston Massacre
was like from knowing the reality of what it is to be in a
situation where you could be shot down by the troops in
your own neighborhood. After a while, the show became
just a bunch of people acting, but sometimes, especially
in rehearsal, there was this great high of being able to
comprehend what the "Spirit of Liberty" is from having
experienced it that week. Something has to be created in
connection with the spirit or it's bullshit.

Q: *The work you've done has had a significant effect on
the general world of popular entertainment. I'm curious
what your reaction is to this.*

SILLS: Of course, you can apply improvisation to television and commercials and the like, and you'll get results,
but I think it's a little like using a diamond to stop
a bottle.

I feel that mere entertainment is not crucial. What happens is that sometime, someplace, you have an artistic work
appear as a response to a necessity, and a form is found in
that response. Once that form is found, everybody can do
it or repeat it or connect with it. So then it can become an
entertainment. It can be sold, watered down successively.
So that you find a well-made play written by a Broadway
craftsman today constructed on formal principles that were
worked out in, say, the nineteenth century by artists. Once
the ground has been broken, once the door is open, everyone can flood in.

Q: *I gather that you don't much care for mass entertainment.*

SILLS: I don't believe in mass culture and mass-pro-
duced culture. I think it's artistically degrading and most
of it is pretense. There are very few instances when it's
true personal work. I think that it's mostly just a business.

It's curious. The best people in society often go into the
theater. The ones with the most heart, the most soul, the

ones most developed in a lot of ways—the cleverest, the best-looking, et cetera. But—I don't know why it is—for most of them the personal liberation doesn't go on. They stunt it. They're not brothers in a journey. They separate from their community.

3.

Roger Bowen

Roger Bowen has been intimately involved with improvisational theater since 1955. *Enterprise,* the first scenario-play David Shepherd directed, was developed from a Bowen scenario and featured him in a leading role. He was in the original companies of both The Compass and The Second City, for which he often wrote, his most famous creation being "Businessman." In the late '60s, he was a member of The Committee, and he has frequently appeared with The Pitschel Players, an improvisational troupe his wife Ann founded and directs.

Bowen frequently appears on television and was a regular on the series *Arnie* and *The Brian Keith Show.* His best-known performance was as Henry Blake in the film *M*A*S*H.*

BOWEN: I was a student at the law school at the University of Chicago in 1954–55. I was reviewing plays at the Playwrights Theatre Club for the *Chicago Maroon,* the campus paper, and I was very enthusiastic. I thought they were really excellent. So I met David Shepherd.

He was very radical politically and his great dream was that you could have a workers' theater. One of the banes of the radical is the lack of self-awareness of the proletariat, so this was to be kind of an educational thing. The proletarians would have their own theater and through improvisation they would create a dramatic form from their own lives and hopes and so acquire a sense of identity. You can see the kind of thing David had in mind today in black theater and El Teatro Campesino. But he couldn't realize his dream back then. Instead of starting a workers' theater, his improvisational concept became the basis of a rather sophisticated medium for college graduates.

The first improvisational theater was something that David and I did at the University of Chicago. It was in May 1955. The University Theatre was going to present a bill of one-acts, so David and I went to the director of U.T. and said, "Put us on your program because we would like to try out some experimental improvised plays."

I wrote a scenario called *Enterprise* which was about four teenage boys who own an auto in common. One day they find under their windshield wiper a notice from a used-car dealer that says, "I have to have one thousand used cars by Friday or I'll be in terrible trouble. I may even offer you cash plus a new car. Don't ask me why. I'm crazy." It was signed "Crazy Jake." The kids start debating. One says, "Gee, we've got this guy over a barrel. We could take our car in and get a new car." And another of the boys says, "Aw, now, let's not take advantage of the poor guy. It says right here that he's crazy." But they overcome their scruples and they go down and, needless to say, the used-car dealer—I played this part—screws them. They end up with a much worse car than they had before plus owing him a lot of money. And then they smash up the car.

So now they're really finished because they have no car at all and they have to pay the used-car dealer and what are they going to do? So one of them suggests, "Well, how about a junk jewelry fad? We'll take the pieces of the car and we'll cut them up into little things and put hooks on them and sell them to the girls in the high school." So they do, and they're successful. You see a scene where they're selling this junk jewelry to a girl using the same techniques that the used-car dealer used to sell them the clunker. They make just enough money to pay off the used-car dealer.

As a result of their work, they get a Junior Achievement Award. It's J.A. Day, and the head of Junior Achievement turns out to be Crazy Jake. So their award is a car, and they're going to drive the car away, but under the windshield wiper they see a notice from still another used-car dealer. And now they fall into a debate—should they trade this car or keep it? And that's where the play ends.

That took about thirty, thirty-five minutes to do, and there was another, even shorter scenario that David wrote that was done entirely with girls. David directed and I assisted him. They were very well received, so we said, "Well, we can go ahead and have a theater because this works."

Q: *Did Paul Sills have any part in putting these on?*

BOWEN: No, though probably David had learned things from Paul and was influenced by him. So Paul's influence on that was indirect and Viola's even more indirect.

In the meantime, Playwrights Theatre Club had been closed down because of fire laws, and so Paul was free. He was interested now. He listened to a tape of *Enterprise* and he said, "I can't understand why the audience is laughing, so it must be good." So he started a workshop to develop techniques. And Viola, who had come out to direct for Playwrights, gave us a workshop for three or four weeks. That was my first acquaintance with acting exercises of any kind. Then she went back to California and Paul took over and we opened The Compass.

The first Compass consisted of two storefronts, side by side. One was a bar, and then you went through a door to the theater next door. The show was always at war with the bar because the guy who started the bar did very well at the bar, but we weren't doing so well selling booze in the theater, so he wanted us out to turn it into a back room. He finally got rid of us at the end of the summer.

Then we moved to a bar called the Dock and that was nice, but no operation where you have a conventional-type bar owner and you're using his room is ever satisfactory. Incidentally, when we moved to the Dock, that was the first time we had a piano. We hired Bill Mathieu. He was about eighteen years old and he's been playing for improv groups ever since then.

I don't remember much about the third place. I was drafted in January 1956, so I wasn't there much.

We started Compass in the summer of 1955. Sills

directed in July and August, then went to England—to Bristol—on a Fulbright till the following spring. But even when he was around he didn't do all the directing. I remember that in August, Elaine directed one, David directed one, and Paul directed one. David was the one who chose the scenarios and helped shape them. We used to do a whole new show every week. That means we were rehearsing next week's show all day and were performing all night.

We'd have some amusing little piece to start the evening. I remember "Love through the Ages: Three Kinds of Kissing." And after the chivalrous romance of the Middle Ages and the noble romance of a later period, there was some modern cynical payoff.

And then we did what we'd call the "Living Newspaper," which was no relation to what was done in the '30s. You see, David had a funny way of doing things. He'd say, "I want to have a 'Living Newspaper,' " and we'd say, "What *is* a 'Living Newspaper'?" and he'd say, "I don't know. I just know I want something called the 'Living Newspaper.' " So I said, "Well, suppose we take a newspaper and break down the speeches so there's one person narrating, and when he gets to what Khrushchev says or Eisenhower says, another actor will speak those lines." And that's what he did.

Q: *Sounds a little like story theater.*

BOWEN: We would do this every day from that day's newspaper, so before the show I'd be editing the newspaper. All the actors would have their own papers, and they would read and they'd get to the end of one section and written at the bottom would be the number of the page they were to turn to next. So we'd do the latest Paris fashions and the summit conference and the comic strips.

Q: *Would you get into juxtaposition of the stories with one blending into another?*

BOWEN: Something like that. It would all add up to one thing. We did all of the newspapers at one time or another. I think we had a preference for the *Daily News*. It turned out to provide the most merriment. We were especially fond of Sydney Harris, who was sort of a vest-pocket Mortimer Adler. Later on, in Compass, we did the same kind of thing with magazines—the "Living Magazine"—using the *New Yorker, Argosy,* and things like that.

After the "Living Newspaper," we'd do our scenario play. The first one we did was a marvelous piece that Paul wrote called *The Game of Hurt,* in which a cigar salesman and his wife go to a bar and they're just in the course of getting drunk, and the cigar salesman auctions off his wife to this very friendly, eager, enthusiastic steelworker from the South who's got a pocketful of money and wants to build a new life with this wife. Elaine May was the wife and David played the part of the cigar salesman. So then you had a scene where David wakes up and realizes what he did when he was drunk and he goes hat in hand to ask his wife to come back to him. Meanwhile, the steelworker, who's a young man, makes an impassioned plea that she stay with him. She replies by giving him this long, long recitation of the story of *Helen Trent,* the radio serial that asked the question: Can a woman past thirty-five achieve happiness? The story of Helen Trent is that she has been engaged to this guy Morgan Thomas for a long time, but they have a fight and break up and she meets a new fella. . . . Anyway, the wife is telling the steelworker the story as if these are real people, like neighbors next door. And in the end she makes the same decision as Helen Trent and she goes back to her husband.

And there was one that David wrote called *The Minister's Daughter.* It's about a minister, himself of an aristocratic family, but who lives in the slums and ministers to the needs of the people. . . . His two children are very annoyed with him for living in this place, and they're always taunting him and tormenting him—you know, they want money for golf clubs and dresses and things like that. The minister finally reveals that they're both adopted children, that they're actually children of that neighborhood he adopted when they were very small. This causes a revolution in their outlook on life. You see, that's the kind of story David liked.

There was another scenario, I don't know who wrote it, called *The Drifters,* about two guys who drift from job to job. They're on the make. They practice small con games on the people they come across, but they themselves are the victims of a much bigger con, the con being society.

And then there was one called *The Fuller Brush Sales-man.* In the first scene, we see a young man off the street, kind of aimless fellow, who goes in and answers an ad for Fuller Brush salesmen. The manager—I played that part—explains to the young man what it's necessary to do to be a Fuller Brush salesman. He equips him with a box of samples and gives him a sales pitch, dresses him up, and sends him out. So the young man goes from door to door and he can't master the sales pitch. He sort of stupidly holds out the samples and the people grab them and they take the things that aren't supposed to be samples and they order a lot of things they never intend to pay for. Halfway through, he realizes that everyone's taking advantage of him—all the housewives—and he says, in effect, the way it is in this society, you either screw or be screwed and he's not going to be screwed anymore. So then we see him visiting all the same women, but this time he comes on like a high-powered salesman. He's learned his lesson the American way and now he's an ace salesman, and he swamps them with brushes that they haven't the faintest use for. The actor, Andy Duncan, had marvelous ingenuity in coming up with weird kinds of brushes. In the end, he is now the sales manager and he's interviewing the new young man who comes in.

Another Compass scenario was called *Concupiscence and Crucifixion,* which is a story about a man faced with the problem of selling out in Hollywood. Mike Nichols played the part of the great European director looking back on the first movie he ever made, the picture that made his reputation, called *Quietly.* He said, "I have made many great films. I have made many important films. But I never made another *Quietly."* Which is kind of ironic in light of Mike's later career.

Then there was one that Elaine wrote called *Georgina's First Date.* It's about a fat, unattractive girl. On a bet from his friends, a very handsome guy invites her to the senior prom. Everybody thinks she's ugly and fat, and he's taking her out on a dare. She sort of knows it. He's got a bet with his friends that he's going to take her out and screw her—ten dollars, twenty dollars, whatever. But what the play is about is how all of society pushes her into this date because it's a "winner" date. He's a "winner" in society. So now her mother, played by Elaine, can go out and one-up the mother of the girl next door. Georgina and her mother go into a store to get her a dress and the mother says to the lady next door, "She's going out with so-and-so," and the lady next door is upset because previously she had been high-hatting the mother because her daughter was going out with a lot of people and Georgina wasn't going out with anybody. You can see the mother and the father sort of egging Georgina on, saying, "Don't worry about what time you come home tonight." It just seems all of society is pushing her into it. So she goes out, has a terrible time, gets laid. She comes back and her mother is waiting and asks, "How was it, dear?" And in a breaking voice Georgina says, "I had a wonderful time, Mother," because society has convinced her that she did have a wonderful time. So even though she has been damaged as a human being, she's accepted the social value.

After the scenario was over, we'd take suggestions from the audience and we'd come back and do some scenes and blackouts.

Q: *Do you remember the first time you took suggestions from the audience?*

BOWEN: Opening night, I think. The idea was to keep them there a little longer and sell them another drink.

Anyway, after a while, the scenario play was replaced by a kind of episodic play. For instance, in our first month we did something called *Five Dreams*. We had five actors who enacted their dreams. One had a dream that wherever he went everyone had paper bags on their heads—one of those noncommunication things. I can't remember the other dreams. But that sort of structure was the exception at the beginning of Compass. Toward the end they did more of that kind of thing as an excuse for doing five rather disparate pieces. Finally they dropped that and, in St. Louis, they actually did a revue. A collection of scenes and sketches and parodies.

Q: *What do you think was behind this transition in the structure of the shows?*

BOWEN: The revue form was developed when people ran out of ideas for scenarios, though David kept looking for scenarios, so, right up to the end, every now and then they'd do one. In the meantime, they'd been doing an improvised set late at night and they'd accumulated material in the form of short scenes and blackouts, and they began to repeat them.

To get back to the scenario plays, there were about eighteen that were performed during a year and a half, and maybe even more. But they all seemed to have a theme in common—how society molds people into the shape it wants them to take. Now this is interesting because it characterizes society as an intelligent force with direction. Whereas the kind of picture you got of society at Second City a couple years later was that society was a blind, meaningless, unintelligent automaton and people would just get lost in it. Second City was about alienation. It was about "How do I get out of this?" About people talking to machines, machines talking to them, everybody lost, everybody looking for a way out, and how it all didn't make any sense. I like the earlier conception because it suggests that man need not remain a helpless victim. That conception of society as a force that molds people into the form it wants them to take is more appealing to me than the conception of society as a machine that's out of control.

Q: *To what do you attribute this difference in emphasis between the two groups?*

BOWEN: Oh, the personality. Compass was David Shepherd's personality. That was the stamp that was put on it. And Second City was Paul Sills's personality. It's the difference between the way they saw the world. You see, these theaters will always have the stamp of the director, or whoever is in charge artistically. At Compass, Sills was the director, but he was lukewarm about the whole venture and he was away most of the time, so David Shepherd was the force who created it in his own image. If you got to know my wife, you'd see how clearly her personality is expressed by The Pitschel Players, even though the six actors in the show are completely different people. Alan Myerson's personality was expressed in the Committee shows, even after he ceased to be the director. Del Close and Peter Bonerz worked as directors under his rather loose supervision, but you could still see Alan Myerson's personality in the show. In this kind of theater, it is very definitely the director's personality that comes out. In straight plays, it's the playwright's personality, but in improvised theater, it's the director's. Because the directors are the ones who pick and choose. They are the ones who say, "Yes, develop this piece of material," and "No, I don't want to see that anymore." Just by this process of selecting and editing and showing the actors the lines along which they want them to go, they assert their personalities.

I think we did something very significant at Compass and hardly anybody knows anything about it. But you know, even when they're involved, very few people are conscious of the larger picture when they're doing something important like this. I mean, if you walked into Compass when all these people were doing these marvelous things, the conversation of the actors would be griping about the pay, or that the place was dusty, or "I'm not going to get up on that stage till they fix this or that," and "Where are we going to have lunch?" and "God, it's so hot. Why don't they fix the air conditioner?" This is what's going on in the actors' minds when they're creating great art. (*Laughs.*) It's kind of an irony, a paradox. Somehow the highest and the lowest are always present in the human endeavor.

I was at The Compass off and on. None of us was really committed to it. Paul wasn't. The only one who was was David Shepherd.

You know, there was quite a difference in the feeling between the replacements and the originals. The original people did it for a reason other than to be actors. We who started The Compass and The Second City had something to say and this was our way of saying it. I couldn't have cared less about being an actor. I never really thought of myself as a professional actor. At every opportunity, I would leave to go and do some writing and live off royalties for scenes I wrote. I sort of became an actor. It turned out to be the easiest way of making a living after a while. I really wasn't so good at the beginning in Compass. Then over the years I think I got to be pretty good, and by the time I got to The Committee, I think I was as good as anybody.

But the whole thing changed at Compass at the end of the summer of 1955, which was when David brought Severn Darden, Mike Nichols, and Mark and Bobbi Gordon into the company. They really were professional actors. He brought them from New York because a lot of our old

33

Compass people had to go back to work. Like Bob Coughlan, who was an industrial relations counselor. He had taken off a couple of months from his job to be at Compass, and then he had to go back. We had other people like that. One guy was a foreign correspondent who had to go back to where he came from. But that was part of what had made Compass good. People had come from different walks of life and they had a lot to bring to it. When it became all professional actors, the quality of the acting greatly increased, but the vision became narrower. People will improvise what they know, and if what they know is the world of theater and commercials and movies, that's what they're going to improvise about. But if they're social workers or lawyers or doctors, they're going to improvise about those things.

Q: *Moving on to Second City, what do you remember went on before you opened your doors to the public?*

BOWEN: Paul intended to open with a scenario play. He had written one—actually half-written one—but he was half-brainstorming it, trying to push it through. The play was to be about an ordinary guy, played by Gene Troobnick, who finds himself in a series of situations in society. Like he's in an employment office and he can't get a job, and then he finds himself at work and he's isolated, and he lies down to sleep and has weird dreams—you know, he dreams about Nixon being President. But the scenario fell apart. It wouldn't hold up dramatically. So we ended up doing a revue with three or four of the scenes from the scenario as separate bits.

One was written by David Shepherd, a thing called "The Dream of Richard Nixon." In it he walks out of the house —this was in 1959—and there's a little girl there, and he says, "Good morning, little girl." And she shrieks, "Oh! You're not Mr. Nixon!" And he rushes back inside the house and looks in the mirror and sees he didn't put on his face. So he opens a trunk and starts rummaging around in it. And he has a face in there for meeting Khrushchev, and then he has a Checkers face, and he tries on all these different faces. And finally he gets on the right face and he goes out and the little girl says, "Oh, Mr. Nixon! There was a bad man here before, but now that you're here I feel much better."

Roger Bowen

Q: *You said earlier that Second City was primarily about alienation rather than exploitation, but "Businessman" was about exploitation.*

BOWEN: Oh well, that was different. That wasn't an improvisation. I sat down and wrote that. I wrote a lot of things for Second City, but they never advertised that because it was supposed to be the theater of improvisation, right?

Q: *Were there others who actually wrote for Second City?*

BOWEN: Oh, yes. I'd say that the people who did a lot of writing for them over the years would be myself, John Brent, Del Close, David Shepherd, Omar Shapli, and Paul himself. In that first show I wrote two things, and Omar wrote a very funny song about FM stations—"The audience laughed,/ The audience cried,/ But Beethoven sells the program guide." David wrote a rather wonderful song in that show. Andy Duncan sang it. It went, "I'm going to school to be a space man./ They wrap you in envelopes of steel,/ Address you to the twenty-first century, /And drop you in the interstellar mail." Bill Mathieu wrote a beautiful tune for it. So there was a lot of written stuff in that first show, and in all the shows. That's how I made my living. I lived in Europe for a year on royalties from what I wrote. I'd write things and send them back to Second City and they'd send me a hundred a month.

Mostly, though, I was the chief source of political satire. Anything about Kennedy. And later, at The Committee, I did a hell of a lot of stuff on Johnson.

I remember I was at Second City in New York when John Kennedy was shot. I didn't particularly like Kennedy. It seemed to me he was a very charming, very likable fellow, but he was just another cold warrior. So I wasn't as deeply moved by his death as some people. I thought we should go ahead and do our show that night. But the others said no, they didn't want to, didn't feel like it. And I said, "I bet you one thing, out in San Francisco, Alan Myerson is doing a show tonight." Later I found out to my disappointment that they called off their show, too.

Q: *You've worked with both Sills and Myerson. How would you compare them?*

BOWEN: Alan Myerson's a real radical. Paul is not very

35

political. He just plays with it. Myerson's very good to his actors. He works with them, encourages them in every way. Paul may not be nice to them, but he certainly understands them. He knows exactly what button to press to make an actor squirm, to make him feel guilty and ashamed and feel that he and he alone is destroying the show. Paul is a virtuoso at that.

Q: *Does he also give absolution?*

BOWEN: In a rough, good-natured way. But very offhand. He has that quality of a charismatic leader to get people dependent on his approval, which is always just a little bit withheld. So he's got them running after the carrot, and meanwhile they're getting it with the stick.

Q: *Do you have any sense of what your contributions have been to improvisational theater?*

BOWEN: I wrote the first scenario, which set the pattern for most of the others. I gave form to David's vague longing for a "Living Newspaper," which, as you pointed out, sounds like the origin of story theater. And I invented several kinds of on-the-spot improvisations: a marriage counselor advising a couple about a problem submitted by the audience, an improvised adventure story woven around a number of audience suggestions with myself standing at the side providing a narrative frame, and improvised poetry. Aside from Severn Darden, I was the first to improvise answers to audience questions in character. I did that the first time as Kennedy. We did Kennedy-Khrushchev debates, so I said, "I'll go out and answer some questions as Kennedy if someone will come out and be Khrushchev and someone will be the interpreter." So I went out and I was Kennedy, and Arkin was Khrushchev and Severn was the interpreter and Andy Duncan was a press-conference guy.

And then Dick Libertini and I invented the spot which Jack Burns and Avery do now where questions from the audience are fed into a computer and the answer comes out.

But the on-the-spot improvisation is truly the most ephemeral of the work we do. It's very rare that you get something that, in addition to being funny and displaying virtuosity, also makes some kind of a statement, has some point of view. You could listen to tapes of hundreds and hundreds of spot improvs and maybe once or twice the actors would stumble on something that was beautifully pointed and had something to say. When you look for the heavyweight stuff, you look in the prepared scenes where someone began with a good idea.

Q: *When you talk about spot improvs, I take it you mean suggestions from the audience you act upon immediately, rather than suggestions that you have a few minutes to sift and discuss backstage before taking a shot at it.*

BOWEN: Right. When you have a few minutes to discuss a scene, it's not that much less of an improv, but it does give you a chance to plan the scene a bit.

Let me give you an example. At The Pitschel Players the other night, we were looking at twenty-five, thirty suggestions. One of the suggestions was "San Francisco chauvinist." Chris Pray said, "OK, I have an idea. I'm your nephew and I'm visiting L.A. from San Francisco and all I do is run L.A. into the ground." And I said, "OK, I know what to do with that. I want to do that, too." Because, ever since we came here, three or four of the guys, including Chris, were really knocking the hell out of L.A. They refused to like the place. Everything was wrong with L.A. Everything was good about San Francisco. I tried to point out nice things to them, but they wouldn't hear of it.

Chris has now reached the point where he has a satirical attitude toward himself for being this way. He has an image in his mind of the San Francisco chauvinist now, so when that suggestion came from the audience, he was primed to go. Taking that suggestion kind of crystallized something for us and we went ahead and did it. Now, if that had been an on-the-spot improv, it wouldn't have been the same because we wouldn't have been focused before we started the scene. Also, we chose to work on that suggestion rather than on the twenty-some other suggestions we got. But in an on-the-spot improv, you take what you get. It might catalyze something, it might not.

Q: *I get the impression that the spot improvs are like sports events. That the audience watches a spot improv differently than a regular scene or a planned improv. They're watching the spot improv to see if you can do it, and part of the interest is that suspense element.*

BOWEN: It's a game. It's a virtuoso feat we perform for

37

the audience. We love it. When it works, the audience loves it. It's not been my experience that during any of these anyone has sent a pipeline through to infinity, you know, and real truth has come out. On the contrary, it seems to me that in content it is the most superficial of the things we do. Certainly a whole evening of complete improvisation wouldn't add up to anything.

Q: *Still, an awful lot of good material has been developed through improvisation.*

BOWEN: Yes, but it's interesting that, to my mind, a lot of the improvised material doesn't stand up very well when transcribed onto the printed page. When a playwright writes and conceives a play, the heart of it is the dialogue and the actor's job is to find behavior that extends the dialogue so that the meaning of the play can be fully brought out. In improvisation it's the exact opposite. The actor creates the behavior and the dialogue is an extension of that behavior. The dialogue is not the heart of improvisation. The heart of it is behavior.

Q: *You've told me that you aren't very much into the theoretical aspects of improvisation and that you don't like doing the exercises and playing the games.*

BOWEN: I wouldn't do them. I nearly got fired from The Committee because I wouldn't do exercises. I said, "If you want to have a rehearsal and create material for the show, that's fine, that's part of my job. But to do 'Mirror,' that's for acting school to acquire concentration. I'm a journeyman now. I'm practicing my craft."

I never had much interest in improvisation for its own sake. For me, the only value of improvisation is that it creates a show. It's one of several different ways of creating a show. It's like a carpenter and his tools. He doesn't fall in love with a hammer and forget about the chisel. It's just one of his tools. But what you have now with some of the people is . . . well, I believe there was a scholar who defined decadence as a tendency of means to swallow ends. And Nietzsche said, "A fanatic is a person who, when he forgets his purpose, redoubles his effort." These thoughts cross my mind when I see the cult of improvisation.

Sure, improvisational workshops can benefit an actor. It's a kind of training, like an alternative school. But a lot of it is mindless. I mean, I don't expect the unconscious to do my thinking for me. Sure, it motivates me, but still, I have to think with my mind. I don't believe this has ever been acknowledged by the purists of improvisation. Sometimes it resembles some kind of Oriental exercise in which you try to tune out your conscious mind and get in touch with the universe—which is mysticism. Anyway, I never saw a theater that satisfied me that came from these exercises, except in the sense that these actors were trained in this way rather than some other way to do the work that all actors are supposed to do.

I remember in New York, when I was working there, Barbara Harris was in the show, and I was sitting talking to her and Arnold Weinstein, and Arnold was getting rhapsodic about Viola's book and saying, "Oh, it's so wonderful! To think that a mighty theater came from this book!" And I said, "Arnold, I've got news for you. Not one scene that was ever done at Second City came from an exercise." He was stunned. He turned to Barbara Harris and said, "Is that true?" And very reluctantly she said, "It's true." Not one. Not even one. Every scene that was ever done came from someone having a good idea.

I will say that improvisation is a very good tool for translating experience into drama very quickly. Something like *The Trial of the Catonsville Nine* had to be written and then cast and rehearsed, whereas through improvisation, though you can't get the same kind of richness of language, you can be on the stage the same day that something happens.

But even in the very best scenes you do not have the complexity of characters that you'll find in just a pretty good play.

Q: *But isn't that because of the limitation of length—having just a few minutes in which to do a scene so that you have to go for prototypes?*

BOWEN: That's true. All the loose ends have to be tied together. The characterizations are necessarily limited to what can be resolved in five minutes.

Q: *Did you find the characterizations were deeper when you were dealing with longer pieces at Compass?*

BOWEN: Well, at that time none of us were really that skillful as actors, and we weren't really prepared to deal with characters in great depth. Also, when the piece itself is

more about society than individuals, you'll get a kind of
flatness in characterizations. When we did *How to Catch a
Tax Evader,* for instance, we were more interested in the
relationship between the evader and society, how all of his
friends cover for him, and how he is very foxy with the
investigator. We were concerned with the *process.* Whereas,
in a conventional play, as a rule you're more interested in
what ultimately happens to the person with whom you most
strongly identify. The consequences of society are secondary. But Compass was about society. The characters
were limned just enough to show how society worked.

We're talking about a series of improvisational theaters
—The Compass, The Second City, The Premise, The
Committee, and The Pitschel Players and others which offer
entertainment to the public, and what they're famous for,
at their best, is not improvisation but satire. They have
something to say about what's going on in the world. That's
what they're there for. The kind of theaters that offer
nothing but games and on-the-spot improvs are not successful and not prominent. When we talk about improvisational
theater, we're talking about a theater of satire.

Q: *Why do you think there have been so few blacks in
this kind of theater?*

BOWEN: I think that satiric improvisational theater is
definitely a cosmopolitan phenomenon and the people who
do it and its audience are cosmopolitan people who are
sufficiently liberated from their ethnic backgrounds to
identify with whatever is going on throughout the world.
They know what a Chinese poem is like and what Italian
food tastes like. But I don't think most black people are
cosmopolitan. I think they're more ethnic in their orienta-
tion, so when they're black actors, they want to do black
theater.

You see, ethnic art tends to emphasize, enhance, and
reinforce certain ethnic values, to say, "Our group is a good
group." But when you get out of that and you identify with
a larger intellectual environment, you say, "Well, gee, that
was pretty narrow stuff." You get a concept of the brother-
hood of man and how much alike people are rather than
how different they are. You become de-ethnicized and you
become a citizen of the world. And the thing you busted

Roger Bowen

out of becomes a chrysalis, a discarded self, and the tendency is to turn on it.

Black people aren't at that point. The ethnic experience is very enjoyable, but it excludes the outer world. It's always "Us against them." In some ways it makes it easier for a person to get along because he doesn't have to fight every single battle.

Now a cosmopolitan has to fight every single battle there is because he can't say, "Me and my tribe say, 'Fuck you,' " because he has no tribe anymore. The cosmopolitan person also, by the way, is in a position of having to improvise a whole way of life, whereas in the ethnic society, much of it is handed to you; it's a received tradition.

Q: *Why do you think so few conservatives are attracted to satirical theater?*

BOWEN: Conservatives like to keep things the way they are, sweep the dirt under the rug, keep the skeleton in the closet. Satirists like to bring it out. "Liberals"—the word means "free." You know, open it up. The open society is a liberal conception. The rigidly structured, hierarchical side is a conservative conception. And yet, some of the greatest satirists in history have been conservatives. Jonathan Swift was an archconservative. I know that occasionally I used to find a clever piece of antiliberal satire in the *National Review.* But I think, on the whole, satire tends to be an antiestablishment thing because it lets the air out of the big balloons and the people who are conservatives have an investment in those balloons.

But it's funny how people react to satire. They love to be satirized. I remember one night at Second City somebody said, "There are Ford Motor executives out there." They'd come in for a convention from Michigan. So we went out and said every horrible thing, cooking up stuff to say how bad their cars were. Well, they came backstage and they loved it. "Oh, we wish the other guys could come and see this! You kids are wonderful!" It was, "Oooh, satirize me again!" (*Laughs.*) So, I don't know. . . .

Q: *So why do you do satire?*

BOWEN: I think it's good because it restores a sense of proportion. People really feel oppressed by people like Nelson Rockefeller and Lyndon Johnson and Earl Butz and Richard Nixon and George Meany—all these guys

41

who are just horrors and take it for granted that it's their job to police the world and decide what's right and wrong for everybody. I think people get demoralized if they can't get some of their own back. And one way to do that is through satire.

People do feel kind of estranged in our society. Not so much in the past few years because a huge counterculture has developed and people can now be at home in their counterculture. But before, there was no such thing, and to be able to go to a place like The Second City or The Compass and see that there were a lot of people who felt the same way you did and you were all having a good laugh at it, I think that was a great tonic for the morale. It increases solidarity among the disaffected.

I remember going to high school in Rhode Island. I lived in conventional middle-class surroundings, and you'd hear the principal telling you what he thinks, and you do something wrong and the teacher gives you a tongue-lashing, and the other kids are pursuing certain values, and the whole thing seems like a lot of shit. It seems that it's all wrong somehow. But you're alone so you feel that you must be crazy. You must be a twisted, distorted person. Then you find out that there are a whole lot of people who feel the same way and they don't look twisted or distorted at all.

Q: *So you think of improvisational theater as a rallying point.*

BOWEN: You know, it may be—and this is something you'd have to be very careful about because it's a very complicated thing and you couldn't really prove it—but it may be that Second City and theaters like it had their place in the counterculture that burst out in 1966 and 1967. A lot of people all of a sudden living a whole different way of life. I think this had to have some precursors, and maybe improvisational theater was one of them.

4.

Andrew Duncan

Andrew Duncan was a founding member of both The Compass and The Second City. It would be simplistic to call him the companies' straight man, though he performed many of the traditional functions of the straight man. He was (and still is) particularly adept at revealing the madness bubbling under the surface of seemingly normal characters. (He was an inspired choice for Lieutenant Practice in Alan Arkin's Off-Broadway production of Jules Feiffer's *Little Murders.*) Among his best-remembered characterizations at Second City were the beleaguered former Big Ten coach who has been lured to Hyde Park to instruct three hopelessly unathletic students in "Football Comes to the University of Chicago" and the eager young social worker who tries to counsel an unemployed Puerto Rican youth (played by Alan Arkin). He and Arkin re-created this latter scene on film in the enormously popular short, *That's Me!*

In addition to *Little Murders,* Duncan's stage work has included *The White House Murder Case* (also written by Feiffer and directed by Arkin). Feature film appearances include *The Rain People, Loving, The Hospital, Network, Slap Shot,* and *An Unmarried Woman.* On television, he was a regular on *The Nut House,* the *ABC Comedy News,* and both the British and American editions of *That Was the Week That Was.* He and a New York Second City alumnus, Paul Dooley, specialize in developing material through improvisation for commercials and industrial presentations.

DUNCAN: I was at the University of Chicago trying to get an M.A. in English, and I did a University Theatre production of *The Wild Duck.* That's how I met Sills and Shepherd. They would always go to these things. Shepherd asked me if I'd be interested in a workshop kind of thing. This was in January or February 1955.

So that spring we started workshops. Viola Spolin had come to Chicago to direct at Playwrights, and she was asked to run them. There were sixty or seventy people in those first workshops, and Viola applied her games— "Contact," "Finding the Where," and the rest. Some of the people could do it, some couldn't. From that they started culling out a company for Compass. They were working against a deadline because they took a lease on a place on the South Side.

We knocked a hole in the wall and built the theater next door to the actual bar. I had been a carpenter and a builder, so I sort of supervised that. Sills and Roger and I did all the physical labor—making the hole in the wall, putting in baffles to minimize the noise from next door. And we did all our own wiring. Charley Jacobs was good at that, too. Sills and I mostly built the stage. It was a platform roughly eight by twelve or thirteen feet raised off the floor about three feet. There were three fixed panels upstage, and in between them were two louvers—panels which revolved on pipes and could be positioned in a variety of ways. You could also peek over the top of them. If you stood on the floor behind the stage with a louver open, you would appear three feet shorter, which is how I would play Toulouse-Lautrec.

Since we had no real set or any kind of production values, I painted the panels bright colors. Then we gelled our lights to tone that down, which gave it kind of a nice glow. There were no curtains on the windows, so you could look in from the outside and it would look very rosy and multi-hued and kind of seductive. Mike used to complain that it was hard to improvise on a "riot of color,"

44

but I thought we needed it. It was primitive, but it worked. As I remember, July 4, 1955, was the night we were supposed to open, but we missed it by one day. The Fourth was hotter than hell and the air conditioner broke down, so we opened on July 5. We publicized it by distributing handbills and flyers during the day.

Q: *When Compass got started, was there a clear delineation of who the company was—who was in, who was not?*

DUNCAN: No, though there were some people who were paid and some who weren't. I think what happened was the people were evaluated in terms of their contributions. I can't tell you offhand who got paid and who didn't, though I can guess about some. Elaine was directing and acting, so she was paid. And obviously I was paid because I was doing so much physical labor as well as working in workshops. But somebody who came and sat around the workshop and maybe walked on that night—probably he didn't get anything.

Q: *How much were the people who were getting paid being paid?*

DUNCAN: At first, $25 a week. I think later it went up to $35 or $40, and then to $60 when we went up to the North Side of Chicago. That was in 1955, when $60 a week went a lot farther than it does today. But certainly, even in those days, the $25 a week we were paid to start with was very little.

David really expected people in the troupe to have other jobs. But to have other jobs meant passing up workshops. Or, if you had a night job, you couldn't perform at night. There was an elitist thing behind his premise, no matter how based it was in Brechtian-Marxist whatever. You had to have money to support it.

O: *You had to have enough money so that you wouldn't have to take a job that would conflict with working at the · theater.*

DUNCAN: Which seemed to me to kind of assume that you had a leisured group of people.

Q: *So the theater was operating on contradictory premises.*

DUNCAN: You'll probably hear me talk a lot about contradictions. I think dialectically. The history of improvisational theater is shot through with all kinds of other things besides who created what and the night so-and-so did something. The anecdotes are fun, but the history also has to do with contradictions between the intentions behind these theaters and what actually happened.

Q: *What kind of people gravitated toward The Compass?*

DUNCAN: They belonged to what I call the *lumpen*-bourgeoisie.

Q: *Could you explain what you mean by that?*

DUNCAN: The proletariat has people who are hangers-on, parasites. They're called the *lumpen*-proletariat. Marx calls them underworld-type people. Criminals, pimps, hustlers. They're capable of heinous crimes, but in a broader context you can see that they're alienated and deprived and so on. That they're just taking the rules of that culture and subverting them for their own purposes.

I think the bourgeoisie, too—the middle class—produced these people. Hangers-on. I know when I went to the University of Chicago, they were all over the place—guys who weren't working for degrees but were there. They couldn't get into the mold of getting a degree. Or, like me, they got a degree and hung around. I remember meeting a professor one day—a guy I respected who was one of my mentors—and he said, "What? Are you still here? Get the hell out there!" That and a few other things sort of woke me up.

(Actually, I should tell you I was from a working-class background—one of the only ones of this group. But I had pretty much de-classed myself.)

But we flirted with academia and we floated around a lot. We generally felt we weren't part of the culture. We felt alienated for some reason. So I call these people *lumpen*-bourgeoisie. We weren't proletarian workers, and we weren't *lumpen*-proletariat. We were kind of misfits. Some people just don't connect. If you don't connect, then you may go insane or drink or whatever. Well, we were enough affected by the fact that we were white and that we were somewhat prone to progressive ideas about growth that we didn't fall apart. We didn't take drugs, we didn't drink, we didn't commit suicide. In a sense we hadn't given up hope of finding a way to express ourselves in something that wasn't a profession or a nine-to-five in an office.

Andrew Duncan

Suddenly there was this place called The Compass. My God, what an incredible opportunity! To suddenly find something that was . . . not elitist, but still an applied form in which to get up and start expressing the things we were thinking about and feeling at that time, with all those repressed political, social, psychological feelings . . . I mean, the *freedom!* We were doing some very outspoken things on sex and politics, saying "shit" onstage, calling a spade a spade. A lot of what we did was very negative in that we were satirizing the establishment's institutions. But a lot of it, too, was an expression of how we wanted to live, crude and pioneering as it was.

And we struck a responsive chord in our audience. We were articulate, we were as educated as they were, and we were as perceptive about what was going on politically and socially and so on. I think it delighted them to have a lot of these repressed feelings expressed. We were their representatives, in a sense.

Q: *So most of the people in The Compass were refugees from the middle class. Though they were brought up with middle-class life-styles and expectations, they couldn't fit into that scene.*

DUNCAN: Right.

Q: *Yet the middle-class way of life was still more their emotional home than anything else. The act of running away from home presupposes there is something in your life you feel is home or you couldn't run away from it. So, despite the alienation, middle-class life was home to them.*

DUNCAN: Though obviously not a perfect home.

Q: *So these people had run away from this, yet even in their social refugeeship—*

DUNCAN: That's a good phrase.

Q: *—they were reporting back to the same people they were running away from.*

DUNCAN: Exactly.

Q: *Don't you think that your audience—these people from whom you had, in a manner of speaking, escaped— just by virtue of the fact they came to see you and supported you and appreciated you, almost felt they became one of you, of your community? That by associating with you, they enjoyed the sense of having escaped, too?*

DUNCAN: Oh, sure.

Something Wonderful Right Away

Q: *Originally there was a new scenario every week.*

DUNCAN: Yeah, and that was impossible. I remember meetings where we said, "David, we can't do this. We physically can't do this." We did so many. Scenario after scenario. Some were good and some were terrible. Roger's scenarios usually held up pretty well. He had a writer's sense of structure. His stuff was very didactic, and at the same time it had a broad sense of humor—almost Marx Brothers.

David's were much more into detail. "How would this guy dress? How would he knock on the door?" He was into that kind of thing. Every day, practically, he would come in with a new scenario. He was pumping them out of the typewriter. He was frustrated in that obviously he was relying on the actors to take off from these, and if what he brought in didn't strike a chord—and a lot didn't —nothing happened. So many of his scenarios just went down the drain.

There was an overt effort on his part to get workers to come to the club. He went into factory areas with hand-bills and sent out flyers to the unions. Well, going to The Compass was cheap, no more expensive than going to a bar and watching television, so some of these big, rough guys would come in once in a while.

Of course, this would affect our work. Normally, in the improv part of the show, we'd do takeoffs on literature, which were favorites with the university crowd. Parodies of Ibsen, Chekhov, Kafka, and such. Say Elaine and I would come out and take a suggestion for a situation, then we would do it as a scene in the style of Henry James. I don't know what it said about political realities and so on. but it was a hell of an entertaining vehicle and the audience loved it because it was their world. Which is how you are in a university—almost bracketed from the real world. But you couldn't connect with workers with this kind of material.

I remember one night there were a lot of steeplejacks in the audience. David had drummed them up from Gary or somewhere. Ironworkers. The scenario that night was called *The War Bride.* Mickey Le Glaire plaved the vet who had come back from France with a war bride, played by Lucy Minnerle. Elaine was in it, too, as a kind of friend up-

48

stairs. It was a really awful scenario, and it wasn't reaching these guys from Gary. As a matter of fact, it wasn't reaching anybody. I suppose they would have been a good audience if they'd gotten something that really touched them—if we'd done something on unions or steeplejacks' problems. But this wasn't. It was so remote to them. They didn't have French war brides. They started heckling and Freddie Ranovitch came into the room and a fight broke out. I was in the back working lights or something. I heard this commotion and got in on the latter part of it, in which one of the workers got laid out with a baseball bat. Finally the fight ended out on the street. Of course it disrupted the show. Cops were called and arrests were made. The charges were later thrown out for some reason.

Q: *That happened after Sills had already left with Barbara on his Fulbright.*

DUNCAN: By that time the group had started solidifying.

Q: *So that first stage of The Compass, when some people were paid and some weren't and the group wasn't clearly defined, was when?*

DUNCAN: I would say July, August, September.

Q: *How did the group become more defined? Was it self-elimination? Did some people sort of drop out? Or did someone actually say, "You're in, you're out"?*

DUNCAN: There was a little of both. Mostly I think it was someone's decision. I don't think it evolved organically. I think Charley Jacobs was more of an influence than people realized. He was the businessman. He would say to David, "Look, David, goddamnit, you've got this audience coming in, and then you put amateurs on the stage and the people walk out on you." David saw Charley's point, reluctantly, probably. So I think it was that kind of economic pressure Charley applied which helped shape the group.

When Sills left, he went to New York and had an open audition. He said the actors were coming out of the woodwork. Actors willing to come out to Chicago and work for $35 a week. Out of the interviews he got Severn Darden and Mike Nichols and Kenna Hunt, who didn't stay very long. So you got a shift from the theater coming out of the principal concerns of the community to isolating the stage with professional actors. Another contributing factor was if you have a sink-or-swim situation, obviously the professional is going to swim, whereas the amateur will sink. So this was another step away from Shepherd's idea of having a place where anybody could get up and do his or her stuff.

Q: *So Compass became decidedly pro. From what I know of David's dislike of professional actors, that must have been a disappointment to him.*

DUNCAN: His quarrel with professionalism is really one of the most amusing I've ever heard. I mean, I know what it stems from—in his mind the professional is linked with commercialism and capitalism and so on. But I don't think that's the Marxist position. A Marxist, it seems to me, doesn't object to the idea that the actor or painter or somebody starts to structure his working procedure into a method to deal with his art. David didn't see that professionalism is a way of dealing with raw material, relating to your material so that you can shape it. It's not necessarily some crass commercial thing.

A lot of David's experiments happened while Paul was in England. He had a Monday-night thing in which the parade of community could come through. It was a fiasco. It was a disaster. Because he was still charging people for beer. We didn't have a cover or a minimum, but still there was an economic premise there. People paid for a drink so they could sit there and watch the show, and on Monday nights, because it was amateurs, the show wasn't working.

So David had the idea that the company would take turns coming in on Monday nights to work with the people who got up. Every week one or two people had to give up their free night to come in and do this, which meant that there were times when you would work every night for thirteen nights in a row. This was a disaster, too. I remember I stayed with Mike Nichols one night and it was horrendous! Poor Mike was onstage with some woman from the community and she just devastated him personally.

Q: *That's another aspect of being in a professional situation—you're protected from that kind of thing.*

DUNCAN: Right.

Q: *What else can you tell me of Mike at The Compass?*

DUNCAN: One night we were doing "Hansel and Gretel" and Mike was playing the witch. I think at the end, Roger Bowen, Bobbi Gordon, and Elaine popped him into the oven; that is, they literally threw him out through a louver and you heard this "Argh!" sort of cry. Little did we know onstage, he had broken his collarbone. Backstage was all a-flurry. They called an ambulance and Mike went off to the University of Chicago hospital. We didn't see him again that night, but he came back a day or two later in traction. He played much of his early days at Compass incapacitated. I often wondered whether that had much to do with his immobility onstage; the fact that he would root himself in a chair and smoke cigarettes. You could always tell when a Mike Nichols scene had been done, because afterward the stage would be littered with Kent Micronite filters.

Q: *In September The Compass moved.*

DUNCAN: Yes. I remember Severn getting up to announce the move saying, "From now on we will be Dump Us in the Cock! Er, I mean Compass in the Dock."

We still did scenarios there. We were doing *Rumpelstiltskin,* which was Elaine's scenario, when Severn finally threw up his hands. He had become drained and was always complaining we did too many scenarios. One year was enough. Severn had played the king and Shelley Berman came out to replace him. One night it was Severn and there was give-and-take, the next night there was this dynamo who was devouring everything in sight. And you'd come off and he'd go, "Was I good? Was I good? Was I good?" You'd say, "Yeah, Shelley, listen to the audience." "Aw, fuck them. Was I good?"

Shelley was a great joke-stealer. We did a scenario about a summer camp that David wrote. Shelley and Elaine were the owners of this camp, Mike was a counselor, and I was a new guy coming up to be hired. There was a scene where we were on the veranda of this big house looking out on the lake. He had a running gag where he'd yell, "Buddies!" and the campers he was watching would hold up their hands in the buddy system. And he'd say, "Where's Number Three? Oh, there he is. Look at him breathe. Oh, he's blue!" Every night he would add a little to this until it became a five-minute legato. One night I said, "Is that one of your campers? He's got a beard." Just to needle him a little, to top him. To put in the spark that makes improvisation. Next night he put the beard in his shtick. (*Laughs.*) "Oh, he's got a beard! Is he one of ours?"

51

He was good. I don't mean to deny that. He had a really tremendous sense of an audience, but he didn't work our way. He wouldn't give an inch. You really had to fight him. I was one of the few who could get along with him and he liked doing scenes with me because of that.

Q: *After the Dock, The Compass moved to the Off-Beat Room where I understand Compass had some ideological differences with the owner.*

DUNCAN: Oh, that was wherever we went. We had it with Freddie Wranovics. He was a strong Catholic and he didn't want to see anything on birth control. I remember there was a young black guy named Bob Patton from the University of Chicago in *Georgina's First Date* and, although it didn't come out at first, I think it bothered one of the bartenders there was a black guy onstage. I mean, this was 1955. Well, it was hollow under the stage, and this bartender would crawl under and pound, interrupting rehearsals, because the whole thing bugged him. Finally, he leaped onstage one night during a performance when Bobby kissed one of the white girls. This infuriated this bartender. He wasn't going to have a black guy kissing a white girl on that stage!

The two guys at the Dock—father and son—they were very conservative Germans. They were unbelievable. They were always objecting to our morality and language. I remember they objected to us using the word "diaphragm" onstage. And yet, they saw the people coming in. . . .

Burr McCloskey at the Off-Beat Room was the best of the owners. He was sort of a nice guy and sympathetic. He had a nice stage with good sightlines, though it was a huge room. We packed them in there, too. Though when the fragmentation started, the audience started falling off. He had a legitimate gripe. That show was falling apart.

What happened was the group really broke up. It was just torn apart. I think the wedge was Shelley. We did scenarios that put us all together, obviously, but in the free-form time we broke up into little groups. I started working with Shelley. Not so much out of Shelley's choice. He really wanted someone more like Elaine because she was terrific to work with. I kind of lost Elaine. We worked a lot together early on, and then Mike came in and she worked mostly with him. But there was some strife between

Mike and Shelley over Elaine. They were really at odds. Meanwhile, Mark and Bobbi worked mostly together doing domestic scenes from their own lives. And occasionally they worked with me.

Sills came back at about this time, and we had fragmented to the point where there was no unity to the show. Lights would come up and there would be a scene, and then the next scene after that would have nothing to do with anything. The show was stagnating, becoming unbalanced. I don't think we were doing any scenarios by the time Paul came back, but I may be incorrect about that.

Q: *What was Sills's reaction to all this?*

DUNCAN: Oh, he was furious! In his typical way—rage and yelling at the actors. Obviously that must have had something to do with the shake-up.

I got fired before the end of it. Actually what happened was that David wanted me to go up to Madison, Wisconsin, and start a Compass there. I was literally supposed to go up there on my own. No capital, no backing from them. I was supposed to get a job in the community, start a workshop, and put together a group that would get The Compass name. Sort of like infiltration. (*Laughs.*) Maybe it was just a way to get rid of me. Maybe there never was any intention of starting a Madison Compass. But it seems a little roundabout to do that. Anyway, if you detect an anti-Shepherd bias in all this, that's the reason—he fired me. The Madison thing didn't work out and I was let go in October 1956. And then Bobbi and Mark resigned. Not so much in protest, but they saw what was happening.

The funny thing is that Mike always felt *he* was the one they were going to fire. He was terrified. Shepherd was taking Mike aside and Mike would tell us. There was a bar out front where we hung out and Mike would come out and say, "David's been talking to me about my work." He thought he was going to get the axe. Instead, I did.

It was a big blow to be let go. I did a kind of reversal thing and didn't even go back to see the show. Around then, Shelley made an overture. We had dinner one night and he suggested we do an act together. I guess we did have a rapport, but nothing came out of that. I remember I asked him how the show was going and he grumbled about Mike.

53

I saw Burr not too long after I left. He said the show was a nightmare and falling apart. Severn and Barbara came back to the company and Rose and Larry Arrick and Walter Beakel also came, but The Compass didn't last long after that. It ran downhill, I remember, to my satisfaction. I had been fired from something I'd been such a part of and had given so much of my energy to.

I wasn't connected with the group again for a while. I did a local job. Social work. I was a counselor. I went into the Cook County jails and worked with prisoners.

While I was there, I would see Sills occasionally. We'd talk in a coffee shop in Hyde Park or I'd see him on the Near North Side. He was working at the Gate of Horn at that time. Talked about starting another group. It wasn't as though he said, "Gee, Mike and Elaine are making it and Shelley, too. Maybe we should start another group." But it was like he felt that this kind of work was more in the air than ever since they hit. That improvisation was still alive and there was still room for it in Chicago. He said, "Barbara's around and I talked to Gene Troobnick. Are you interested?" I said, "Yeah." It was to be a lot like Compass but more finished. We talked at that time about it being much more of a cabaret in the German sense and that it would hit politics much more.

So we started workshops in the Chinese laundry on North Avenue and Wells, across the street from Lincoln Park. It was just a bare floor with wires sticking out of the ceiling and debris, and you'd have to sweep away plaster. We started work and some nights there'd be two or three of us, and some nights the whole group. Meanwhile, behind the scenes Bernie was getting the money.

They hired the guy who'd decorated the St. Louis Compass to put Second City together. He bought up a warehouse of doors, painted them black and lined the walls with them. Then he brought in red plush velvet. There was something sexy about the look of the place. A sin kind of thing. You came in there and it was all black with red plush.

The stage was tiny at the first Second City. It was a little postage-stamp kind of thing, smaller than our first Compass stage. It had drapes on either side, and the piano was tucked up in the corner upstage left. The only entrance was stage right so we were very limited in terms of entrances and exits.

What was evident at Second City was the completeness of the presentation. Rather than the anarchy which reigned at The Compass, Sills planned every second from the minute the light dimmed to the applause and bows. Also, whereas in Compass scenes would start without introductions, at Second City they would often be set up. I don't know where we got that convention of making introductions, but somehow it fell on me to come out and say, "Good evening. Welcome to Second City. Tonight we'd like to bring you our show, *Too Many Hats*"—or whatever the title was. Severn was constantly coming up with titles from Shakespeare. He got a number of them from *The Tempest*.

Sills insisted very strongly that the audience get to know the actors very early in the show, so that by the end of the first act they could identify who the people were and pretty much what they did—who was the kook, the square, et cetera. The first act would have a lot of group numbers like "Great Books" and "Football Comes to the University of Chicago." And then, at the end of the first act, I'd come out and say something like, "That completes the second part of our program. After a brief intermission we'll bring you the first part."

The second act would have more of the heavy stuff. The "people" scenes were always second-act scenes. like the museum scene Alan and Barbara did. The stuff that relied on character and place, when you knew the audience was really with you. Part of the fun then was to turn the audience's expectations upside down in terms of what they anticipated from the individual cast members. Like Barbara would come out and play old ladies. But very rarely would we start the show with people playing something very far away from themselves.

Sills wanted a variety of cast and a balance of cast. He would rarely have two scenes in a row with the same people. He insisted that if you saw Barbara and me in a scene. if it came back to us again. the audience would still be carrying the previous scene with them. He would want a break in between. That's what we used blackouts for. Also songs. Of course, the songs weren't improvised. Those we rehearsed with Bill Mathieu.

We often did operas. Severn and Barbara and I had done this kind of thing at Compass and it was a great crowd-pleaser. The first opera we did at Second City was improvised. After that Sills insisted that they be written, so that he and Mathieu could work out musical parodies to put on top of the actors parodying opera-style performing.

We had a pretty rigorous schedule. We were open six days a week. We'd come to the theater at ten o'clock and work till about two, then have lunch and come back and work till about six or seven—sometimes right up almost until nine, showtime—get a quick bite and then do a full Second City show, then take an intermission and come back and do improvs. So a normal day could be fourteen, fifteen, sixteen hours. Saturday worse. You didn't usually have a rehearsal on Saturday, although there were times we did. Saturday night we did two full shows. We were open Sunday so we'd rehearse on Sunday. Monday was off.

You'd fall into a rhythm, and sometimes it was easy because of that rhythm. It was almost like going to the office. Your perceptions were out in terms of what was going on—reading the papers. And you'd be thinking of ideas for scenes, storing them up for the improv set.

It seemed that every three months there was a crisis because that was when the new show would come in. Then the tensions would mount. Sills would be screaming, walking out. He and Barbara would fight, Howard and I would fight, Gene would be sulking because he didn't have enough material. Then the show would open, we would get great reviews, and then you'd fall into the rhythm again.

Q: *Can you go into a little more detail on Sills?*

DUNCAN: The Paul Sills syndrome would tend to operate this way: He would start out terribly enthusiastic and excited about what we were doing, laying it out for us. Then we'd start the rehearsals. You'd hit the block that you always hit with anything. You have a time pressure, you can't step back and reflect, you've got to work it through. Well, that would produce these rages in which he would throw chairs, sometimes at you. All kinds of juvenile behavior, all of which he'll admit, I'm sure. He's supposed to have changed. He says he doesn't work that way anymore. But I know I won't risk it. He wanted me to work with him in Washington a year or so ago, and I didn't do it because I couldn't face it.

Sills would say to us, "Goddamnit, we're not a theater where you go out every night and give the same performance by the numbers, and the audience has a certain relaxed assurance that the actor knows what he's doing. The whole point of Second City is the unexpected. You've got to have your creative juices going. *Do* something onstage." "Don't drop your pants," he'd say, "but if you do, make sure your ass is painted blue."

You'd get caught up in that and you'd go out onstage and maybe you'd try something and maybe it wouldn't work. You'd come offstage and he'd grab you by the arm and say, "What the fuck are you doing out there? What do you think you're doing?" You might be coming off to make a hat change, and suddenly he's grabbing you! He would do this to everyone, not just me. He did it to Arkin. You could tell one night that Arkin came that close to hitting him. Paul sensed it somehow and let go. But you can imagine how upsetting that would be. Sometimes it produced paralysis onstage. I can recall going out and shaking in a combination of anger and frustration and sadness, unable to speak. When he would come in and sit in the back, you could just feel his presence. The whole tone of the show would shift, sometimes from a thing that was working with a relaxed, witty brilliance to a very tense, slick pro thing. Suddenly the air would go out of it, and there was a sudden depression or terror.

Because you didn't have the usual cushion of preset lines and because this kind of theater came so directly out of people's personalities, and because sometimes there were tense things going on backstage, some of the offstage tensions would get mixed up in the onstage work. And sometimes ugly things would happen. I remember Harold Clurman saw us at such a time when we gave a terrible show, and he panned us. This kind of thing would be less noticeable in the group scenes. If I were having a fight with Howard, we could still do "Football Comes to the University of Chicago" well. What it really affected were the small scenes. For instance, if something were wrong between Alan and Barbara, you could sense it in the way they played the museum scene.

Q: *What are your thoughts on Bernie Sahlins?*

DUNCAN: As far as I was concerned personally, I thought Bernie was very sweet, genial, and probably a better boss than ninety-nine percent of the people you can work for. But there's that old contradiction of the guy who's both accountable to his backers for profits and sympathetic to the creative side. Even though there was a veneer of liberal humanism involved, the actors still got fucked. The owners really got a lot. When we left Second City as individuals, we didn't have anything except the experience and a certain amount of prestige. But they were left with the name and reputation of Second City, which would continue to draw crowds and make them money. We could say we were with them and that might be a credit on the résumé, but it was never anything you could go to the bank with.

The problem of ownership of the material was a major concern. The actors were advised to get a lawyer to prepare some sort of a legal contract in which management would get theirs and somehow we would get ours. The idea was that this material would be catalogued. Say we're talking about the museum scene. We knew that Barbara and Alan had improvised this one night in front of an audience and that it had been worked on in rehearsal, and that it was their scene, so they would get royalties if it were done again.

There were problems with this, of course. Say there were seven people in the company and four were very active in a show and three weren't. Do you pay all of them the same royalty? If you had a body of literature that was saleable, let's say you sold four Barbara Harris scenes and two Andrew Duncan scenes, would Andrew Duncan get two-sixths? Or say a scene that started between me and Severn at Compass. Then, years later, Steinberg does it with Severn and adds something to it. And then Steinberg does it on television and is paid for it. I don't think that was right. On the other hand, it would be very difficult for Severn and me to claim total ownership of the scene.

We never did get this cleared up.

But you couldn't help but like Bernie Sahlins. He was hardly the devil incarnate. It's just he was the boss.

Q: *How soon did the idea of going to New York come up?*

DUNCAN: We opened in December 1959, and by February there were people in from New York. I remember we had a vote when it came time to decide whether we were going to stay in Chicago or go to New York by way of L.A. I think the vote was five to four to leave. I voted to go. I've often wondered what if I'd voted the other way. . . . Part of my vote had to do with thinking that maybe if we escaped that pressure cooker of Sills and Alk. . . . Of course, we didn't escape because they followed us, and in some ways the pressures got worse.

Paul would play groups off against each other. He'd come to L.A. when we were playing the Ivar and say, "Jesus, the Kennedy-Khrushchev conference the other night in Chicago! Someone asked Bill Alton something and he said this or that. And Del Close said such-and-such. Maybe you guys can use that." Then he'd go back and do the same thing to the people in Chicago. I got this from Tony Holland, who is a close friend. And again, when we got to New York, there was the constant playing-off between us and the Chicago group.

Paul really had problems of relating. He had an affection for all of us, I'm sure. More than affection. But at the same time, he was under such pressures! And the more the groups proliferated . . . he had to get a group ready for London, cast replacements in New York, put together a new show in Chicago. The pressures of coming up with a new show were pretty hard on the actors, so you can imagine what it was like for Sills. So, if the Chicago group came up with a good scene, he'd bring it to New York. Well, there was no way to be assured that the New York audience would accept that scene or that the actors could take it over and make it theirs.

Something else that was part of this problem was that Paul didn't understand that the kind of surreal "head" humor that some of the Chicago people were coming up with then didn't fit me or Severn or Tony Holland. So it

59

was not good to try to make us do their scenes because they weren't right for us.

Q: *So he was extending his belief that anyone could do this kind of theater to the belief that anybody could do any scene out of this kind of show. But that doesn't logically follow.*

DUNCAN: That's right. I'm glad we got to that, because I think that relates to what I was talking about regarding contradictions.

The breakup of the troupe in New York was probably historically rooted to when we left. There was no way we could have this vast universe of Second Cities all over the world operating from the brain in Chicago or wherever Paul was. Groups tend to take their head, which is what we did in New York. Well, then we were accused of taking over. Larry Arrick, who was our director in New York then, was fired. So the whole group—Arkin, Zohra, Tony, Gene, and I—went and said, "OK, then we're going, too." I knew in the back of my mind that we were writing our notices because in doing that we forced their hand and they hired Larry back. We had a very close relationship with Larry, because he was *there* and Sills was in Chicago.

Larry left soon after, Arkin went off to do *Enter Laughing,* and Zohra went off to do *Mother Courage.* You could see the end coming. I didn't have a thing to leave for until way into 1963. When I was fired, I had a TV series in Hollywood called *The Nut House*—a thing like *Laugh-In* that didn't make it—to go to. Tony came with me.

But the group didn't last long after that. I think Sills really did destroy it, for whatever reasons, though I don't think they were overt or conscious. I don't mean to make him the villain. I just don't think that anybody could do it in that position—be the head of a multicorporation and still expect every facet to be in your hands. The good administrator puts people in charge in these places. But he seemed to have a mania for wanting to be . . . even though he couldn't do it physically, he wanted to be in charge of it all.

Q: *Having come out of Second City helped your career after you left, didn't it?*

60

DUNCAN: Sure. If I had come to New York and studied with Berghof or Strasberg and then started making the rounds, trying to get an agent, of course it would have been more difficult. My entrée was paved, as is true for everybody who came through Second City and The Compass. Of course, by now there have been so many people who've come out of Second City. It's astounding the number who really did. But, beyond that, there are a lot of résumés listing it who never did.

You and I were talking before about the total involvement of the individual in the making of improv scenes. He's not an "actor" in the Broadway or traditional sense of assimilating a body of material that's written with a director who has a point of view and a producer who's trying to achieve a certain effect. The actor in Second City and The Compass invested his sensitivity, his knowledge, his total person, and because of that, when you left the group, the effect would be one of . . . I'd put it as a crisis.

The two main crises in my life were when I left Compass and Second City. I left Compass after almost two years of emotional involvement, and I felt as though part of my life had been lost. It was an emptiness. I remember almost going into a retreat kind of thing. I was in a small room on Chicago's South Side and I just withdrew socially. I read and became very morose and unhappy. Totally distraught. It was as though a meaning had gone out of my life. Like a divorce.

When I left Second City, there was a period of being very busy immediately afterward which covered the separation. Doing *Nut House* and touring and playing Vegas with Bill Dana. But throughout these experiences, I really missed that kind of company—the community, working together, respect. I did pictures and TV and I'd meet people and do scenes with them without really knowing them, and after shooting I wouldn't see them again. And then again I went through an emotional thing of how incredible it was. I don't mean to say those were the good old days, but they were intense moments in your life that had meaning, that somehow you knew you'd never experience again. Which is both good and sad.

Again, in contradictory terms—there was the good and

the bad. What I have said may sound negative, but I take it for granted you've gotten all the positive from the others.

Thomas Jefferson once said he thought heaven would be the legislature. I guess for me it would be The Second City.

5.

Barbara Harris

Barbara Harris got her start as an apprentice at Playwrights, where she eventually worked her way up to leading roles. She belonged to the original Compass and Second City companies.

While at Second City, she had a hand in creating what I believe to be two of the finest scenes in the troupe's history:

In "First Affair" the teenage daughter of a University of Chicago academic (played by Severn Darden) reveals to her father that she has had her first sexual encounter with the son of one of his colleagues. Her father is distressed, not so much at the loss of her virginity, but at her seemingly dispassionate, academically analytical attitude toward the experience. When he asks her what she feels for the boy, she refers him to Erich Fromm. When he talks of Juliet's passion for Romeo, she characterizes it as a neurotic dependency. Finally the father gently breaks through his daughter's shield of jargon, revealing the vulnerable child underneath who, as the lights fade, buries herself in his arms and tearfully confesses her fear that the boy doesn't love her.

In "Museum Piece" a coed who has (as she puts it) "numerous problems in the area of spontaneity" encounters a beatnik (played by Alan Arkin) in Chicago's Art Institute. He encourages her to drop her inhibitions and charge full-tilt into stream-of-consciousness self-expression to the accompaniment of his guitar. She spends several minutes hilariously wrestling with her inhibitions, but the battle is hopelessly lost when the boy puts the make on her. Trying to remain polite, she beats a frantic retreat, leaving the beatnik alone and at loose ends at the scene's close.

The performance of these and other scenes quickly brought her to the attention of the New York theater world, and she went on to star in *Oh Dad, Poor Dad, Mother Courage, On a Clear Day You Can See Forever, The Apple Tree,* and *Mahagonny.* In films she starred in *A Thousand Clowns, Who Is Harry Kellerman?, Plaza Suite, Nashville,* and *Family Plot,* among others. Generally acknowledged as one of this country's best actresses, she is also a director of considerable ability, as evidenced by her staging of Elliott Baker's *The Penny Wars* on Broadway in 1969.

Q: *How did you join the gang?*

HARRIS: Friends of my family told me about Playwrights, and I went there as an apprentice to fill my extra time. I was going to school, but I was curious about theater, too. Curious about it more than serious, at that time. The theater scene in Chicago then was mostly road companies and that sort of thing, not easy to get into, even as an apprentice. I wonder now, had I not gotten into Playwrights, would I have gone into the theater? If I had apprenticed in, say, summer stock. I don't know if it would have been as stimulating for me. Playwrights was more than a summer stock company, it was kind of a way of life. Or a school of life. And a repertory company.

Q: *What do you remember of the Playwrights audiences?*

HARRIS: They were mostly from the University of Chicago—students or members of the faculty. They were staunch supporters, i.e., they made the hour-long trip from Hyde Park, they would climb a long set of unlit stairs to be seated in saggy canvas chairs (the chairs were sometimes still wet as we hand-scrubbed them too near to curtain time), and without air conditioning or ventilation, they would sit sweating and puffing, furiously fanning away with hankies and programs during one-hundred-degree heat waves. The crowds came in all numbers, from three hundred to three, to watch Sartre, Eliot, Brecht, Büchner, Shakespeare, et cetera. Despite our clumsy, unprofessional ways and the conditions which prevailed, they magically appeared again and again.

Q: *What was the effect of the McCarthy era on Playwrights?*

HARRIS: We were rightly disturbed, but it didn't prevent Paul Sills and David Shepherd from choosing the plays they wanted to do, whatever the political tone. I think I remember we were a little uptight about letting our theater be used by a group of lefties for a showing of a Communist film, *Salt of the Earth*. We voted on that one, because there was some chance we would be closed down if it ran there. After we caucused for a couple of hours, the majority felt, yes, of course, we had to run it. We would have been awful hypocrites if we hadn't. It finally came down to a matter of conscience. We weren't closed down, but some of the more paranoid among us had a few sleepless nights.

Q: *How soon did you start appearing in the shows?*

HARRIS: After about four months of apprenticeship. They needed people for crowd scenes.

Q: *I understand that when you did* The Dybbuk, *since there weren't enough men in the company for a minyan, some of the women put on beards. Were you one of them?*

HARRIS: No, I played the role of Bassia. Just a couple of lines and a simple folk dance. Later I did larger parts, without beards, which was just as well; they were awfully warm and too dark for my complexion.

Q: *Do you remember Paul running any of the games during rehearsals there?*

HARRIS: I don't, but then again I wasn't there for every rehearsal. I know for sure he was a serious student of Brecht—his concepts, methods, and ideology. He called us there on nights off to lecture about Brechtian philosophy. There was a religiosity to Paul. His principles were inviolable. He gave us the spark, the fire that kindled the group's spirit. It was a spirit which transcended individual, private, selfish concerns. He was an idealist and a perfectionist. "Stardom," for example, was totally out the window. Stardom, critics, petty ego all fell by the wayside in the face of his larger example.

It seems to me that improvisation came with Compass.

Q: *What do you remember about Viola's workshops before the opening of Compass?*

HARRIS: I remember with the advent of Viola's workshops—which, if I remember rightly, Paul and David also ran occasionally—that something very "gamey" was going on, i.e., the games, which none of us actors understood at all. In fact, in an ethical way, and quite suddenly, we actors were seemingly "brainwashed" out of our roles as actors. Our conventional suits were cast off. The technique, which was new at that time for us, namely, improvisation, swept us into another realm, another consciousness. It was hard. It was hard because it was new, because it was a totally unknown quantity with a new vocabulary, a new language, which asked for spontaneity and freedom on strata that followed nothing I had ever heard of before. I'd heard of *commedia dell'arte,* but that was about it. It was difficult at first. You think you'll never learn it, and you think you're an awful, awkward, cumbersome person who's just taking up space, but, as when you keep playing your scales on the piano, one day it becomes something you can feel—a learned faculty—and something easy comes about: You forget yourself as the process takes hold. You sort of become part of the form itself. It's suddenly so natural, like going from crawling to walking.

Q: *What did David have to say about where all this was leading?*

HARRIS: Months before Viola's workshop, when David's Compass idea was in the incubation stage, he had a couple of meetings where he made attempts to describe to a handful of us what he had in mind. As he put it, improvisation was to be used as a method to promote a non-middle-class theater. He talked about a radical departure from traditional theater, including traditional community theater where they did traditional plays, e.g., *Bell, Book and Candle.*

He spoke of establishing neighborhood cabarets. There the audience could watch and—equally important—participate in scenarios reflecting their own values, experiences, and life-styles. His idea was to incorporate the needs of the community into the life of the theater. We would be acting alongside lawyers discussing taxes, steelworkers discussing unions or their wives, ministers discussing their parishes, delinquents discussing their motorcycles and their girls, et al. It was to be the living truth of the community placed on the stage for them to gain insight into their own environment. In that theater, you got the feeling from David that it was more important to be a living person with a "real" occupation than to be an actor. For example, if there was a scenario with a part for a waitress, he would rather cast it with a real waitress than an actress, or vice versa.

Q: *David has conflicting feelings about Compass. . . .*

HARRIS: He has a right to them, I think. He had a good idea, he started it, and then it kind of turned into something else. When you say "conflicting feelings," that's right. He wanted it to go and be successful, yet, on the other hand, he knew it was a mutation of what he wanted.

Q: *The thing is, I think he actually accomplished what he set out to do. . . .*

HARRIS: Yes, at the University of Chicago, he did. But what he really wanted was a people's theater for all different classes. Instead, because the people he worked with were from the U. of C., they gave the theater to the U. of C.

Q: *Do you think Paul was as concerned with these contradictions David wrestled with? Or was his attitude more one of doing the work at hand?*

HARRIS: I think Paul understood and was sensitive to what David was saying, but it's almost as if there were a volition . . . as if the determining forces were too strong. His attitude had to be one of doing the work at hand. We weren't particularly successful initially, so the main struggle was just to keep it alive in whatever form. David talked about opening other cabarets in proletariat communities, but we had neither the money nor the energy nor the people to realize that. It was kind of like "Next year in Moscow." The priorities were simple—we had to keep our business going. It wasn't uncommon to find that at the end of the evening we'd only taken in twenty dollars. The proletariat were less hungry than we were. To think that we could sally forth and open a lot of other places was a wonderful thought, but, considering the realities of the situation, hardly practical.

Q: *I get the impression that, despite the lean times, you were having fun.*

HARRIS: I think you could say that. Nobody knew what was going to happen, but it *was* happening. We were creating our own standards as we worked and that was fun— win or lose. We were in a game of blind exploration. I really can't verbalize it. It was an existential need almost. Once it began, there we were, and like little ants or beavers, we *did it.* Like ants or beavers, we just kept *building!* Even if what we did fell down. There was nothing else to do but work hard.

Q: *Mike said he remembered times when, if something really didn't go well onstage, you'd literally run out and jump in the lake.*

HARRIS: Yes, Lake Michigan was about three blocks away. Between sets we would dive in out of sheer frustration. It was as good an answer as any in moments of total despair. That and playing chess were our big escape numbers.

Q: *If it failed as frequently as you say it did, why do you think people kept coming?*

HARRIS: I think the sense of watching something which might or might not work was interesting for the audiences in the beginning. What was going to happen? What *was* this? What could this form do, what did it do, what didn't it do? I think that may be why people would come back, even though half the time we were doing things that just didn't take off.

Also, in the beginning, it didn't cost much money to go to The Compass. It was a student hangout. Really, there was no place else for them to go. They were sitting in their residence halls; if they wanted to go someplace, they'd stop by to see what we were doing. It was sort of a place for intellectuals to slum. Later, as it became more professional and as salaries were being paid, the attitude of the audience changed and it became less informal.

Q: *You left Compass after the first ten weeks or so. When you came back, what was your reaction?*

HARRIS: When I came back, they had made something different out of it. Much more professional-looking, more groomed. For one thing, the long scenarios were pretty much gone, and two-people scenes had pretty much taken their place. Nichols and May were the dominant talents, and Shelley Berman would do his single scenes. . . . It was a surprise.

Q: *So there was a wide gulf between the way David and Paul had originally conceived it and the final form The Compass took.*

HARRIS: Let me draw an analogy. Say a physicist needs to have some concept of what an atom looks like in order to approach his work. So he makes a working sketch of an atom and works on the basis of that. David and Paul wanted to start a scenario theater, and so they constructed a mental picture of what a scenario theater was. As they went on, experience modified that picture.

Q: *Did you have debates on scenarios? Such as, "No, we shouldn't do this because it doesn't underscore the right social values?"*

HARRIS: We were guided by David's political ideals in the beginning. He would bring newspapers to work and choose things to deal with—what was happening with atomic bombs, what was news current in the '50s. Whatever the political issues of the time were.

We were like archeologists who were trying to unearth things without really knowing what, if anything, would come up. Sometimes we got lucky. It was experimental and naive. As I say, it just evolved slowly.

Q: *As opposed to The Second City, which I hear caught on like a house afire.*

HARRIS: Not really.

Q: *I was under the impression it was an instantaneous success.*

HARRIS: Instantaneous in the sense that we were patronized by our friends from the University of Chicago and people from Northwestern and people from our community. But that was it for a while. It took a while before our reputation extended beyond the people we had always attracted.

In the beginning, I would just sort of fill in, say when they needed a secretary in a scene. They'd say, "You may go now, Miss Pisk." I'd say, "Yes, sir," and sometimes that was it. But gradually, as I felt more comfortable, I began to explore more types of roles. I forget the specifics, but there were some characters I was unable to do and scenes where I felt lost. One never knew about a scene, however, until it was too late.

The worst was when a scene was absolutely terrible and there was no way to find an ending—no logical place for a blackout. So sometimes you'd find yourself stuck onstage with something awful for what seemed like forever. The reverse was also true. You would begin a scene which seemed to promise something wonderful, and just as you got started, the lights would black out and it would be over.

Q: *Who took the lights out?*

HARRIS: Whoever wasn't onstage at the time.

Q: *So sometimes you would end a scene prematurely?*

HARRIS: Yes, and the others would come back saying, "Why did you take the lights out? It was just getting good."

Q: *Do you remember any turning point in the work when you felt, "OK, now I've got it?"*

HARRIS: I'm afraid that there's something about improvisation that . . . you never do really have it. Shelley Berman, for instance, who is almost flawless by himself, could get into an improvisation which just wouldn't go, despite his talent.

Q: *A lot of the people I talk to give Andrew a great deal of credit for making Second City work so well.*

HARRIS: Deservedly. He was the objectifier of the group —the analyst. His strength, besides acting, was in devising, selecting, organizing, and casting the scenes for the sets. He was the midwife, in a sense . . .

Q: *I find it curious that, while you were tentative and shy about the work, you did some of your best work with Severn, who was the least predictable and the craziest in his choices.*

HARRIS: He was wonderful to work with. That unpredictability was interesting. We were all unpredictable in the sense that improvisation is unpredictable. It was all problem-solving, with Severn or any other member of the group.

Q: *What were some of your favorite scenes at Second City?*

HARRIS: Oh, I liked so many. I think the beatnik scene

Alan Arkin and I did was fun. And Severn and I did a nice father-daughter scene.

Often one would come up with a scene with someone, and then, after a while, that person might say he or she didn't want to do it anymore. When people didn't want to do things, they had their reasons and you didn't ask why. Besides, something more interesting might come up instead. Another thing, if we were putting together a new show, Paul would look at the scenes and decide which fit into what he was aiming for in that particular show. And if a scene didn't fit, it fell by the wayside. There were lots of scenes we did that were wonderful that we never repeated.

Q: *Do you still feel part of that community?*

HARRIS: Yes, of course. It became like a family.

6.

Mike Nichols

Mike Nichols began his association with Sills and company when a student at the University of Chicago. For a while intent on pursuing an acting career, he appeared at Playwrights and Studebaker. But it was in improvisational comedy that he first made his reputation. Performing with The Compass Players, he established a special rapport with Elaine May, and within a few years they were recording hit records, appearing in the top clubs, and walking away with every television and radio program on which they were guests. Abandoning nightclubs, they apppeared on Broadway in *An Evening with Mike Nichols and Elaine May*, which played to packed houses for a year. Shortly after, they split up the act to carry on separate careers.

Nichols quickly became one of the hottest directors in the history of the New York theater, scoring hit after hit with *Barefoot in the Park, The Knack, Luv, Plaza Suite, The Odd Couple, The Apple Tree, The Prisoner of Second Avenue, Streamers, The Gin Game*, and the star-laden revivals of *The Little Foxes* and *Uncle Vanya*. He has also directed a string of remarkable films: *Who's Afraid of Virginia Woolf?, The Graduate, Catch-22, Carnal Knowledge, The Day of the Dolphin*, and *The Fortune*. In addition, he produced the hit musical *Annie* for the stage.

Mike Nichols

NICHOLS: I met Sills in the University of Chicago coffee shop when he was a busboy and I was eating the leftovers on the tables. There were two ways I could eat. One was to eat the leftovers on the tables of the coffee shop, and the other one was to enter the cafeteria backwards as if I were on the way out and had already paid.

I think that just about that time Sills was directing *The Duchess of Malfi* for the University Theatre. He got bored with it in the middle and rewrote some of it, and all of the university's great scholars were there but nobody noticed the changes. So we were fooling around in the University Theatre at the same time.

Q: *Wasn't there a breakaway group you and he were involved with called "Tonight at 8:30"?*

NICHOLS: "Tonight at 8:30" was a "revolutionary" group, which just meant that the guys in "Tonight at 8:30" didn't like the faculty head at the University Theatre very much. All it really came down to was that you had a choice between doing a play in some little place and calling it "Tonight at 8:30" or doing it on a big stage in Mandel Hall. The first thing I ever directed I did at "Tonight at 8:30." I directed my roommate Ed Asner in Yeats's *Purgatory*.

Elaine came along during the "Tonight at 8:30" days. I was in a production of *Miss Julie*. Paul had taken over the direction from another guy toward the end. It was a pathetic, awful production. And a terrible thing happened. A man from the Chicago *Daily News* called Sydney J. Harris came to it, and for reasons of his own decided that it was wonderful and he wrote about it in the *Daily News* with the result that we had to play it for months. It was a huge hit and it was terrible. It got worse and worse.

And one night, there was this evil, hostile girl in the front row staring at me throughout the performance, which was in the round. I was about four feet away from her, and she stared at me all through it, and I knew she knew it was shit, and there was no way I could let her know that I knew it also. Oh, this was before the Sydney Harris piece because I remember a day or so later I saw Paul walking down the street with the hostile girl and I had just bought the *Daily News* and read this Sydney Harris thing, and I said, "Paul, look at this!" He read it and Elaine read it

73

over his shoulder. She just said, "Ha!" and walked on down the walk.

She hung around school. She sat in on classes. She never registered. She once convinced an entire philosophy class that everybody in Plato's *Symposium* was drunk and that was the point of the *Symposium*. She used to go into classes and do things like that and then leave.

Q: *How did you and Elaine finally become friends?*

NICHOLS: One night I saw her in the Illinois Central station, which was the way one got from downtown Chicago to where we lived on the South Side. I sat down next to her and I said, in a German accent, "May I sit down?" And she said, "If you weesh." And we just started a kind of foreign-agent conversation for the few people on the adjoining benches and ourselves. And then I think I went home with her and she made me her specialty, which was a hamburger with cream cheese and ketchup that was the only thing she cooked. And then we became friends.

We both had big reputations on campus as being danger-ous-to-vicious depending on the stimulus, and so we were both interested in each other from that point of view, as well as others. Once we'd had that meeting, there was that strange thing which is true to this day—that in some way we are safe from each other forever. We can't do each other any harm or say anything wrong to each other. But gen-erally it was unwise for people to start trouble with her.

There was a bar called Jimmy's near the university where we all hung out. One day, the wind was blowing and her hair was wild, and as we walked in some guy said, "Hi, Elaine, did you bring your broomstick?" And she said, "Why, do you want something up your ass?" Without pause for breath or thought.

Q: *What happened between your days at the University of Chicago and your involvement with Compass?*

NICHOLS: I never graduated. I got a job on an FM radio station, playing classical music and talking in between. Then Paul started Playwrights with Shepherd and Gene Troobnick, and they did a couple of plays, but I didn't want to give up my job at the radio station. They did *Wozzeck* with Zohra Lampert, who was sensational, and they did *Threepenny Opera* and a few other things. And then I was in *La Ronde*.

Mike Nichols

Not too long after, I went to New York to study with Lee Strasberg. It wasn't The Actors Studio, it was his class. I was with Strasberg for two years. By this time, I had no money at all and no possibility of any kind of work, and Paul came and said would I like to come back and be in Compass? It had already started while I was in New York.

The reason I think Compass was interesting was that you had a group of six or seven people and they were thrown onstage with no idea at all behind it. There was no plan. There wasn't even exactly a positive aim. There was the negative aim of doing something without a playwright. There were no tools or methods or technique, except Paul's spectacular theatrical imagination.

What I think happened was this—you had a group of people who were not actors, really, and didn't have a lot of theatrical experience, but who were very intelligent and, in some cases, highly educated. And they were thrown in front of an audience with very little help. What came from Shepherd was rhetoric, and what came from Paul were concrete and specific theatrical ideas. But I think what shaped it was the audience. I'd done improvisations with Strasberg, but none of us had ever been in a situation of having to improvise with the pressure from the audience. I think that over the months, and finally over the years, that pressure from the audience taught everyone to answer the unspoken question the audience asked—"Why are you telling us this?"

You learn various answers to that main question. "Because it's funny" is a very good answer. If you can't answer, "Because it's funny," then you'd better have a damn good other answer. You can't have *no* answer. I still resort to what I learned then having to do with what makes a scene. For instance, if we're improvising a scene and you choose a position, if I want to make it a scene, I've got to take the opposite position. If I agree with you, we don't have a scene.

We came up with certain vulgar rules. By vulgar I mean something to catch quickly. This one's vulgar in both senses: Elaine would say, "When in doubt, seduce." Because that was a scene.

You learned there had to be a core to a scene. It didn't

75

matter how clever the lines were. If they weren't hung on a situation, you were only as good as your last line, which was never good enough. But if you could grab a situation, whether it was a seduction or a conflict or a fight, once you had that spine, then things could come out of it. And what was so good about it was that after doing it months and months and years, it became almost a reflex. And there was a remarkable thing about Compass—whoever left, somebody would instantly rise to replace that person. *Anyone* could do it if he just did it long enough. When Barbara Harris first came to Compass, she didn't speak for two months. She couldn't do anything. But by simply doing it and doing it and doing . . . well, you know what happened. I was the same way.

I was a disaster! For a month I cried in scenes because that's what I thought I'd learned from Strasberg. That was my only contribution. I remember one night I was fooling around onstage with Elaine. We were doing a riding scene of two English people on a bridle path. Somebody went running into the bar for the guys who weren't onstage, shouting, "Come quick! Mike has a character!" And I guess my character was that I was English.

Q: *If you were blocked for a month and Barbara didn't say anything for two months, what was it that allowed you to be kept on?*

NICHOLS: Ah well, that brings me to Paul. The most striking thing about Paul is that he's one of the two people I've met who doesn't stratify people into important people, less-important people, unimportant people, people he likes, people he doesn't like. He takes everyone equally seriously. He'll get pissed off, but he'll get pissed off at anybody. He had terrible tantrums in Chicago. But he doesn't dismiss anyone ever. That attitude also extended to all his theater. Anyone could be in it and anyone could have any part. He didn't divide people into the talented and the less- and the untalented. Everyone was the same to him. and so everyone was equally gifted after a while. And people would walk in from the street.

In fact, that was how Barbara Harris joined the gang. She walked in from the street. She was fifteen years old and said, "What are you doing?" We were cleaning up a

Chinese restaurant for Playwrights Theatre. We said, "We have a theater. Do you want to be in it?" She said, "Sure." I remember I came back to Compass once after a vacation—every now and then you had to get away—but I came back and they were doing an incredible scenario about a personality course called *The Real You*. It was complicated and wonderful. I was watching it and Severn was sitting next to me, and we were watching Andy Duncan do something and I said, "He's terrific," and Severn said, "Yes. I was supposed to play that part, but I went out for a cup of coffee."

It was Paul who made it possible for me and Barbara to stay. I kept saying, "I want to go home. I'm terrible." He'd say, "Stay, it's all right. You'll be fine." And it did happen that whoever stayed long enough was fine. I think it was a combination of this gift of his with people and the process, which was constant learning. As I say, there was no way to be onstage like that and not learn about the structure of scenes, about the connections with an audience.

And what it finally gave us, and something I felt with Elaine always when we were in front of an audience, was almost arrogance. A feeling that "I can handle you guys." I got to where I was completely comfortable with an audience. That has since left me to such an extent that I can't do anything in front of an audience anymore. I won't do a TV interview. I won't do anything as a performer because I've lost that feeling of connection and the ability to handle the audience as myself. I can do it with actors when I'm directing. But when I could perform like that, that had to do with the daily, weekly, monthly, yearly intimacy with an audience.

The great joy of Compass and then, after, working with Elaine was that once every six weeks you would be possessed. At the end of our show, Elaine and I would do an improv, like at Compass, and once in a while you would literally be possessed and speak languages you didn't speak. . . . I don't mean to sound mystical, but such things did happen. Like doing twenty minutes of iambic pentameter that we had not thought of but just came pouring out. That was thrilling, and you'd be drained and amazed afterward, and you'd have a sense of your possibilities.

At the time we were doing this stuff, somebody told me

of some experiments they did in the paratroops which determined that there were two kinds of personalities—those who become less than themselves under stress, and those who become more. I thought about it at the time because we were doing improvisations and what happened after some time was that you had access to everything you knew and some things you didn't. You got so that under the stress of performing and improvising for an audience, instead of being crushed by it and made smaller, as one is to begin with, you could actually become more than yourself and say things you couldn't have thought of and become people you didn't know. Certainly not all the time, because for every one of those times there were, let's say, ten when you relied on certain tricks and certain things you'd done before and certain gimmicks you knew always worked. But that tenth or eleventh time when there was a dybbuk, when you suddenly didn't have to think at all, that was the most, the *only,* exciting thing about it.

Q: *Do you have any idea what brought times like that on? Were there nights when you were about to go on when you just knew, "It's going to happen tonight?"*

NICHOLS: Oh, quite the reverse. You never knew when it was coming. It had something to do with. . . . You see, that was the difference between Elaine and me. She could do it with several people. I could always do it only with her. I never did a good scene of any kind with anybody else. I mean, I did some good group scenes. But for me it depended on a certain connection with Elaine and a certain mad gleam in either her or my eyes when we knew something was starting and then the other one would jump in and go along.

Q: *Do you remember the first really satisfying scene you and Elaine performed together?*

NICHOLS: I guess the first complete scene was "Teenagers." I said, "Let's do two teenagers in the back seat of a car," and we did and it was a terrific scene, and then it kept changing and growing and we kept adding to it. It's hard to describe. It's just two kids screwing around in the back seat and getting their arms tangled up, talking about what they talk about. and it had the line in it when she says. "If we went any further, I know you wouldn't respect me," and I say, "Oh, I'd respect you like *crazy!* You have no *idea* how

Mike Nichols

I'd respect you!" It was never recorded. The two best things we did were never recorded—"Teenagers" and "Pirandello."

"Pirandello" was good. It was really something. And we fought about it steadily all the years we did it.

"Pirandello": I came out and said, "We would like to do something in the style of Pirandello, which has to do with reality. . . ." And I'd get all mixed up describing it. "Holding a mirror to a mirror. . . ." And I'd say, "We'll show you." We started out as two little kids. I was sick in bed and she did this staggering little girl—pulling on her dress and forgetting what she was going to say—and we started to play house. We got big laughs from insulting each other like Mom and Dad. You know—"Get your ass in here," and "What do you want, you drunken sot?" and "Be quiet in front of the kids," and all that stuff. Then we got quite angry with each other within the game. We had a Mom-and-Dad fight, and the angrier we got, we sort of slipped into *being* Mom and Dad, which was quite neatly done. You couldn't tell when it happened. Suddenly we were grown-ups yelling. Also big laughs. Then, at one point, I would improvise something. I would say something like, "Oh, that's very witty. I'm really shriveled," and she would say, "Yes, I've been meaning to talk to you about that," which would get a *huge* laugh, and I would get pissed off at her and start to say something—while she was talking—under my breath. And then we had a few more moments like that, and then the audience really got scared because it was clear we were having trouble with each other. And then we had a fight, but it was real. It consisted of a long pause and my saying, "My partner will now. . . ." And then they were really scared, and she'd start to walk offstage, and I'd grab her. I'd grab her, and her blouse would rip and she'd start to cry. And then she'd say, "What do you think you're doing?" And I said, "I'm doing Pirandello." And we'd take a bow.

Well, we fought about this scene because I was always saying it was time to move on to the next point and, "You stretched this too long," and "We should have done that." I mean, friendly fights, but we argued about it, and we had a weird experience. . . .

We were out of town with the show we were going to

79

bring to Broadway. And the one thing I thought wouldn't
have happened did—the fight got away from us. I must
have blacked out because I suddenly found that I had her
by the front of the shirt and I had been hitting her back
and forth for a long time, and my chest was pouring blood
where she had clawed it open. And they brought down the
curtain and we cried a lot. It never happened again. But
that one time, it suddenly actually did take us over. When it
happened to Ronald Colman in *A Double Life,* I thought it
was bullshit, that that had nothing to do with acting.
But. . . .

A funny thing happened in Compass. You were not
meant to repeat things. You had a new program every week
or two weeks, a scenario and new improvisations. But
Elaine and I found ourselves developing pieces and people
would start asking for them, so we repeated and added to
them. The more that happened, the more I wanted to keep
doing the established pieces, and she wanted to do new
things. I kept wanting to work on the ones we had already,
because I'm a chicken and I don't really like performing
and I don't like doing something new because what if it
doesn't work? So she got bored with the old pieces and I
kept wanting to do them. This always remained true, even
when we had our own act.

One thing that distinguished Compass was that the people
in it were not interested in being in the professional theater,
at that time. I mean, right down to when Elaine and I
auditioned at the Blue Angel, we knew we weren't going to
be in show business. It was just something to make a living
until we decided what we were going to do. For the first
year, in which we ended up on television and everything
else, we thought it was a big joke. Because everybody
thought we were in show business, but we knew we weren't
because we never could be. So that everybody back in
Compass had that mentality of a group of . . . I don't know
what . . . oddballs who didn't know what they were going
to do, but they knew it wasn't going to be the theater because the theater was so dumb. We were snobs.

Q: *Did this frame of mind help you be any more relaxed
and/or daring with what you did, because maybe you didn't
care quite so much?*

NICHOLS: Well, Compass was, after all, a cabaret that was

designed for a very parochial neighborhood university in-group. All the choices of subject, all the jokes, and all the serious things were based on a very specific and narrow frame of reference having to do with the University of Chicago. The frame of reference among these people had nothing to do with show biz, Broadway, nightclubs, or anything like that. Also, as you say, none of it seemed to count very much. I mean, the worst thing that happened was that maybe we did a rotten scene and then we ran out the back door and down 55th Street and literally jumped in the lake. We would do that on some nights. If it was really terrible, the audience never saw us again.

Q: *Could you give me some impressions of some of the people you worked with at Compass?*

NICHOLS: Well, Severn always eats his handkerchief during rehearsal. He claimed that once, during a gigantic assembly at the University of Chicago, he stood up at the back and screamed at the top of his voice, "Mike Nichols fucks pigs!" He then managed to get "pigs" into as many sketches as possible. I would say, "Where have you been?" and he would say, "I've been in Africa—pig-sticking!" And of course, he got me to the point that whenever he mentioned pigs I would break up, which he took as an admission of guilt. He would try to use it as proof to the others that I did indeed fuck pigs. He would say, "The way you can tell is if you just mention pigs onstage, he'll go to pieces." That was Severn's little foible.

Once he went into the Ambassador East in a sweatshirt with a whistle around his neck and with a hard-boiled egg in a brown bag, and when they wouldn't bring him coffee to go with the hard-boiled egg, he stalked out under the marquee, blew the whistle, and Ted Flicker drew up in a Rolls-Royce, he got in and drove away.

I remember the first time Barbara Harris ever spoke on-stage because it was extremely touching. As I said, she didn't speak for months. Well, we had a spot called "Story-Story." At the end of the show, we all lined up and somebody in line would begin telling a story. Then Larry Arrick, or whoever the director was that night, would stop that person and would point to you and you would have to pick up the story and continue it. and then he would stop you and point to somebody else. Then, after a while, at a certain point he would stop it and say, "And the moral of the story is . . ." and we'd raise hands if we had something and he would choose someone. With Barbara, the story would move on from her in a matter of seconds, and she would never raise her hand at the end. Till one night, she did raise her hand, and there was this whole line of people staring because Barbara had her hand up, and Larry called on her and she said, "Love is the key that opens every door." And we all went—*Aaah!*

Q: *I read someplace that most of the material you did with Elaine was created during Compass and that you didn't do a lot of new long pieces after.*

NICHOLS: Very few new pieces.

Q: *Any idea why?*

NICHOLS: Fear. The more we became the talk of the town, the more I was afraid to try something new when we had so many things that worked so well. I told you I'm a chicken. After all, other performers repeated their act. Why the hell should we have a new one every night? We did improvise every night. The last thing in the show was always improvised, where we got a first line and a last line and a style to play the scene in from the audience. We never skipped that. But we finally found that the safest thing was to stick with the set pieces, which changed a little bit anyway, do the improvisation, and then get off with some set thing we had prepared.

We did develop a piece on funeral parlors then. That was almost new. We'd done it in some club in Chicago for the first time and they said that if we ever did it again, they'd close the club and throw us out. And we did one about the emergency ward in a hospital that was new because Elaine had had it happen. She'd hurt her arm and went to the emergency room and of course they said, "Where's your Blue Cross card?" I'd say we did maybe four or five new ones, but not a lot.

Q: *Can you talk a little about the chemistry between you and Elaine? Who was more or less responsible for what? Or was it such a blend that. . . .*

NICHOLS: Well, it *is* a blend. It's hard to sort it out except that by and large I would shape them and Elaine would fill them. It's still true in our work now. You can see it. What she's interested in is character and the moment. What

I'm interested in is moving on and giving it a shape. I was always very concerned with beginning, middle, and end, and when it's time for the next point to be made and when it's time to move because, after all, we're telling a story. I was forced into that since she was a much better actor than I was. She could go on and on in a character. I could not. I could make my few points, I had my two or three characteristics, then I had to move on to the next point because I was out. I couldn't do any more.

Q: *How did the Broadway run happen?*

NICHOLS: We did a concert at Town Hall which was a success, and then we decided to do concerts instead of nightclubs because we hated nightclubs so much. We went to San Francisco to do a show, and it was totally fucked up. We didn't go over, to our amazement. It was the first time anything had not been a success. We were so spoiled. We just assumed we would go do what we wanted and everybody would say it was great. Then we got to San Francisco, it didn't go well at all, and I charmingly blamed the manager and said that it all had to do with the sound system. At that point, Alexander Cohen said, "Let me be the producer and get you a sound system and help you with the physical part of the show and put it on in my Nine O'Clock Theater." We said, "OK."

Q: *How long did the Broadway show run?*

NICHOLS: A season or a little more. And then we stopped because Elaine couldn't stand it anymore. The longer you go, the harder it is. I now think, when I listen to our record of the show, that what happened is what happens to all long runs. It got so dehumanized and so unreal by the time we'd played it for a year. I listen to myself in the telephone sketch, and I'm not a person at all, just doing various voices and squeaks and pauses and noises that you begin to do by rote. . . . I would start playing games like, "Let's see how fast I can make it go."

Q: *In his book,* Ladies and Gentlemen, Lenny Bruce, *Albert Goldman says that Bruce wanted to write material for you and Elaine, but that you said, "No, thanks."*

NICHOLS: Lenny Bruce, although he was a friend, never offered to write anything for us, so, of course, we never turned him down. The Goldman book is completely inaccurate about everything as far as I know but very "artistic."

Q: *What did it feel like when you and Elaine broke up?*

NICHOLS: We didn't break up when we closed the show, because we did some more TV and stuff like that. We broke up over Elaine's play. She wrote a play for me, as it were. It was also *about* me, which made part of the problem. We were meant to be in it together. Arthur Penn was going to direct it, and he wanted her to cut it and work on it. And he went to Europe saying, "I want you to do this and this and that," and Elaine chose to hire Fred Coe as a director, because he *didn't* want her to cut it. She then decided she would not be in it, that she would be better off if she could have the distance of watching it and judging me. It was disastrous. It didn't work for me, it didn't work for the play, it didn't work for her. If we had had Arthur, or somebody who knew how to work on a play, it might have helped us.

For the first time, Elaine and I really had a fight because we were so disoriented by no longer being together against everyone else. It divided us in some terrible way, and we never quite recovered from that. It's like that thing in *1984* —once they betray each other, they can be friendly, but it's never the same. And we did, in fact, betray each other. She was trying to get another actor. I was saying to people, "Get her to cut the play or I'm leaving." Once we'd gone through that experience of trying to screw the other one, out of panic and discomfort on our own parts, it was sort of over.

Q: *How did you make the transition to director?*

NICHOLS: It didn't feel like a transition. I was coming home in every way. Now this is theater direction I'm talking about. Movies felt very different and still do. But directing a play, it was as if I'd been getting ready for it all my life without knowing it. Here at last was the thing I knew all about. That was the feeling. It certainly wasn't true. But I came into the first day of rehearsal after all the years with Compass and Strasberg and Elaine and not knowing what I was going to do, and on the first day I thought, "This is what I've wanted to be without knowing it."

Q: *Can you differentiate what you learned from Strasberg and Sills?*

NICHOLS: As you know, everybody learns different things from people. What I learned from Strasberg has nothing to do with what he supposedly teaches. People aren't really very good at reproducing what he teaches. What I learned from Strasberg was much more about directing than acting. There are some good Strasberg rules that come up again and again when you're directing. For instance, he'd say to an actress, "The scene says it's after dinner. What about the dishes?" And she'd say, "I did them already." And he'd say, "Well, that's so uninteresting. Why not do them now?"

Another example: I mean, he never said it quite this way, but I came away from him thinking like this—I was talking to Lee Grant about a scene she was doing in *Shampoo*. In the film, Warren Beatty's just fucked Lee's daughter, and she said, "Warren wanted me not to know. What should I do?" And I said, "You should *always* know. There's never a time in a play or a movie or a scene when it's more interesting not to know something than to know it." The answer to "Should I know?" is always "Yes," but then maybe you have to dissemble "No," or maybe you have to do something about not showing you know. But you must always know. If someone's onstage and a second person comes onstage, of course they know. They see each other. It's stupid to pretend they don't know. If they're supposed to deal with it as if they don't know, the thing of it is to know and then find some reason to act as if you don't know. Such things come from Strasberg and they're basically useful ideas. Like about the dishes—it's always more interesting not to have done it before the scene or plan to do it after the scene. Do it now.

On the other hand, Paul never taught me, except as a person. There's a lot to learn from him as a man. But what I learned from The Compass has to do with dealing with the audience. Not catering to it, but understanding a story and telling a story to a group of people. You know, how do you tell a story? There's a thing you learn from Compass—if you're doing a play, or a movie, you have to say to the audience, first of all, "You feel fine, you're not worried. We know what we're doing. Everything is OK and you don't have to worry. It's not Judy Garland." You must do that in the beginning in one way or another. You must tell them that they're in a situation in which people have the confidence to begin the story they're going to tell.

Q: *And then you hit them with "Pirandello" and you scare the shit out of them.*

NICHOLS: Once you've reassured them.

Also there's the thing of finding the style for what you're doing. You have to find a way to tell the story that will permit the things that later happen to happen. If they're very bizarre or extreme things that happen later, you have to make that possible within the beginning.

Q: *You mean to create a world or an atmosphere in which the events that follow are logical and consistent.*

NICHOLS: Right. That's true for Strasberg and it's true for Sills. It's just true.

Q: *Do you find that you use improvisational techniques much in your current work?*

NICHOLS: Some. We improvised a lot for *The Graduate.* We improvised their whole childhood. In *The Graduate* we decided that Benjamin's father had had an affair with Mrs. Robinson, and we did some of the early childhood of the kids and the families together and stuff like that. And in some of Neil Simon's plays, we did a lot of improvisation, like the poker game in *Odd Couple.*

Q: *Did you find things you ended up using?*

NICHOLS: Yes. Not very much dialogue, because Simon had written that so well. Mostly behavior. I've never really used it to find dialogue, although there were some scenes in *Carnal Knowledge* that were improvised. Some short scenes. For instance, the offscreen stuff in the scene where Candy's laughing. I started them off on an idea, but then it was improvised. I don't think there was much other actual dialogue improvised. But sometimes behavior.

I've gotten more and more formal and controlled. I don't know why. Robert Altman is doing what I would have expected me to be doing. When it works for him, it's better than anything. When it doesn't work, as with all of us, it's not. Every time I decide that I'm going to go in that direction, something pulls me into a style that is much more spare and not so free.

As I've learned more about movies technically, I'm more and more interested in simplicity. I can be very excited by the kind of richness of texture of, say, *McCabe and Mrs. Miller.* I admire it immensely, but I'm just drawn in another direction. I can't explain it. But I don't seem to have any control over it.

Q: *If someone introduces an actor to you and tells you*

that this person was really terrific in Compass or Second City, what do you automatically know about him?

NICHOLS: That he has what few actors have—a sense of character observed from without. The ability to comment on a character with some humor and a little bit of distance and, at its highest, with genius, like Elaine; to be able simultaneously to comment from without and fill it from within. That's Compass at its highest, to me personified by Elaine's best stuff—that she's doing both simultaneously. Being completely real, saying things for the first time. She's clearly just thought of them and she's really feeling the things, but also she's outside saying, "Did you ever notice this about this kind of person?" That's what I associate with Compass.

Q: *Was there ever a time when you did a piece, with Compass or with Elaine, when you'd hit a target that jolted the audience?*

NICHOLS: That we'd gotten too close to something about them?

Q: *Yes.*

NICHOLS: No. Because, as Elaine always claimed, if you were in the audience and I did you exactly, you would say, "I know somebody just like that." That was always the reaction. Elaine's mother always thought it was my mother we were doing, and vice versa. If you have a group of middle-aged Jewish ladies and you do the mother sketch, they all say, "I know a woman just like that."

You know, all the stuff Elaine and I did, everybody always thought we were making fun of everybody else, but of course we were making fun of ourselves. It was our attitudes we were kidding because we had nobody else to go by but ourselves. People would say that we were putting on this or that kind of person, but it was always us.

7.

Severn Darden

Within the improvisational community, a reference to Severn Darden is akin to using a secret handshake with a Freemason. He is the improviser's improviser, possessor of a unique comic intelligence. He is also the center of an impressive body of esoteric folklore. Stories about his exploits are traded with the same relish with which one imagines Germans traded tales of Tyl Ulenspiegel.

Son of a former district attorney of New Orleans, Darden is yet another University of Chicago veteran. He was a member of The Compass Players in Chicago, St. Louis, and New York; was a founding member of The Second City, appearing with it in Chicago, New York, Los Angeles, London, and other cities; had a productive stretch with The Committee in San Francisco; and frequently performed with Ann Bowen's Pitschel Players in Los Angeles. His most famous creation is Professor Valter von der Voegelweide, an academic so consumed by the minutiae of scholarship he loses sight of the sense of his subject, which doesn't inhibit him from lecturing extensively on anything at the drop of a hat. The "Metaphysics Lecture," on his Mercury album *The Sound of My Own Voice*, is a masterpiece of surreal pedantry. WFMT, a Chicago FM station, tells me that when it solicits requests for comedy recordings, the "Metaphysics Lecture" is always the single most requested routine.

In addition, Darden has amassed considerable "straight" acting credits. He has played leading roles on and Off-Broadway, at Stratford in Connecticut, and with the Barter Theatre. On television he has guest-starred on virtually every major series. In movies he has been featured in *Dead Heat on a Merry-Go-Round, The Day of the Dolphin, The Mad Room, The War Between Men and Women, Goldstein, The Virgin President,* and as a big baddie in a couple of *Planet of the Apes* films. Probably his most memorable performance was as the sympathetic Russian spy in Theodore J. Flicker's brilliant paranoid fantasy, *The President's Analyst.*

The following chapter was drawn from three separate sessions. Eugene Troobnick was also present at one of them and Roger Bowen at another.

Q: *I understand you went to the University of Chicago, too.*

DARDEN: It was the only real Bohemian university in America. They had a system where you went in and took a placement test, and it found out everything you knew and everything you didn't know, and then they took all the stuff you didn't know and taught it to you, so that when you left you knew everything.

TROOBNICK: You should know that while he was there, Severn drove a 1930 Rolls-Royce around the campus, wore a cape, and became legendary for many of his incredible activities. For example, going into Rockefeller Chapel at the university after hours and playing the organ, and when the campus police came to get him, throwing himself across where an altar should have been—it was a nondenominational chapel so it didn't have one—and claiming sanctuary.

DARDEN: And then running out the back and hiding across the street in a girls' dorm.

Q: *Did you hang out with the theater people there?*

DARDEN: Yes, I can remember doing *Volpone* there. I knew some of the people slightly. And I knew people who knew people. I lived with Sills's aunt, Beatrice Stronsdorf, while I was there. I knew Bill Alton somewhat. I had met Mike Nichols a couple of times. But to me the university was such a cold place. Or maybe it was just that I was an outsider. But I never found any real group except for about five friends.

Q: *Did you graduate?*

DARDEN: No. It was thought crass to graduate. But I got my education there. What there is of it.

Q: *Ted Flicker remembers going to Bard with you.*

DARDEN: Yes, I went to Bard for about seven weeks once. Then I got sick and went into the hospital and they gave me cortisone, and they gave me too much and I got sick again.

Q: *After that I know you worked with the Barter Theatre. How did you get into The Compass?*

DARDEN: I drove into New York one afternoon at four, after a summer at the Barter. At four-thirty I met David Shepherd, who was in New York to look for people. Mike Nichols and I went to Chicago the same time. That was in 1955. Mark and Barbara Gordon came a little later.

I was just thrown onstage. I still remember the first line I heard spoken there: "Adventure is a small town at the mouth of the Essequibo." I think David said it. They were doing a "Living Newspaper" and he was reading from *National Geographic*.

Q: *Let's talk about some of the scenes you did at Compass and Second City.*

DARDEN: I used to do a scene with Elaine called "Doors." I call her on the phone in the beginning and I say, "I've just been to the doctor," and she says, "Yes, Max, how are you?" "Oh, it's fantastic. I have a surprise. I've got to show you." "Good, can you come here now?" "No, no, I want you to meet me. You go down the street, you turn right, you go over the bridge, you turn left, you go up the flight of stairs, into the little green door, into the big room, through the little brown door, into the little small room, turn right, go up the stairs, walk onto the roof, crawl over the ladder onto the other roof, go down the stairs, cross the street. . . ." I'd give her endless instructions! And then we'd carry them out endlessly, miming and climbing and crawling. Sometimes I would carry a bass drum case

90

through the whole thing. At one point, I pictured that we'd
get into a basketball gymnasium, but with water in it, and
it's very dark.

TROOBNICK: Of course, nobody in the audience ever knew
it.

DARDEN: No, we were just going (*shouts, with echo*),
"It's very big in here! Where are you?" I go on and off and
on and off and I come back on and the audience doesn't
even notice that I don't have the drum case anymore.
Elaine and I finally meet and she says, "What's your surprise?" And I say, "I lost it." And that was the end.

A wonderful thing happened one night. I think Barbara
Harris was playing it with me. I decided to do something
different, and so I opened the door to the alleyway and
went out into the alley shouting, "Emma, where are you?
Emma!" And a cop comes up with a flashlight and a drawn
pistol! Barbara's standing onstage alone, and I thought, "I'll
never get back. I won't be able to explain this." There was
a little curtain there by the fire door, and I pulled it down,
so there he was, aiming at the audience! He was furious!

Q: *Did you work well with Barbara?*

DARDEN: Yes. The best work I ever did I did with Barbara. She was my favorite, after she became unstuck.

Q: *What do you mean, "unstuck"?*

DARDEN: She didn't talk for a long time. Mike Nichols
was similarly paralyzed, although he talked incessantly. He
couldn't move or think for about two months.

I remember we were doing a scene called "The Fifth
Amendment" and I played his lawyer, and he's being called
before a Congressional subcommittee. I'd come onstage at
one point and tell him the good news that he's not going to
be . . . well, whatever the good news is. Mike would just
sit there. Later I said, "Mike, you didn't move? I've got
this good news and you didn't say anything?" And he said,
"I didn't believe you." And so, one time I came in and I
said, "Hurrah!" and I stood on my head and told him the
news. He looked at me and—right onstage—said, "I still
don't believe you." It took him about a month to get into
the spirit of it, which is not too long at all.

Q: *One of your favorite characters was Professor Valter
von der Voegelweide. How did you come up with him?*

DARDEN: You know who Valter von der Voegelweide was, don't you? He was a medieval minnesinger. That's where the name came from. I did him first at The Compass. I got up and would lecture on any given topic.

Q: *Did you base him on any of the professors at the University of Chicago?*

DARDEN: Oh, all of them. It was no particular one. I used to mention some of them occasionally. I used to announce that Bruno Bettelheim would be giving a lecture entitled "Some Positive Aspects of Anti-Semitism." He loved that. (*Laughs.*) And there was one professor I mentioned who was really obscure. At one point in a scene with Barbara she would say, "You can never get along with anyone," and I said, "I can, too. I can get along with Dr. Davis at the hospital, and *nobody* can get along with him, he's such a nut!" Well, there were always a few doctors in the audience, and we'd get laughter and applause on that line because they knew I was referring to M. E. Davis.

I used to get hung up on nuns. I used to talk about them all the time.

I remember there was a psychiatrist scene I did with Mike. I think it was with Mike. Anyway, the psychiatrist said, "I want you to go back in time. What do you see?" And I said, "It's dark. It's *dark.* It's *very* dark." He said, "How dark?" "Dark as the inside of a nun." (*Laughs.*) Which is pretty dark. We got a letter from the dean of Loyola University asking me to stop referring to nuns.

Q: *Did you stir up any other controversy?*

DARDEN: I was looking for a group that hadn't been insulted, so I used to make anti-Danish remarks. We did a scene about Ingmar Bergman movies at Second City. We got a review from a Chicago paper about that scene. It said, "The scene about Ingrid Bergman didn't quite come off." (*Laughs.*) Anyway, I played this Swede who worked with Bergman. Somebody asks me, "Don't you think Mr. Bergman owes something to Carl Dreyer?" And I say, "No! Carl Dreyer is a Dane!" The interviewer asks, "What do you mean?" "The Danes are pigs!" I say. "It's a well-known fact. Ask anyone who's ever met one. They are pigs! They are filthy people. Thieves and liars and cheats." I used to get letters from Danes all the time.

Q: *What did Sills say to you when he was first putting Second City together? Any statement of intent?*

DARDEN: No.

Q: *Just, "I've got a thing going. Do you want to be part of it?"*

DARDEN: That's roughly it, yes. Not quite so articulately, though.

Q: *Was Bernie very much in evidence at the beginning of Second City?*

DARDEN: We saw him frequently.

BOWEN: He was kind of a benefactor. I have been helped by him.

DARDEN: There have been a number of people in dire trouble Bernie has helped out.

BOWEN: But he'd rather scrimp on your wages and then perform a generous act. I guess it balanced out. But if Bernie had any thoughts on what improvisational theater was or ought to be, he kept them very much to himself.

Q: *How was it for Howard Alk to be both an actor and a coproducer?*

BOWEN: Nobody took him seriously as a producer.

DARDEN: And he never thought of himself as an actor.

Q: *How about impressions of some of the other people, like Andrew Duncan?*

DARDEN: Andrew Duncan, among other things, I think, was the best straight man ever, which is extremely difficult improvising. You would go onstage with Andrew and he would make you look very good because it looked like you were making all the jokes. Roger Bowen was another great straight man.

Q: *His being here doesn't have anything to do with this opinion?*

BOWEN: Of course not.

DARDEN: Straight men have to know what you're going to say, more or less. They have to psych you out. They have to know where the joke is. A good straight man, for example, would make an excellent lawyer or a diplomat or a used-car salesman.

Q: *Because they all know where the joke is?*

DARDEN: No, they all know what the other person is going to say next. A good straight man can set it up so that you have only a fifty percent chance of not getting a laugh. In other words, if you say, "Yes," you'll get the laugh. You *have* to make the joke. It's a highly meta-physical point as to what the straight man does.

BOWEN: My description of the function is that the straight man creates the reality and the comic plays off it. The more reality the straight man creates, the bigger the balloon gets blown up, so the greater the pop when the comic sticks the pin into it.

DARDEN: Bill Alton was good at that, too. Speaking of Bill Alton, I remember he did a scene with Mina Kolb where he gives her a drink and she takes it, and he gives her another drink and she takes it, and she says, "Oh my! It's the second drink that makes the first drink possible!"

Q: *I get the impression that Mina was there to provide a contrast to the intellectual U. of C. wits.*

BOWEN: Mina was there because she was the best actress Paul could get. He had some actresses in his workshop. Karen Black was in his workshop in Chicago and she wanted the job, but he decided on Mina.

DARDEN: Mina was unique in that, when onstage, she had a very deep insight into what she was like. When she did a takeoff, she did a takeoff on herself. I don't think anyone else on that stage had that insight. We were always doing takeoffs on other people. Mina was always doing takeoffs on herself.

BOWEN: Exactly right. She was more mature in that respect.

DARDEN: Much more.

Q: *That's curious, because she says that the woman she played was nothing like her.*

DARDEN: I mean Mina was a proper Catholic, suburban wife who played the part of a proper Catholic, suburban wife.

Q: *Mina's comedy was characterized by a unique brand of illogic. She would say something which at first sounded reasonable, but then you'd realize there was something off-kilter about it and you'd look at it and it would explode into nonsense.*

DARDEN: I've seen smart-asses try to put Mina on. I happen to have *been* one of the smart-asses who tried to put Mina on. (*Laughs.*) Once you've done it and been destroyed utterly, you take double delight in watching it happen to other people. They think, "Ah, here's easy fodder! Watch this!" And then they wither before this absolutely incontrovertible illogic that you can't approach any . . . no possible . . . no one! (*Laughs.*) St. Thomas would weep.

Q: *How about working with Arkin?*

DARDEN: Alan Arkin was always very easy to work with. A little bit grouchy offstage, but onstage very pleasant. Teaching scenes were always good with him. Teaching scenes were always good with Shelley Berman, too. They both made very good teachers.

Shelley Berman was one of the hardest-working people ever in improvisational theater. We would work out a scene in the afternoon and then everyone else would go out for dinner. But he'd go home and work some more, and by the time he came back for the show that night, he'd added forty new good ideas.

I remember a great scene Mike and Collin Wilcox and Shelley and Elaine did. They played two guys and two girls who were going to the Catskills. The guys were going there to meet girls, and vice versa. Shelley played the smart-ass guy and Elaine played the smart-ass girl. At that time, Elaine and Shelley had been having a running fight for a couple of months. So there was this point in the scene where Elaine and Collin are onstage and there's a knock at the door. The girls know it's the guys who've come to pick them up. Shelley and Mike were offstage on the other side of the door. So Elaine winks at Collin and she says, "Who is it?" Shelley says, "It's Santa Claus!" Elaine says, "Have you got something for me, Santa Claus?" He says, "Baby, have I got something for *you!*" And she says, "Shove it under the door!" (*Laughs.*) He's offstage and she's just gotten that laugh. I was sitting in the house and I could almost *see* him ready to claw his way through the set and kill her!

Q: *What about Elaine?*

DARDEN: Well, I'm *terrified* of Elaine! (*Laughs.*)

Q: *Why?*

DARDEN: I don't know.

TROOBNICK: A very common reaction, I think.

95

Q: *How does she terrify people?*

TROOBNICK: Well, she's about fifty percent more brilliant than she needs to be, for one thing.

DARDEN: But that isn't it.

Q: *Then what is it?*

DARDEN: I don't know. You have a feeling that at any moment she might kill you. Outside of that. . . . (*Laughs.*) When Elaine and I worked together, we had such arguments that a good deal of the time we wouldn't even go onstage together. It's hard to explain. She's just terrifying.

TROOBNICK: I think their outlooks on humor are diametrically different. Severn always sought the bizarre things in human behavior or speech that commented on the human condition. Elaine always sought the human expression that turned bizarre. And somehow they couldn't do it together.

Q: *Were there any subjects you would stay away from?*

DARDEN: Yes, we tried to keep away from making Jewish jokes and fag jokes. That was one of Sills's rules and it was very good.

TROOBNICK: I think we had a good deal of taste, largely because of Sills.

Q: *Were you aware of the sort of audience you attracted?*

DARDEN: Unh-hunh. Jews. When I said that to Sills, he said, "No, we attract audiences whose names are Neumann and they all have money. Some of them are Jewish Neumanns and some of them are Catholic Newmans, but their names are all Neumann."

Q: *You played with Second City in Chicago, New York, and London. Was there much difference betwen the suggestions you got from them?*

DARDEN: The company I was with in London was forbidden by the Lord Chamberlain—who used to censor plays—from doing any suggestions. The first company that went to London did take suggestions, and the English audiences would make *filthy* jokes! Incredible.

Chicago was the best audience we played for. Chicago liked watching things being built. New York audiences like to watch things that are already completed and polished. New York audiences are extremely unsophisticated in that way. It's very hard to get New Yorkers to suggest anything. They're sure, they're convinced, that every suggestion you take is planted. Nothing will convince them otherwise. But most audiences are convinced of that. The audience generally doesn't believe we take their suggestions seriously. I remember at one time we actually would work up things on *most* of the suggestions. Many nights. It grew less and less, though. The others were always getting on me because I wanted to do the suggestions rather than do old stuff. They thought it was some kind of feeling of honor or purity on my part. It had nothing to do with that. I was *bored* with the old stuff. I wanted to do new things, even if they failed. I wanted to go ahead.

My idea of the way it should work is to do improvisations until you find something that works. Then you keep adding stuff to it until it finally gets to fructification, and the fruit is ready to fall off the tree and it's eaten and that's it and it's over with. It would be like painting a watercolor of some half-remembered fruit, but that's not very Chicago. We don't have the colors.

I don't think the point of this theater is perfection. What is important is to be up there and open to what is going on in the audience, rather than do something perfectly no matter what the audience feels about it, even if the audience walks out.

Q: *Alan Arkin said that Sills's genius was in putting together a well-balanced troupe.*

DARDEN: That was one of the things. Another was to be completely inarticulate. Once Bill Mathieu, our musician, was playing some very good variations on Mozart behind a scene and Sills said, "Will you stop playing that thick Jewish music?" Bill said, "What do you want, Paul?" Sills said, "Play music like from the glider movie." And Bill thought for a long time and said, "Paul, *what* glider movie?" And Paul said, *"If they had made one, schmuck!"*

Q: *That's one of the interesting things about talking to the various people—to get their different perspectives on Paul. Whether they like him or not, they always call him extremely talented or a genius.*

DARDEN: Actually, I feel he has no talent at all. He's just an opportunist in it for the money. Paul Sills is in it for the buck. You can quote me on that.

BOWEN: God, did he line his pockets! Those apartment buildings on the South Side!

DARDEN: Yes, and the Portuguese bank accounts. Well, *that* went. (*Laughs.*)

Q: *Aside from that, how was he to work with?*

DARDEN: Marvelous generally. Like anyone else he had moods, but he never bothered me a great deal.

BOWEN: It wouldn't have done him any good and he knew it. Severn had more dignity than the rest of us.

DARDEN: I don't think I've ever had any dignity that I know of.

BOWEN: That in itself is a kind of dignity.

Q: *You are above dignity.*

DARDEN: You can write that down.

Barbara once said that Paul was the only person who had ever stopped me cold in a conversation. He called me stupid at one point. (*Laughs.*) My mouth fell open, my eyes went blank.

Q: *Sills commands the greatest sense of loyalty that I've ever known anyone to command.*

DARDEN: Of course he pays a far greater price than anyone I've ever known. He himself is so dedicated. I mean, Hitler was a simple megalomaniac. Sills *believes* it! Can you imagine the hell he goes through! I mean, Hitler's was a quiet, simple bourgeois world. (*Laughs.*) But Sills suffers with his soul and with God all the time.

He used to walk out on rehearsals regularly.

Q: *Why?*

DARDEN: Rage. He'd go over to the Lincoln Hotel and I'd have to go and calm him down. Everyone else was too bored to.

TROOBNICK: We were Bohemian people for our time and the people who had the Lincoln Hotel hated us. They were Greeks, weren't they?

DARDEN: They said they were Greeks. They were secretly Danes.

We were always directing each other at Compass and Second City. It was very rarely that somebody in the company said anything to me that I didn't listen to very carefully.

TROOBNICK: That's true. It was a constant communal

directing. You'd come offstage and say, "Listen, there's something I want to try in that scene next time. When you do so-and-so, let me do a thing," and he'd say "OK," and you'd do it, and something would develop or it wouldn't. But for that moment, you were directing.

DARDEN: We also had workshops all the time. We used to have workshops even in New York at Second City, though not as regularly as in Chicago. Workshops are very important. Viola ran workshops in Chicago. I enjoyed what little work I did with her. I never understood her. She was too vast.

Q: *I have a theory that one of the reasons why Paul and Viola are so into the games is that they find it difficult to make contact with people in unstructured environments. So they created games to create a structure in which they feel secure to communicate.*

DARDEN: Yes, but on the other hand, that's true of almost everyone. Take a public figure at random. Quickly. Someone.

Q (Trying to think of a public figure): *Uh, Jesus Christ. . . .*

DARDEN: OK. Now that's one of the more elaborate games ever invented! (*Laughs.*) But anyone you might ever have heard of works from some kind of game. Politics is a game, religion is a game.

Q: *Being in an environment in which there are rules, and the rules make contact possible.*

DARDEN: Hopefully. . . . Sometimes working here in L.A., I think about Second City. When you work in television, you work with such *assholes* a lot of the time. Second City spoiled me. It was so much pleasure and such a challenge. Also, once you got it over with, it was finished. It was an empty stage and there was nothing anyone could hold you to. Here, you do some damn television show and they play it twenty years later and there you are being prime asshole number one, and there's nothing you can do about it!

BOWEN: Let me ask you a question. Did you have any political point of view? Doing Second City or Compass, did that have anything to do with any political statement you wanted to make, or did it seem to fit into . . . I'm trying to find out if you had a strong reason for doing it.

DARDEN: Oh, yes! (*Silence. No elaboration.*)

BOWEN: OK. (*Starts to laugh.*)

DARDEN: You see, a perfect straight man! Perfect! We described it and we did it! (*All laugh.*)

8.

Mark and
Bobbi Gordon

Mark and Bobbi Gordon spent the first year of their marriage in Chicago, where Mark directed and they both appeared with The Compass Players. Subsequently, Bobbi appeared with the short-lived Compass Larry Arrick directed in New York. When it closed, she quit acting, and a damn shame that was, too, for the tapes I have heard of her Compass work indicate she was quite something.

Since The Compass, Mark has kept very busy as an actor, director, and teacher. On Broadway he appeared in *The Devils* and the celebrated revival of John Steinbeck's *Of Mice and Men* and directed *Before You Go*. Off-Broadway he was a member of Elaine May's improvisational troupe, The Third Ear. On film he appeared in *Take the Money and Run* and *A New Leaf*, and he is constantly visible on television in guest roles.

The Gordons' son Keith is keeping up the family tradition, having already embarked upon an acting career.

MARK: As was always my wont—along with acting and directing in New York—I was conducting an acting workshop. I was going with Bobbi at that time, having directed her in a play with Marty Landau and Shelley Berman and fallen madly in love with her and her work. Well, what happened was Elaine and David came into town, and I think they were looking for a director. Elaine did a scene from Strindberg in my workshop and I criticized it, and then David said, "Would you be interested in working in Chicago?" I said that sounded fine, but that Bobbi and I were going to get married. They said, "We'll have something for her, too." We were married on October 14, 1955, and left for Chicago immediately after the ceremony.

I was hired to direct *The Devil's Disciple* for Playwrights. I remember them saying the money for the production would be coming in from their *Hamlet*. So I went to see *Hamlet* and there were about three people in the audience. This was when Playwrights was on its last legs. I said, "The money's coming in from *Hamlet*? How? It's losing money." And they said, "We know. That's the way we function." I suddenly felt very stranded and scared. I worked for a few weeks on *Devil's Disciple,* but they never did raise the money to do it. So I was asked to join Compass as workshop director and actor. Bobbi was already working there, so I consented to do it.

Q: *Let's backtrack a little and talk about your arrival in Chicago.*

BOBBI: We got there at twelve midnight. We'd been driving for two days, and I couldn't see.

MARK: As soon as we got there, we were taken to The Compass.

Q: *If you were both so tired, why did you go to The Compass immediately?*

BOBBI: You see, David had completely forgotten to get us a place to stay, so we had to go to Compass and hang around while he tried to find someplace. We ended up staying at his apartment that first night. Where he stayed, I don't remember.

MARK: It was quite a honeymoon!

Q: *What was your first reaction to Compass?*

BOBBI: Terror. I must tell you that when I came out, I had no idea of what I was going to. They told me I was going to be in an improvisational theater. I didn't know what it was, but it sounded interesting. I was a very "serious" actress, right? So you can imagine what it was like to walk into this place, half dead with exhaustion. and see this madness that was going on. And to know that I was committed to being part of it!

Mark and Bobbi Gordon

Q: *Who was in the company then?*

BOBBI: Severn, Andy, Elaine, Mike, and Kenna Hunt.

MARK: Kenna didn't stay very long.

BOBBI: I guess they must have sensed my terror because everybody began to reassure me as I met them. Everybody kept saying, "Oh, you'll see—we have rehearsals and it's wonderful. You'll come tomorrow and you'll rehearse. Don't worry about a thing." Mike came over to me and said, "Listen, I've come from New York, and I've studied with Strasberg and I know what you're going through. Don't worry, it'll be fine. Really. Because I want to do some really serious scenes and. . . ."

I came in the next day to rehearsal, and everybody was sort of sitting around and yelling at everyone else. Somebody said, "Let's do a scene about Chekhov or something," and the others said, "No." And somebody said, "Let's do a scene about a thief stealing a wallet in a park," and somebody said, "No."

Q: *Was this the way Compass rehearsals usually were?*

BOBBI: All the time. The problem was that everybody was too full of incredibly good ideas, and everybody was so articulate in the company that so much of the time that was supposed to be spent rehearsing was spent airing and fighting over ideas. Rehearsals were chaos because there was no rehearsal process. What we would jokingly call rehearsals would usually end up in an argument with very little actual work being done. I was very disturbed by the amount of conflict that always went on. It was an incredible waste of time. Yet, I guess maybe not, because at night, when it really got down to it, brilliant things could happen.

So, very briefly, that first rehearsal was a series of "Absolutely not," "I will not do that," "No," "What do you mean? We certainly can't do *that!*" A lot of yelling and screaming. And then, "OK, see you tonight."

I came back that night. The way I thought it would work was I'd watch the show for maybe a week, right? And after I'd kind of got the drift, I'd join them. But what happened was they just threw me onstage immediately. "OK, the Chekhov scene!" they told me. "What Chekhov scene?" I said. "The one that we didn't want to do this afternoon. Do it! We need it!" And then there I was onstage with Severn doing the Chekhov scene.

MARK: I remember that. Sevvy was supposed to be push-ing Bobbi on an imaginary swing, and every time he pushed her, he touched her ass and made a face. I was standing with David and he was saying to me, "Oh, Mark, isn't she marvelous! She's such a good addition to the company!" I said, "David, when the scene is over, she's going to be crying." He said, "What do you mean?" I said, "Because her ass is being touched in public and she doesn't like it." And sure enough, the scene ended, people applauded, and she ran into the bathroom and cried.

BOBBI: Now I'd be mad at Sevvy if he *didn't* touch my ass!

Q: *That first time you worked with him must have been a little scary.*

BOBBI: But I had that reaction to everyone! They were the strangest group of people I ever walked into. Each in his or her own way was terrifying to me. So it was a growing process of getting used to them all. When I finally got to know them, I got to love them very much, because each one had something so special.

Q: *OK, let's talk about the people. Andrew. . . .*

BOBBI: I felt very safe with Andrew onstage. Andrew was always very sensitive to things I was frightened of. I always felt he would avoid situations uncomfortable for me. I knew that in the middle of a scene he wasn't going to turn around and say, "Oh, by the way, do you realize that the porthole just broke and this ship is flooding?" when you've been doing the whole scene under the assumption that you were in a living room. The others did this kind of thing constantly—pulling these things from out of left field.

MARK: We all knew that kind of thing was wrong, but some of us did it anyway.

BOBBI: Andy never did that to me. Ever. So I always had a sense of trust onstage with him.

MARK: Except that one time. . . .

BOBBI: Yes, that time. . . .

MARK: It was a scene where we played people who had just gotten married and moved into a house, and the others brought us gifts. Like Mike gave us a Vivaldi recording. Everybody gave us the kind of things you'd give a suburban *nouveau riche* couple. So Andy came in with something.

We said, "What is it?" He said, "It's an egg poacher. But if you want, you can keep your diaphragm in the little cup." Now, *that's* a scene-stopper, especially in those days. Well, at that, Mike did his trick, which was to turn his back on the audience and shake his shoulders like he was breaking up, which made the audience go hysterical. We saw that and figured, "That's a good way out," so everyone turned and shook their shoulders and the scene ended. That's the only crime I remember Andy doing as far as a scene-stopper.

Q: *He talks a lot about Marx now. Was there much of that then?*

MARK: No, he wasn't overtly political then. What I remember about Andy was that he was always there and able to *do* things. I know he told me he had been a forest ranger, had worked on a boat. . . . He could do practical things with his hands. It was the same kind of thing with his scene work. He never did anything that would overwhelm you, but he was always there for the scene.

Q: *Mike?*

BOBBI: I felt very close to Mike immediately. He had a great need to be an actor at that moment in his life. That's what he was all about. Michael *cared*. He understood immediately that I didn't understand what this theater was all about. He reached out and let me know he was uncomfortable, too. We both had a great deal of trouble at the beginning. We wasted a great deal of time trying to be "real."

Q: *What about Elaine?*

BOBBI: I didn't meet her when she came to Mark's class. The first time I met her was at Compass. She was chewing apple cores, her hair was down to her knees practically, she was in these old jeans. My first impression of Elaine— I was frightened of her. She was very distracted, very removed, rather annoyed about everything that was happening at the time. You knew that she and Mike could destroy you with a word, but neither of them was out to do that. In fact, they were both most helpful and sweet. Mike more so than Elaine initially. I don't think Elaine ever recognized the massive discomfort I was going through. She was so much in her own place at that point.

There was a quality of Elaine—of this *grande dame* of

105

letters. With people sitting around her feet, staring up at her, openmouthed in awe, waiting for the Word.

MARK: Where was that?

BOBBI: I'm talking about my first days of working with her. When you weren't there yet.

MARK: Oh, you mean when I was rehearsing the Shaw.

BOBBI: Yes. That was my first impression of Elaine. Many people would come into the place, and Elaine was always the center of a great deal of activity and attention.

Q: *So people outside the group would come in and be part of the workshop?*

BOBBI: From time to time, yes. And a lot of people sort of hung around. There was a magnetism about Elaine. There were at least five men around her at any given time. You sort of had to push them aside to talk to her. There was something very strange about it to me, because here was this woman who made no effort at all—I mean *less* than no effort at all—to be attractive, and yet guys were drawn to her like a magnet.

There was one guy who was madly in love with her —one of many—who was constantly pursuing her and would run onstage and profess his love, bring gifts, and scream and yell at her from offstage.

Q: *He had no sense of embarrassment about jumping onstage?*

BOBBI: No, he was totally insane.

Q: *How did she deal with that?*

BOBBI: I think by incorporating what he did into the scene. But Elaine was constantly pursued by the oddest assortment of people in the world. I mean, really.

MARK: How strange that I felt so comfortable with her! I really did.

Q: *Was Elaine doing a lot of writing then?*

BOBBI: She was bringing in a lot of scenarios. Every week she'd come in with a new one.

MARK: I don't think that anyone ever said it was good. Every time she came in with material, it was. "Oh my God, it's awful. It'll never work." Everyone would come forty minutes late to rehearsal, and then someone would kind of grudgingly say, "OK. we'll try it." Then we'd do it for people at night and the audience would be hysterical loving it. And then somebody maybe would say, "Oh, I guess it's

Mark and Bobbi Gordon

all right." But there was never a recognition that Elaine's stuff was fantastic.

Q: *And Severn?*

MARK: Sevvy was like a Robert Benchley who was a good actor. He could do many characterizations, but he was like Benchley in the sense of being able to get up and do a lecture at a blackboard on *anything.*

BOBBI: I loved working with him because for the most part he wanted to do something good. Even in his insanity and his way-outness. He really related in a scene, really talked to you. He really tried to say something. Of course, what was said was beyond understanding sometimes. . . . He had this marvelous freedom and would jump in with both feet to see what would happen.

Q: *Andrew remembers a black guy named Bob Patton in Compass in the first theater. Do you remember playing with any blacks while you were there?*

MARK: No, but I remember blacks being in the audience.

BOBBI: Rarely, though.

MARK: It was mostly a college crowd, but there were blacks now and then.

Q: *Did you ever deal with racial issues in the scenes?*

MARK: Yes.

Q: *Do you remember in what way?*

MARK: Bad ways. What I remember was people not afraid to play black.

BOBBI: I don't remember that.

MARK: I do. I wish I could be more specific. But I remember I was very sensitive to it. I felt that we should have had a black actor if we were going to do it. Anything that came out of improvisational theater would have to be a recognizable cliché.

Q: *A stereotype or prototype?*

MARK: Yeah, so it could be recognizable. So, if you were playing an old person, you had to do it "general old."

Q: *What?* (Quavering voice:) *"Hello there, sonny"?*

BOBBI: Exactly, but without teeth.

MARK: So, if someone did black, they would do black in stereotype. I remember that being done. I don't know who did it, but I remember it being done, and it used to offend me. Also, I remember that it was very difficult to find women for improvisational theater.

107

Q: *Because it was related to what was going on socially —that women were more restricted in the roles they could play in society.*

MARK: Yeah, and we reflected that. It's interesting that almost all improvisational companies had five men and two women or four men and one woman. I don't think that's changed even today.

Q: *What kind of women did you find yourself playing, Bobbi?*

BOBBI: I felt most comfortable in the stereotyped roles, I guess. In a lot of the scenarios I was the wife or the mistress. Elaine, on the other hand, was always the psychiatrist or something like that. I tended to play traditional women. Elaine always went against that.

Q: *Was there much of a sense of community between the actors?*

MARK: Of necessity it was there, but never was it what I heard later—how much we loved one another. I don't remember the love. I remember we had to read each other, which may be love, really love. But we never used the word. There was a lot of healthy fighting.

BOBBI: I cared about everybody very much, but I knew the minute I set foot in there I didn't belong. It was clear to me this would never work, and why wasn't I back in New York. I'd do something very badly onstage—really badly, where I'd be embarrassed to show my face—and the others would say, "Very nice." I knew they were bolstering my ego, but even I couldn't be fooled that much.

What I liked to do most were the structured things. Like "Living Newspaper" and the scenarios. I *loved* the scenarios. Everybody else in the company was always screaming, "Not another fucking scenario!" But they saved my life. They were tangible and I could really work with them and develop things that at times I was pleased with. It was the suggestions I hated. The on-the-spot stuff. It really killed me. I never got used to it.

MARK: I've got to say something about Sevvy. . . .

BOBBI: Mark, I'm talking. . . .

MARK: I'm sorry.

BOBBI: I resent this intrusion. (*Laughs.*)

MARK: When I would argue with her. . . .

BOBBI: That was the worst part.

Mark and Bobbi Gordon

MARK: I would say, "Gee, that's a good scene. Let's do a scene about this fight."

BOBBI: He would do that to me. We would have a fight like any normal human beings who live together have fights. Then, in the middle, Mark would say, "What a scene this would make!" Do you know what that does to somebody?

MARK: I bought this candle. It was in a glass, and I lit it and it was our fireplace. So we were cuddled in bed watching the candle and I said, "Gee, that candle will never go out." She said, "Why do you say that?" I said, "The wax will melt right back into the glass, so it will just keep burning." She said, "There's something wrong with that." "No," I said, "it will keep burning." She said, "It has to go out." I said, "Stop being silly. What happens to the wax?" "It melts." "And where does it go?" "Back into the glass." And I said, "Where's the wick?" She said, "In the glass." I said, "Then it will last forever." Well, we had such a fight! And as the yelling and screaming was going on, I said, "This is a great scene." I insisted we do it at Compass. It worked very well and became part of our repertoire, but each night that we did that scene, when we got offstage, we'd have the same fight.

BOBBI: Why we did not get divorced I still don't know, because it was so painful. Not only painful living through the first year of marriage, but to know that everything I said when we fought made a good scene! And then to have it brought onstage that night for the world to say yea or nay! It was terrible! Mark would literally make us do scenes onstage about our life.

Q: *Did that . . . ?*

BOBBI: Yes, whatever you're going to say, it did. (*Laughs.*)

Q: *When you had that kind of scene, did you find yourself sort of arguing your real-life case to the audience through the scene?*

BOBBI: Oh, absolutely!

MARK: Well, that's what was wrong, Bobbi. (*Laughs.*) I was just saying that relationships are funny.

BOBBI: *I* didn't think it was funny.

MARK: I thought the behavior we got into was funny. I wasn't trying to win the argument onstage.

109

BOBBI: Funny it was not. Painful is what it was. Very painful. For you it was funny. That was what was wrong. That you could laugh at. . . . (*They both laugh.*) We're doing it again! Enough!

Q: *I understand at one point the two of you did a scenario based on* The Execution of Private Slovik. *That's hardly the kind of humorous work that people came to The Compass expecting. Did you run into any hassle with the audience about that?*

MARK: No, the audience loved it. I played Slovik and Bobbi played my wife. The book, you remember, was in letter form. So we started from the letters and found scenes out of them. The scenes we liked we kept. It was really beautiful. It wasn't until we had been playing it for about two weeks—this was at the Dock—that the owners came to us and said, "They're not buying drinks."

BOBBI: They were very upset. They wanted us to stop doing it.

MARK: Anyway, here we were stuck with all these crazy people on the South Side of Chicago doing these crazy things. It always felt to me like taking your pants off in front of an audience. A little terrifying. And yet, the audience seemed to love it.

The actors were doing things never done in a so-called Method approach. It was a mistake to try to get them to do what actors do when approaching a written part. I became aware after a while that there was no way we could do that because that kind of approach involves working backward from given material and endowing that material with personal meaning. But at Compass, the material was being made up as you were performing. There was no way of working backward, except maybe the next day to go over it in rehearsal.

BOBBI: Once in a while we got to do things we really could act, but for the most part, I think my contribution was that I didn't talk too much. If I said something funny, I didn't resent it if somebody else said it the next day (which happened a lot). I was very good when I was working with somebody who really had an incredible idea for a scene and could take off. Then I didn't feel that the responsibility of making the scene work was on my shoulders. I didn't mind being there *for* somebody. In fact, I worked a

110

lot because I got along well with everybody. So when people wouldn't work with anybody else, they would work with me. But if somebody said, "This is going to be funny . . ." —forget it. I really was no good at that.

I remember when Barbara Harris came into the company. She was this incredibly beautiful, quiet little dandelion-puff child who didn't open her mouth. I thought, "Oh my God, she outdoes me!" My fear was always that we would be onstage alone together, and there we would sit and nothing would happen! Poor Barbara, I avoided her like the plague.

MARK: Little did we know the development that was going to take place. Years later, when I was doing The Third Ear in New York with Elaine, on Tuesday nights we'd invite people to come down and improvise with us, and Barbara Harris would come down. She had nothing to do with the Barbara I had watched many years before. She was on top of everything. I knew she was still quiet in real life, but when she got onstage, it was look out! I was in awe and couldn't believe it was the same girl.

Q: *Anyway, you were talking about conducting workshops.*

MARK: Right. I realized that we needed to do a lot of group exercises that would make people work together so they could read each other as quickly as possible. So I started running some of the standard exercises, and these crazy people turned them into some of the strangest things I had ever seen. I had never seen such imagination.

For instance, there was a simple exercise I had done in basic classes. It was about the use of objects. It's supposed to take only two minutes. You put down a broom and say, "You can change it into anything you want—any object except a broom—and use it." In my old classes, people would make it a snake or a baseball bat—very basic stuff. It would take a second.

Well, Sevvy got up and didn't go near it. He kind of looked at it for a second, then he went to another part of the room and started climbing imaginary stairs. He must have climbed forty or fifty flights. It went on forever. I was on the verge of going to sleep, and I kept thinking, "Maybe I should stop him. He's going up and up, and it has nothing to do with this broom I put down. But he's got something in mind. I've just got to see where it goes. I don't care if it takes all day!" Something made me watch it. It was just awful! Finally, he got to the top of whatever he was climbing, and he stood and smelled the air so you knew he was outside and on top of something tremendous. Then he went and picked up the broom and blew it. Blew into the stick end. Then he put it down and said, "I'm finished." I said, "What was that?" And he said, "I'm Gabriel." It was then I realized I couldn't teach them anything.

The first thing I directed at Compass was about a rainmaker. Severn was going to bring rain through all kinds of mystical incantations. We worked on it in workshops and I said, "We'll go through the audience. We'll have a demonstration for rain with drums and cymbals and signs." Everybody thought that was fine.

BOBBI: Everybody *hated* it.

MARK: We made the signs and got the drums. On Saturday night we opened. The cast was in the back of the theater because they were supposed to march through the audience to the stage, right? Only the place was so crowded, there was no way to get through. There was no place to walk, and we were climbing over tables and it was a disaster.

Q: *You told me that The Compass got some outside gigs?*

MARK: A couple of times. Once the PTA asked us to do something. So we learned what we could about the PTA and put together a scene for them with Elaine playing a PTA speaker. She later played that with Mike on Broadway. I think we were paid $25 for that.

And then the scientists at the atomic project at the University of Chicago wanted something. We spent a day with them to prepare for it. They showed us the cyclotron and demonstrated how it worked. The thing that overwhelmed us as actors was not the miracle(?) of the atom bomb, but these little badges they wore.

BOBBI: These badges would turn a different color when you were exposed to too much radioactivity.

MARK: Actors seeing that—oh my! Life and Death! So we did a scene where everybody died.

BOBBI: I remember it going on and on about people looking at each other's badges. It was probably one of the worst scenarios. . . .

MARK: But the scientists had the time of their lives that evening, because here was a group able to grab their essence.

Q: *In a sense, you were being their comic mirror.*

MARK: Right. The point is that the group was facile enough that I think it could have gotten the essence of any group and then would have been able to come up with a scene that would be meaningful to that audience. Too bad we didn't explore that further, but we just thought of it as a way to make an extra buck.

We also went to an insane asylum. Not to do a show, just to observe. Doctor Jim Sacks, who was a fan of Compass and would sometimes improvise with us, worked at an asylum and asked us if we were interested in coming out to visit.

BOBBI: We interviewed about five different patients. There was one woman I recall who spoke only in stream-of-consciousness. Each person who came in had another category of illness wrong with him. They were very open with us, very easy to talk to. When they left, we discussed what was wrong with them with the doctors. We all decided that the last guy who came in was the craziest of them all. It turned out he was the head of the institution.

Q: *Did he act outrageously?*

BOBBI: No, he just told us the truth. He said he was in charge and we thought, "Delusions of grandeur!"

Q: *What did you think about Compass at the time? Were you aware that you were doing something new and important?*

MARK: No, as a matter of fact, it was like we were entertaining in a living room. I never could understand why people enjoyed it so much. It always felt like kidding around to me. David would always speak of it in such lofty terms.

BOBBI: I never understood what he was saying. I knew he was saying something and it was important to him, but I could never translate it into workable terms. I heard the word "community" a lot. And "group." Good words, but I never really saw what that had to do with the work. There was something very beautiful and sad about David. I felt he had a tremendous need—a tremendous drive—to make this into something very special. The problem was I never saw his vision.

MARK: When he talked of it, it was as a theater of the proletariat. It would be about the immediate area we were in and the problems those people are confronted with, and that meant people would come from that area and identify with what we were doing, and we would be part of that community. And it would be tremendously important to them because it would be about their rent struggle or some other struggle, and we would have a point of view and it was going to be a theater of the people. Coming as I did from an old Marxist-socialist background, that appealed to me like crazy. Whenever I listened to him I would think, "Oh, we're doing something very important." Then I would look at what we were doing and realize, "Wait a minute. It's not important at all." I kept looking at Mike and Elaine and Severn. They had nothing in common with the people who were struggling in the community. They were intellectual people, well-read, so the audience they naturally got was the University of Chicago. So the whole thing was kind of words, but it was not reality. The possibility was there. It could have happened maybe, but we never did it.

BOBBI: From my point of view, it could never work because I never had anything to do with the community. There was no *time*. I remember working all day long in what we laughingly called rehearsals, and then all night long till twelve or one onstage. The only thing I remember about Chicago is that it was so fucking cold in the wintertime. I remember going from my house to Compass thinking I was going to die. So that stuff about reflecting the community's needs, wants, et cetera, was a total fraud because I couldn't possibly reflect the community. I didn't know anything about it. I knew a great deal about my New York community that I came from, which is what I brought with me. But that's it.

MARK: Talking about purpose, when I first came there, Paul Sills was in Europe observing the Brecht theater. He sent us a letter that said that this Brecht theater has a Communist philosophy which gives them a purpose, and that's what we need. I had to laugh. It implied to me,

Mark and Bobbi Gordon

"Everybody work on being a Communist," which struck me as funny.

Q: *What do you remember about the move from the Dock to the Off-Beat Room?*

MARK: They just said, "You'll get more money and we're moving." We got $55 at the Dock and, I think, $75 at the Off-Beat Room. Also, I remember that suddenly we had a doorman and a place to park a car.

Q: *Was it a matter of moving from the underground to aboveground?*

MARK: That's it exactly. It was an old nightclub going back to Prohibition days. Supposedly it once had a swimming pool underneath it, if you pushed a button. We felt like we were moving into Chicago society. We weren't really, by the way.

The change in the audience from the Dock was night and day. It was no longer just the young college crowd. Now we had Northwestern people and grown-ups.

There was another difference in the tone of Compass. It went from being a potential theater to a nightclub act.

Q: *Shelley Berman came in toward the end of your stay at the Dock. Do you think that his arrival had anything to do with the change in tone?*

BOBBI: Yes.

Q: *He told me that he felt pretty much alienated from everyone but the two of you.*

MARK: That's because we brought him out. I had directed Shelley in New York, and he was a fine actor. I remembered that after rehearsals he would take out material he had written or improvise some pantomime. and we'd laugh. So when David said they wanted another actor, I said, "I'll get another guy out here that'll be a good actor." But what was in my head was that he would come out. and I knew he would be very good and very funny. but I also knew that he wasn't just going to fit in. And I figured from that something would happen.

BOBBI: Shelley, had he trusted his talent and ability. had he trusted who he was a little more had he trusted that he essentially had a lot to offer—not just in the way of being funny and verbal parrying and "I can be funnier than you. . . ."

I don't know. This is so hard. I don't want to put down

115

Shelley. I felt he was a very talented man. *Extremely* talented. But he was insecure. He was out to prove himself, and that's what I felt was wrong in what happened. He didn't have to prove himself. He had a marvelous mind, a marvelous sense of humor, great improvisational ability. Had he gone with that and trusted that that was there, he would have been an incredible addition to the company. In fact, the moments he did do that, sensational things would happen. Unfortunately, maybe out of this need to prove, when he would go back to do a scene which had initially been touching and beautiful, he would turn it into jokes. It became funny time and it was a shell of what was there.

Q: *Around this time, you had pretty much stopped doing the scenarios.*

BOBBI: There was always so much dissension with every scenario presented. Now, as I said, I liked doing the scenarios. I felt most secure with them. But, generally, the others didn't like doing them. Mark and Andy and I liked them, but I think Michael didn't, and Elaine balked at doing other people's scenarios.

MARK: What I think Elaine balked at really was doing old scenarios again, scenarios that worked before. Because that was safe ground..

Q: *That sounds right. As I understand it. Elaine always preferred to work on new things.*

MARK: Right.

BOBBI: There's another consideration, and that is that the scenarios were the only things we'd really have to rehearse. They required preparation, whereas the scenes didn't. The scenarios were a lot of work, and if you were up late the night before—sometimes till two or three if there was a big crowd—you didn't want to have to come in at eleven or twelve the next day to argue through a scenario. And remember, usually we had to come up with a new scenario a week. So what I think it came down to was people saying, "I don't want to work this goddamn hard."

Q: *So you went pretty much into a straight revue format.*

BOBBI: And then it was funny time and who could be funnier than who. I never felt as much competition onstage as around this time. What started to happen was almost like—OK, you'll do your turn, then Mike and Elaine will do their bit, then Shelley will get up and out-funny Mike and Elaine, and then Mike and Elaine will get up and out-funny Shelley. A lot of marvelous things were still happening, but I felt totally inadequate on that level. I could never compete at that, never pretended to. With the scenarios gone, I felt that my usefulness in the company was so limited that I wanted out.

Q: *Then Sills came back and hit the roof.*

MARK: If he hit the roof, he didn't show it to us.

BOBBI: Yes, he did. I remember one afternoon when he first came back and he'd seen the show the night before. There was a tremendous explosion with the company.

MARK: I might have blocked it out.

BOBBI: There was nothing very subtle about it, I can tell you. I don't remember what he said, except that he thought the whole idea of Compass had gone awry, that he didn't like what he saw, felt that it was funny for funny's sake. But I don't recall Sills solving it at that point.

MARK: No, as a matter of fact, he revived an old scenario.

BOBBI: But it was no longer the place for that kind of work. We were now in a nightclub situation, not a theater. So going back and recapturing the stuff that had worked for the University of Chicago crowd wasn't applicable.

Q: *Andrew said he thought that his getting fired around that time might have been a contributing factor to your leaving.*

BOBBI: In a way, yes, because the funnymen stayed. Andy was like glue. He held people together. . . .

MARK: And we thought, if Andy could be let go, then we knew where Compass was headed. Andy was not a funnyman. He was a *rock,* an unselfish rock. He was there for everybody. He did anything, everything. I felt that if he could go, then there was no place for us either, since we weren't really funny-people and didn't wish to be.

I think we gave plenty of notice we were leaving. We had made our decision a month before we went.

Q: *Did the company draw together and say, "Gee, we're sorry to see you go?"*

MARK: I don't think so. What about you, Bobbi? Did you think so?

BOBBI: I felt something different. I really felt a tremendous amount of love from everyone and a lot of "I wish you weren't going." There was talk from Elaine about, "Listen, I am going to come to New York, and we're going to have a company together because this is not good. It will be us and we'll do it the way we want to." I felt very close to everyone in the company.

MARK: I think you were loved in a very special way. I think I was making a demand in leaving. A hidden demand of "I'm leaving because this company is no longer a company," and that if it didn't get changed I was going to stay hostile.

BOBBI: I was happy to leave. I was relieved. I felt a tremendous burden was lifted.

Q: *How long did you stay there?*

MARK: A year. Then we went home to New York. After we came back, Bobbi was in a troupe that played near the Cherry Lane in the Village.

BOBBI: It was a company headed up by Larry Arrick with Rose—who was then his wife—Severn, Del Close, and Paul Mazursky. We played in the restaurant next to the Cherry Lane and it was good, that's all I remember. We worked very well together and enjoyed each other and it was much fun. We got some absolutely marvelous reviews, and then we had all kinds of problems. It had to do with unions and with the house itself and the bar, and there were all kinds of underground and underworld wheelings and dealings, comings and goings, and whatever. Whatever it was, it became too difficult to cope with, so it was "Oh, fuck it," and that was the end of it.

Q: *But out of this you got an offer to be regulars on the Steve Allen summer replacement show with Steve Lawrence and Eydie Gorme.*

BOBBI: Right. We were consulted on the writing of it and were asked what scenes of our own we wanted to do, and everything was fine. Nobody raised any objections about anything. Then, something like two days before the first show was going to air, Del didn't come in for rehearsal. Everyone said, "Where's Del?" Nobody knew. We went through that day, and the next day we all showed up but Del didn't. So they saw it wasn't going to work and said, "Thanks a lot, fellas." Del never called, never showed,

never said why to anybody or contacted anyone. Just never
came.

Q: *He told me the reason was he didn't want to do a
sketch he considered anti–United Nations on TV.*

BOBBI: None of us would have. But there wasn't any. . . .
Oh, I know what he might have considered an anti-UN
sketch. It was with Sevvy doing the interpreter bit—trying
to understand people and. . . . Oh, it wasn't an anti-UN
skit! That he might, after all these years, justify it that
way—OK. The point is, everybody had an equal say, and
he never said anything.

I saw Del many years later when Mark went to Playwrights at Second City to do *The Caretaker,* and we hugged
and kissed and it was hello. I mean, I love him, so who
would carry on about it? But it would have been nice if
he'd shown up and said his piece.

MARK: Something interesting about a lot of the people
influenced by the U. of C. background—some of them have
the sense that if the public likes something they do too
much, then there must be something wrong with it. So
sometimes it's like they purposely fail. Wow! What a
generalization! But, yeah. . . .

Q: *Bobbi, was this your last contact with improvisation?*

BOBBI: Yes, in fact I still think it was one of the contributing factors to my leaving the theater entirely.
(*Laughs.*)

Q: *Talk to me a little about The Third Ear.*

MARK: Elaine May gathered an improvisational company
to go into the theater where The Premise had played. That
company was amazingly talented. Reni Santoni, Peter Boyle,
Renee Taylor, and Louise Lasser. They were very bright
people. Renee had already done a nightclub act, and Reni
could introduce scenes and be funny as an emcee. Peter
could do hundreds of imitations. I was a little afraid because I was still just an actor.

Elaine wanted to do something topical on civil rights.
There had been a black protest at the World's Fair in New
York where they were putting themselves in front of trains
and on the highways, stopping all traffic. She said, "Let's
do a scene about that." So the first time we did it, everybody made jokes about how the trains stopped and how
terrible it is. Elaine said, "That's not what would happen.

What would happen if you were really on a train and it stopped?" Well, you really don't know what's happening when a train stops. So you read the paper or something. So we just sat there, and after about ten minutes I think it was Reni took it on himself to be the conductor and he just walked through the car. This improvisation went on for about forty-five minutes and Elaine said, "Let's keep it in." Everyone said, "You can't do that." She said, "Well, they waited all this time and they're rebelling. Maybe we ought to experience a little what the waiting is like."

We did a lot of political material. We would read the paper every day for new material. I thought I was pretty aware, but I was getting an education in current events then, because you really can't improvise unless you know what's going on that moment. We started out with a set show that had places in it for spot improvisations from the start. She had us do spots on opening night. I was terrified because I thought it would flop. And it did. It fell right on its nose.

Q: *How would you contrast her with Sills as a director?*

MARK: From the little I worked with Paul—remember, it was *very* little and many years ago—with him there were orders given. Elaine never gave orders. She thinks if an actor's having trouble, then something has to be wrong. Maybe it's the actor, maybe it's the material. But she will keep experimenting and letting the actor make things real for himself, if necessary even change the material. That's unique.

She'd audition actors and she'd say, "OK, you try to pick me up at this bar." I would play the bartender and a cat would come in and order a drink, and he'd say to her, "You want a drink?" She'd say, "Yes." And he'd say, "What do you want?" She'd say, "Go to your place?" And he'd say, "You're really very pretty. You have beautiful eyes." And she'd say, "Go to your place?" And it would be like the actor auditioning didn't want to get offstage and he didn't hear what she was saying. Well, an actor who didn't hear couldn't be in the company. These guys would get up and think that they were supposed to make funny jokes and do verbal shtick. What Elaine was saying was, "No verbal shtick. This scene should be over in ten seconds. If your task is to pick me up and I say yes right then, you've reached your objective, so go out!"

Q: *Do you have an idea of what improvisational theater has meant to you in terms of your work?*

MARK: The knowledge of the audience I never would have gotten elsewhere as strong as I did in improvisational theater, because there the audience guides you, which doesn't happen when you're dealing with a play.

BOBBI: You had the right to fail at Compass. You were not placing the obligation to be good on yourself, therefore you allowed things to happen. You couldn't do that in New York, because here you knew you were being judged. But in Chicago, you could experiment. Once you eliminate the element of maybe, make something safe, it cannot be good. Rather, it can be good, but it cannot be great.

9.

Shelley Berman

Everything I have heard indicates that when Shelley Berman was a student at Chicago's Goodman Theater, he was a remarkable actor. But initially he had a very rough time of it. Then he was asked to join The Compass. Through his work there, he discovered and developed his flair for comic monologues. Shortly after Compass closed, that talent brought him to the fore of solo comedy. He, along with Lenny Bruce and Mort Sahl, profoundly changed the character of the art. But whereas Bruce and Sahl specialized in jazz-like improvisational essays on political and social themes, occasionally sketching quick caricatures to people their routines, the bulk of Berman's work rests firmly on his ability as an actor. He creates full *characters.* His humor is mostly based on accurate but compassionate observation of human behavior rather than on a string of verbal wit. For this reason, I find his albums stand up better than those of most comics. Most comedy records consist of a series of jokes, and how many times can one laugh at the same jokes? In contrast, Berman's routines, being in actuality dramatic pieces, lend themselves to the continuing sense of discovery that characterizes any good theater piece.

The Liars, which Berman discusses in this chapter, was a particularly well-received piece presented during the last

Shelley Berman

few days of The Compass. Directed by Walter Beakel from a scenario by Isaac Rosenfeld, and also featuring in its cast Beakel, Mike Nichols, Severn Darden, and Barbara Harris, it told the story of a Jewish refugee named Lieberman (played by Berman) who teaches in a public school. He is abrasive and egotistical and thoroughly disliked by three fellow teachers with whom he rides to and from work every day. These three (Beakel, Nichols, and Darden) decide to get their revenge by preying on his gullibility, making up progressively more outrageous fictions which he swallows whole. At the culmination of the most elaborate prank, Lieberman finds himself on the bank of a river being called upon to toss in a bag containing what he believes is the mutilated body of a Chicago gangster. He breaks into tears. The others shamefacedly confess to him that they've been having fun at his expense. He forces a laugh and claims he knew it all the time and was just going along with the gag to be a sport. In the final scene, the three confederates are obviously ashamed of their cruelty, but at the end it is evident that the situation between them and Lieberman will resume as before.

The tape of this piece twenty years later still packs a hell of a punch.

BERMAN: I was with a group of actors in New York who were starving, and I met a fellow there by the name of Mark Gordon, who was at that time an aspiring director. We sweated out a good deal of time together, and we did a couple of readings for producers of a play that we had and were trying to get backing for. Nothing came of it.

I started to write free-lance, trying to make a living. At the time, Steve Allen had The Tonight Show, and I would write material and submit it and they'd buy what they wanted. At the same time I was looking for acting work, which was impossible to get. I was always too short or too tall, and I froze in auditions. Today I think I would freeze. I'm terrible at auditions.

Then, one summer, I got a call from Mark saying he was a member of a group called The Compass Players in Chicago. They were on the South Side of Chicago at a place called the Dock, earning something like $40 apiece a week, and they needed a replacement for a man who had to do a

123

summer season at the Barter Theatre. That man was Severn Darden. So I went in as his replacement. As it turned out, I stayed. I was earning very little, but I realized that this was the place to learn my trade. To learn acting, to learn comedy.

For all that I had trained—and I'd trained many years —for all the stock that I had played, for all my experience prior to that, I never really did anything that came close to the kind of work I was able to do after being with Compass for just a few months.

Q: *What were your first impressions of Compass?*

BERMAN: That they were a bunch of smart-asses. They were extremely young. A little bit younger than I, and I was embarrassed by that because I had struggled for so long and hadn't gotten anywhere and here I was.

Q: *Do you remember the first scene you improvised there?*

BERMAN: Oh yes. It was an improvisation on a fairy tale. I can't remember which it was, but I played a king. I played him well because I didn't think I had too big a job and I didn't think that I had to star or shine or be funnier than the rest. All I had to do was play the king. which I did, and it was good. Then it dawned on me that some of the people *were* shining. I wanted to shine along with them, so I imposed my mother wit upon that and started to screw myself up something awful.

At first I thought the idea was to go up and ad-lib funny. It took me at least a month, I think. to learn that you don't go up with the intention of being funny. You go up with the intention of playing out an action. If you have funny in you, the funny will happen. To trust that and not to work for funny was the thing I had to learn, and I did learn it. I learned how to work out of an action. I learned all the language that had been so mysterious to me when I studied with Uta Hagen for about two years, like what is your first beat. what is your second beat. what are your needs, what are your wants. what is your action, what are your obstacles. All these things, all of this language, had been a problem for me before. But suddenly, as I worked in improvisation, I began to realize how to go about getting some of the things I had done intuitively in the past.

It seemed to me the work was very intellectually ori-

ented. Some of our sessions together, which we called rehearsals, were largely intellectually steeped conversations.
I was never really intellectually oriented. I had worked
more viscerally, intuitively. All I wanted to do was to get up
onstage and explode, you see. But these sessions were good
because I learned a great deal from these people. I had no
idea how much there was to learn. I learned more than the
craft of acting and comedy. I learned on an academic level
things I never knew. I thought I'd read everything there was
to read, but I hadn't read what they'd read. I tried to catch
up, to at least have some acquaintance with much of what
was being said. I'd never heard of Kierkegaard. His name
came up in conversation and therefore I went to read
Kierkegaard, which destroyed me because I didn't understand him. But I recall going out to get a book by Kierkegaard. I didn't know what book I wanted. I just wanted a
book. There were several instances like that. I wasn't by
any means unschooled, but they had a more specific knowledge. It was esoteric and I wanted to be part of that, and
so I tried.

I could never be as beautifully informed as Mike
Nichols. I thought he was an exceptionally informed man.
I immediately took to Mike on the first day that I met
him. There was an immediate love-hate relationship. I
never felt that same kind of hate with Elaine May. I
found a love relationship there. With Barbara Harris, there
was a love, but I would find myself irritated with her because I found her an elusive personality. I couldn't quite
grasp her thinking. Mark Gordon and Barbara Glenn, who
eventually married Mark—I felt they were dummies like
me and I felt good in their company. And there was Andy
Duncan, who I thought was like myself in many ways,
trying to be on the inside and yet not quite reaching it. Yet
I thought he was very good onstage. Super-reliable and he
had a super wit.

With Mike, as I say, it was a more strained relationship.
But there was no way to deny his brilliance. There was no
way to deny how much I admired him and how much I
enjoyed working with him. But it was difficult for me to
reconcile myself to the fact that I recognized in him a
superbrilliance. I thought that I was the possessor of a superbrilliance myself. We would approach things in such

diametrically opposite ways and yet arrive at almost the same conclusions. Though I found myself a bit more vulgar than Mike. As a matter of fact, a bit more vulgar than all of the others. I mean in choices, in selection. I found myself certainly working more from my gut than from my head than did the others. But I tried to develop techniques which would allow me to work in their way, and I did.

I would work with anybody on anything anytime because I loved to get up there and do things. Just loved it. After I learned how and was good at it, I couldn't wait to get onstage. I really was a stage-hog.

I think after my first month there, I went to Mike and Elaine and I said to them, "We can make an act together. The three of us can go out and become professional comedians." They said that they did not wish to do that. They didn't think it was a good idea, so we let it go. It was good we let it go because there was more to be done, far more to be gained from working with Compass before leaving it.

Q: *Were there any scenes you particularly enjoyed?*

BERMAN: I think "The Panhandler's Apprentice," which was a scene I did with Severn Darden, would have been one of the great classic scenes of burlesque theater. He was a new panhandler, a young guy who didn't know how to approach anybody. I'd teach him a few pointers on how to approach somebody for the few cents you'd say was for carfare to get to the job that was waiting for you at the other end of the line. Then I would stand back and watch him panhandle. Severn was so surprising on all occasions. I recall one occasion he tipped his hat and said, "Excuse me, Sisters, but could you. . . ." I had to pull him away from these nuns, whom of course you didn't see until after he said, "Excuse me, Sisters. . . ." And then he went after a midget, the tiniest little man in the world. I think he asked him for a half-dollar and I scolded him and said, "That man doesn't have room in his pocket for a half-dollar." Then we tried using the handicapped bit. I said, "Now you put your arm inside of your coat and we'll button it so that it looks like you have only one arm." So he went and stopped people with his left hand, but you could see his hat stuck to the outside of his coat. Obviously his other hand was holding his hat from the inside. Although scenes became set as we repeated them, there was

126

no way that Severn would not surprise you. He was a true improvisationist.

Elaine May was also a true improvisationist. Pure. It was a cause of friction many times between her and Mike when she would deviate from that which had already been set. Mike knew a good thing when he came upon it and he wanted to stay with it. Mike as a director now does not insist on these results and does not insist on going for a laugh moment. His idea is that you be true to the action. It seems to be a contradiction of what I had noticed in him much earlier when he worked with Elaine. If there was a laugh to be gotten and she didn't set up the feed line, he would work with her until she did. He did everything but lasso her. That's how Mike worked at that time.

Another of my favorite scenes was called "Mountain Climbing." I didn't create this. It was one I moved into. I was a mountain climber, the head man on the rope, and I was trying to belay the line. Originally David Shepherd had done this part. I understand he used to do a slide back across the stage when one of the other climbers had fallen. He was top man and you'd see him literally slide across the stage and you didn't know what was pulling him. I tried to do that and I think I eventually got that movement. The second man on the rope could barely be seen. His head would poke out through this louver door. The third man on the rope was a pain-in-the-ass. He would want to know if it was time for tea. That sort of thing. He would shout a question up to the second man on the rope who would shout something up to me. I'd shout the answer back to the second man. the second man would shout the answer back to the third man. and the third man would have his comment. Really the funniest man was the third man, but you never saw him. That was Mike. He did one of those British types. He was really a drag. Literally a drag. He'd yank us. The end was when I took a knife and handed it to the second man on the rope. And then you'd hear Mike's voice trailing off as he fell.

I took over roles that had been played by others, just as people in Second City took over roles that had been played by others, and took some of the lines and ideas. They never seemed to belong to anyone in particular. They were the domain of our group. So, many of the lines that some of us created, many of the actions we created, many of the sketches we built became the property of others eventually. A few of the things that even today I do as a stand-up comedian came out of my original days at Compass.

Sometime after I joined, Sills came back. He was marvelous, though he'd also get off on those damn rap kicks, sit around rapping for hours. That would drive me crazy. "God damn it! Let's get on, let's *do* something!" But I wasn't altogether right in my impatience. The fact is that Sills frequently came up with *brilliant* things. He would give us an activity and we would have to come up with a specific for that activity. Like once selling was the activity, and I came up with the idea of selling myself to myself.

It was a soliloquy. I opened with a brief telephone conversation in which I found out there'd been a party last night I hadn't been invited to and that the girl I'd had a date with last night who'd stood me up was at that party. I hung up the phone and then I did this thing to the mirror in which I sold myself to myself, talked about the good qualities I had. And it was rather moving and interesting. I think then I went back to the phone to call my friend and tell him to go to hell. The only reason I used the phone was to establish why I felt disliked and why I felt there must be a reason to dislike me. I didn't feel, since my idea was selling myself to myself rather than selling myself to somebody, that it would be a good idea to have another person to improvise with. Yet I had to establish my plot. Although improvisation isn't playwriting, you still have an action to pursue and it has to be clear. So you took certain liberties. You were really playwriting to some degree.

Anyway, I was doing this scene at The Compass, and the phone conversation was getting more involved every night. It got to be a little better and a little longer, and one night, when I finished the phone conversation, the audience applauded as I hung up. So I stopped right there. And that became my first actual telephone monologue.

Portions of our show were improvisations that were already set, and portions were improvisations of the night. We'd take suggestions from the audience, take a ten-minute intermission, pick partners, pick ideas, talk them over, and go out and do them. On a New Year's Eve, somebody in the audience yelled out, "The morning after the night before." I went back and said to Elaine, "I have an idea about a guy who's carried on something dreadful at a party the previous night. You're going to tell me what I did, and my action will be to fight belief." She said, "I'm doing a thing with Mike." So I decided, since I'd already done this phone thing, that I could go out and improvise another phone thing.

Well, I did. I set my hangover by having the worst possible headache. The first words out of my mouth were, "Oh God, God, God, God . . ." and I felt around for the rest of my head. "Oh God, where is my Alka-Seltzer?" Then the pantomime of the Alka-Seltzer and water. "Don't fizz!" Then I got on the phone, dialed my friend, and found out what I'd done to his household. Well, on the first night I did it, it was just that I threw a lamp through his window and vomited on his rug. That, I thought, was a little strong, to have thrown up on his rug. A rather tasteless idea. So on future occasions I took that out.

One night, after I'd done this two or three times, Severn Darden came to me as I was just going out to do it again. "Not his lamp," he whispered, "his *cat.*" So I said, "OK." I was game for anything. What the hell, I had nothing to lose. And so I threw the cat out the window. And it became one of the most requested routines that I have in my act today. People are still requesting "The morning after the night before," or they say, "Do the hangover," or sometimes, "Do the one with the cat." How casually it was said. "Not a lamp, Shelley, a cat." Just whispered in darkness. How casually that became a routine which earned me great, great sums of money and considerable importance in a difficult field.

Eventually Mike and Elaine and I did try to become a trio. This was while we were still at Compass, but we knew that Compass was going to break up soon. The problem was Mike didn't want to do things with me. He admired my work, as far as I knew. I think he did admire my work. But our personalities were so involved. Occasionally we'd quarrel. I would be enraged sometimes at some of the things he would do. And yet, when I was good, Mike would come to me and say, "That was good." And when I did a thing that was bad, he would say, "I thought that

129

was the most tasteless thing you ever did." He would say it. Almost as if it was therapeutic, as if someone had advised him, "If you think of something like that, say it." I don't know if that was the motivation, but it would sound like that. I didn't think of this at that time. I'm coming to conclusions rather retrospectively.

The interesting thing was how much I wanted to work with him. *God,* I loved working with him! When we did work together, it worked out fine, but there was resistance. Eventually, when we tried to become an act together, I was asking them to please think up some things with me included because they had too many things they were doing together. I did do two things with Elaine. One was "The Driving Lesson," in which I taught her how to drive. It was very funny. Eventually there was a driving lesson done by another comedian who came out of Chicago and was not part of Compass. A lot of things Compass did somehow this comedian thought of at exactly the same time or a little bit afterward.

I also did a thing with Elaine we created one night at Compass, an improvisation called "The Lost Dime." I was a man whose car got stuck and I was stranded miles from nowhere and Elaine was a telephone operator, and my dime was deposited and I didn't have another dime and she couldn't return it. Eventually that routine became Mike and Elaine's. I made a single out of it called "Franz Kafka on the Telephone," but it was never really a dynamite routine. But the duet version was a dynamite routine.

Anyway, we weren't doing things as a threesome, which made it difficult for us as a trio. We had no three-person scenes. I did do one thing with them in "Pirandello." I was a stage manager who originally began it by describing it and then came on later. But "Pirandello" was essentially a two-person scene. It didn't absolutely require the other character. So we had no real three-person scenes and we abandoned the idea of doing the act together.

Q: *What do you remember about* The Liars?

BERMAN: I wish that *The Liars* wouldn't be used as any basis of discussion of my work. I disliked what I did. It was a job and I played the character as I saw it and was directed to play it. I found the characterization quite distinctly anti-Semitic. I found that in an effort to make him

Shelley Berman

an unlikable man I had succeeded too well. Yet, as much as you disliked him, when you understood what was being done to him, the story became far more valuable.

Q: *I thought it was as much a negative comment on the others.*

BERMAN: Yes, one could be angry at the others for what they did, but I don't think being angry and disliking someone is the same. No matter what they did, it still didn't make you like the character I played. You could feel sorry for him, but that ain't going to make you like him, and that, I felt, was the major flaw. It could have been because of my choices. My accent was extremely thick, my attitude, my manners were extremely pushy, extremely vulgar. The character had no tact. He wasn't nice. He was an uncomfortable man to be near. To portray a Jew in a way that fits all the unfortunate notions about a Jew, regardless of the outcome of the play and regardless of the fact that it shows that others can be awful—I don't think that does the Jew any good.

Q: *Did you find that you got a negative response on it?*

BERMAN: No, as a matter of a fact, I got a lot of positive response on it from people who looked at it as a work of art. If you want to look at it esthetically, I did nothing that was terrible. I'm not sure that everything I did was good, because I'm sure I could have played the character with greater grace I think I could have come across with a better piece of work, generally speaking. Yet, as an overall piece of art, it was accepted on its esthetic value by our audiences.

Individually there were those who found what I did was not good. Geraldine Page and David Pressman, the director, came to see it. They didn't like what I did. They liked Mike Nichols enormously. I was hurt by that. I wanted them to like me, of course. To have them dislike me was bad enough. But to like Mike Nichols so much really rankled. But, of course, that was the immature part of me being upset.

The important thing was why I had been disliked. On that particular night, incidentally, I wasn't getting the laughter I should. I always did get my laughs in that show, but on that particular night, I did not get my laughter. The others did, I didn't. It was a strange performance.

But I was unhappy with it anyway. You have to like the character you're playing, but after the first few nights I realized, "I don't like what I'm doing here. I don't like this man." I tried very hard to get back into it and tried to like him. You must like the character you play. You can't say, "I am a villain." You can't say, "I am an ugly person." You play a person with a problem, but you can't stand off and make a comment on him. You must *be* that man, and people don't generally dislike themselves.

Q: *What about the kind of life you were leading at Compass?*

BERMAN: It was the loneliest goddamn existence. I was just plain lonely-miserable. I was married and away from my wife. I had struggled for longer than some of the others. I wondered if anything was ever going to come of me. The age thirty was looming up on the horizon and I was getting scared. I wondered where I would go from here.

I recall a moment in my life which I will not ever forget. We had a little dog, a little toy poodle whom we called Lilliput, and I found out one night when I talked to my wife that my dog had a disease called hardpad. I talked to her long-distance, and she was telling me that the dog was going to die and there was nothing that could be done. I loved that dog more than I can tell you. At that time, there was also a young man with the company whose name I forget. And he wanted to use the phone and he kept knocking on the phone-booth door, saying, "How long are you going to stay in there?" I turned to him and said, "Please, man, please. My dog is dying." And he said, "What do I care about your goddamn dog? Get off the phone."

Well, I did get off the phone and I ran toward him with my right hand back and shot it forward as I reached him and hit him somewhere in his belly, as hard as a man could hit another man, and I tried then to hit his face. He didn't want to fight with me. He got frightened and started grappling for my arms and I realized, "I don't want to hit him anymore." And so I pushed him away from me. I said, "You don't know. If only you knew." The owner of the place took me off into his office where I sat and cried for a while. And then we were to go onstage and do a scene, and as we walked backstage—we were walking up a few steps—Mike, whom I'd thought before was without emotion, touched me on my shoulder and just looked in my face. He knew, you see. *He* knew. The boy that I'd hit couldn't ever. But there was a communication in that little split-second that, for all of his brilliance, I don't think Mike would remember now. There was a communication and a kindness that I won't ever forget.

There was much about Mike I'd learned to love prior to that. There was more to love after that. He can't know how much affection I feel for him. He can't possibly know because we were at each other's throats so much of the time, and then, as our careers went their separate ways, we were almost in competition with each other. It shouldn't have been. There was room for all. So I haven't really expressed myself ever to Mike in the way that I would like. I expressed myself to him in all kinds of other ways. In anger, petulance. That was so many years ago.

Q: *What do you think there is about the improvisational experience which has encouraged so many directors?*

BERMAN: You are so complete as an improvisationist. You understand the working of an action. You understand it thoroughly. You understand the beats which make up the action. You understand the entire structure of an entertaining or communicative action. You understand it all. You know it from every possible viewpoint. You know it as a playwright would know it, you know it as an actor knows it, and since you are self-directed, you know that, too. Since you are performing publicly, you've also learned how to give and take in terms of blocking. And you learn about the value of lighting. It's all there. So yes, they're all, all of them directors. Anyone who really functioned well in that atmosphere became a director, or *should* be a director.

Compass sort of dissolved and moved to St. Louis and I remained in Chicago because I felt I had the beginnings of an act. So I auditioned in a nightclub and got the job. Then I recorded my act and everything came together.

Q: *Do you still draw on improvisational techniques today?*

BERMAN: My routines are pretty much preset now, but I work on a highly improvisatory level on the in-betweens. Rather than just go up in front of an audience and pick up a phone and go into character, I found it was essential for me to reach the audience. You can't just ignore them. So I had to find in-betweens to talk to them directly. These, as I say, I largely found improvisationally. It was not separate jokes. It was always thematic. That is my working process. Not to work for one thing, then another thing, then another, but to get onto something and then really talk about it.

Q: *Have you ever felt the urge to improvise again with a company?*

BERMAN: Oh, yeah. Sure. I always want to work that way. I haven't had much opportunity to do it since then. I used to do it when I'd go on television on the talk shows, before they made you practically write out everything you were going to say.

Q: *It seems that there has been a sudden resurgence of interest in improvisational companies lately. There are so many new troupes around.*

BERMAN: That's because there are no places for young actors to work. So they get together and form little groups. But eventually, the awful thing that happens to all of these companies is that they find several pieces and they canonize them and then sell themselves as a revue, which is eventually what happened to Second City. And once that's done, it's done.

It's hard to retain that freshness of approach, particularly when you are bombarded by criticism whenever you take a chance. You need the good word, the reassurance of the critic. You need it commercially to survive. So you cease taking chances. Once you cease taking chances, you've lost your craft. You really have. Because one of the most important ingredients of improvisation on a professional level is derring-do. You know, fuck them all and get out and do! But once you know that if you die this particular night and so-and-so walks out and says, "They were *terrible!*" you could lose everything, you start freezing pieces. Then you standardize your methods. You get so that you're very tricky. You act like it's an improvisation when the fact is you know goddamn well what your tricks are going to be, where you've got your safeties. Many's the time that happened. We sometimes fell into that trap in the good old days. We'd start an improvisation and all of a sudden we'd find ourselves in an old routine. What started out to be pure

134

and really good and marvelous on-your-feet entertainment
—really on the moment, spontaneous, and exciting—eventually began to disappear because we lost our nerve.

Q: *Do you go back to see any of the troupes now? For
instance, when you play Chicago, do you see Second City?*

BERMAN: No, but then Second City doesn't come and
catch me. You see them when you can, but you don't always have the time available to see other performers. I'll
tell you, I have seen them at work, and I've visited, but I
don't feel like I belong to it anymore. I don't feel that pro-
prietary sense that I did feel earlier in my career. I felt a
kinship and a certain amount of desire to protect it, to keep
it going. Maybe I don't now because when it finally did end
at Compass, I felt that it was over. Even though Second
City was an extension of it and did very well, for me it was
over.

On a few occasions I've dropped in to see an improvisational group and visit with them and maybe get up
onstage and work with them. It's interesting to get up on
that stage and truly improvise. It throws them. It absolutely throws them because nobody is listening to anybody.
Nobody's responding to anybody. Everybody's waiting to
get the *joke* told. We didn't do that. We let things happen
to us at Compass. When somebody said something, we
didn't twist it around to absolute garbage.

On a few of these occasions when I've gotten up with
one of these groups and worked with them a little bit . . .
well, say somebody suggests, "Walking your dog." OK.
You're walking your dog and another person is going to improvise with you. He walks onstage and says, "Did you see
a tall man walking by here a minute ago?" Well, goddamn
it, why can't that person come on that stage and say,
"That's a good-looking dog"? Walking the dog is a present
action. You are open to a million things, like "Does that
bite?" Anything, anything in the world. But I see these
young improvisationists and it's really, "Let's see how
much we can screw each other" rather than playing the
obvious. If you play the obvious and *do it*, you'll see that
it will be all right. It will be. Invariably.

Improvisation is going along with the subject at hand.
Maybe if you're onstage with "Walking your dog" and a
girl comes along, starts a conversation with you about your

dog, maybe the two of you will find love. But it began because you were walking your dog. And your dog can then become a marvelous little obstacle to the smooth discourse which will lead to love.

Q: *Have you ever entertained the idea of doing an improv show on TV?*

BERMAN: Say you sold an improv show to a TV company. All that TV is interested in is the result. So what happens if you improvise? All it does is get put on tape and eventually, when it reaches the viewers, it's either a good or a bad sketch. They don't give a shit if it's an improv.

Improvisation seems to have its fullest impact only live. Because there's a sense of suspense as to whether it's going to work or not. You see, failing is part of it.

You know, nobody paid attention to us in Chicago. When we were there, people could have seen us for nothing. We were doing our best work then. We were doing some great things.

10.

Del Close

Del Close appeared with the first St. Louis Compass under the direction of Ted Flicker. He also acted with The Second City and The Committee, has directed the latter company and, for the past several years, has been directing the former. Along the way, he has taught workshops like crazy, out of which have sprung a number of improvisational groups, including Los Angeles' talented Synergy Trust. His other stage work includes appearances with the Barter Theatre and the famous Julius Monk revues, and a well-remembered, if short-lived, performance on Broadway in *The Nervous Set*.

In addition, he has had a large measure of success as a stand-up comic. Two of his records, *How to Speak Hip* (which he created and performed with Second City alumnus John Brent and which was produced by Bernie Sahlins) and *The Do-It-Yourself Psychoanalysis Kit,* have acquired well-deserved underground reputations; they are not only wonderfully funny albums but are also two of the earliest "concept" comedy discs. For a taste of truly brilliant improvisational acting, check out his work as a drug addict in "The Cleanup" on The Committee's *Wide World of War* record.

A man of many gifts, he can also swallow fire and do

magic. He keeps threatening to write a book on how to create improvisational comedy.

CLOSE: I was seventeen and didn't know shit. I came down to Chicago with a friend—I'd been doing summer stock in Wisconsin—and found an agent. While I was waiting for something to turn up, I took a room in a hotel, and when they discovered I couldn't pay for it, they said, "Well, all right, you can start painting hotel rooms." While I was painting hotel rooms, I went to Playwrights and saw a production of *Volpone*. I thought, "This is pretty sleazy, but this kind of rings a bell somewhere. These strike me as the kind of people I'd like to work with." I went backstage afterwards, complimenting actors on their performances, and they all walked right by me. They wouldn't even tell me who their director was. Finally, I got somebody in a corner who told me they were going to be auditioning soon for a production of *The Glass Menagerie*. But before that, my agent came up with something, said, "Want to go to North Carolina?" I said, "Why not?" So I missed my first chance to get involved with Paul Sills.

I toured North Carolina for nine months, got sick of it, and went to New York where I was very precocious and was able to get every role I ever auditioned for. Did some Off-Broadway and children's theater. One thing led to another, and I did a rather spectacular audition for the Barter Theatre in Abingdon, Virginia, and was hired.

Severn was down there, and he told me, "There's this action going on in Chicago." The Compass. They were having auditions, so one weekend I took a twin-engine plane up. They had moved twice by that time; they were in the Off-Beat Room on the North Side. I remember I auditioned with Elaine May, and what I was supposed to do was, I was a businessman who had to catch a plane and had to get this chick in the sack before a certain period of time. I really didn't know what to do up there, but Elaine brought me through the scene and made me look good. I guess I kind of charmed them. I mean, here was this extremely high intelligence and very high reference level combined with absolute fucking naïveté—Kansas innocence right off the farm. Anyway, I was hired. The unfortunate

138

thing I had forgotten was I'd already signed a contract to
go on tour with the Barter, so I couldn't take the job.

I helped put together and acted in a show at the Barter
about the history of the theater that went from *Antigone* to
Death of a Salesman. We took it around to colleges and
places like that. It was a big success. Ted Flicker saw me
in this. Since we did a Flaminio Scala scenario in the show
—*commedia dell'arte*, you know—he got the impression I
knew something about improvisation. Ha. He was putting
together the first St. Louis Compass, so he hired me. And
we chose two women to work with us—Nancy Ponder and
Jo Henderson.

We rehearsed and were feted by the St. Louis maniac
crowd. We played in the Crystal Palace, which was run by
the Landesmans. The name Landesman must always loom
large in the history of improvisational theater.

We went to work, and the first night we opened, nobody
knew who we were or what the fuck was going to happen.
We decided to begin our improvisational career with a
scene that. . . . The lights went on onstage, nothing
changed, came time for the performance, a slight ruckus
began at one of the tables. Somebody started insulting
somebody else. It got a little louder, and louder, and people
were saying, "Shhh!" Of course, it was us sitting at the
table. Nancy Ponder and I fought our way onto the stage,
having this argument. In the middle of this, Ted Flicker
comes out and says, "Freeze!" And *boing!*—we do. And
suddenly the audience is aware that something slightly unusual is happening. And he says, "All right, what happens
now? You tell us." The audience suggests something, we
do it, the audience goes "Hooray!" and suddenly we're off
to a tremendously good start.

We would do twenty-five-minute sets. and then we would
take suggestions from the audience and then retire for five
or ten minutes. It was a requirement then that we come up
with a scene for *every* suggestion. So we'd come back. do
a set, take more suggestions, retire. come back, do another
set, et cetera. On Saturdays we would repeat the best of the
week. On Sundays, we worked at some slightly more free-
form thing.

I remember sometimes we would improvise from paint-
ings. I remember doing that Rousseau picture of someone

sleeping in the desert being guarded by a lion. I don't know what the hell went on in the scene. Some pretentious garbage. I remember being particularly disturbed about having to do that because that was one of the scenes we did when Paul Sills and Howard Alk came down from Chicago to take a look at what we were doing. "Oh shit, I'm going to have to do this dumb-ass thing for Paul Sills." And it turns out that something else I did in the show impressed Paul so that he thought I was a likely candidate for Second City later. So that's how I was first seen by—though didn't get to meet—Paul Sills. I didn't meet him until I finally got here to Chicago.

Severn came through town with a girl friend. I had convinced him to buy a hot-shit motorcycle. So he bought a BMW Double Twin Cylinder 650-CC, which is like having a Rolls-Royce. (He also had two Rolls-Royces, incidentally.) He had his initials on it: F.X.S.T.D.—Francis Xavier Severn Tekel Darden—and how magnificent they looked! He asked me if he could borrow my crash helmet for his girl friend. I said sure. About three days later we got information that Severn had run a stop sign and was hit at about sixty miles an hour by a car that had literally crushed him from hip to ankle. They sent me back my crash helmet that had a dent about an inch and a half deep in it. Thank God that girl had a crash hat or her head would have splattered like an egg all over the highway. She came out of it OK.

Then we used to get long incoherent tapes from Severn. We would sit there listening to them, drinking from the dusty bottles of never-touched aperitifs from the Crystal Palace. (Have you ever had *crème de violette?* Can you *imagine* such a thing?) So we'd be drinking and listening to these tapes from Severn, who was under nineteen different kinds of medication for pain. They were like communications. Sometimes he would have his cousin read one of his latest compositions, a poem or something. Or they would have a conversation on a subject they thought we would be particularly interested in. Pretty soon everybody but me got tired of listening to the tapes, and then I got tired of listening to the tapes, and then Severn turned up. He turned up with his leg in a brace, and by a brace I mean a *brace!* It was an engineering marvel! He looked like a bionic man. He called up Ted and said, "Can I have a job?" Which he got.

I think what was happening at this time was Ted Flicker and David Shepherd were in communication about the possibility of opening up a New York Compass, and this required Ted's presence in New York. Which required a replacement for Ted as an actor and director, which meant hiring Mike and Elaine, which meant firing Jo Henderson, which was a pity because she was just getting very good.

So Mike and Elaine arrive. Mike is in St. Louis for one purpose and one purpose only—to work with Elaine. Elaine is in St. Louis partly to get away from a guy in Chicago. Also because she needed a job, of course. Anyway, Elaine and I became close. I would write scenarios and she would direct them, and we would work together, which I think infuriated Mike. Mike and I just didn't hit it off, which was a pity. It was probably for artistic-ideological reasons. We weren't mature enough to treat each other properly.

Anyway, here we were doing Compass and we discovered we were successful without knowing what we were doing. We were absolutely fearless about going on to do the world's most abysmal bullshit. Let's not say fearless. Let's say fearful, because Ted Flicker forced us out there to do it, though if we were not willing to be forced, we wouldn't have gone.

We would come out after shows, though, burning with humiliation because we knew what we'd done in front of the audience was a con. We didn't know what the fuck we were doing up there. It was all intuitive. So, for our own self-respect, and so we could have a conscious technique to rely on, we came up with three principles of improvisation that seemed to work for us at the time:

1. Don't deny verbal reality. If it's said, it's real. "What about our children?" "We don't have any." That's wrong. Same is true with physical reality. If another actor physically establishes something, it is there and you mustn't do anything that says it's not there.

2. Take the active as opposed to the passive choice. Of course, this means a great deal. It means you are free to choose on the stage. Which, if you choose to ponder that

for a second, means you are in an existentialist state of living your life in public.

3. The actor's business is to justify. What this came out of was a time when one of the actresses in St. Louis said, "The character I'm playing in the scene wouldn't *do* that. How can I justify doing that?" Elaine's response: "The actor's job *is* to justify." In improvisation, the "character" is illusory. Everything starts from yourself. For "character," read: "You—with a few *characteristics* tacked on." Or: "One aspect of yourself emphasized over others." Paul used to say, "Wear a character as lightly as a straw boater and be prepared to tip it and reveal *yourself*."

These directions are followable. They are understandable by anyone who speaks English, and they formed a kind of tripod upon which I was able to base a much more complex and probably not very much more profound theory or system aimed at the professional theater, which is opposed to the way Viola's book is aimed at the amateur and personality development. I mean, the two systems essentially face different problems.

After St. Louis, at just about the time Mike and Elaine were making it—1956, I think—I got an offer to take a group down to Miami. So I thought, "Whom have I got available? Who in the world knows about improvisation at all?" I'd never met Larry Arrick, but I knew his name as having been one of the Compass gang. So I called him up, told him about the Miami proposition. He said he wanted to think about it. Finally he said no deal because it sounded a little precarious, to say the very least.

About two weeks after that, I got a call from him. He said, "I'm going to put a Compass together in New York. Do you want to be in it?" I said sure. Shepherd didn't have a hand in the show for a change, which was a relief, since he tended to confuse things more than anything else. He's a magnificent catalyst, but if you left him around, he'd just confuse you to death. It ended up being me and Severn, Rose Arrick, Bobbi Gordon, and Paul Mazursky. We opened in spring going on summer, 1956. Everyone in the theater flipped over us. Geraldine Page was there every night. The joint was jammed. But there was a union problem and wham, we were closed in two weeks, though we had these fantastic reviews.

142

We got an offer to go on Steve Allen's show, *The To-night Show*. Steve Allen was going off the air for the summer and Steve Lawrence and Eydie Gorme were going to have the summer show and we were going to be a resident company. Then I finked out. I really don't exactly know why, because my political convictions aren't all that deep, but I felt that one of the pieces we were putting in the show. . . . I didn't feel that in 1956 we should be attacking the UN. What was beginning to happen to me was that I was beginning to develop a political consciousness. Like I had joined SANE that year, and the Village Independent Democrats. The upshot of it all was that I screwed everybody and everybody was thoroughly pissed off at me except Severn. My disappearance from the show canceled the group's opportunity for appearing on the show, so they did not . . . we did not. . . . Nobody appeared on the show from Compass. Only Severn seemed to have some understanding of what I was doing and why.

Anyway, as I say, Mike and Elaine were doing their act, and Shelley had a nightclub act going, so I thought I might as well get a nightclub act, too. So I took some material from the Compass days, put together some new stuff, and I had an act. It took me two years to get a single going. Two years of absolutely humiliating defeat. I don't know how I kept alive. Elaine helped me with money part of the time. I took jobs typing. I had to buy a tuxedo. The sleazier the joint, the fancier they wanted the comics to dress. Like Mort Sahl could wear a T-shirt in Mister Kelly's; I had to wear a tux in this toilet in New Jersey.

About this time—I guess it was '58 or '59—I was taking acid for the Air Force. They were investigating REM—rapid eye movement—and I started as an experimental subject. The point is they would take me to the dream lab in Brooklyn, hook me up to this machine, I would dream, and when REM indicated dreaming, they'd wake me up and say, "Are you dreaming?" "Yes, I am, you motherfucker." "What were you dreaming about?" "I don't know. Bunny rabbits." I didn't like it. I grew tired of it real fast. About this time, Ted Flicker offered me a part in *The Nervous Set*, so I split for St. Louis. I left a forwarding address, and I got a letter that said, "Dear Mr. Close: You still owe the United States Air Force one dream."

The Nervous Set was brought to Broadway. Mike and Elaine came to the opening of the show. I think Mike and I were sort of on nodding terms at that time. Actually, speaking terms, as a matter of fact. I remember we went to see *The Horror of Dracula* together—Mike, Elaine, and I —and Elaine gave us a detailed Freudian analysis of it later, and she was right on the button! God, she must have been born with the total knowledge of the working of the human psyche!

I remember sometime during this time Elaine came by Ted's apartment and we were trying to turn her onto grass. And she was at her least social. She wanted to do this irrational thing or that irrational thing. Said, "Let me draw a mural on your wall with this felt-tipped pen." And Ted said, "No, that's a really dumb idea." "If you were really stoned," she said, "you'd let me do it." So Ted says, "OK, go ahead." So she did this atrocious mural on the wall, and I think it took nine coats of paint to finally cover it up.

Meanwhile, my act was pulling together, and I started getting booked into clubs like the Hungry I, the Blue Angel, the Village Vanguard, and the Bon Soir.

I was working in the Club Renaissance in Hollywood when I got a call from Howard Alk. This was in the summer of 1960 and Second City had opened the previous winter. He called and said, "Communication has temporarily broken down between Paul Sills and the company. Will you come be the director for a while?" So I did. I remember this was around the time of the Republican Convention, which was the occasion of one of the finer hours of the Public Cretinization Program.

Q: *Public Cretinization Program? What is that?*

CLOSE: Severn and I have done many public acts whose meanings were opaque. Practical jokes. And the more you tried to understand them, the less you could figure out what was really going on. We called it our Public Cretinization Program.

Q: *How did this involve the Republican Convention?*

CLOSE: Severn and I were both Stevenson men, and we were very disappointed that he hadn't been nominated. They nominated Kennedy, as you'll recall. One afternoon, we were walking along the street and we thought, "Since the Democrats didn't nominate him, wouldn't it be nice if the Republicans did?" We thought this was a great idea, so within a matter of hours we got something like thirty people—waitresses, bartenders, actors, friends—to call their congressmen or representatives and get credentials to get onto the main floor of the convention.

It was the first day of the convention, and Senator Walter Judd got up to make the keynote address, and whammo!, out came our banners and placards—INDEPENDENT REPUBLICANS TO DRAFT STEVENSON! And there was a picture of an elephant with a blanket draped over him, and on the blanket was a shoe with a hole in it—the Stevenson emblem, you know. And we started parading. The only sound in the entire place was the television camera crews cracking up. All the cameras swung our way, and for just a second this thing was blasted across America. Of course, the cops threw us out. Can you imagine if we'd tried that in '68? We would have been *killed!* Everybody tried to figure out what it meant. "Are these guys Stassen men? Are they trying to sink Nixon?" They never considered the fact that it had no meaning at all.

Q: *What were some of the other activities of the Public Cretinization Program?*

CLOSE: Severn told me about one from before I came on the scene. About the time of the Rosenberg trial, he was walking in the Loop just at about the time the theaters let out—this was when there *were* legitimate theaters in the Loop, before it had turned into the jungle it is now. Anyway, Severn was walking around there carrying a briefcase, when suddenly two burly men jumped out of a limousine and grabbed him. As they grabbed him, Severn tossed this briefcase into the middle of the crowd, and it opened, and a bunch of calculus test papers from the University of Chicago flew out of it. He shouted out in a foreign accent, "Quick, get these to Dr. Oppenheimer!" Then the two men slammed him into the limousine and it drove away.

We would have contests, too. Mind contests. Like the one for the most outrageous Christmas present. Severn won that with a one-to-one scale model in plaster of paris of the Notre Dame Cathedral shipped to your home town. You could picture three or four of them sitting around Omaha.

And there was a suicide contest, which I won. My winning entry was I was going to hang myself from a weather balloon and fly over the city of Los Angeles, and as I strangled, my sphincter would relax and I would dribble all over L.A. The authorities would be very busy trying to figure out whose jurisdiction I fell under, and what they should do about it. I mean, if they shot me down and I landed in a playground, it might be a bringdown for the children. Severn came in second. He was going to rent offices on the highest floor of the Empire State Building and, piece by piece, bring up a Rolls-Royce Phantom II and assemble it. Then from the inside he would remove the bricks and drive out through the wall of the Empire State Building in a Rolls-Royce.

Q: *To get back to Second City. . . .*

CLOSE: I didn't stay too long that first time. I ran some workshops for them, and then they had a vacation, and I split to do something else.

Q: *Just when did you rejoin Second City?*

CLOSE: In 1961. I had gotten a taste of what doing a stand-up act was like and I didn't like it. I had a choice between continuing at it or coming to Second City at a considerably smaller salary. Actually, it wasn't to be in the Second City show, but next door in Playwrights at Second City, which was doing Jules Feiffer's show, *The Explainers.* John Brent and Hamilton Camp joined around that time, too. Also, I remember we did our own version of *The Beggar's Opera*, from a scenario by David Shepherd with music by Bill Mathieu, called *Big Deal.* Alan Arkin played Macheath and Avery Schreiber was in it, too. Dick Schaal joined the company around this time.

I took over directing *Big Deal* after it opened. Paul had directed it, but it needed more work, so he told me to go ahead. He took me out of my part and put someone else in and I tidied it up some. So my first job at Second City was as a director, then as an actor, then as a director. Then they decided to put me into the improvising company. I didn't do a tremendous number of improvised scenes. I mostly did interviews and stand-up stuff. Gimmicks where I could exercise my wit rather than my improvisational ability. which was really rather slight until I started working with The Committee later. But I did some clever stuff.

I developed a character called Brigadier General J. C. Clevis. I got the name from a friend of mine who said if he ever wrote a play with a general in it, that's what he would call him. The clevis is the least essential piece of military equipment there is. It's the little ring you hang up a mess kit with. I used General Clevis three times.

The first time was in an interview near the Berlin Wall. He's being interviewed about Communist brainwashing techniques, which he's warning against. But during the course of the interview, it becomes apparent that he has been brainwashed himself. He tells the interviewer that the way you teach the men to resist brainwashing is to teach them brainwashing techniques. "How do you teach them?" the interviewer asks. "You pound it into their heads, day after day." The interviewer: "After one of your recruits goes through your anti-brainwashing school, what'll you have?" "Pabst Blue Ribbon."

The next one was in 1961. Paul came in and said, "Hey, there's a war going on in Vietnam. We'd better do something." So we read the papers and started putting together what our military posture was in South Vietnam. We figured that out pretty fast. So we started off with an extremely reluctant brigade of Vietnamese soldiers going through these fucked-up maneuvers. Demonstrating not their incompetence but their extreme reluctance at being driven to war. We wanted to show America lending the wrong kind of assistance. And here was Brigadier General Clevis as an "advisor." He was teaching courses again. Preposterous stuff. It was a guerrilla war being fought, and he was teaching tank maintenance in a swamp. The interviewer asks, "What happens to tanks in a swamp?" "They sink." Clevis also pointed with pride to the fine audiovisual program which the Vietnamese were enthusiastic about. They particularly liked a film called *Industrial Canada*.

Brigadier General Clevis returned again in a scenario play called *My Friend Art Is Dead*. At the end of the first act, a peace maniac—played initially by Severn and later by Dennis Cunningham and Camp, I think—is looking for something to handcuff himself to in protest. First he thinks maybe a flagpole, but he finally ends up handcuffing himself to General Clevis. A bunch of people start pulling Clevis away from this maniac, and a bunch of peace freaks start pulling the maniac the other way, resulting in a great Marx Brothers moment when we were lifted off our feet connected only by handcuffs. Sometimes it was terribly painful. I would often bleed. When we were finally released from the handcuffs, we would be interviewed by the audience. Oh, General Clevis was always willing to be interviewed.

This third time around, he turned out to be a rather serious character. Although he devoutly believed in his extremely right-wing military stance, he turned out to be a completely vulnerable human being. Some scientists play a practical joke on him in a radiation laboratory, telling him that something he's handled—actually a child's toy— is a nuclear device he's done something wrong with. They convince him he's got a fatal dose of radiation. His first thought is to save the men. "Get them out of here! Get them away! Stand back! I must be hot! What's the count in here? Can you get my wife on the phone? How long have I got to live?"

So there was a progression in the three appearances. The first time he was merely the tool of a joke. The second one, he had a certain amount of irony. And the third one, without changing his political posture, he became a person with a certain amount of depth.

q: *When did you first have contact with Alan Myerson?*

CLOSE: He was the first director at Second City after Paul. Apparently he had contributed a little to a group Paul and I were very impressed with in New York called Stewed Prunes. On those credentials he was hired. He didn't start off very brilliantly, but, in fairness to Alan, we gave him a lot of trouble. His first idea was, "Let's do a *commedia* piece." We thought, "Oh God, *commedia!* If the guy's first thought in improvisation is to do a *commedia* piece . . . I mean, we all thought of that years ago, right? If this is the way the guy's going to start off. . . ." He forced some people to do stuff they really didn't want to do. Like he had me eating fire, which I did when I was a kid at carnivals. I really didn't want to do that because I burned myself every time I did it. Actually, I must say the first show he put together was quite good. That had the first General Clevis scene.

q: *The way he described the dynamics of the situation was that there was some tension between him and Bill Alton and you. He said you and Bill wanted to direct the*

*company and were upset that he had been chosen instead
of you.*

CLOSE: No, I didn't want to direct the company. I was
probably making noises like a director, because I was
redirecting his mistakes.

He did one fatally uncool thing. We were going to do an
industrial show for Max Factor that Alan was going to
direct. Then Alan said, "Let's really jack them off and put
those people down through our interpretation of the material." Well, I didn't agree with this. I think once you take
on an assignment, you do it to the best of your abilities.
So instantly I became extremely critical of his work. He
lost my sympathy with that.

Q: *Do you remember how he left?*

CLOSE: Paul was in town at the time. Alan was directing
a scene and he gave some direction to us and we sort of
looked at each other and I said, "It's all right. Wait till
the director gets here," meaning Paul next door. What a
hostile bastard I was in those days! There was a flare-up,
and at this point Paul walked in and I went over to him
and said, "Look, it's either me or him. I can't work with
this guy." Which was a ratty thing for me to do. Then
Alan and Paul talked a mumble-mumble. Then Paul started
directing and Alan was sent to New York.

Many years later, when I was directing The Committee
—Alan having hired me for the same job I had gotten him
moved from at The Second City—I went to him and said,
"These actors are giving me trouble. They're driving me
out of the theater." He said, "You once drove me out of a
city." I said, "Right," and went back to work. Of course,
if I hadn't had that fight, he wouldn't have gone to New
York, left New York, and then started The Committee.

Q: *I understand you were in London with Second City
during the Cuban missile crisis.*

CLOSE: Yes, that was interesting. When we first heard
about the missile blockade, we were all huddled around
the radio at eleven o'clock. This was in the back kitchen
of a restaurant next door because we didn't have a radio.
Five of us. It looked like an underground cell in World
War II huddled around the shortwave. The President of
the United States was talking about the missiles and we
looked at each other and said, "Holy shit, this is it! This

is World War III and here we are in a foreign country." We had to almost physically restrain Dick Schaal from getting on a plane and flying back instantly. We all had the impulse to return, to be under the Bomb with our friends.

It's very hard in a foreign country in that kind of situation to know what posture to adopt. We had to figure out a posture to take, not only for our show—which was secondary—but for ourselves, for our own sanity. "How are we going to behave now? We don't have a director with us. We're five foreigners in London. Five political satirists. And suddenly the political situation has blown sky-high."

We always used to consult the *I Ching* in situations of extreme crisis. This was obviously a terribly important moment. There was insufficient data for us to figure out how to think or what to do. Was Kennedy being a maniac? So we cast the coins and got *chien,* number one, the creative, which transformed into another trigram, the taming power of the great, which seemed to have specific lines in reference to the East and the paper tiger and the superior man conquers through this and that. So we decided, all right, we realize this is being arbitrary, but this will be our posture, that Kennedy is not insane. That in all likelihood there *are* missile sites in Cuba. We had to go on what we knew, which meant that we decided to have faith in Kennedy rather arbitrarily. At the same time, Alan Myerson and his company were back here picketing things in Chicago. We were behind Kennedy in England and he was attacking Kennedy here.

There was one night that was a little tense. I went out and defused the audience by talking about Cuba, saying things like, "I'd like to remind you that we're all members of NATO, so if we go, we're all going together." When Avery and I did the IBM machine that night, a large gentlemen stood up very grandly and said, "Would you tell me, sirs, the difference between Cuba and Suez?" I snapped my fingers, which meant an immediate answer from the machine, and said, "The difference, gentlemen, is that we're strong enough to bring it off." This got us a standing ovation—for sheer balls, I suppose.

During this time, you'll remember that the Communists were saying the photos were faked and things like that. But every day, more information came out. I went to Hyde

Park where this Communist speaker would get up on a box and spiel that day's party line. Because of what was coming out, the party line changed every day. So I got a box and stood next to him and announced, "Yesterday's party line repeated here," and while he did his spiel, I did the spiel he'd done the day before, which bugged the hell out of him.

Q: *Let's talk about Paul.*

CLOSE: I would have to regard him as the master—not in any mystical-guru bullshit sense, but as a master craftsman. I was his apprentice, in effect. When I first started to direct, I would imitate some of Paul's most glaring flaws, such as yelling at the actors, terrifying everybody. What was missing in my imitation was his incisive ability to set things right.

Q: *I understand that he's soft-pedaled the yelling in recent years.*

CLOSE: Oh, I don't know. He still does a pretty good amount of it. He doesn't yell at *me* too much because he knows I go into a catatonic fit.

I remember at one point—Paul may say this didn't happen, but I'm pretty sure it did—I remember he had Schaal on the floor and was banging his head against the floor and punctuating the sentence with thumps. "If (thump) you ever (thump) get a job (thump) anywhere else (thump) don't you ever (thump) dare (thump) tell anyone (thump) that you (thump) worked (thump) with *me* (thump)!" Schaal got up and walked away, shaking his head, came over to me, and said, "Gee, I sure hate to get yelled at." That was the feeling we all had. "Oh God, we're going to get yelled at."

A couple of times I yelled him down. Once he was coming backstage during the middle of a show to grab actors as the performance was going on. He was coming up the stairs and I stood at the top like the Colossus of Rhodes and told him, "Don't you *ever* come backstage and give notes during a performance!" He said, "Right," and turned around and left.

The other time was when we were doing the scene that eventually became "Family Reunion." We were rehearsing it, not under Sheldon's direction, but sort of under his supervision. At the time Sheldon referred to himself as a monitor and hall guard. He would take down what we said.

Oh, I've got to tell you, we'd done all these Jewish scenes.

Q: *What do you mean?*

CLOSE: Well, you know, everybody was Jewish and the scenes kind of reflected that. In rehearsal, Paul used to say, "All right, Jews, get onstage. Close, you might as well get up there, too." I think I was the first *goy* in the company. Maybe Schaal.

Anyway, what I'm getting to is that "Family Reunion" was different. It was a W.A.S.P. scene. We were dealing with what being a W.A.S.P. was all about. We were doing a scene in which everybody was demonstrating repression like mad. It was such an emotionally charged scene that sometimes we would have to wait five minutes between lines for people to cool off. I was essentially playing my father in the scene, which was rather emotionally wearing because my father was a suicide, and he would come alive inside of me and it was rather frightening. Paul came into a rehearsal while we were putting it together. He was sort of sitting off to the side watching us playing all this repression, and he called out in the middle of it, "People don't behave like that!" I spun on my heel and said, "Per-fucking-haps and per-fucking-haps not!" And Paul spun on *his* heel and went to New York for four months.

Q: *What about your relationship with Viola?*

CLOSE: I had a few disagreements with Viola. As a person, I think she's marvelous, but I didn't enjoy working with her. I never managed to find my way through "the space." I'm much more interested in immediate results. It's not that I had anything against Viola. I just felt that the use of her work was slightly misplaced in a professional theater company. There's a great deal we can take from her work, of course. On the other hand, we do have slightly different problems which are not solved by walking through space. My major disagreement with Viola may have been based on a misconception. I had the feeling that she wanted to take theater and reduce it to the level of a game. At the same time, I had independently of Viola cooked up various theories of my own. Since then, I've had to . . . well, not exactly eat my words, but on the other hand, I am using more of Viola's work now than I have in the past.

Q: *Why did you leave Second City in 1965?*

CLOSE: Actually, I was fired. I was too high too often and it was affecting my work. Some people told me that some Loyola students were thinking of demonstrating in protest in front of the theater, so I went and found the people who were talking about it and told them not to. The management was absolutely correct in firing me.

Q: *It's interesting that they were so aware of you and obviously related strongly enough to what you were doing at Second City that they would consider such a protest.*

CLOSE: Well, I'd been there quite a while, after all, and visible publicly. I must say I didn't have the feeling that Bernie fired me. I had had no relationship with Bernie previously. He was a gray eminence back in those days. Nobody really saw much of him. So I didn't really feel that my being fired was his doing. Now he's around all the time. Of necessity, he's had to direct several shows, and it turns out he's quite good at it.

After I left Second City, I spent an awful lot of time analyzing what had gone before. I've got quite a good memory and went through the scenes beat by beat and started figuring out the rules of the various processes we were involved in, or tried to. And then I went to The Committee and got the chance to apply some of these things there.

Q: *I find it kind of remarkable that after the trouble you gave him, Alan hired you. You'd figure that he would have been less than favorably disposed. How did it happen that you made peace?*

CLOSE: Well, I was in California and in pretty bad shape, really at the end of my rope. And my old lady at the time said, "Why don't you call Alan?" I said, "I can't call Alan." Then I thought, "Why can't I call him? OK, I'll call him. All he can say is no." I just took a mighty gulp, thinking, "If he's willing to give it to me, I'm willing to swallow any bullshit I might have to put up with to pay off the karmic debt." I asked for a job as an actor. He said he'd give it to me if I'd direct, too. So I ended up directing and acting simultaneously.

The thing that finally got us together again as civilized

people was the fact that the first show I directed for him was wildly successful. Obviously I was not out to screw him if I had done an extremely good show, right? So I had the feeling that from that moment on, all was forgiven. Of course, I worked with a terrific company. Peter Bonerz, Garry Goodrow, Leigh French, Chris Ross, Howard Hesseman, Morgan Upton, and Nancy Fish.

Q: *From the perspective of having worked with both Second City and The Committee, what comparisons would you make?*

CLOSE: The Second City is not nearly as politicized as The Committee. I have always felt that we can say some of the things we say here because nobody's figured out our political stance. It's quite possible we don't have one. Sometimes we'll turn around and attack the liberals, which is our audience for the most part. This couldn't happen at The Committee. It would never have occurred to us there to do an antiradical scene. But here, we reserve the right to lash out in any direction. That's why when Alan was directing here and wanted to get the Second City actors as a group to go out and demonstrate, I would not be one of the group. I felt it would not be wise to commit the theater to a particular political policy. I don't think it would have been proper for Second City. I do think it was absolutely proper for The Committee.

The Committee was mostly concerned with national politics because so much of its audience was tourist. What the fuck would they know about local San Francisco politics? But here at Second City, we're more concerned about politics on a local level. Second City is a Chicago neighborhood theater. Lenny Bruce once said, "Chicago is so corrupt it's thrilling." We deal with that.

Q: *Yet, at the same time, The Committee seemed to have closer ties with the life of the community than does Second City, in terms of actual contact. The Committee got involved in protests and opened its facilities to the Red Guard and the Diggers and assorted other groups. I can't imagine Second City doing that on a day-to-day basis, though I understand there was heavy involvement here during the Chicago riots.*

CLOSE: We are a different part of the community in Chicago from what The Committee was in San Francisco.

Del Close

I think if the proper circumstances arose, Second City would respond to the community as The Committee did, but it has not been required of us to do so. Actually, we are involved with the community, but we're more involved with the artistic community than the social community. You can see the distinction in the way I run workshops here and the way I ran them there. There, the idea was that we had a responsibility to feed back creatively into the community by offering improvisational workshops at little or no cost, mostly for social good. Here, the workshops are more self-serving. We use them to develop and scout new talent to put into the touring and regular companies. So you see there is a different focus. But I think it's partially a matter of environment. I think if Second City had been in San Francisco at the time, it would have behaved similarly to The Committee.

When Judith and Julian Beck got busted in New York with The Living Theater for income tax evasion back in '64 or '65 or whenever, there was only one theater in the entire country that did anything about it—Second City. In three days we threw together a benefit that raised $1,200 that got them out of the country. It also got our ass in a sling with Equity. "You can't do that. It's not an approved benefit!" We had Studs Terkel emceeing, we had Irwin Corey and the lead singer from Mr. Kelly's. All these artists were concerned about the fate of another theater! We had a jam-packed house. Equity said, "You can't do an unapproved benefit." We said, "OK, in that case we'll withdraw from Equity." They went mumble-mumble and said, "OK, go ahead, but don't do it again."

Q: *How did you get back with Second City again?*

CLOSE: I'd been directing The Committee for four and a half years and had developed a case of tunnel vision. Partially burned out. I needed a break—a different kind of work. I'd hear Paul was on a new trip, something called "story theater," so I called him up, asked him if he could use another actor. Paul said, "Who'd you have in mind?" I said, "Me." He hired me for his company at the Body Politic.

I pretty much stayed away from The Second City, remembering the circumstances of my leaving, until a delegation of actors from there came up to me to ask me to run

155

some workshops for them. (Bernie was on one of his extended vacations.) I said, "Sure, for $50 a shot." I was sure they would turn me down. They didn't. The actors themselves hired me. When Bernie came back and saw what was happening he gave me his official blessing, validated the actors' move after the fact, and suggested I continue.

A new show was coming up and he asked me to direct one scene—a satire on *Hamlet*, of all things. Well, I did and it worked. Spectacularly. This prompted Joyce Sloane, the associate producer, to offer me the Second City directorship several months later, after I got stranded in Hollywood when Paul dumped his *Story Theatre* actors after an engagement at the Mark Taper Forum. I accepted gladly and here Ah is. I've been here since 1972.

My job here now is covering home plate. If Chicago falls, the whole thing falls. To some degree it's a Red Queen's race—you run so hard to stay in the same place. We have a constant turnover of actors. It's amazing to me the level of quality we've been able to maintain.

You know, at the beginning, in Compass and the first days of Second City, we had a definite sense of being part of the process of history in the making—hanging ten out there in the front of something forging away into the unknown. Now, to some degree, the thrill of discovery is gone.

Q: *Do you have any overall summation of what it's meant to you? Pardon the* This Is Your Life *tone of the question, but you've been in improvisational theater for the better part of twenty years.*

CLOSE: Let's say it started off as a gig and turned into a career.

11.

Theodore J. Flicker

Theodore J. Flicker directed and appeared with the first St. Louis Compass in 1957. Subsequently, he appeared with and produced and directed The Premise, an improvisational troupe which flourished in New York and played successful engagements in Washington, D.C., Los Angeles, Miami; Westport, Connecticut; and London. His nonimprovisational stage work included early stints with the Barter Theatre and directing and sometimes acting in a number of avant-garde plays in St. Louis, one of them the musical *The Nervous Set,* which he brought to Broadway. In his post-Premise days, he has distinguished himself as a writer-producer-director. His films include *The Troublemaker* (a fictionalized comic account of his legal hassles operating The Premise), *Three in the Cellar,* and the prophetic satiric gem, *The President's Analyst.* His television credits include directing episodes of various series, directing *Playmates* (featuring Alan Alda, Severn Darden, and Roger Bowen), one of the few truly funny made-for-TV movies, and creating (with Danny Arnold) the popular *Barney Miller* TV series.

q: *How did you get involved with improvisational theater?*

FLICKER: Through Severn. He and I were old friends.

We went to college together—Bard. Then, when I was studying at the Royal Academy, he came over and roomed with me in London. God knows for what reason, but it was fun. Then I came back to the States.

I realized with horror that the Broadway theater I had been trained for had ceased to exist, only nobody had bothered to tell me. It wasn't that temple you were supposed to serve. It was in the hands of the charlatans.

So I decided to try to build a popular theater. I was going to call it The Rolling Theater. The idea was to have a really elegant, comfortable theater that would fold up into six trucks almost automatically and move from town to town. Unfortunately, it was too expensive to pull off. It would have cost a million and a half to build the theater— this was in '53 or '54, God knows how much it would cost now—and even then the engineers couldn't guarantee that the wind wouldn't knock it down. So that was the end of that.

Then I decided I was going to create a regional theater in New York. I found an old theater on Third Avenue at Thirtieth Street—the oldest standing legitimate theater in New York City; it had been turned into a movie house— but I was going to raise the money to turn it back into a legitimate theater. I worked very hard at it and had most of the money raised, but it required real concessions from all of the unions, which they refused to grant, so that didn't happen.

At about that time, Severn had come into contact with David Shepherd and Paul Sills and that whole group. He introduced Shepherd and me, and we liked each other very much. Our aims were the same. Popular theater. Though I always felt that he was a touch too visionary, and he always felt that I was a touch too crass. He really did believe you could do improvisational theater on table-tops in a lunchroom of a Gary, Indiana, steel mill and that the workers would adore it, when, in fact, what the workers really wanted to do was have lunch and "Stick your theater up your ass, who the hell are you?"

But it seemed to me that with improvisational theater, David had come up with the best possible idea. That maybe this was the answer to everything. So I scrounged around New York and I got a guy who promised to give me thirty grand to open an improvisational theater in New York. I got hold of David and told him about it and he was very excited.

By that time, The Compass had been opened and had moved from the South Side, where it had had some success, to the Off-Beat Room in the Argo Hotel on the North Side near Loyola University. They were in deep financial trouble then. Walter Beakel, who's still a good friend of mine, was directing the company. He was married to Collin Wilcox then. Well, I came out to see what it was like, and I spent five or six weeks there. It closed pretty soon. It was a financial disaster. I also thought it was a lousy show. David and I had many a disagreement about that. I thought it was very undisciplined, too intellectual, too precious. Also, the actors wore onstage whatever they wore on the street, which David adored, and they all smoked during the performance, which offended my classical training. I didn't think it was much of a show, but it was fascinating. It's just that I felt it was wrong.

So a schism was developing between David and me. I think David's feeling at the time was that I was a financier and that I had no business interfering in the art of it. But we had this partnership to open a Compass in New York.

Anyway, I got an offer from some lunatics who had a bar called the Crystal Palace to open a Compass there. We thought, "How terrific. We'll open one in New York and one in St. Louis at the same time. Then we'll rotate companies so the show will always be fresh and the two will feed off each other. It will be a glorious new age of theater!" We offered Walter St. Louis, and he turned it down, so we said, "The hell with New York, we'll open in St. Louis first." My idea was that we would try it out in St. Louis, then take that company to New York and put in a new company in St. Louis, and then do the trading thing like we'd planned before. I told my New York backer this, and he said wonderful.

So I went to St. Louis and opened The Compass Players at the old Crystal Palace. I had Del Close, Nancy Ponder, Jo Henderson, and myself. I insisted we wear costumes. Del and I wore dark pants and white shirts with cuffs rolled up, collars opened with no ties, and the girls wore black tights (both had great figures) and belted shirts like dance rehearsal outfits. We played on a tiny stage, thrust into the middle of this nightclub with crystal chandeliers. Marvelous!

The thing that makes improvisational theater so fascinating, and something which happened then but I was unaware of at the time, is that each company takes on its own character and the character of its audience. For me, the only reason for doing theater, as opposed to making films, is that in the theater you have live people. If you can't use that aspect—really *use* it—what the fuck is the point? Why do a play for a year and a half, saying the same words, playing the same emotions? (Oh well, I guess that can be fun, too, and if someone offered me that right now, I might get a kick out of doing it.) But the *real* kick was in talking to an audience, taking what they said to you —how they reacted to you—and returning it to them through the prism of your vision of the world. Anyway, we were very successful at the St. Louis Compass from the start.

David was disgusted with my show. It was the first improvisational theater that had been a financial success, but he was horrified with the decadence of the Crystal Palace and horrified that I kept insisting that it be a *show* and that I put a time limit on improvisations, and that we'd do some things just for laughs. He thought I had ruined his child. His worst suspicions of me were confirmed. So, when the money in New York disappeared, he dissolved our partnership.

Q: *I understand Mike and Elaine and Severn joined you later in your run there.*

FLICKER: Elaine and I, I think, did something extraordinary during that time. All of us lived in the same boardinghouse, and every morning she and I would sit down and say, "What is it we're doing? How do you improvise? How do you not fail the way we have all failed in the past?"—the risk of failure being a major part of public improvisation.

First, we divided improvisation into two categories: private and public improvisation. Private improvisation is classroom improvisation, which is what actors use to tune their personal instruments. With private improvisation, no one gives a rat's ass if you bore each other to death because

Theodore J. Flicker

the purpose is not to entertain the class but to sensitize yourself to your inner creative force. The problem was that
too much of what had been happening on our stage was
that kind of private improvisation that bored the piss out
of an audience. So we decided that public improvisation
first of all had to entertain. At that time we were very
Brechtian, so it also had to edify, and perhaps at times even
frighten, all of which came under the heading of entertainment for us.

Out of these conversations, Elaine and I worked out a
series of techniques, a set of rules for teaching public improvisation.* We would take these into rehearsal during
the day and, in the evening, try them on the stage. We
experimented with them, and they proved out one hundred
percent of the time. One of the reasons I don't go to see
improvisational theaters anymore is they violate all the
rules and they bore the shit out of me. They make all the
same mistakes we made when we were kids in Chicago
and St. Louis, mistakes that don't have to be made anymore.

We came up with all of these rules in a two-week period
of white-hot creativity. It was an incredible period. Last
time Elaine and I talked—it's probably been ten years since
we had a real conversation—we still were stunned by what
we had done together.

Q: *What were some of the rules you came up with?*

FLICKER: That's an eight-week course. But they had to
do with three things: place, character, and circumstance.
All I know is that in explaining these three things to you
and giving you the exercises to do, if you are a talented
actor, you are going to come out of it a good improvisational actor. If I were putting together a company today, I
would spend a good ten or twelve weeks working with the
people on this technique before opening, and keep working
every day as well as performing every night for the next
three months. The freer the form, the greater must be the
underpinnings of discipline.

So, after Elaine and I invented these things, we changed
the show and it got much better. Then I went off to New
York to raise the money to bring us all to New York. That

* See Del Close's chapter.

161

was one of the worst periods of my life. To put it briefly, I didn't raise the money.

In the meantime, while I was gone, a tremendous war had developed among the players in St. Louis. When I came back, it was nightmare time. The company had dissolved into clashes of ego and ambition—everything that ever destroyed any theater company that had any success. This taught me a profound lesson.

Q: *Which is?*

FLICKER: First you have to understand that it is far more dangerous for an actor to improvise than it is for him to play Arthur Miller or any other script. Yes, in any kind of theater you risk failure, but there is nothing like going out there and not knowing what you're going to do next, relying on your own inventiveness and bombing. Unless you've actually tasted what improvising in front of an audience feels like, you can't *imagine* the horror of it. You have a company of talented people facing this strain night after night, and that's likely to break out into some kind of warfare unless . . . and this is what I learned: In order to cast a company that's going to live together in that crucible, you have to devise some means to protect them from themselves.

So, I decided that my next improvisational theater was going to be an exercise in group dynamics, which is a phrase we didn't know at the time. What I developed, without knowing it, was an encounter technique for rehearsal. When I cast The Premise, it was not only a matter of the actors being talented, but it was also my hunch as to whether or not their personalities would mesh. I tried to pick people who would never be competitive at the same level. People each having something that the others didn't, but who would be so balanced that they would be able to get along with each other and not be jealous.

So, putting into practice both my ideas on group dynamics and the techniques Elaine and I had come up with, I started The Premise.

Q: *And it worked.*

FLICKER: Yes, it worked.

Viola Spolin (*Courtesy of Viola Spolin*).

David Shepherd taking suggestions at The Compass, 1955 (*Photo by Stephen Lewellyn*).

Paul Sills at the University of Chicago, 1953 (*Courtesy of the University of Chicago*).

Mike Nichols and Elaine May at The Compass, 1955 (*Courtesy of Nancy Nugent*).

Mark and Bobbi Gordon at The Compass, 1955 (*Courtesy of David Shepherd*).

Mark Gordon, Shelley Berman, and Andrew Duncan at The Compass, 1956 (*Courtesy of David Shepherd*).

Alan Arkin, Jerry Stiller, Nancy Ponder, and Anne Meara at St. Louis Compass, 1959 (*Courtesy of David Shepherd*).

Barbara Harris and Paul Sand at The Second City, 1960
(*Courtesy of Playboy Magazine*).

Front, Mina Kolb and Andrew Duncan; middle, Eugene Troobnick, Howard Alk, and Severn Darden; rear, Paul Sand and Barbara Harris, at The Second City, 1960 (*Courtesy of Playboy Magazine*).

Alan Arkin, Paul Sills, and Anthony Holland at The Second City, 1961 (*Photo by Morton Shapiro*).

Theodore J. Flicker, Joan Darling, Tom Aldredge, and George Segal at The Premise, 1961 (*Courtesy of Theodore J. Flicker*).

Back, Ron Weyand, Diana Sands, Alan Alda, and Reni
Santoni; front, Honey Shepherd, at The Hyannisport Compass,
1962 (*Courtesy of David Shepherd*).

Avery Schreiber, Joan Rivers, Bill Alton, and Del Close at
The Second City, 1962 (*Courtesy of Avery Schreiber*).

David Steinberg at The Second City, 1965 (*Photo by Morton Shapiro*).

Joan Bassie, Robert Klein, Fred Willard, and Sandra Caron in "The Amateur Hour" sketch at The Second City, 1968 (*Photo by Fred Schnell; courtesy of Robert Klein*).

Standing, Martin Harvey Friedberg, Ira Miller, J. J. Barry, and Burt Heyman; on floor, Peter Boyle (*Courtesy of The Second City*).

Musical director Fred Kaz, Bernard Sahlins, and Del Close, 1972 (*Courtesy of The Second City*).

Richard Schaal and Valerie Harper in an edition of **Paul Sills's** "Story Theatre," 1971 (*Courtesy of Lincoln Center Library of the Performing Arts, New York*).

(left) Roger Bowen as Henry Kissinger
(center) Bill Alton and Mina Kolb.
(right) Severn Darden.

The Second City reunion at the University of Chicago in October 1976. (*All reunion photos by Bobbi Gordon.*)

From left, Eugene Troobnick, John Brent, Bill Alton, Paul Sand, Mina Kolb, and Tony Holland.

(*left*)   Anthony Holland.
(*right*)   Paul Sand (as a dog) and Eugene Troobnick.

Severn Darden, Barbara Harris, Roger Bowen, and Del Close.

Gilda Radner and Rosemary Radcliffe at The Toronto Second
City (*Courtesy of The Second City*).

12.

Anne Meara and Jerry Stiller

Anne Meara and Jerry Stiller, with Alan Arkin and Nancy Ponder, were members of the second Compass to play St. Louis. From that experience, they discovered they could improvise comedy together, and, after The Compass disbanded and a year in a revue at Chicago's Happy Medium, they formed the act which made them famous, leading to nightclub appearances, record albums, and innumerable guest shots on television.

In addition, both have kept their hands in as actors. Stiller had a prominent role in the film *The Taking of Pelham 1-2-3,* and was starring on Broadway in Terrence McNally's *The Ritz* when I taped our conversation. Shortly thereafter he starred in the TV series *Joe and Sons,* and in the film version of *The Ritz.*

Anne Meara created the role of Bunny Flingus in John Guare's *The House of Blue Leaves.* She starred in the television series *Kate McShane,* and has been a regular on *Rhoda.* She also starred in the films *Lovers and Other Strangers* and (with her husband) *Nasty Habits.*

MEARA: Jerry had worked with Nancy Ponder for a while, trying to do a comedy act. Nancy had already been with The Compass in St. Louis with Ted Flicker. So, evidently when David Shepherd wanted to put together a new Compass, he contacted Nancy and Nancy got Jerry involved. And he had Alan Arkin, so there were the three of them. Then they needed another woman. At the time I was doing a Brecht play in Boston with a repertory company, which we were hoping to take to New York. Jerry kept saying he wanted me to audition with him for this group and I kept saying no, hoping the Brecht thing would go Off-Broadway. It never did, so that spring I said, "All right, I'll go and audition." So that was how I got together with David and Nancy and Alan and Jerry. This was in 1959.

It didn't take me too long to understand what we were doing. Having studied acting for quite a while, I was familiar with improvisation. Classroom improvisation. Improvisation for acting purposes.

Q: *Did you find much of a difference between classroom improvisation and working with Compass?*

MEARA: At Compass we learned to go for the comedic moment, which was something we were never ever supposed to do in acting class, where we were never supposed to go *for* the result. But since we were performing before people in a nightclub, it would have been fake of us not to go for the moment. There was an entertainment value that had to be respected.

Before Compass, I always had the safety of being in plays where the proscenium arch was respected. You know, the fourth wall. Actually, with Compass, we kept the fourth wall when we were doing the scenes. But between the sketches, the fourth wall would come down, and, for the first time, I had to deal directly with the audience. I would *tummel* with them. *Tummeling.* It's an old-fashioned word comics use. What it actually was was dealing with the audience specifically as you would another actor. I'm using acting terms explaining it, but when I was doing it, I was *performing*. Performing and acting being slightly different. Dealing with people in a nightclub is different from doing it in a theater. In a theater, you don't have to win them over because they made their commitment when they bought their tickets. In a nightclub, your first objective is to get their attention. Your second is to keep it. And there's an obligatory response demanded throughout, namely, laughter. Unless you're singing "The Lord's Prayer." So I'd say I learned performing at Compass.

Also, I found it cultivated onstage a humorous sense I'd always had offstage. I started to think in terms of . . . (*laughs*) punchlines. As an actress, that's terrible, but, like I say, when you're performing in nightclubs it's quite necessary. I found myself onstage thinking up funny lines. Not that I'd start an improvisation with the idea of going for a joke. But I would find funny things out of the situations we were playing.

I found the spot improvisations the most fun, even though they were the riskiest. They never really failed. Even if they didn't always work, they didn't fail.

Q: *Because the audience, understanding the risks you were taking, was on your side.*

MEARA: They knew we didn't have any time to talk anything over. What we did were truly spot improvisations. We would get a suggestion and instantly, without any talk between us, do a scene. Also, the audience was always curious about how you were going to work their suggestions in.

Another thing is that you had some security because you developed a repertory of characters. Each of us had our own characters. It seemed Nancy and I each had three or four ladies we could pull out of a hat.

Q: *I'm interested in how The Compass and Second City reflected the changing roles of women. What do you remember about the kinds of women you played then?*

MEARA: I do remember I was the interpreter in the UN sketch. And there was another scene in which Alan and I played psychiatrists. Oh, I played mothers, I played sweethearts. and I played . . . nervous ladies. I used to do a takeoff of Geraldine Page sometimes.

It being 1959 and women not having as much access to certain professions. whenever we got a suggestion from the audience—sav. "A dentist in the Alps"—it would instantly be funny if either Nancy or I started by playing the dentist.

Q: *It must have been interesting to face such different audiences in St. Louis, Columbus, and New York.*

MEARA: I wasn't with them in Columbus. That was just Jerry and Alan and Nancy. It was the first booking. St. Louis was where I joined them, and then we played the

Quadrille in New York. I was with them four months—
June, July, August, September.

Q: *Was there much difference between working at the
Crystal Palace and the Quadrille?*

MEARA: The Quadrille was a commercial nightclub. We
would use a word like "hypothesis" and it would go over
like cancer. The Crystal Palace was more of a theatrical
situation. You'd get the kind of laughter which let you
know that that audience was on the same wavelength with
you mentally. It was as if they were saying, "I got it. I'm on
that cerebral level. I got the joke. Sure, I know 'hypothesis.'
I know Jung, I know Freud, I know all that stuff." It was
that kind of laughter—knowing. Where the Crystal Palace
was—Gaslight Square—was a hip place to go in St. Louis.
It was where the in-group would go. In fact, the first
time I ever heard an apartment called a "pad" was in St.
Louis that summer.

I don't think we went over too well at the Quadrille.
They didn't know what we were doing. I think we were a
little ahead of our time. I think we took fewer suggestions
there, because. of course, the more frightened you get. the
more you pull back and tend to do your set pieces. There
isn't much room for experimentation in nightclubs.

It was disheartening when we played the Quadrille. We
disbanded after that. Because actually we had no more
bookings. David was not really a businessman. He was
more of a person who thought up things. He was not someone who could propel it. Have you talked to David about
all this?

Q: *Yes.*

MEARA: What did he say?

Q: *He said that in a way he thought he'd betrayed his
own values by trying to make Compass a commercial enterprise. What he wanted to do with Compass was to create a
kind of folk theater.*

MEARA: Gee. *I* never was after that! (*Laughs.*) I'm glad
I didn't know that.

Q: *What he originally wanted to do was play in factories
and slaughterhouses.*

MEARA: I'm glad he didn't pursue that idea with us. I had
no eyes to go to factories or slaughterhouses or do a *St.
Joan of the Stockyards.* I really didn't.

166

Anne Meara and Jerry Stiller

I was born during the Depression. I did all of my reading when I got out of high school because I didn't want to go to college, I wanted to *act*. But as I look back on that period of history and what I read, it seemed like an awful lot of educated people seemed to think that they knew what was best for other groups, and that seems to me a little patronizing.

You know, I think it's much harder to do the same play every night than to do improvisations. I think it is comparatively much easier to be different every night than to do the same thing and make that appear as if for the first time. That's really an art. Once your mind and imagination are oiled. I think improvising is more stimulating and easier. Can you imagine how much more difficult it is to do eight performances a week of *Long Day's Journey into Night?*

STILLER: Anne and I were married and had a dog and two cats. The best I could do at the time was get a job at the New York Shakespeare Festival with Joe Papp, playing a great variety of Elizabethan clowns in Central Park. I did very well with these roles. The rapport with the audiences made the $55 a week I received for my nightly endeavors seem like a gift. I remember hearing them yell at Romeo in perfect Spanish, "Give it to that Juliet!" The TWA flights overhead just as my scenes started were welcome interruptions, giving me chances to ad-lib in iambic pentameter. But actors do not live by Shakespeare alone.

So one day Larry Arrick approached me and said he was looking for someone to replace Shelley Berman in a backers' audition for The Compass in a New York hotel, in a sketch called *The Liars*. Larry told me, "This is the part of a German refugee and you're kind of being hazed by these people." I said, "Where are the lines?" "There are no lines. You make them up as you go along." I said, "You've got to be kidding." He said, "No. I feel you're the kind of actor who can do this sort of thing." He started to describe how it was done, and I said, "That's *commedia dell'arte*."

So I went out and did this thing, not knowing what was going to happen. What I remember is that people laughed. They did handstands out front. They laughed from their diaphragms. I was never so happy as an actor in my entire

167

life. I could feel a connection with the audience I had never felt before. My mind had been freed! The audience was with me. I didn't know what I was doing, but it was working. And this fellow I was working with, Mike Nichols, was unbelievable because no matter what you said, he had a line to come back with. It was a miracle. A miracle of the craft of acting.

When it was over, I was shocked to find out that the backers didn't like it. They didn't put a dime into it.

About a year later, in 1959, Larry Arrick recommended me to David Shepherd for a company he was going to put together. He already had Alan Arkin and Nancy Ponder.

I remember one night David took us to perform as a kind of tryout in a club on the East Side. Lenny Bruce, Milt Kamen, and Mike and Elaine had played there, so we thought it would have the kind of clientele that would be friendly to us. We asked the audience for a suggestion for a scene, and someone said he wanted to see me play a politician. So I came out and began, "My name is Carmine DeSapio. . . ." And at that, a man in the first row got up. A giant. He says, "You son of a bitch!" He was with two women with beehive hairdos. They grabbed him and said, "Sit down, Joe! Sit down!"

Well, he did and we started to go on with the scene. I think I was doing it with Alan. So he turned to speak to me and said, "Carmine. . . ." The guy leaps to his feet again. "Don't ever say that!" He was livid. Well, somehow we finished this little scene and went offstage, and this guy ran backstage after us and—I'll never forget this—he picked me up and held me up against the wall at full arm's length. "I told you not to say that!" "What did I say?" I said. He said, "You said, 'Carmine DeSapio!' " "What's wrong with Carmine DeSapio?" I said. He says, "I didn't say there was anything wrong with him, but you can't say that name. Don't ever use his name again, you son of a bitch!"

Meantime, the women he was with were saying to him, "What are you doing? Let him down!" He says to them, "You heard what he said, didn't you?" I was scared. I didn't know what he was going to do to me. I thought maybe if I reasoned with him I might be able to get through to him. I said, "Don't you understand? We're actors. We're making fun. . . ." He says, "We know that! We *don't like that!* We don't want that! Don't you understand? We don't *want* that!" Finally, the women stopped him. They cooled him off. They said to me, "We think you're very funny, fella. Very good, what you did. But don't ever say that again." I said, "I promise. I really won't ever do it again." And now the guy says, "Hey, can I get you a sandwich?" I said, "No, thanks, I'm not hungry." He says, "How about a drink?" And I'm thinking, "Is this what happens when you're an actor in improvisational theater?"

The first place we were booked was a place in Cleveland called the Alpine Village. It had a unique stage—a rising stage, like the old Paramount Theater. The man who ran this place was being indicted for income tax evasion and he was just able to pay the help. We worked on the bill with a lady named Beverly who was a baton twirler. I remember her telling us she used to work the Globetrotter games. Between the halves. Her big number was "The Ritual Fire Dance," which was a smasher. So we followed Beverly and her flaming batons. She destroyed the audience, and during the applause, the owner, who also emceed, asked us how he should introduce us. I said that it was our first engagement, and he went out and introduced us, "Ladies and gentlemen, those international favorites—The Compass Players!" We went out and did our act. At the end, as the stage sank into the floor, people threw rolls at us! And knives and forks!

Q: *What happened when you asked for suggestions from the audience?*

STILLER: They gave us suggestions. Like "Go home!" We told them, "We want real suggestions." And they said, "That *was* real!" After the show, the owner came up to us. We expected to be fired. He said, "You've got to remember the first show is always like this."

Q: *So you stayed?*

STILLER: One or two weeks, I forget. It was the first taste of misery in show business. How do you play to those people? We survived it.

Q: *How did Anne join?*

STILLER: I told David that if he wanted to hire me, he had to hire her, too. "I can't leave her in New York." "What does she do?" he asked. "She's an actress." I told him. "Does she know how to do this kind of acting?" "She'll learn." "Well," he said, "I can only pay her $75 a week." The rest of us were making $125 a week. I told this to her and she was grossly insulted. "You get $125 and I get $75? Whoever heard of such a thing?" She was hired just before we went to Cleveland, though she didn't come along for that engagement.

Q: *So the first time she played with Compass was in St. Louis?*

STILLER: Yes. We went there in David Shepherd's car, which was a Volkswagen. There were the two cats, the dog, Anne, and myself. We took shifts driving. I don't know how we ever managed to take this menagerie out there. I do remember piling luggage on top of the Volks and the wind almost blowing the car over on Route 80. And also that our dog threw up in Columbus.

Q: *You seem to have great luck in Ohio. How did you go over in St. Louis?*

STILLER: We were somewhat shocked. I wouldn't say we were instantaneously successful, but we were instantaneously accepted by the St. Louis audience. We could do no wrong in St. Louis. If we said hello, they'd cheer. They wouldn't throw money, but there was never any hostility. They waited patiently for whatever you came up with.

Q: *What do you remember of the material you did?*

STILLER: I remember one set scene we had was called "War." It was set at the UN, and one person was a Russian and one was an interpreter for a Russian . . . I remember Alan doing Russian very well. So it was about us having an argument with the Russians, and at the end we announced we'd found a way to settle our differences: We were going to have war.

Another was a father coming to find his hippie son in the Bronx. He's with a guitar and a girl. Alan was the hippie, or I guess then he was a beatnik. I played the father.

Mostly David Shepherd put pieces together with a mind to utilizing our own particular personalities. Alan played the guitar and had a great John Wayne imitation, so we were always trying to find a place to put that in. I was a great Jewish father and a great camel driver.

We did instant improvisations—spot improvisations. The

170

audience would throw a thing up at us and immediately we would start to do it. We didn't go offstage to discuss it first, so they knew there was no fakery. So someone would have to take suggestions. Alan and I were afraid to do it, and Nancy was shy, so Anne went out and did it. She was terrific at this. She had never done anything like this before, had never broken the fourth wall, and was initially very fearful, but when they threw the gauntlet down, she picked it up. Maybe it's Irish courage. The way she answered the audience was sometimes so funny that we often never got to the sketch. So all of a sudden I saw that I had a wife who was really something else.

Q: *What was going on between the actors and David?*

STILLER: What happened was . . . everybody was supposed to have about the same amount to do. It was supposed to be an ensemble. We were almost sworn to anonymity, like the Moscow Art people. Nobody was supposed to stand out. But I remember within three weeks a man named, I think, Miles Standish on the St. Louis *Post-Dispatch* wrote a review, and he singled out Alan as being terrific in one scene and said Anne was very funny. But he didn't mention me. So David had to find a way of dealing with the egos of these four people so that we had equal standing. But there's no way to keep everyone equal. It was unfortunate because David's motive was terrific, but the audiences of America don't work that way.

I want to say that the credit for so many of the good things that have happened to me since must go to David. He really taught me what it was like to be part of an ensemble and to be able to give on the stage. And not to be afraid that if I didn't have words in my mouth I was going to disappear onstage.

David has never really gotten his due. He's a bright, brilliant guy. A philosopher of the theater. He established this idea for this kind of theater, and so many people were able to take pieces of what he said and their lives were changed as a result. That's what happened to me. But he himself never got what he should have out of it. It's like he's up there in bronze, but he never got the Academy Award he deserves.

Q: *What happened after St. Louis?*

STILLER: The next booking was New York—the Quadrille, which was formerly the Moroccan Village, on Eighth Street, across from the Bon Soir. It was owned by some men who were of the, uh, organization. They were very nice to us. We opened with Maxine Sullivan, the great jazz singer. The audience came to see Maxine and we just about survived.

We got some criticism from the owners. They said, "The trouble with this group—you got one guy in there, he don't do nothing. That kid there, Alan. He don't talk." "He's a little shy," I said, "but he's very talented." "That's no good," they said. "You can't have a guy like that in the show. You gotta have people who talk up like your wife. It's all right what she does." (*Laughs.*) That was the end of the four of us as an act.

Q: *Was it a question of everybody saying, "This is the end"? Or David saying, "I've got no more bookings"?*

STILLER: A combination of those things. It's almost like, how do you lead a revolutionary group and keep all the factions happy? Nightclubs were not the environment for social satirists, at least not the ones we were playing. Each place we were booked into emphasized this. Oh, it would have been great if we could have played St. Louis forever—like never leaving the womb. But you can't always choose your audience.

So, the group broke up.

Q: *Was this when you and Anne started the act?*

STILLER: No, first we went to Chicago and appeared in a revue at a place called the Happy Medium. At about the same time, Second City got started and was a tremendous success. The money at the Happy Medium was good—we started at $225 apiece a week and went up to $300, which was a lot of money for two actors who were used to making $55 a week—but we were driving ourselves up a tree because we were doing the same thing every night, two shows a night, and we weren't improvising at all. But the money we were making gave us the wherewithal to start a family. Anne became pregnant and went up to 185 pounds in her fifth month and, after forty-six weeks of being at the Happy Medium, they asked us to leave. After Amy was born at Mt. Sinai Hospital, we decided to do an act.

Anne Meara and Jerry Stiller

In 1962 we opened at the Phase II in Greenwich Village, at the slow end of Bleecker Street, with no act, coming in just after Vaughan Meader had left on his way to the Blue Angel with his Kennedy routine. We got up in front of the audience each night and made up little things. After six months of this, we had thirty-five minutes of material which we tried out for Max Gordon at the Blue Angel on one of their Sunday guest nights. We were hired for a three-week engagement and kept on for fourteen weeks—a house record for a comedy act. We also found we couldn't keep the same stuff at the Angel that was successful in the Village. We needed more jokes and had to come to the point quicker. We cut half the stuff we had and it made us twice as funny.

Q: *So not only were there changes in audiences from city to city, but even within a city.*

STILLER: Max Gordon once told me, "Lenny Bruce was great downtown at the Vanguard, but when I took him to the Blue Angel, he died." You have one crowd in one place, another in another.

We made the *Ed Sullivan Show*, and when we got there, we found to our surprise that the stuff we'd done at the Blue Angel was not always right for his audience. So we changed some more and by the time we appeared regularly on the Sullivan show, we had traveled a million light-years from the Crystal Palace in St. Louis. Our approach and delivery now were totally different, and not all of the changes were for the better.

We did Ed's show so often, we were running out of material. Finally we came up with the idea of doing something based on our different ethnic backgrounds—that Annie was Irish and I was Jewish. Computer dating was coming in then, so we did a sketch where two people from these different backgrounds were matched by a computer that thought they were right for each other. As I say, we had done a lot of his shows before, but that was the first time people really began to know who we were. Up to that time, we were just an act. But now we were the Irish girl and the Jewish guy.

Q: *That makes me flash on something Sills said—that*

when you are improvising truly, you become more your-self.

STILLER: The glory of this improvisational business was that you found something you could never do in a role as an actor. You all of a sudden were making a direct connection with your audience from your innermost feelings, because there was no time to prepare or fabricate or give anything that was less than true. Coming on at that moment with an instant selection, the audience was watching you, watching your mind think. You were exposed. You were absolutely open. There was nothing you could hide, and the audience recognized that. If you allow yourself to be totally open, the audience will respond in a way you won't find with any other format. That's why so many improvisational people were so absolutely successful.

Q: *Do you have a sense of being a part of the community, a part of the improv gang?*

STILLER: I don't feel like I'm part of the group, if that's what you mean. Certainly improvisation helped me find things, but I never felt I was an innovator. Not like some of the people who were really trying to say things and were very pure and beautiful, like Severn. He was a guy who utilized that particular sphere of consciousness to bring out something of himself that was never said by any artist before. I think I was more conventional, in a sense. I was looking for a joke. I was trying to make something happen that was funny.

It was still fun and exciting, but there are people today who are really the beneficiaries of the improvisational heritage. Like Andy Kaufman, who works at the Improvisation a lot, doing absurdist humor. It's taken twelve or thirteen years for audiences to accept this kind of humor. We started too early to really be a part of that. Years ago, when we tried to do that sort of thing in a club downtown, Anne and I got fired, so we had to change, conform. It would have been nice if we could have pursued the really unique, but we're all victims, in a way, of having to do what's necessary for survival. I'm a lucky survivor.

I feel very sorry I never did join The Second City group. Paul Sills did ask us once. He saw Anne and me at the Phase II and said, "I'd like you to be part of one of the Second City troupes," but we didn't take him up on it. We were just putting our act together, and we were so intent on following through on it that we didn't take him up on it.

13.

Bernard Sahlins

Sahlins was a coproducer of Playwrights Theatre Company and produced two seasons of plays at the Studebaker Theatre, which employed a good many of the Playwrights-Compass crowd during its brief life. He opened The Second City with Paul Sills and Howard Alk, and now, more than eighteen years later, is sole producer. He has occasionally made excursions into other fields, including television and film (he does not deny responsibility for *The Monitors*). Within the past several years, he has directed a number of successful editions of Second City, either alone or with Del Close. He is also an executive producer of *Second City T.V.*, a television series featuring members of the Second City casts.

Not everybody loves Bernie Sahlins, as some of the other conversations in this book attest. But then, how many universally loved producers are there? If, however, one accepts the idea that an institution reflects the character of its management, he must be doing a considerable amount of something right.

SAHLINS: There had been a lot of theater in Chicago before the war. Progressive theater. That is, the theater that grew out of the Depression: the WPA, the theater of social consciousness. You know, Mr. and Mrs. Zero and this kind of sentimentality that people are basically good and all you have to do is give them a chance and the world will be all right. The people who had been involved back then were still involved in anything theatrical that took place after the war. They were around as a sort of cultural nexus when the new people came along—the people who either had been too young to go to war or maybe had just come back. We were the new generation. (I was almost too old for the new generation at that point, but before that I had not really participated.) We inherited the values of the older people, the liberal-progressive theatrical tradition.

Q: *Did you meet Sills and Shepherd while you were a student at the University of Chicago?*

SAHLINS: I was at the University of Chicago much before the others. When they were there, I was manufacturing tape recorders, but I was very interested in what was going on at the university, especially in theater. You never actually leave the U. of C. I knew all these people—Paul and Mike and Elaine. Though I wasn't involved with them at the university, I was actively interested and would come down and see their work and talk to them. After they started Playwrights Theatre Club in 1953, I became one of the administrative directors and found myself saddled with the chores. Then we were closed by the city in 1954 for violations of building codes. We didn't have an asbestos curtain. sprinkler systems, et cetera. We fought that, but lost. Sills and Shepherd went on to start Compass, and I started a big theater downtown at the Studebaker, which lasted a year. People filtered back and forth between the two. I'll never forget a production we did of *Lysistrata* with Mike and Elaine and Severn and Gene. which Paul directed and [newspaper critic] Claudia Cassidy said was the worst production in two thousand years.

Our first work was totally snobbish in the way the peace movement was snobbish. We played for the elite and were the elite. This observation, of course, is hindsight. Looking back, all of our democratic impulses were arrogant in many ways. We were educated, interested in high-level reference. While our hearts were in the right place politically and socially, we were nevertheless snobs, cultural snobs.

The theater has always been an upper-class preoccupation, with only two or three percent of the population interested. Even the Elizabethan theater we look back on as being so rich in common appeal—eighty percent of London never went to it. And of the remaining twenty percent, maybe ten percent or twelve percent were regular theatergoers.

But don't minimize David Shepherd's contributions. The social notions of his had nothing to do with the work.

My memory of David Shepherd, the one that's symbolic, is from when we were opening the new Playwrights Theatre. Things were totally disorganized and a crowd of people was waiting to get in. The box office was bollixed and the actors were desperately scrambling for their props and costumes. Totally disorganized. And in the middle of all this, with tremendous concentration and diligence, David was off in the corner scraping away a little piece of dirt that would never be seen by anybody.

And yet, he was sort of the conscience of the theater, which I think is necessary for every theater—someone who maintains a certain floor of integrity, of standards, of steady worth, and who says, "This is good," "This is no good," and "We can't let it slide by." Invaluable and totally necessary.

Q: *What about some early impressions of Paul?*

SAHLINS: I think most of my early impressions of Paul are very much like my later impressions of Paul. I don't think he's changed a lot.

I think there are two kinds of directors. One kind is the director who conceives an idea and then tries to fit everything in the production into his concept. He will push and shove and lop off any corners that don't fit in order to make the play conform to his preconceived idea. That seems to me to be the least successful kind of director because, while sometimes he may come up with good work, if the concept goes against the reality of the material, he won't notice.

The other kind of director—of which Paul is the epitome —is one who doesn't have any real notion of what the work should be but does have an unerring notion of what works.

Q: *You mean the kind of director who finds a production's style organically out of the material, rather than doing violence to the material by making it conform to a preconceived style?*

SAHLINS: Right. Paul is able to do that. That's his gift. And when something is going wrong, he's able to spot that and communicate somehow that it's going wrong. Also, he had then and has now a tremendous gift of being able to call on people's highest ideals and aspirations in terms of selflessness and serving art, and he's able to act on these feelings and organize them into a theatrical result. He had that in Playwrights and he has it now, so he hasn't changed all that much. He's just been sharpening and improving.

Q: *What can you tell me about the beginnings of Second City?*

SAHLINS: There was a two- or three-year hiatus between the end of Compass and the Studebaker and the start of Second City. Paul and I were in contact all that time and we discussed opening some kind of thing. We weren't particularly definite in our plans. We knew it would be nice to have a coffee shop where people could come and sit and watch a show, and we knew we would be working with a lot of the old Compass people and that the show would be developed out of the kind of work that had been going on with this group. Well, I had some money. Enough to be poor for a long time; I had sold my business. I think it took about $6,000 in cash to open. We owed a lot. Paul and Howard and I were the total owners of Second City. I loaned them the money. So we built it. We hired some amateur carpenters and did a lot of work ourselves. It wasn't very stylishly done.

None of us had any notion that we were doing anything revolutionary or significant. What we knew we were doing was getting the place ready and rehearsing, painting, hammering. Working almost twenty-four hours a day. I remember distinctly all the inspectors from the city coming and saying, "That's nice, when are you opening?" and our saying, "Oh, about three days," and their laughing. Because to any external eye, looking at the shambles, we were six months from opening. Though, from our experience with Playwrights, we could see the order coming out of the chaos.

We were insecure right up to opening night, between deciding what the show would be like and getting the

179

place ready. We had bought the carpeting from an Armenian rug dealer named Kalujian, and as people came walking in that night, he was still nailing down the carpet. The audience was stepping over him. He was still tapping when the opening song was going on. I remember his tapping in time to the chorus. At the same time, Paul and I were in the kitchen, still in our work clothes, making hamburgers.

The place was jammed. Hundreds of people showed up, attracted by our reputations, and, of course, because a great many of them were friends. The house held only 120 so we had to turn away a lot of people. It's a prestigious thing now to have been at the opening night of Second City. I've personally met thirteen or fourteen people who claim to have been at the opening of *The Threepenny Opera* in Berlin, so it wouldn't surprise me to hear a lot of people claim having been at our opening. We were an instant success. Instant.

We were never as political as people remember us. We didn't have any great political content, but we had great topical content. The excitement of those days was the recognition of what we as people had been reluctant to say about ourselves before. It wasn't so much our cleverness in saying it, but the sheer fact of saying it.

In our highest work we consciously recognized that we ourselves were the proper target of our humor. We ourselves and our community were what was under discussion. The most gratifying part of the work was not when people were laughing at the KKK—though God knows we wanted them to—but when they were laughing with the joy of recognition. Saying, "Oh yes, that's us!" The truth can only be about yourself.

o: *Andrew Duncan made comments about the tensions which existed between the actors and the management. What is your perspective?*

SAHLINS: When we started, I identified myself totally with actors.

Q: *You felt it was almost a communal situation, with you just happening to be the person who helped make the wheels go?*

SAHLINS: Right. I was crestfallen and disillusioned to find fairly early on in the game that I was separated from them because I was taking on some kinds of responsibility that inevitably made me the focus of free-form paranoia and any discontent that existed. I discovered that people I considered to be friends and intimates were not. I went through a kind of crisis personally in terms of defining my ongoing role at Second City, and I found myself having to make some conscious analyses and conclusions about my ultimate relationship with everybody. How vulnerable I could leave myself. And I realized that there's a certain amount of distance and a certain kind of loneliness necessary to keep it going. I decided what I would do would be straight in terms of equity. I would be aboveboard and accept the fact it wouldn't suit many of the people much of the time.

Q: *There has been a good deal of speculation about Second City's profitability over the years and some question about how much you personally have made out of it.*

SAHLINS: I think my big failure in this is a certain kind of secretiveness, a certain kind of unwillingness to say to everybody, "Look, this is our situation." I do want to say, "This is a separate compartment, I'll take care of it. Forget about it. Let's do the work."

Q: *Another bone of contention has been ownership of the material. Robert Klein told me he's of the opinion that the actors who created the material should be able to use it outside Second City.*

SAHLINS: That would be terrific, but the reason I don't allow that is that it's all we have to keep going.

Q: *But there have been so many examples of Second City material being used outside. Steinberg has used a lot of it on television, for instance.*

SAHLINS: Because I'm not diligent about . . . I don't want to get into hassles particularly. You must understand I don't sit up here, make rules, and follow them. I'm not thorough and precise about everything. As a general rule, if I can stop it. I will. If they go ahead and do it, I'm not going to hire lawyers and sue people particularly. I may someday. I'm not here to hurt anybody, but I do feel strongly that whatever we have we should hold onto for our own survival. If our survival means my survival, so be it. But Second City's survival has been chancy and I've been juggling bills and creditors and existing from day to day for so many years, I'm going to kill anybody who tries to get away with stuff I feel is ours.

Q: *I understand there was also some discord when Alan Myerson was directing.*

SAHLINS: We all objected to certain simplistic political notions of his. We didn't agree with him that the world is divided into just goodies and baddies, and we didn't buy the sentimentality of the have-nots being good and the haves being bad. So we were always editing him in one way or another. We weren't ready to hand over total control of a company to him to follow that approach.

Do you know what a resultant is, in mathematical terms? The resultant is the direction something moves in as a result of all of the forces acting upon it. Perhaps in any given Second City company, some forces are stronger than others. The director might weigh at four and each actor two and the producer one-half. The resultant of these forces is what you see up there, and everybody, including the audience and the waitresses, has some input in this resultant. Now Myerson came along with such a strong notion that he tended to steer the work in such a way that everyone else's input was more minimized, and that's why we clamped down.

It's true for actors, too. When you have a very strong actor of a destructive or noncooperative nature, his input then becomes too strong. It then minimizes others' contributions. It's not a matter of rocking the boat, it's that it prevents others from contributing. For instance, I like David Steinberg very much. But I would no more think of having him in a company now than the man in the moon because he uses the other actors for his own advancement with the audience, his own advancement in life. He's a user. He's totally self-involved. He's a Duddy Kravitz. And I *like* him. I love being with him. He's charming, he's sentimental and sweet, but he's a prick in that way.

I like thinking of this kind of work from the point of view of vectors and resultants. In the first company most of the input was Paul's, with some from the actors. When Sheldon took over, there was a little more from the producer and more from the actors and less from the director. In the Myerson company, it was in the beginning heavily the director, and later, because we clamped down, less.

Bernard Sahlins

Q: *After Paul and Alan Myerson and Sheldon, who directed?*

SAHLINS: After Sheldon left, Mike Miller directed a show or two. He was sort of a warmed-over Kazan-type director. I wasn't living in Chicago at the time. I was in New York and came in maybe once a month, maybe more often. I was in New York for two years, but Second City was kind of declining here, so I moved back. When Mike left, we had another fellow who tried but didn't work out, so I finally said the hell with it and came back and directed myself. That's when I did everything—directed, produced, kept books, et cetera. I was alone here for about four years is what it amounted to.

Q: *That must have been a little schizoid for you. After all, a director's relationship to his cast is different from a producer's.*

SAHLINS: I found it fairly difficult, but not impossible. I tried to keep the producing half out of my work as a director. I'll never forget how nice it was when I went to New York to do a show and I had a company manager to do the shit. (*Laughs.*) And I was able to divorce myself from it. Terrific! But the director needs to share with the actors the hostility against the producer. (*Laughs.*) I enjoy directing.

Q: *Let's talk about Del.*

SAHLINS: Del's first appearance at The Second City was a ploy on my part. Paul had done two shows and was exhibiting the all-too-familiar signs of losing interest. At that time I was not active in the day-to-day esthetics; I was operating strictly as a producer. From having worked with Paul before, as I say, I recognized the symptoms of disinterest, so I brought Del in, really as a goad to Paul. In fact, I think Del was Paul's suggestion. I went to Paul and said, "Who should we get? Because you're obviously tired." Del was around for a few weeks, working with the cast, and then Paul suddenly got re-interested. So it worked.

Later, about the time Paul left with the first troupe for New York, Del came in as an actor. He stayed for two or three years, but he got progressively less able to cope with the work, or with life, and really cracked up seriously.

Q: *Now he's back again as director.*

SAHLINS: I always valued Del in terms of his ability, his

183

intelligence, and always somehow felt he was rescuable. He wasn't in good shape when he first came back, but lately he's been in wonderful shape and it's been a pleasure.

Del's strength lies in the immediate moment. He's interested in the effect of scenes and also the overall moment-to-moment truth of the playing and the work. I'm much more organized and much more likely to pare away superfluities.

I learn when I direct. I remember I directed a scene called "Fifties" which was done in 1969, way before *Grease*. When we were putting it together, the cast of that show sang me a hundred '50s songs, none of which I'd ever heard. And I suddenly realized that at the same time we at Playwrights and Compass and Studebaker were doing what we were doing, these kids had been going to drive-ins and been singing these songs. And since then, these kids had come out of their drive-ins and become the dominant culture, and their music and life-style were now being co-opted by the entire country. I really learned something out of that experience. That was when I realized how much I learned from our casts about what was going on in the world. The point of this work or form is that it allows you and them and me to express what's going on now and it allows you to learn.

Q: *It also allows you to be a vital part of the times.*

SAHLINS: Right. Because we are directly relating to our preoccupations and our audiences, we are of the time. As the times change, we change, and that's why we've lasted eighteen years.

Q: *Because you have the techniques and skill to react instantly to whatever happens in society.*

SAHLINS: I think it goes beyond that. I think we *are* what happens and the audience is what happens. And so we're just expressing ourselves.

Q: *What about Second City's relationship to the City of Chicago?*

SAHLINS: Chicago is in many ways a producing city and always has been. We have more resident theaters right now than any city in the country. This is a hell of an interesting city.

Q: *I understand that Second City used to be a watering hole for Chicago progressives.*

184

Bernard Sahlins

SAHLINS: Nelson Algren and Studs Terkel used to come around, but we're not their meat anymore. We aren't exciting enough for them anymore. They're not finding that antiestablishment kick. Perhaps it isn't as exciting now as it was at first, but that's easily explained.

Q: *The novelty is off.*

SAHLINS: Not only the novelty of Second City, but the whole novelty of getting onstage and saying things that hadn't been said onstage before. When we first came on, it was like an orgasm because nobody had been addressing the immediate political and intellectual situations, current events, relationships. So when you got onstage and said anything, it was like violating taboos. We were coming out from under McCarthy and everything he had represented. And here we and people like Mort Sahl and Lenny Bruce were doing things that people really got off on. They don't as much now because now this kind of humor is common currency.

But, because we are indigenous to Chicago and have become such a part of it, we are relatively critic-proof, and even relatively bad-show-proof. When we announce the opening of a new show, the audience comes. We have built an audience.

Q: *How is Second City structured now?*

SAHLINS: It's a little like a baseball league here. We have workshops taught by Del, Jo Forsberg, and Roberta Maguire—four or five workshops a week, each with twenty people or so. In addition, every Thursday high school kids from Metro, the open school we have in Chicago, come in and they have a workshop. So we have maybe 120 people in workshops at any one time. Del and I and the others keep our eyes open for promising people in the workshops. If a spot opens in the touring company, we invite that person to join.

The touring company plays here on Monday nights, when the regular company has a dark night. They also take college dates—two or three a month. Not too long ago they played five weeks at a dinner theater in Kansas City. We keep our eyes on the touring company for when a spot opens in the resident company. In fact, in the last five or six years, we've not gone outside our own ranks—except for one person—for an actor for the resident company. I

185

decided the hell with going to New York to hunt for people, so we develop them here. So they go from workshops to touring company to resident company. It's a moment of great joy and trauma when someone from the touring company moves up. Occasionally a whole company will move up at one time. I'd say our average actor stays with us about three years, with the average length of time in the touring company being about a year and a half.

How people use The Second City is dependent on what kind of people they are. For some, the work represents nothing more than a stepping-stone to the work they really want to do eventually. There are other people in the company for whom the work represents more of an end in itself. They wouldn't turn down outside work, but still the prime thing is doing the work here; they generally leave only when the work begins to pall, as it must eventually. Of course, there were and are some people better than others, but I don't really think of it that way. Because, again, the work allows you to use what each performer has.

I do think there are some drawbacks for an actor in working at Second City. The problem with improvisation for an actor is that it deals in shorthand. When you're improvising you tend to run for external characteristics, to make quick choices to get the scene going. You don very quickly a partial characterization that has the trappings of reality, but through which you show. That's why Severn Darden shows through any of the characters he plays. In anything he does, it's the essential Severn you're interested in, not the character he plays. He just wears the character like a hat. Or a cape. (*Laughs.*) It really isn't full character work.

So, what happens in this work is that you develop the facility required to make your point in five minutes, to make your character in five minutes. But that kind of creative process is certainly different from building a character organically over the course of a play or movie. A play or movie requires maturation over the length of the work. Here you have to hit it and hold it. I'm not saying that Second City people can't do other work. It's just that when they do they have to approach it differently than they do the work here.

Bernard Sahlins

I think Second City has taken up the thread of a kind of work that I feel has been going on for centuries; we represent a kind of demotic form. As opposed to the great tragedies or those times when the really creative minds of a generation are drawn to the theater as a means of expression. But those times are very rare. The Greek theater lasted ninety years. The next theater of the kind I'm talking about—the great tragic theater—was 120 years in the Renaissance period, then nothing. You try to name me five important plays written between the seventeenth century and the nineteenth century, what do you come up with? Sheridan, *The Rivals, The Beggar's Opera, She Stoops to Conquer.* And then a few years of creative outpouring in the late nineteenth century in Northern Europe—Strindberg and Chekhov and Ibsen—and that's it. So that kind of theater—the theater that drew the writers to express themselves—is very rare. If it's existed for three hundred years out of the last thousand, that's a lot.

But our kind of theater, the kind that Second City belongs to—the demotic, the burlesque, the theater without heroes, the theater of everyday life—has continued unbroken. I feel strongly about Second City being directly in the tradition of the *commedia,* the strolling players, the Roman farce, and before that the Greek harvest things. We do the same things in the same ways. Our stage looks like the Greek stage. There's a scene I have from a Greek vase painting that could be our stage with our people on it. Whether it was spontaneous regeneration or unconscious or whatever, we're in that tradition both in our methods and our material and in the way we view the world. I feel that is our function, to preserve that thread and the thread of theater in general. What we represent is a sort of holding action for the time when the real theater will return. But I don't think we've done anything particularly unique here.

I think that Viola's book is wrong and that Paul's emphases are wrong in the sense that I do not believe that we are leading to another form or part of the classical theater. I think what we have done and will continue to do is to revive an old form. I think all of the other aspirations for improvisational theater are unfair to the notion of the work. Improvisation is a functional device to achieve a

187

goal other than itself. Just as fencing is. I know there are
people who will want to string me up for saying it, but improvisation is a tool for arriving at . . . (*laughs*) Second
City material. It hasn't proven viable for anything else.

14.

Eugene Troobnick

Eugene Troobnick coproduced and appeared with Playrights Theatre Club. He was one of the original cast of The Second City, where he inspired American youth as Businessman, gave Chicago a taste of things to come as a multifaced Richard Nixon, and did his best to protect Sophocles' interests as the discussion leader of "Great Books."

Since leaving Second City, Troobnick has worked as an actor in all media. On film he starred in *Harvey Middleman, Fireman,* and appeared in *Funny Lady* and *California Split.* The last time I saw him on television, he was being murdered and stuffed into a car trunk on *Kojak.* On the New York stage, he starred in *Before You Go* and *Dynamite Tonite!* He teaches, acts, and directs at Yale.

TROOBNICK: I went to the University of Chicago to major in English lit. While I was there, I got involved with a theater group called "Tonight at 8:30." I remember very early on I met Paul. That would have to be about 1952.

A number of us got the idea of starting an Off-Broadway theater, which Chicago did not have. I guess through attrition and apathy after a while, most of them stopped working on the idea, leaving Paul, David Shepherd, and myself. So we ended up producing the Playwrights Theatre Club. I remember David and I touring around in my car, trying to find a place, and one day we walked into what had been a Chinese restaurant above some stores, and we looked at it and turned to each other, smiling broadly. It turned out he was smiling because he was thinking, "How bizarre!" and I was smiling because I thought, "This can work!" We showed it to Sills and we all agreed we could make a theater out of it. Jeez, it seems like a miracle now, but we made a theater out of it.

We slept in the theater when we started because we had so little money. Since it had been a restaurant, it had little alcoves and each person took an alcove as a sort of room of his own. We ran for about a year before we were bringing in enough money to become an Equity company.

In addition to the plays we did, there were also workshop performances. One of the people around at the time was Tom Erhart. He's very tall, and with the proper make-up can look very like Lincoln. So, for one of the Monday-night workshops, he and Ed Asner did the Lincoln-Douglas debates.

I gather now, in retrospect, that a lot of people told the Chicago authorities that we were "pink." We were certainly liberal. We did plays by people like Brecht and Büchner, so the city, in reaction to the Red Scare at that time, sent around every inspector you could think of. We couldn't possibly afford to rectify all of the violations they insisted were there, so they closed us down.

Q: *You weren't a member of The Compass, were you?*

TROOBNICK: I wasn't a member in the sense of being there night after night and performing. At that time, I was working as an editor for Sears Roebuck and Company, and I would very occasionally go down there and work with them. But they did consider me still a member of their group.

At the time of The Compass, we knew someone who worked on a Milwaukee television station, and he or somebody came up with the idea of having us go up and do a television show, which we chauvinistically called *The Milwaukee Revue*, trying to attract local backing. Mike and Elaine did their "Teenagers" scene. Shelley Berman did what would later be one of his famous telephone monologues. A fellow named Vernon Schwartz and I did a scene, and Barbara Harris was a weather girl. Paul Sills directed. We could not get a sponsor.

I remember seeing Mike and Elaine do "Pirandello" at Compass. I was completely taken in when I saw the scene. I thought Mike and Elaine had flipped and were really taking out some backstage venom onstage. Of course, at the end I realized I had been taken in.

Incidentally, Mike Nichols is the fastest verbal human being I have ever known. He's not been given credit for some of the things he's said. Like, to my understanding, he originated such wonders as, "Way down deep inside, you're shallow," and "Death is nature's way of telling you to slow down."

Mike thought of himself as a verbal comedian and me, in contrast, as a physical comedian. When The Compass was disbanding and he and Elaine had their first nightclub offer, he thought that they wouldn't be able to make it alone, so he invited me to join them and make it a threesome. Well, their first offer was, I think, $60 a week apiece, and I was already making an enormous $150 a week at Sears as an editor, and I had a wife and child, so it was impossible. And that's the big story on how I did not go with Mike and Elaine.

Not too long before this, we had all appeared at Bernie's Studebaker in the worst production of *Lysistrata* ever seen by the eye of mortal man. There were a lot of good people in it, but the original director was not able to cope with it and us and he left, and Sills came in to direct it in about a week. Besides Mike and Elaine and myself, the cast included Barbara Harris, Severn Darden, and Andrew Duncan. Mike Nichols was the head of the old men's chorus and Severn Darden, of all people, headed the old women's chorus. When Paul came in, Severn had had no direction. A day or two before we opened, Severn went to him and said, "Paul, for heaven's sake, I'm a big hulking man and I'm cast as head of the women's chorus and nobody's given me a single direction. Tell me something!" Sills looked at him. Then he said, "Well, uh, Severn . . . do it like Dylan Thomas." And he walked away.

Being with The Second City we all had to be on top of the news because, when we took suggestions from the audience, the great majority of them would invariably be right on top of what was happening that day. And I would say that the best-informed were Andrew Duncan and I. I know I would read a couple of newspapers and listen to the news on the radio and watch it on TV because I felt a great obligation. Andrew and I would pretty much know about anything that was going on, and Howard Alk was very close to us in that. And then Severn and Paul Sand and Alan Arkin and the girls. Sometimes they would know all about something esoteric, and then something everybody else knew all about they wouldn't have heard of.

We used to do a spot in which we asked the audience for a subject that one of us would then come out and play being an expert on. I don't remember once when we got a suggestion from the audience that someone backstage didn't know what it was about so that somebody could be an expert on it. You should have heard Severn speaking on hagiology—the study of saints. He invented saints you never heard of—black midgets who did incredible things off in Uganda. It was really marvelous. Some of it he claimed was true. Of course, there were so many saints, it could have been true.

There was another spot we did where Andrew and Howard and I pretended to be an advertising agency and we would get from the audience a suggestion for a product. The object of the improvisation was that we then had to come up with a name for the product along with a motto and an advertising campaign. I can remember one night the audience gave us mint-flavored tuna fish and I came up with the name "Finny Mint." Severn was backstage for the first part of the scene, and after we'd kicked the audience's product around for a little while, he would come in, playing the head of the agency. We'd all get very obsequious and grovel a lot. He would always come out with a product idea in addition to the audience's that was even more outré. For instance, an olive the size of a watermelon, and he'd say. "I don't think we're going to have any problem selling this, but packaging may give us trouble." There was another time when he came onstage with a soft drink or something and said, "We're going to have a little bit of a problem with this one because our scientists have discovered that it's pretty addicting." And I came up with the campaign—free samples.

Eugene Troobnick

Severn used to love to play a maniacal doctor in any scene that called for a doctor. He was doing this maniacal sadistic doctor in a scene with a very nervous Mina Kolb one night, and he was browbeating her and she said, "Goodness sakes, Doctor, but you're hostile," and he said, "Don't give me any of that hostile crap or I'll hit you!"

Also, Severn, I think, had the distinction of being the first man ever to say "shit" on the American stage and have it accepted and laughed at. We did a scene—one of us on one side of the stage and the other on the other side, both miming steering the wheels of great ships. He hailed me, "Ahoy! What ship be you?" And I told him and then I said, "What ship be you?" And he said, "The *Pequod.* Have you seen anything of a great white whale?" "Yes," I said, "three days ago. We killed it." And he said, "Shit!" and the lights went out.

When we were in New York, Larry Arrick, to get our juices flowing, would sometimes have us do an exercise called "Crisis." One of us would sit on the stage and just wait, and the other person had the responsibility of running onstage with a crisis and trying to engage the first either in helping him or giving him advice. The idea was the first person had to be involved, and from this, presumably, a scene would start. One time, Severn was sitting on a stage waiting and Barbara was supposed to come on with a crisis. She ran on yelling, "Sevvy! Severn!" Oh, he *hated* to be called his own name onstage. But she ran on yelling, "Severn! You've got to help me. I just found out I'm pregnant! What am I going to do?" And Severn turned and instantly said, "Whom do you suspect?"

I like to say that David Shepherd and I defeated Richard Nixon for the presidency in 1960. Nixon lost Illinois by one-tenth of one percent of the vote. Had he carried Illinois, he would have won the election. There was a good deal of talk about scandal and ballot-stuffing, but the thought of such a thing happening in Mayor Daley's Chicago is, of course, preposterous. Anyway, at the time I was doing a pretty strongly anti-Nixon scene which David Shepherd had written and in which I played Nixon. It was about his various faces and how he never seemed to have one of his own and he would always adopt a face for whatever audience he had to face, et cetera. I think that

David and I must have convinced at least one-tenth of one percent of the voters not to vote for that man. Right? And so we were the ones who brought Kennedy into the presidency. You can thank us for that and the Cuban missile crisis and the Bay of Pigs.

I remember when Charles Percy came to see us—he was then vice-president of Bell and Howell—and he was at that time a big Nixon supporter. When he saw that scene I told you about, he laughed and winced at the same time. It was something to behold.

Q: *You mentioned Mayor Daley. Did he ever come to the theater?*

TROOBNICK: Not to my knowledge. I don't think he would have understood or enjoyed us. He probably would have resented us. In fact, if he had been in the audience, we surely would have directed as much material at him as possible. And when we got to the improvs, the audience would have helped us by suggesting things to enable us to get at him, and he wasn't the kind of man who enjoyed being criticized or caricatured.

Q: *Do you remember getting much in the way of protests regarding your material?*

TROOBNICK: No, except we were bombed once. I can't remember how long it was after we opened—I think maybe it was two months or so. Somebody, after hours, after everybody had gone home, at like two in the morning, broke windows and got in there and threw red paint over everything and wrecked the inside as much as they could and set off stink bombs. At the time I was also getting threatening mail, though, strangely enough, I was the only one. I can't remember now what it said. I threw it away as soon as I got it. I do remember I was scared. The reason I brought this up is because of what Severn did. I would park my car in what was at night a very lonely place, so Severn went out and bought me a blackthorn stick to carry with me when I was alone. I still have it. But that was the big bombing incident. We never did get conclusive evidence as to who did it or why.

Q: *Talk about Sills.*

TROOBNICK: The kind of directing that Paul has always sought for, and it's one of the things I think has made him important as a talent, is . . . well, if he has an insight, he

194

doesn't try to give it to the actor. He tries to lead the actor to find it for himself so then it's the actor's insight and it's so much more important to him. If you hand me an insight, and if I'm lucky enough to realize it's important, even so, I might feel some irritation or hostility that you had to give it to me. Whereas, if you lead me to finding it for myself, then I think I've done something.

One of my chief functions in the early days of Playwrights, besides being a member of the board of directors and an actor and very rarely a director, was to interpret what Sills meant to the actors. I seemed to be on his wavelength and understand what he meant before or more clearly than other people did. I'd say, "Paul. you mean so-and-so and such-and-such?" and he'd say, "Yeah!" and the actor would say, "Oh!" As time went on, he became more coherent and intelligible, except that part of his thing, as I say, is not to be too explicit.

I don't think he's ever been given the recognition he deserves, especially grant-wise. God knows. he should have a school someplace right now so that other people who have a lot of talent could come out of it and be more than they otherwise might have been.

He could also be unbearable. I found him to be irascible. There were often terrible fights. Not physical fights, but arguments. I remember one time there was a big argument at the Chicago Second City. I don't recall who was in it— I know I wasn't. And I know Paul Sand wasn't in it. It was very unpleasant and taking a long time, and he and I were waiting to work. Finally Sand turned to me and said, "Gene, I think I'm going to go inside for a while." What he meant was to go inside his head. And he did. He was still there, looking pleasant and everything. but he was inside his head. thinking his own thoughts and having a good time. He has that ability.

Paul Sand joined us a little after we opened, and the next notable addition wasn't until Alan Arkin came along. You know what would happen is that we would find that we would tend to work with the same people in the improvisations. That's how Mike and Elaine got together, because they could work really well together at The Compass. They more and more gravitated together. I had a special rapport sort of like that with Alan Arkin and Paul Sand.

I remember one night at The Second City when Severn was ill. He did the set show, but he said, "Listen, I feel rocky. I'll go out and sit in the audience and watch you improvise, but I won't go on." So he sat down. That night Alan and I improvised a scene called "The Egg." He played Attillio Setembrini, this Italian, and I was a Brooklyn fellow named Murray Fischer. We were both workers on the top of a steel construction thing, riveting the building together, and the lunch whistle blew. And all the scene was, was us sitting together on our lunch hour and talking about various things and finally getting around to this egg. The character I played remembered that when he was a boy he read in *Ripley's Believe It or Not* that the way an egg is constructed is so perfect that if you hold an egg in your hand, in the very middle of your palm, and apply pressure on it evenly, you cannot break the shell of the egg. Of course Alan pooh-poohed this idea until I finally challenged him to do it, and he couldn't do it. And then I took the egg back and was boasting, crowing about how he couldn't do it when, *crack!* there was a little chick inside. It was a fertilized egg. And the scene ended with us making plans to make a pet of it, feed it, and have it following us around on the girder.

Now I personally feel that improvisation is a means and not an end. I think it's a means of finding and developing scenes. However, when an improvisation is working, there's nothing more exciting to watch. The greatest compliment we ever got as improvisers was from Severn that night. He walked back after Alan and I had completed that scene, he looked at us, and said. "I was among those in the audience who could not *believe* that scene was improvised."

We did another scene with those two characters where Alan was the man in one of those pizza places, you know, who throws the dough up in the air and a crowd gathers and watches him. I was playing Murray again, and I was hired as an apprentice. And the whole scene was, of course, him teaching me how to make pizza. The thing I remember about it that was so marvelous was that Groucho Marx and Harpo were in the audience the night we first did it, and by a great happy stroke of luck it turned out to be a Marx

Brothers scene. Without props or scenery or anything else, we had the audience understanding exactly where the pizza dough was and everything else. We were covered with the dough, we got stuck to each other. It was marvelous. Then there was one Paul and I did on the suggestion, "Lie down with dogs, rise up with fleas." We made an Italian movie out of it—*cinéma vérité.* I was an old Italian bum fumbling around some garbage cans and he was a dog. Paul Sand is the greatest dog you've ever seen onstage. All the scene consisted of was me finding things in the garbage can and not sharing them with the dog and then finally breaking down and sharing with the dog, and then sitting on the park bench. Finally, I started to nod and doze and he came over and turned around three times, right?, and then leaned up against me and started to rest. But then he started scratching, then more and more. And it turned out that the dog was getting an incredible amount of fleas from me, the old bum!

I was used very heavily in the scenes at the beginning of Second City, but I discovered after a few months of working eight hours a day at *Playboy* magazine, where I was an editor, and whatever it was at Second City—six hours a night?—and trying to be a father and a husband and all the rest of it, I was going out of my mind. So I asked them at Second City to give me less important things to do, which is why, when we hit Broadway, I had virtually nothing to show off in.

We accepted Max Liebman's offer to produce us on Broadway, but first we went to Hollywood, which was supposed to be a sort of tryout. Alan wasn't with us. Although he had worked with us in Chicago, he had been hired to stay as part of the replacement company. But Barbara, Severn, and I kept pushing for him to join us because we thought he was so valuable to us, and we finally convinced Sills and the others, and he did join us in L.A.

The most important thing about the L.A. engagement was that it was the end of the real group feeling at The Second City. What we had had was this incredible group effort in which nobody felt singled out or above or below anyone else. But when we got to Hollywood and opened, the critics said, "They're all great, but two of them are going to be stars—Barbara Harris and Paul Sand." That couldn't help but change things. It was never quite the same after that.

The reason we didn't make it on Broadway was because our producer, Max Liebman, didn't have the courage to allow us to do what we were unique in doing. He was terrified to allow us to improvise in front of critics. He wouldn't even let us do the Khrushchev-Kennedy thing. A week or so after we opened, in desperation, he let us put that into the show and it instantly became the hit of the show, but the critics never saw it. They never saw us do any improvisation whatsoever on Broadway.

The Second City group I think was the best in terms of working together was Zohra, Andrew Duncan, Tony Holland, Alan, and I—Off-Broadway. We were asked to appear on David Susskind's program. We were on it for two hours and we did many of our scenes and also some improvisations. Anyway, what happened with the program was that he'd had Khrushchev on shortly before with very high ratings, but it turned out the ratings he had with us were higher than the show with Khrushchev. Not only that, it was a fairly late-night thing and it went on for two hours and what the ratings people were particularly impressed by was that it did not fall off during the second hour. We held the attention of the audience. So Susskind got very excited about the commercial possibilities and boiled the show down to a pilot and took it around to the networks. The report we got from him was that the network people all laughed very much but said, "We couldn't show that stuff. People would be offended. That's satirical!"

One day in New York, a girl came by who wanted to be with The Second City. We didn't actually have an opening for her, but she had so much charisma or something that everybody in the company wanted her in, including Sills. We told her she had a job. The next day she was institutionalized. But when she came in and saw us, she was at some point in craziness at which charm just blazed from her. You could not resist it.

Adlai Stevenson came downtown to see us and loved us and asked us to perform for his guests at the United States Mission to the United Nations. He was then ambassador to the UN. We did it and it was pretty successful. The thing that was surprising to us was that the Kennedy-Khrushchev scene was not nearly as successful with these diplomats because there was some amount of resentment from them at the idea of us playing heads of state. Some people are offended by that.

Q: *Do you remember any other interesting people who turned up in your audience?*

TROOBNICK: Feiffer used to come. I remember once he was sitting with us after hours and a fellow came in—Eichmann was being tried in Israel at the time—and this fellow came in wearing a large button that said "I Like Eich" on it. And everybody sort of laughed except Feiffer. And someone sitting next to him nudged him and said, "Come on, Jules. 'I like Eich.' It's funny, isn't it?" And Feiffer looked at him and said, "Well, up to the first five million I can laugh."

Marcel Marceau came to The Second City in Chicago and liked us very much. He sat around and talked with us afterwards. As you know, we used neither props nor scenery at Second City. We pantomimed everything. Well, I finally got up courage enough to ask him, "What did you think of our pantomime?" And I thought he gave us an accolade. He said, "Oh, it did not bother me."

Groucho Marx came two or three times and liked us very much. He not only would talk to us after the show, but when we took improv suggestions, he heckled us unmercifully. We were doing the Kennedy-Khrushchev scene one night and Tony was acting as the Russian interpreter. But we couldn't get a word out because Groucho was heckling us. Finally Tony stepped forward in character and said, "That will be enough. You've had your chance, Mr. Engels."

When we went to England, we couldn't do the Kennedy-Khrushchev scene because, at least at that time, there was a law that you couldn't portray the living head of a state onstage. We finally ended up doing just Khrushchev because technically he was not the head of the Russian government. He was the chairman or the secretary of the party and somebody else was the president so we were able to get away with doing him. But we could not portray Kennedy there.

There were two English tours. The one before I went was sort of an Off-Broadway tour and played at a nightclub called the Establishment Peter Cook had. I went over with another group a year or two later. We played the West End and got incredible reviews. Just remarkable raves. Better than *Beyond the Fringe* had gotten before they went to the U.S. And nobody came to see us. We never could figure out why. All we could think of was that they were sick and tired of satire by that time. That second tour was Erin Martin, Paul Sand, Dick Libertini, Severn, Sandy Baron, and I.

All told, I was with Second City for about four years. Played with them in Chicago, Hollywood, on Broadway, Off-Broadway, London, and, once, for a TV show, in Dublin. When I got back to the States after that, I figured that was it, and that was the end of my being with Second City.

Q: *Did you keep up contact with the improvisational crowd?*

TROOBNICK: Dick Schaal not too long ago got infuriated watching *Stand Up and Cheer*—you know, the Johnny Mann TV show?—so he got me and Severn and J. J. Barry and Buck Henry and about eight other weird men, including the writer Pat MacCormack, who's almost seven feet tall, and we got together and rehearsed and performed a few nights at the Comedy Store, which is a club in L.A. where comics get up and perform for each other and test out material. What we did was *Stand Up and Blow*. We whistled. We had twelve men standing there whistling a medley of popular American war songs. When we did "The Marine's Hymn," Pat MacCormack, this enormous man, played the mountain on Iwo Jima and the rest of us raised a flag on him. We were all in evening dress, except for Severn, who turned up in a priest's cassock.

I still do get recognition from having been at Second City. As a matter of fact, it's amazing how many people will remember having seen me there ten years ago.

But the reputation of having been with The Second City was not always a plus. For a long time I couldn't get read for a serious role because I was known as a nightclub comic. Also, when I was in *Before You Go*, a couple of the critics talked about the improvised quality I gave to the lines because they'd read in the program I'd been with Second City. When you think about it in terms of acting, what does that mean? It means you're saying the lines as if they're being said for the first time, which after all is what acting is all about.

I think I would say that the people connected with Second City were intellectuals. One of the things that made us intellectuals was the demands of our audience. We had a very hip audience. We were known as informed people so the smartest audiences would come to see us and make us stretch ourselves even more. I use the term intellectuals in the sense of people who not only have ideas but whose ideas help to shape their time. I don't mean we moved the country or the world or anything by what we did. But I do think that we did help start changing the consciousness of the country in the direction of being a good deal more aware of the reality of things than before.

15.

Mina Kolb

Mina Kolb was the only non-Compass/Playwrights veteran in the original company of The Second City, and she cannily turned her initial "outsider" status into a distinct comedic advantage. Many of her scenes seem to have an *Alice's Adventures in Wonderland*–like pattern, depicting her confrontations with eccentric characters whose peculiar logics she was, despite considerable effort, unable to comprehend. The *Alice* analogy goes only so far, however, because, in contrast with Lewis Carroll's conventionally sensible heroine, Kolb had a personal logic every bit as *outré* as those of any of the characters she confronted (but *outré* in a different way). In one scene in which Andrew Duncan remarked on her habit of leaving the front door unlocked, she explained, "Well, the kids are in and out all day, and besides, you know, burglars always come through the window." I think it likely that an encounter between her and the Cheshire Cat would leave the latter quite baffled.

Since leaving Second City, she has appeared in films (*Loving* and *Every Little Crook and Nanny*) and on the stage (*Story Theatre*). In addition she appeared in and directed some of the episodes of the *Story Theatre* television series. It is in the field of commercials that she has achieved true eminence, however. Ad agencies speak of

Mina Kolb

"the Mina Kolb type," a phrase which amuses me because the only Mina Kolb type I know is Mina Kolb.

KOLB: I did the *Ray Raynor Show* on TV in Chicago. It was a teenage record show. They would play records and the kids would dance, and then Ray and I would pantomime to the records. I did that for five years. Then Paul Sills called me up. I didn't know who he was. He said he was putting together something called The Second City, and it sounded kind of fascinating. We'd meet in this abandoned Chinese laundry on Wells Street, a bunch of us. I didn't know what it was all about. It was just kind of get up there and say a few words about something. I really had no idea what was happening.

Q: *You were unique in the company in that most of the others had come out of the University of Chicago-Playwrights-Compass crowd. Do you know what it was that got Sills so interested in you that he went outside of his crowd and cast you?*

KOLB: Maybe I helped make the balance because I was different. I was way off from their thinking. I had my middle-class, square-straight way of thinking, and they had the University of Chicago kind, analytical-psychological . . . they had lots of *terms* for things.

Q: *So you sort of played Margaret Dumont to them? Acted as a kind of foil?*

KOLB: Perhaps. I seemed to do the clubwoman type of person a lot. I figured that if I couldn't deal with subjects in a knowledgeable way, it was better to have my head someplace else altogether.

Q: *You mean, to play a person who couldn't deal with the subjects and find comedy out of that?*

KOLB: Yes. Rather than try to match what they knew about whatever was being talked about, I would react with non-sequitur kinds of things. Kind of foolish remarks, yet sometimes with a certain amount of truth involved. For instance, Andrew Duncan might start describing some famous sculptor's work, and he'd say, "How do you feel about it? Can you feel it? You *do* understand it. don't you?" Well, I wouldn't know what he was talking about, so I'd say something like, "No. I haven't seen it. I've been out of town." Because I just didn't know where I was. He'd swamp me with a lot of information, and it was my panicky remarks that made for some kind of a dramatic scene. Mostly, I think I would make comments in scenes. Barbara, Alan, Severn, Paul Sand, and some of the others could really develop scenes dramatically, but I don't think I was very good at that. Perhaps I should have worked more on Viola's games.

You know, I was never the person that I portrayed. I always played the clubwoman type of person. But really I had no idea, *no* idea, of what that kind of woman really thought of. I mean, I had no conscious idea. My mother was never a clubwoman, and I was never a clubwoman.

Q: *But you grew up on the North Shore in Wilmette, one of the ritzier suburbs of Chicago. From having grown up in that area, I know those attitudes are in the air up there.*

KOLB: But I was really far away from that.

Q: *But somehow you were able to portray that kind of person well.*

KOLB: I think I was able to portray it only because I didn't know anything about it. If I'd known anything about it, I don't think I could have. Fact is, I had sort of an idea what it was to be a clubwoman. I thought it was a kind of snobby dumbness. A haughty arrogance. And so that's what I played. If I had known real clubwomen, I probably couldn't have done it. I probably would have had some sympathy for them.

Q: *You've played that character a lot since, in commercials and films.*

KOLB: Yes, and I'm really tired up to the eyeballs and over the earlobes because I think I'm really a lot brighter than that character.

Q: *How much did you make at the beginning of Second City?*

KOLB: $50 a week.

I can recall way back when everything was going to be rosy because we were all going to be partners. We were going to share in the royalties for the material we came up with. The scenes were going to be taped and patented and stamped out in steel, for God's sake. The idea was that as other groups came along and used our stuff, we would be entitled to a small percentage and so on and so forth.

I said—and I recall it clearly because I happen to be

Mina Kolb

the daughter of an attorney—I said, "This is a lot of b.s." I didn't say it in that way exactly, because I was a very nice person at the time, you see. But I said, "There's no way we'll ever collect a dime out of this. It's a lot of nonsense. Let's not get into it. Rather, if there's any settling to be done, let's settle now. Get the money now. But don't let's sign something in the belief that there will ever be a residual in any shape or form." It turned out, of course, that there never was. Certainly not for the players anyway. I mean, you cannot nail a thing like that down. It cannot be done. It's much too loose. It's like a comedian's routine—all you have to do is change a couple of words and it's somebody else's routine, right? I figured that out right away because, of course, I have this fabulous mind.

But we were told, "Listen, don't ask for a lot of money up front because you're going to get it residually, every time another company comes along." But that's so dumb, because you have to come up with new material at Second City, particularly if you're dealing with politics.

Oh, but there were lawyers! The place was *covered* with lawyers! Lawyers for the actors, lawyers for the producers, lawyers for everybody. I kept sitting in the corner, shaking my head and saying, "Please, this is a *waste!* Forget it! It doesn't matter what we claim because we'll never be able to collect." I got insights, you see. I mean, you grow up in a family where your father's an attorney, you get to know what's collectible and what's not collectible.

Anyway, we opened and people came and started laughing and they wrote things about us, and I couldn't understand it at all. I had a song which began, "When Beethoven wrote his *Eroica* . . ." and I didn't know what an *Eroica* was! I hadn't even heard of it. So I was singing about something I had no idea what it was all about. But the audience thought it was just swell. Thank God there are more educated people in the world than myself.

Q: *Something I find curious is that you and Barbara never did a two-person scene together.*

KOLB: Oh, we probably did a couple.

Q: *Maybe in sets, but no scenes that were put into the final, rehearsed shows.*

KOLB: Curious. We never did find a common ground to work something out.

205

Q: *Was it a difference in chemistry?*

KOLB: It's very hard to take apart why.

Q: *Well, let me toss out a couple possibilities, and if something sounds right, let me know. One, perhaps because Second City wasn't as interested in exploring relationships between women at that time. Or, maybe neither you nor Barbara was particularly keen on initiating ideas but rather would develop others' ideas, and, since the others were all men, their ideas would tend to be all-male or male-female scenes. I mean, it would stand to reason that there would be some people who tended to initiate concepts for scenes, and others who would go along with and develop others' concepts.*

KOLB: Actually, the problem was more "Where do you stand?" and "How dare you?"

Q: *What do you mean?*

KOLB: I mean, what position did one hold? I mean, it was almost always that a man instigated a scene.

Q: *Did you and Barbara feel that if you came up with ideas you were out of line?*

KOLB: Well. . . .

Q: *Was it that you were sort of subtly discouraged? Or did you never think of this then?*

KOLB: Oh, I thought about it all the time. You want to know what I really thought?

Q: *Yes, very much. I think this relates to what was going on in society in general.*

KOLB: Sure, I had a lot of thoughts, a lot of ideas, a lot of approaches, but they weren't always acceptable or agreeable to who was in power at the time.

Q: *So, if you put out an idea, it would be less likely to be used than, say, if Andrew or one of the other men had suggested it?*

KOLB: You had to make it somebody else's idea. You had to play a funny game. It was like playing with a kid. You had to coax them. It was much harder to get them to do one of your ideas than it was for them to get you to do one of theirs.

Q: *So you had to play that game with the guys in the company and with Paul?*

KOLB: I've been playing that game all my life.

Mina Kolb

Q: *What you're saying is that it was a sexist situation then.*

KOLB: Isn't it now?

Q: *In the sense that there are still always more men than women in improvisational companies, yes. But there are often scenes between two women, and, from what I've seen of what's going on backstage now, the women feel as free to initiate ideas as the men. They don't seem to have to play that game.*

KOLB: Oh yeah?

Q: *That's my impression.*

KOLB: I'd like to see that. I'd like to see a complete show where the women were stronger than the men.

Q: *You've been out of Second City for several years now. Do you still feel part of the gang?*

KOLB: Yes. As a matter of fact, Andrew and I just did something for 3M this past weekend, and he said to me, "Could you have imagined fourteen years ago that we would be doing this stuff after all this time?" And I said, "No, I wouldn't have guessed that we'd still be doing the same old stuff."

16.

Paul Sand

When Roger Bowen left the original company of The Second City to devote all his attention to writing, Sills brought in Paul Sand. At first glance, Sand may have seemed an odd replacement. Bowen's strength was in words, Sand's—as a result of work with Marcel Marceau—was in mime. Sills knew what he was doing. With the addition of Sand, Second City's balance shifted perceptibly, becoming a bit less preoccupied with verbal wit and more aware of the gentle and tender possibilities in the Second City situation.

"Phono Pal," the scene to which Sand refers in this conversation, concerns a lonely young man who buys a record designed to teach him how to make friends with people. The voice on the record (Gene Troobnick) makes comments designed to elicit responses from the man, and soon they are "conversing." For a moment, the man has the illusion of enjoying a warm relationship with another, but then the needle hits a scratch in the disc, the illusion dissolves, and the man is aware of his isolation once again.

After leaving Second City, Sand went on to parts on and Off-Broadway, including Neil Simon's *Star-Spangled Girl* and *The Mad Show,* in which he appeared with others from the improvisational community—Linda Lavin, Richard Libertini, and MacIntyre Dixon.

Paul Sand

Sand rejoined Sills in *Story Theatre*, in which he made an enormous personal success. Subsequent to that, he was seen in the TV *Story Theatre* and all but stole the film *The Hot Rock*. In 1974, he starred in his own TV series, *Friends and Lovers*. Working with him on the series were Viola Spolin and Paul Sills, who ran workshops for the cast.

SAND: My mom called UCLA and asked "Who's a good teacher?" and they said, "Viola Spolin." I was brought up by her. I was eleven years old and I just got it every day. And I figured that's all there is to it. I mean, that's what acting *is*. I had no other training. When I saw that's what I wanted to do, then I went to this amazing teacher and she taught me all these amazing things that seemed very simple. Everybody must learn this, I figured. So by the time I got to Paul Sills, I knew what he was talking about.

Q: *Had she formalized her games then?*

SAND: I think they were being developed at the time. I think we were the guinea pigs. I was trying to think what it is, and I guess it's to learn how to have the courage to allow yourself to do anything you feel like, but at the same moment, to be your own director and your own editor and kind of your own judge.

I was always embarrassed telling a joke or a gag or making a face for a laugh, only because that was part of my nature, I guess. And also because Viola would hit anybody —not *hit* anybody, but yell at them if they would do anything . . . is "cheap" the right word? Uh, simple, easy. Yeah, easy. And Paul's the same way. I mean, he would throw people down on the floor and shake them and say, "That's a *joke!* No jokes allowed here!"

Q: *To go back to Viola, do you remember what kind of work you did with her?*

SAND: We did plays a lot. We would rehearse plays mostly. One was *The Clown Who Ran Away*, and I was the clown who ran away.

Q: *How did she rehearse them?*

SAND: She'd have us do gibberish. Then she would pin the curtain up so that just our feet and ankles would show and we wouldn't use any dialogue; we'd have to show with our feet and ankles what was happening. And she would yell out, "Stage Picture!" which means to be conscious of where you are in relationship to everyone else, which creates the balance. During *Story Theatre,* a lot of the reviews amazed me because they wondered who did the choreography. What it was, was we all just *moved,* and we were conscious of each other.

Q: *Where did you go after studying with Viola?*

SAND: I'd seen so many French movies, like *The Children of Paradise*—I'd seen it six or seven times—I wanted to be a French movie star. So when I got out of high school—I was eighteen—I went to France, and I found Marcel Marceau. And I said, "I would like to study with you." Marceau said, "Well, come back in two weeks and audition for me." I met a girl on a boat and we went to Spain, and I saw my first bullfight. There was a young man there who looked just like me, and the lady I was with said, "This must be his first fight." I saw him standing in back of that wooden thing, holding the sort of cape thing in his mouth, and he was just standing there, watching it all. So I came back to Paris and Marceau, and said, "This is called 'The First Fight.'" I stood on the middle of the stage, really going through it. And I became a member of his company.

He's very competitive and very jealous like flamenco dancers are. I'm sorry if he reads this and is upset, but it's true. He did something—mimed being a horse—and I wanted to know how he did it, and he said, "Ah, you would like to know, wouldn't you?" And I said, "Yes, what do you think I'm doing here?" (*Laughs.*) No, I didn't actually say that.

After about a year, I was sitting on a bus, and I was thinking in French and looking out the window and worrying in French, and I suddenly knew, "I've got to get out of here." I had found out I wasn't a mime. I didn't want to be a mime. It was much too restrictive. But I had learned a lot of technique.

I came back to the States and did a lot of sitting on the beach. Then I met Judy Garland. I auditioned for her, dancing and doing mime and stuff to her records. She said, "Do you sing?" I lied and said, "Yeah." And she said, "I'd like you to come and do this thing with me," and so I went and took singing lessons and traveled around with her being her partner doing "A Couple of Swells." I did that for a while. It was terrifying. The comic in the show sort of wanted to do my part, and he was saying all sorts of hideous things to me about how they were going to fire me if I didn't shape up. I was throwing up all the time and weighed about eight pounds. It was just a terrible life. So I quit the business. I did a lot of quitting the business.

Q: *How did you join The Second City?*

SAND: Sills wrote me a letter. He remembered me from when I was a kid. He sent this letter saying, "Do you still do what you did when you were fourteen years old?" I called up Viola and she said, "It's wonderful. He's got this wonderful company. You ought to go." I guess he wanted someone like me to help balance it out. So I went.

I remember walking in and seeing that show, and I saw Severn Darden on the stage. I couldn't believe my eyes, my ears. I thought it was the most wonderful thing I'd ever seen. And I still do. It's amazing! And Barbara Harris! I was *terrified* by Andrew Duncan's intelligence, intimidated by his knowledge of what was going on in the world. I saw all these really bright people up there on the stage from the University of Chicago with real *background*, and I didn't have that sort of background at all.

So I couldn't talk for the first year. I wouldn't open my mouth. I became "the mime." There was this terror because I was really scared because I couldn't compete with the brilliance of Severn Darden and Andrew Duncan and all these people who really knew what was going on. So I kept very quiet until I began to catch on to what moved me. And then when I started sort of creating things that moved me, I started talking. And then I couldn't keep quiet.

Q: *As Second City went on, it got more and more into "people scenes."*

SAND: Yes. I was around for that. When I started talking, I did people stuff. The first time I started talking was "Phono Pal." The mime speaks! I was sitting on the bus and saw someone actually reading *How to Win Friends and Influence People,* and it moved me beyond belief. So I did a scene about that, only I turned the book into a record because it was easier to do onstage. So it was about someone trying to learn how to make friends from a record.

211

There was a period when I couldn't do that scene. When I was tougher, I guess. I didn't care about anybody who was like that, and I sort of tried to kill off that person in me. I didn't want to be that sad and self-pitying and all that stuff.

Oh, I'll tell you the funniest thing that happened. I was onstage, and I was doing something quiet. Probably some mime thing. And I heard somebody in the audience go, "Tsk!" It wrecked me completely. I retired again. I went offstage thinking, "Oh my God, how can I be that bad that somebody was moved to go *tsk!*" That was really the saddest experience. It was so horrible! "I won't go on again. I won't go back onstage." I went to the back of the theater where the audience was drinking and eating, and then somebody went "Tsk!" And I realized it was somebody trying to get, like, a piece of pumpernickel out of his tooth! (*Laughs.*) This one guy was doing it to everybody and everybody was going offstage wrecked! Boy, was I relieved! And I went back out there.

I'm sort of a bad person to talk to about Second City. Yes, I come from Second City, but I didn't really feel like I *got* anything until *Story Theatre.* I didn't feel as though I were in the right show really. I just felt like I didn't really belong. I felt as though I were getting by by the skin of my teeth.

Q: *Why? Because so much of it was so heavily verbal?*

SAND: Yes. They'd have me do stuff that I didn't understand. I would say, "I don't get it. It's not funny." And they would say, "Get out there and do it," and I would do it and the house would fall down with laughter.

Like one—I played a Vietnamese farmer plowing and an American soldier says, "You should learn how to work with a bayonet." Andrew Duncan played him. "You take this bayonet, and you see this dummy here? You do *this* and *that!*" I don't want to, but he makes me, and I kind of begin to like it. I'm tearing into this dummy, tearing it to pieces and he's saying, "Yeah, yeah, go on!" Then I turn and get him. So in this short scene I went from this innocent farmer to a murderer, and I thought, "Oh come on, it's such a heavy message." But it worked.

Paul Sand

During improvised sets, we would take suggestions and the audience would shout out things. Like "a piece of string" or "a sponge diver." One night, someone yelled out "a shaggy dog." We all lived in the neighborhood, half a block from the theater, and Tony Holland said, "I've got a dog at home." So we ran through the snow, and we got it and we put the lights out and whispered to it, "Stay, stay!" And we announced, "And now, on your suggestion, 'shaggy dog'. . . ." And the lights went on and there was this dog in the middle of the stage! And then lights out! (*Laughs.*) We had just looked at each other and run through the snow. Didn't even put a coat on. We *ran* for this gag! It was wonderful.

You know, what the great thing was was that when we were there, there was no ambition to get the hell out and become a big star. We were just *there*. From morning till night, that's all we did was improvise. Barbara and Severn and I would get up at eight o'clock in the morning, we'd eat something, get on the bus, go see the first showing of a Bergman movie, come back, eat lunch, and we'd do the Bergman movie on the stage. And everyone would laugh.

Q: *You said there was no ambition as such at that point, that you were just there and doing the work and living the life. Do you remember when that started changing?*

SAND: We got ambitious. We had incredible publicity.

Q: *You were instantly so successful. Articles in all the magazines, record albums, TV appearances, Los Angeles, Broadway. . . .*

SAND: I remember hardly anything from those days. Even the Broadway thing.

Q: *What happened between Second City and* Story Theatre?

SAND: God, I hardly know. Off-Broadway stuff, love affairs that would wreck me completely, and I would live for love and live for making love. It was just crazy abandoning myself. A lot of that. I was in Rome and in some more love when Sills said that he was going to do something called *Story Theatre* and would I like to do it?

We got to pick the things we wanted to play. Sills said, "Who wants to play what?" There was no fighting over roles. There was even one I didn't want to play—the simpleton role in "The Golden Goose." And they all said, "Play it!" So everybody was happy.

Q: *You just began with the stories as written in the books?*

SAND: Yes, and we stood around like untalented, immovable, impossible, noncreative people who couldn't do anything for over a week. Then we started to slip into it. I don't really understand how. It's amazing.

I had to play a murderer in one scene, and rehearsing, I couldn't catch onto the role. I was doing everything an actor does when he can't get it. I was going, "Shit!" and . . . that's where all my energy was going—into acting like an actor who couldn't catch onto how to do a part. And so Sills comes up to me and says, "Listen, Sand, I'm convinced you've been an actor for at least five thousand years. So you're going to screw around like this and make us all wait for about three weeks, and then you'll get it and you'll be good, and we'll open and you'll get good reviews. So why don't you just do it *now* instead of making us all wait?" And I did. (*Laughs.*)

Q: *Could you talk a bit about Sills as a director? I understand he's not wildly verbal in rehearsal, yet his message comes across.*

SAND: I understand everything he says, and I don't know how. I hear it. I can't look at him when he talks because otherwise I won't understand it. He's saying these words, but you don't really listen to his words.

First, Sills assumes you know how to act. When he calls you up and says, "Do you want to work together?" that's assumed. So all he wants is something wonderful right away.

Q: *That's all?*

SAND: That's all he wants. (*Laughs.*) And it's wonderful to try to do it. "Just be wonderful!" That's one of his rehearsal notes. "Make it better." That's all. Not saying, "I think you should work on the motivation of this" or something. You know all that anyway.

Q: *I hear he has a habit of walking out on rehearsals.*

SAND: Yeah, he'll work for a while, and then he'll get angry and he'll leave and then Viola will come in and she'll nurse us, right? We're her babies and she'll nurse us. And then he'll come back and say, "Yeah, yeah, that's right." They work great together, separately.

Q: *Do you feel a sense of community with the people who came out of the same improvisational background?*

SAND: A few of us are so close you cannot even . . . it's like your mother and your father, your sister and your brother. It's really like that, this closeness.

Q: *A sense of family.*

SAND: Yeah, really. But just very few of us. We all have an underground hot line on the telephone and call each other when we hear about parts. There's some competitiveness with some of the people, but a lot of the time, there's more of a generosity.

You know, by the way, improvisation had a terrible name for a while.

Q: *I didn't know that.*

SAND: Because a lot of people started doing it, only they didn't *really* improvise. They showed off. They pretended to improvise. The carnival types came along and tried to take advantage of it and didn't know what they were doing, and it was cheap and unfunny. I'm not going to name names or anything, but I remember seeing some stuff that came up later that was a drag to watch as an audience. It became ego trips and go to L.A. and Broadway as fast as you can. It became really unattractive, and people didn't want to hire improvisational actors.

Q: *Why?*

SAND: I think it was an ego thing. I think probably a lot of improvisational actors sort of said that their heads were better than what was written down, or they couldn't memorize lines. There was no discipline. Now it's good. Now something really good is happening.

The ideal life-style for all of us would be to be a really good rep company. It would be my perfect dream to always be together. It would be wonderful if we could have a theater like the Mark Taper Forum and work there and touch into any medium we feel like. That would be a great way to spend the rest of your life.

It's *really* amazing to be sitting here doing this! Just amazing! To really be flashing on all of these things. I mean, I have a *past!* I actually have a past now! And I didn't ever . . . that's really interesting. I have a past. You know what I mean? A past that's sort of exciting to talk about and that someone's interested enough to put a tape recorder on to hear about . . . all our pasts.

17.

Alan Arkin

After appearing with Jerry Stiller, Anne Meara, and Nancy Ponder in the second St. Louis Compass, Arkin joined The Second City, where he played a dazzling variety of characters. He appeared in film versions of two scenes he helped create, *That's Me!* and *The Last Mohican*, and made his film-directing debut piloting Bill Alton and Barbara Dana (to whom he is married and with whom he also appeared at Second City) in *T.G.I.F.*, which was based on a scene Alton created with Joan Rivers.

His appearance in the New York Second City led to starring roles on Broadway in *Enter Laughing* and *Luv.* Then he made the switch to films, becoming an instant success with *The Russians Are Coming,* and following this role up with memorable performances in *Wait Until Dark, Catch-22, The Heart Is a Lonely Hunter, Popi, The Last of the Red Hot Lovers, Freebie and the Bean, Rafferty and the Gold Dust Twins, Hearts of the West,* and *The Seven-Percent Solution.*

He has also built an enviable reputation as a director, with stage credits including *Eh?, Rubbers,* and Jules Feiffer's *Little Murders* and *The White House Murder Case,* Off-Broadway, and the original Broadway production of Neil Simon's *The Sunshine Boys.* He made his debut as a feature-film director with the screen version of *Little Murders,* in which he also appeared.

As if all this weren't enough, he writes charming songs with Dana, has a fine singing voice, and plays a number of instruments. His sons, Adam and Matthew, are also talented actors.

Q: *I understand that when you were very young, you worked with Viola Spolin.*

ARKIN: Yes, I was with her for about six months when I was eleven. We'd just moved to L.A. and I had wanted to act since I was about five. My aunt knew Viola and recommended me to her and she gave me a scholarship. I did a production with her called *Once Upon a Clothesline,* which she directed, and my recollection of it was that it was an extraordinarily professional production. I was also in an acting class there, but I don't have the vaguest idea what I did in it.

Q: *How did you get involved with The Compass?*

ARKIN: Well, it was a very fortunate accident. I was at college with David Shepherd's wife and we were both studying drama. I did very good work in college and then nothing happened to me for years after that. David was starting this little group and she recommended me. She kind of pressured him into taking me, I suspect. I don't really know.

I was very good at character, but I don't think I had any sense of comedy at all. It took me about six months of working with David Shepherd before I had any handle on any kind of comedic thing. I had had a background of improvisation in college, but it wasn't the Second City type of improvisation. It was experiential improvisation, the whole purpose of which was to create an experience for the actor—a kind of living experience. The sort of improvisation you're talking about in improvisational theater is the exact opposite of classroom improvisation in that there your intent is to create an experience for the audience. If you do it for yourself, that's terrific. But the main thing is to give something to the audience.

I wasn't with The Compass in Chicago. I was with a subsidiary one David Shepherd started with Anne Meara and Jerry Stiller and a girl named Nancy Ponder. It was not a very happy time for me. I just felt it wasn't a well-matched group. The four of us weren't on the same wavelengths.

We performed in New York at a couple of places and then went to the Crystal Palace in St. Louis. Paul Sills came down from Chicago to look at the group, and that's where I met him for the first time. He told me at that point that if I ever wanted a job in Chicago I should look him up.

Q: *You took him up on that later and joined Second City. How would you compare Sills with Shepherd?*

ARKIN: The main difference was Sills's genius for putting a group of people together who somehow set each other on fire. The other thing that I felt was genius was his ability to mount a show. He would spend twenty-five hours a day at it. When we had enough scenes to put a show together, he would spend days and nights sometimes putting them in order to make a show out of fifteen or sixteen totally disparate pieces of revue sketches.

We did exercises forever with Sills, trying to find new forms that would work. Trying to find new ways of improvising. Trying to break down the acting process into elements and doing exercises for the specific elements. For instance, a scene is made up of who, what, when, where, and how. So we might do scenes for weeks on who. Or do scenes with just the where given.

Q: *What do you remember of your own work at Second City?*

ARKIN: The first couple of nights there I did *terrible* work. Well, it wasn't that bad. It was just that I reverted to what was most easy and comfortable to me and I was turgid and serious onstage for a couple of nights. Then Sills yelled and screamed at me and I shifted gears and things got all right.

I was always playing some kind of extreme character all the way through Second City. I was never myself.

Q: *I know you did a lot of characters with accents, ethnic characters. Sheldon Patinkin told me that in the first show or two you played an Irishman, a Chinese waiter, a Puerto Rican, an Italian . . .*

ARKIN: . . . an old Jew. . . .

Q: *Where did all those characters come from?*

219

ARKIN: Who knows. Movies. (*Laughs.*) It was a way of escaping from myself. It was a way of getting as far away from myself as I possibly could. I did that until *Catch-22*. I was afraid to unleash my own personality on an audience until *Catch-22*, and I only did it then because Nichols really wanted me to do that.

Q: *Do you have any idea why Second City clicked so well?*

ARKIN: I could be very sociological and say it was the beginning of the breakdown of form in the country altogether. It was . . . no, that's not really true. This is when that's happening. (*Laughs.*)

Q: *Did you have any sense of Second City being part of a movement of humor? For instance, were you aware of Lenny Bruce and Mort Sahl?*

ARKIN: Oh yes, I was very aware of them.

Q: *Did their being around help reinforce your work in Chicago?*

ARKIN: No, I was totally wrapped up in it as a way of life. Not in any movement sense. Just the *doing* of it was my entire life for several years. I didn't care what anybody else was doing. The thing I was wrapped up with was making a living in the theater for the first time in my life. And it was such a pleasure. Most days, I would be at the theater sixteen hours a day. I'd go to sleep and then come back to the theater in the morning and stay there until the last show at night. I remember I didn't leave for months and months.

Q: *What about the way you came up with scenes?*

ARKIN: There was no, there is no, there never has been and, as far as I'm concerned, there never could be a formula for how to come up with material. There are, however, formulas for what makes scenes work. Scenes work for very specific reasons.

Q: *Can you think of a specific specific?*

ARKIN: Scenes work when the actors in them are involved in their tasks rather than being funny. Say the director sets up a scene—this is a common one—with a single person onstage doing something and no one else knows what he's doing. Another actor watches for a minute and then he's supposed to go in and join in the experience as soon as he has an idea of what it is the first guy is doing, or maybe he's gotten into the rhythm of the activity and the rhythm will suggest something. But you know the scene is going to die immediately if that second person comes on and says, "What are you doing?" You know that's the end. There's no possible way that scene is going to work because all you'll get is an explanation of what the first guy is doing while the second guy makes wisecracks about the first guy's activity. The only way a scene can work is if the first person comes up with a very strong objective and the second person comes on with a very strong objective and they hang onto very strong ideas of what they want to accomplish in this scene. If two people have very strong objectives, you have to have a scene and it has to work, provided you have actors with some kind of talent.

Q: *How much of the material did you find coming out of the sets improvised in front of the audience?*

ARKIN: Almost all of it. Almost everything I ever did came out of improvisational sets.

Q: *I guess maybe the best-known one you did was the one with Barbara Harris about the beatnik and the girl in the art gallery.*

ARKIN: Yes, that was an improv.

Q: *How did you hold onto what happened so that you could recapture it in other performances? Did you have someone out front with a tape recorder?*

ARKIN: No. What happened after a while was that we all got rather brilliant at being able to re-create what had been completely improvised the night before. Part of the director's job was to sit out front and watch the improvs for scenes to work on and make sure we rehearsed them as the days went by and also to remember what the key elements were in them. But after a while, most of us got to the point where, if the scene really cooked, with just a ten-minute discussion the next day, we could virtually repeat it word-for-word.

Second City was the most competitive situation I've been in in my life.

Q: *I was under the impression there was a great sense of teamwork.*

ARKIN: Yeah, but we fought tooth and nail. The stage was a battlefield. We didn't take it out on each other personally, but it was a battlefield.

Q: *What about Severn?*

ARKIN: What was his way of working? No one will ever be able to tell you, including him. God knows how Severn works! Severn was like working with cybernetic Jell-O. (*Laughs.*) It's like working with an abstraction. He's not like a human being.

Q: *How did you relate to that?*

ARKIN: You couldn't. It was like playing Ping-Pong into a sponge. An enormous wet sponge. Whatever you threw at it would stick. (*Laughs.*) I don't know how to describe him. He's not like any person I've ever known.

Q: *What about Andrew Duncan? He has the reputation of being a great straight man.*

ARKIN: He was a lot more than a straight man. The year when I was in Chicago, sooner or later everybody had a vacation or got sick and was out for a while. When I left the company, people would say, "Jesus, what are we going to do? Arkin's out of the company. It's going to fall apart." Didn't fall apart. They said the same thing with Barbara Harris and with Severn and with Tony Holland, and each time one of us left, the company just picked itself up and rolled along very happily. Then finally Andrew got sick, and the thing almost totally fell apart. He was in a lot of ways the glue that held the whole thing together.

Q: *What about Troobnick?*

ARKIN: Troobnick's major asset to me was that I always thought he was a great clown. I'm not sure he's crazy about that idea. I think he'd rather think of himself as an actor. But I thought he was a brilliant clown.

Q: *And Roger Bowen?*

ARKIN: He was always on sabbatical somewhere, and he would send in material.

Q: *Was there a different way of working on the material he sent? Different from the material that came up in the workshops and sets?*

ARKIN: It tended to be highly technical and needed learning word by word. We didn't do terribly much of that kind of stuff, but every once in a while, just for tone, just to show that we knew how to speak four-syllable words, we'd do something like that.

Q: *Did you know Alan Myerson when he was at Second City?*

Alan Arkin

ARKIN: Yes. I liked him. I got a lot from him. He wasn't there terribly long, but I enjoyed working with him. The only thing I know that he specifically did with me was that he slowed me down. My God, I was very high pressure. I was up until a couple of years ago, actually. I had to have my action, and I blasted. Well, he got me to try slowing my tempo down. Consciously. It was very interesting.

Q: *What scenes do you remember as being your favorites?*

ARKIN: "Phono Pal," the beat scene with Barbara Harris, "Clothes Make the Man" with Tony Holland, a scene in which I played Noah, and there was a scene Gene Troobnick did which used to destroy me every time I saw it called, "How to Get Out of the Army." Oh Christ, it was funny! And I did one with Gene called "Garbage" about an old garbage man and an apprentice he was teaching the trade to. And I did a thing with Severn called "Irish." It was very Joycean. About two old Irishmen sitting talking about the wonderful old days which, as they describe them, you see are horror upon horror. There was a Chinese restaurant scene I loved. There was one I did with Tony Holland about a kids' camp that I loved. He was a kid in camp who didn't want to participate in any of the activities and I was a counselor trying to get him cooking at something.

Q: *It strikes me that a great deal of the Second City material was based on class differences. For instance, the museum piece about the beatnik coming in contact with the very rigid middle-class girl.*

ARKIN: That wasn't class at all. That was temperament. I don't know what he looked like or sounded like, but my character came out of me and I was middle-class and not terribly far away from that character.

Q: *Maybe "class" isn't the right word. Maybe I should have said "culture." The conflict between cultures.*

ARKIN: Yeah, that sounds right. Yeah, there was a lot of that.

Q: *Were you aware of subjects that Second City would not handle?*

ARKIN: The material never got heavily sexual or terribly dirty. It wasn't that it was an issue at any time with anybody, it was just that we kept away from it. I don't know why that should be.

Q: *Much of the material was political. Having begun in the Eisenhower years, did you feel any kind of shift in emphasis when you moved into the Kennedy years?*

ARKIN: No, because all of us were jaundiced enough to see all the paradoxes and foibles of the Kennedy administration. The only thing I felt good about in those days in the Kennedy administration was that there was a kind of emphasis on culture that Washington had never seen before. But aside from that, politically, none of us were really that . . . we felt kind of hopeful about the possibility of what he would represent, but nothing terribly extraordinary materialized as far as we could see.

Q: *Would you say that the basic viewpoint was a kind of skepticism?*

ARKIN: Yeah, very much so.

Q: *Did you ever find that you had any kind of political feedback from what you did?*

ARKIN: The answer to this is that Tony Holland did a monologue at one point on satire and the great influence satire has had on the world. He said, "Here's a letter from Mrs. Jerome Whatsis from West Jesus, North Dakota. She says, 'Dear Sir: I don't know what I would do without satire. When my husband is home sick in bed and my children are screaming for food and there's no money, I thank God there is such a thing as satire!' " And then he said, "Well, this is only one of the influences of satire. We all know how much satire did to stop the rise of Hitler in Germany in 1931." (*Laughs.*)

Q: *If there was the feeling that you were having no political effect. . . .*

ARKIN: No, none of us had any effect. Nobody was paying any attention to us at all, except the audience laughing.

Q: *So, on the one hand you had a sense of social purpose —social commitment in that you were making political statements through the work. . . .*

ARKIN: Yeah.

Q: *On the other hand, at the same time you were very aware that what you were doing wasn't going to make any difference.*

ARKIN: I don't think that was much of an issue. It never got much discussion around me, anyway. I don't think any of us were terribly deluded about the great social impact

224

Alan Arkin

we were having or that the world was going to be a better place because of us.

Q: *It was more a release valve, then?*

ARKIN: Yeah, that was how I perceived it. It was a way of screaming endlessly and getting paid for it.

Q: *Do you have any sense of what you've gotten out of Second City?*

ARKIN: Oh my God, yes! It's been of endless value. Out of all the films I've done, there were maybe one or two in which I haven't done a substantial amount of improvising. What Second City did was give actors a place to fail. Actors have that very infrequently. The audience came to a show knowing, suspecting that thirty or forty percent of what they would see might not work in an improvisational set. You know, we'd first do our set material, and then we'd improvise. The audience would know that a lot of the improvs wouldn't work. So we had not only the opportunity, but were virtually *encouraged* to fail.

Q: *So you were creating a very hip audience in the sense that they understood the process.*

ARKIN: Oh yes, they understood the process and were very excited. It was like verbal-physical jazz. I think we had the same kind of audience which appreciates good jazz musicians. The people who came to see us were obviously upper-middle-class professionals. I think that subtly there was a great sense of pride in us for the audience we were attracting.

One of the things that was extraordinary was that we played in bars, in saloons—drinks were being served all night long—and for the three years I was working with Second City, they were absolutely the most respectful audience I've ever worked for. With all the booze and things that could have been going on in that kind of situation, they were an extraordinarily attentive, quiet, interested, and interesting audience.

I remember we did the *David Susskind Show* once. It got a very high rating and got us tremendous publicity and suddenly everybody knew us. For about a month afterward, we got the mink-coat crowd. They were coming because it was the thing to do. They reacted differently. They were one step below anyone else we had played to in

225

terms of the quickness of their response. We were all furious about it.

Q: *When you went to Second City, you weren't part of the first company....*

ARKIN: Well, I really was. I didn't *start* with the first company. I came in a year after the first company got started. They had vague plans then of sending the company off to New York. My purpose was they wanted to integrate me into the first company long enough so that I would develop the techniques they had learned, and then, when the others went off to New York, I would head a second company. But I fit so well into the first company that they kept me in Chicago long enough to get the second company started, and then they sent me to join the first company in L.A., just as it was about to come into New York.

Q: *So it was taken first to L.A. and then to New York and it was plunked down in a legitimate theater.*

ARKIN: It felt strange and stilted. You didn't get a sense of tone from the audience on Broadway. I remember that it was just a big mass of blackness out there. You'd get a laugh or you wouldn't get a laugh. You didn't have a feel of who was out there particularly. Whereas in a nightclub, even when there were as many as four hundred people out there, you could see them and feel them and get a sense of what kind of a crowd it was.

The Broadway run was also the beginning of the fragmenting of the group, which was very bad. People got singled out for the first time and they were offered other things. A kind of paranoia settled in. Then, when we closed on Broadway and got the club on the Lower East Side, it smoothed out and it got a lot more exciting and more like a group again.

Q: *After that you got the lead in* Enter Laughing *on Broadway, which I've read you weren't wildly overjoyed with.*

ARKIN: Well, it was scary because it was really the first time I'd been away from my crowd and on my own. I felt very closely tied with those people.

Q: *Did you find you were using some of the things you got from Second City in* Enter Laughing?

ARKIN: Not with the words so much. I didn't improvise verbally. But I did an awful lot of physical improvisation. After that I went back to Second City again with Severn and Barbara [Dana].

Q: *That was the one titled* A View from Under the Bridge. *I understand that was put together very quickly.*

ARKIN: Yeah, six days.

Q: *Barbara had never done improvisation before, had she?*

ARKIN: No.

Q: *So at the same time you were rehearsing, you were in a sense having to train her.*

ARKIN: Yeah.

Q: *How did you do that?*

ARKIN: I don't know. (*Laughs.*)

Q: *Do you have any kind of impression of what went on?*

ARKIN: Panic and hysteria. The way we did everything!

Q: *I remember hearing about your takeoff on* After the Fall, *which was playing right down the street.*

ARKIN: We would get screams and bravos. The scene wasn't all that terrific, but everybody hated *After the Fall* so much that they just went crazy over ripping it apart. That was my last experience with Second City.

Q: *After that you did* Luv *on Broadway and* The Russians Are Coming. *I hear that you got* Russians *partly through improvisation.*

ARKIN: Yes, my screen test was improvisational. I insisted on improvising, and they let me do it. I just knew I was going to play a Russian seaman, except I couldn't play a seaman because I didn't know any naval terms. So I played a Russian seaman who had just become a seaman and up till then had been a musician. And I got the part.

Q: *To get to your directing, I saw in some of the old* Variety *reviews of Second City that you were given credit for directing some of the shows.*

ARKIN: Jesus, I don't even remember. Oh yeah, I *did* direct for a while. But that was really just a high-class stage-managing job. I didn't really direct Second City. I was the titular head for a while, but it didn't really amount to anything. I was too much into acting in the company to have an outside eye of what was going on.

Q: *What do you consider your first real directing job?*

ARKIN: The first thing I directed was *Eh?* Off-Broadway with Dustin Hoffman, Elizabeth Wilson, and Dana Elcar, who had been with The Compass, I think. Directing was never anything I had as a goal. It's nothing I ever thought about. I never *dreamed* of being a director. The only thing I ever wanted to do was act. I directed *Eh?* because someone asked me to, and I was just helping out some friends. And when that was successful, I got asked to do other things and I started to enjoy it a lot.

I don't feel like I have anything emotional at stake when I direct. It's a very pure thing for me to do, unlike acting, where I have a lot of ancient neurotic patterns that aren't very strong anymore but still have hooks in me every once in a while. I don't feel like I have any of that when I'm directing. I feel I'm in service to the play and the actors.

When I direct, I work the same way I work for acting— I work from general concepts. Long thematic lines. I'm very conscious of details, but not until the moment I'm doing them. My main concern is that I have a very good grasp on what I want the whole event of the play to be about.

Q: *Do you draw on improvisational techniques much when you direct?*

ARKIN: I don't use improvisation in a straight play unless the actors are in a hole and can't get out of it. Then I'll improvise, if they want to. If they don't, then I'll just keep talking.

Q: *What value do you find in using improvisation when directing actors in prewritten parts?*

ARKIN: Sometimes a person or a group of people will not understand what a scene is about. I can talk till I'm blue in the face and they still won't understand organically what the scene is about. So then what I'll do is I'll go off for ten or fifteen minutes and try to figure out a situation I can put them in, an improvisation that will paraphrase the situation in the play, so that after a few minutes of playing the improv, what I'm getting at will become crystal clear.

Q: *Can you give an example?*

ARKIN: The first scene in *Little Murders,* the play, gave the actors terrible problems. After we got past the first

228

scene, everything was fine. But the first scene was murder for them, and the reason it was murder was because the actors were performing for someone onstage. It was a scene where a girl was bringing home her boyfriend to meet her family and they were all performing for him, because that's what people do in a social situation—they put on performances. But actors, particularly if they're good actors, don't like to *perform* onstage.

So I created a situation which was not very far from this, but they didn't realize how close it was. I said, "We're going to do an improvisation. You're another family entirely and you've been chosen Family of the Year by President Johnson"—he was President at the time—"and President Johnson is coming to visit you. You're preparing dinner for him and it's like it's going to be the night of your lives." And so they prepared, and it was a big party, and then I had Fred Willard—who was playing Alfred, the boyfriend—come in and just not say anything. He was President Johnson and he didn't say anything. After a few minutes, the family got more and more hysterical and, in an attempt to get him to join in the festivities, they began putting on this incredible, hysterical regalia. After about four or five minutes of that, they all started laughing hysterically and understood what they were doing and what it was they had to do in the scene in the play. From then on they could have a terrific time with it and it worked.

Q: *I heard also that there was a lot of this in the rehearsals for* The White House Murder Case. *Was it a conscious decision to use all those Second City and Committee people?*

ARKIN: Oh yeah. I mean those are my favorite actors. I love these guys. I could work with them forever.

Q: *This gets to the question of what it is about the Second City actor that makes him someone you'd want to use.*

ARKIN: There's something that's special about the best ten or twelve Second City actors and that is they don't work from their own parts. They work from the whole event. They'll read a play and they'll be interested in the play as an event and fit themselves in immediately. They'll know what their roles are in that event and be able to play them with very little effort. If I'm directing, I can say one sentence to them and from that one sentence they'll be able to go for twenty minutes. Whereas ninety-nine percent of the other actors I know in the world look at a play and are concerned only with what their part is. It becomes twenty times as much work because they don't know what the whole picture is. If you look at the whole picture, then your part in it—your reason for being connected with it—becomes quite clear. Also, in the case of *The White House Murder Case,* they'd worked with each other before and knew how each other worked. Paul Dooley, Andrew Duncan, Tony Holland, Peter Bonerz, J. J. Barry—these are people who had had long experience in keeping something alive as a group.

Q: *Do you find that Second City actors are more trusting actors?*

ARKIN: In what sense?

Q: *In the sense that when you're in that kind of improvisational situation, it isn't the kind of theater in which when someone gives you a cue you have a preset line to respond with. So, because the lines aren't set and you're so dependent on the other actors, you have to really listen, you have to react, and you have to trust the instincts of the other actors.*

ARKIN: Right. Every once in a while you run into an actor who can do that and you say, "Hey, that's a Second City actor," even though he never worked with Second City. Like Jimmy Caan is that kind of actor. Fluid and loose and available.

Q: *I remember when you were shooting* Catch-22, *I looked at the list of the people who were in that and there were so many people from Second City or the like. . . .*

ARKIN: Yeah, but that was word for word, period for period, comma for comma. It's the way Mike wanted it.

Q: *When you were down there, because so many of you were from the same background, was there much of a sense of. . . .*

ARKIN: There was a great sense of catatonia from everybody involved. It was an awful experience.

Q: *That's funny. At the time I thought that you must be having a hell of a time, that off-camera everybody was improvising like crazy.*

ARKIN: Nobody had a good time on- or off-camera.

Alan Arkin

Q: *Would you ever consider going back to doing something like Second City again for a refresher?*

ARKIN: I'd die first. It was so taxing emotionally. Grueling.

18.

Sheldon Patinkin

As did so many others, Sheldon Patinkin met and first worked with Sills and Shepherd when a student at the University of Chicago. He continued with them, working as a jack-of-all-trades with Playwrights, then, after a spell as a teacher, returned to theater as business manager of The Second City, subsequently becoming director and, for a while, part-owner.

After leaving The Second City in 1968, he free-lanced in theater, film, and television in various capacities. One of his more interesting credits was as director of "background improvisations" for Irvin Kershner's *Loving,* in which capacity he worked with Second City alumni Andrew Duncan, Mina Kolb, and Martin Harvey Friedberg to create supplementary material to give the picture added texture. He also wrote two as-yet-unproduced screenplays with Alan Arkin and ran an excellent improvisational workshop in New York (one of his students was Adam Arkin).

He moved to Toronto after recording the main body of this chapter and directed the Toronto Second City for a year. He is now one of Toronto's busiest directors of plays and cabaret entertainments. He has worked on *Second City T.V.* as a writer and editor.

PATINKIN: I was sixteen years old, in my second year

232

at the University of Chicago. My first year, I didn't do any theater work at all, just tried to get my bearings. My second year, I discovered I desperately needed an escape and went into the University Theatre, which Paul sort of controlled. It was around that time he started running his workshops in the games. What he was really doing with those workshops was training us to become a company, giving us a common terminology and work process. He was also helping us in plays we were doing that he wasn't directing. He would come and give notes to us after performances, which, of course, any director would *kill* another director for doing. He was protecting his investment in us. At the same time—and this I didn't know then—he was grooming me as his assistant. I don't know if he knew it either. We just sort of grew together. I was his assistant director for the production he did of Brecht's *Caucasian Chalk Circle*. It was an extraordinary production. It was essentially the same production which opened Playwrights Theatre Club.

The length of the rehearsal for a play at Playwrights was determined by the success of the previous play. We originally planned that each would run two weeks. But we rehearsed *Volpone* in one week because the play we put on before that was an original by Paul Sills called *The Coming of Bildad*. It was directed by David Shepherd and was one of the maybe dozen worst plays ever written. And I still have a copy of it, Paul! *Volpone* was just as bad as Paul's play. We had no more business doing *Volpone* than we had cutting off our heads. It was insanity to do that play. And in a week! We were children!

Playwrights existed for two years. Then the place was closed down by the fire department.

Q: *Did the group feel that the closing had anything to do with disapproval of your politics?*

PATINKIN: Yes, we were very left-wing. After all, we did Brecht. This was February of 1955. We were from the U. of C., and the U. of C. was pinko. It was. You could sign up for the Communist Party anywhere you wanted at the University of Chicago. There were petitions and stuff around all the time. Actually, we weren't all that political at Playwrights, except for David Shepherd. I mean, we were liberals, I suppose. I was a Youth for Wallace in high school. (Henry Wallace, that is.) But politics didn't enter into it until The Compass, which was an attempt to create a political cabaret theater.

Q: *You weren't part of Compass.*

PATINKIN: No. I quit Playwrights at the beginning of 1955 after an argument with David, and, except for social things and going to see performances, I had no contact with the group until I started working at The Second City six years later, around the end of 1960. Second City had been open about a year by then.

When it first opened, they did two shows a night, Tuesday through Thursday and Sunday, and improvised after the second show. On Friday they did two shows and no improvs. And Saturday they did *three* shows and no improvs. That was an incredible ordeal. I remember about a year after it opened, one night there were a few empty seats at a second show, the first time there'd been any in a long, long time. Paul said, "See that? We're a failure!" As time went on, we got more empty seats for the second show, so we eventually shifted the schedule so that if there were X number of reservations for the second show, we would do the show. If there were less, we'd do only the first show, then a set of improvs, and charge a buck rather than full price for the people who'd reserved for the second show.

Most of the material originated in the improvs done in front of the audience. If an improv looked promising, we'd pull it into a rehearsal and work on it, and then put it into the improv set again to find out how it was working, and then pull it back into rehearsal. Finally, it would become part of the set show. That was our work process.

For instance, "Museum Piece," the famous scene Alan Arkin and Barbara Harris did set in the art museum, was first improvised in front of an audience. It was spectacular the first time. Unfortunately, in those days they didn't tape the sets, so they lost it and had to go back to scratch. It took three weeks of screaming, cursing, and tearing hair to get it back again.

It's exciting building material that way. Some of the pieces, though, were actually constructed in rehearsal. Especially a lot of the longer pieces.

Q: *Did you get much reaction to your political material?*

PATINKIN: Oh well, our audiences already agreed with us, so we didn't have to try to convince them. The one thing the audience got turned off by was being hit over the head. Anything that hits you over the head is saying, "We're better than you." They would resent that, and so we would lose them for two or three shows, or sometimes forever if the show was bad enough. There was one full-evening piece called *My Friend Art Is Dead* we did from a scenario. It was terrible. It was about scientists and protestors and bullshit, the most heavy-handed bullshit imaginable. It was Paul saying we would never cop out. It just hit the audience over the head for an hour and a half.

The other thing the audience resented was when the show got too dumb, which was frequently the problem during the early days of J. J. Barry, Marty Friedberg, and Burt Heyman. That was later. In fact, it got so dumb at one point that I brought David Steinberg back for a little bit to bring back some smarts. David's smart as all hell.

Q: *We were talking about the long pieces.*

PATINKIN: There were a few full-act pieces. *Peep Show for Conventioneers* was about two conventioneers coming to a house thinking they're going to find prostitutes, and what they find is room after room fulfilling their real fantasies—like being in a Salem ad. Paul's last piece at Second City was called *The Trip*. It was about a family birthday party where suddenly Timothy Leary appears and feeds them acid. It was interesting, but it wasn't very good. Most of our audiences were bored by it. The one full-act piece I did was also a flop. It was a musical called *The Super-Humans and I*. We did it about a year before the Broadway musical about Superman. We had a lot of fun doing it, but it was too dumb and we lost a lot of money on it.

The one long piece I love that came out of improvising in rehearsal, as opposed to finding it first in a set, was a piece called "Family Reunion." It was about a boy from a small town in downstate Illinois who has moved to Chicago. His parents and older brother come up for a funeral and visit his apartment afterwards. It was a scene about him trying to tell his country family that he was homosexual and about their not hearing it. It was both very funny and very painful. That was with Del Close, Jack Burns, Ann Elder, and Dick Schaal. It was in the first show I directed. They came to me with this idea they had tried doing once before with Paul two years earlier. They had the premise and the characters. It sounded too risky to try it in front of an audience, so we improvised it in rehearsal. I think it's still my favorite Second City scene. It's a one-act play.

If you were truly improvising in the improv sets (sometimes we copped out), it was mandatory you frame the improvisations with a certain amount of blackouts you knew worked, or works-in-progress that were already working well enough. Because, if an improvisation bombs, you want to have something to pick the audience back up again. I'd say if one out of four or five improvisations worked at all, it was terrific. And our audience *knew* that. The regular audience for the improvs knew the chances were good they were going to see a night of disaster.

I remember one night Barbara and Alan improvised a scene in which she was a social worker visiting a condemned man in his prison cell. It went on for twenty-five minutes and nobody could find a way to end it. (*Laughs.*) It was one of the two worst scenes I've ever seen.

The other one also had Alan in it. This was long after he was already a movie star. He came back to the New York Second City one night, and we coaxed him into going into the set. He did a scene with Steinberg. Well, Alan was a little rusty, and Steinberg was totally into a competitive thing. Alan is not competitive onstage, ever, at all. He doesn't believe in that. He understands that to be competitive is to destroy what it is to be onstage with other people, to truly act. Anyway, the scene ended with Alan just walking off and leaving David alone onstage.

That was Severn's first introduction to The Compass, too. I don't know this firsthand, but I've heard it from enough people to know it's true. The first time he went onstage at Compass, he was doing a scene with Elaine and she walked off and left him alone. (*Laughs.*)

Some of the best scenes were about people of different orientations colliding, such as "Museum Piece" and "Family Reunion." One of the scenes we took from The Compass and redid for Second City was called "The Exurbanites," which was about a couple of would-be newcomers to the intellectual heap and their two guests who are dreadful snobs. The party is interrupted by the arrival of a truck driver who has taken literally the host's suggestion, "Why don't you stop in sometime if you're in the neighborhood?"

And the truck driver just behaves like a truck driver in the middle of all these people as they quote Gerard Manley Hopkins and listen to Vivaldi. That was about a social clash, except it was a three-way clash because the people who were giving the party were a step below the guests in the socioeconomic scale.

When Second City began, all over town people were getting together to have discussions about the great books. So we had our great-books group. There were a number of versions of that scene. They discussed *Das Kapital* and *Crime and Punishment* at different times, but *Oedipus* worked best. Part of the fun of the scene was to see how these different people with different backgrounds misunderstood the book under discussion in different ways. Barbara played Miss Belden Stratford, who was quite vacant but had a store of intellectual-sounding words she'd throw in. Mina was Stella Dallas with a new hat and not a brain cell working. Severn was Genghis F. X. Khan with a Southern accent and a mother fixation. Andrew was an ad man with a dreadful case of the smarts. Gene was the discussion leader faced with the chore of trying to get a serious discussion out of these people.

Then there was a piece, which I believe was invented by Roger Bowen, which was about whether *Jack and the Beanstalk* should be banned from grammar school shelves. Mina was the president of the PTA, a suburban housewife (she was never used enough or in great enough variety), and she introduced two experts, one of whom was a psychologist and the other an expert on Marx. Of course, the psychologist gave the story a Freudian interpretation, and the other expert gave it a Marxist analysis. It was a very funny piece and it made the point that it *is* possible to see *Jack and the Beanstalk* as either a Marxist or Freudian parable. By the end, they had proved their points so well that it was decided that it was a very dirty, subversive book, indeed, and had to be kept from schoolchildren.

Q: *A lot of the material seemed to be about the misapplication of "intellect."*

PATINKIN: While we had that original spurt of creativity, yes. Later we had scenes between J.J. and Marty about selling vacuum cleaners. Subtext was a word they'd never heard of. God, what a piece that was! One of the most embarrassing things in my life was to have that piece in a show with my name on it! J.J. was a department store man and Marty was a customer who had bought a faulty vacuum cleaner and was trying to return it. J.J. spent the scene trying to prove to him that he couldn't return it because the machine was perfectly good. It was dumber than The Three Stooges. Today, if I'm working with them, when I want to shut them up or when they're getting too big for their britches, I say, "Oh, go do 'Vacuum Cleaner' and leave me alone!" And they shut up instantly.

There were always two or three pieces in every show I didn't like. I don't think you can possibly like every piece in any revue ever done. Certainly the director can't possibly like every scene. Not when you've got to turn out four shows a year. Paul wasn't satisfied with a show unless he liked seventy-five or eighty-five percent of the material or more. There were periods when I was pretty happy if I liked sixty-five percent.

Q: *How did you become the director at Second City?*

PATINKIN: I was Paul's assistant, and one day during rehearsal, Paul got fed up with the actors and stormed out for the umpteen millionth time. On his way out, he turned to me and said, "See what you can do with them, Sheldon." When the rehearsal was over, I called Bernie and said, "Have you heard from Paul? He never came back to rehearsal." Bernie said, "He's on his way to New York." I said, "What are you talking about?" and Bernie said, "You're directing now."

By the time I started directing Second City, it had become a place where actors came to become stars. That happened very quickly to Second City, within two years of the opening. I rarely had a company that knew how to play the games or was willing to learn. They didn't come thinking, "I want to learn how to do this kind of work," but, "I want to be discovered here."

You know, there were some awfully bad performances in the early days, but it didn't matter because the material was so good and the energy was so fantastic. Oh, back then we were really good. We got terrible and sometimes got pretty good again and sometimes stayed terrible for a long time and sometimes stayed good for a long time. Basically, when we were good was pretty directly related to the length of time that company had been together.

Every time we had to change the cast, it was terrible for a good six months. Three times Bernie made the same mistake, moving entire companies to New York so that they would be replaced in Chicago by entirely new people. Now, the first time he did that, they were replaced by people who had been around with us all the way back to Playwrights—like Tony Holland. And Alan stayed for a little while as a holdover to help. Even so, the second company's first show was dreadful, the first really bad one done at Second City. It took a couple of shows for that company to get into shape.

Later, toward the end of the time I was directing, I'd beg and plead to get one of the old Second City actors to come back for just a few months, just to have somebody there who knew what he was doing to help the others learn how to do it. That was when we got Steinberg back for three months. He pulled us out of a jam.

Steinberg was box office in Chicago. There were a few actors who were box office in Chicago: Barbara, Severn, David, and J.J. Alan didn't become box office until New York. Some of the original Second City people would be box office today because they were original Second City people, though they mightn't have been box office at the time they were first in the company. But Severn, Barbara, David, and J.J. were celebrities during the time they were actually in the company.

When it came to getting new people for the company, we had two choices. We would either go with absolutely unseasoned beginners, train them a bit, and throw them on, which usually turned out disastrously, or we would take seasoned nightclub performers and try to teach them to work our way, which didn't always work. Nor did taking actors and trying to make them funny. So I started the touring company, I think in 1965. We didn't want to have to keep going to New York to find new talent, bringing them back to Chicago to train them, and then having them get good enough to leave for New York again. I hired Viola Spolin to run the workshops and hired Jo Forsberg to be her assistant. Eventually I had to fire Viola because she was really saying terrible things—justified though they may have been—and creating a lot of dissension about the way the place was being run. She hated the way Bernie and I were doing things and said so all the time.

Q: *What were you doing that she hated?*

PATINKIN: By that time, Second City was just a commercial venture. There wasn't any art about it. And the games, if they were being used at all, were being used badly and incorrectly.

Q: *Let's talk about Paul.*

PATINKIN: I have to say a few things first to color the things that I'll say. I love Paul very much and respect his talent as much as anybody I've ever met. He has also given me more hellish times in my life than anyone who is not a relative. And I have been just as rotten to him.

Q: *What was he like in the early days? Was he pretty much a no-nonsense guy, or was he fun to be around?*

PATINKIN: Mostly sitting around talking about serious things seriously. I guess we were all mostly like that, including Bernie. We're not very good at small talk and we don't usually sit around telling jokes. And gossip lasts for only a little while. So we spent a lot of time talking about acting, theory, plays, playwrights, and theater in general, and ideas and politics and literature. The problem with all of this is that Paul is basically a nonverbal person when he's directing. Most of his directing is through a series of grunts and groans and peculiar outpourings of language. You either learn to interpret it or find someone to interpret for you. Or quit.

Q: *He's obviously got a strong quality of leadership or he wouldn't have been able to assemble such a loyal band.*

PATINKIN: The word that's used today is charisma. He had then and has now, though less often—we do get old, older (oh, we were so young!)—a drive, and excitement about what he knew and where he was going. And an almost dangerous sense of his personal magnetism that either turned people on or repulsed them. He's got an incredible ego, but with a talent to match it.

He's a fucking genius, and there isn't anybody from all of this who doesn't know that, whether they love him or hate him.

I've seen several stages of Paul. The first stage I met him in was what led him to Playwrights and its destruction.

The second stage was The Compass, the proletariat improvisational theater stage, which was meant to reflect the community that it was in, and did reflect the university area to a very large extent. Then he went off on his Fulbright. I lost touch with him for a long time, what with his Fulbright and coming back to Compass and the Studebaker. That was also the time he was married to Barbara.

When I came back in contact with Paul again, he was in the Second City bag. Actually, it was a year after Second City had started and he was getting out of the Second City bag. He was no longer married then. He was older, more assured. He was crazier. He had a violent temper. He was already getting bored with Second City.

Q: *What happened from there?*

PATINKIN: He gradually descended or ascended to St. Paul. That was when he started walking out on things. The day of the opening of Second City on Broadway, after the rehearsal he told the actors they were all full of shit and couldn't possibly do it and walked out. He got an opening-night performance out of them by putting them in a rage. (*Laughs.*) Somewhere I have tapes of when we were doing the improvised musical version of *Beggar's Opera, Big Deal.* When we were rehearsing. I would listen to the tapes to catch whatever came out of rehearsal each day, and I have at least three three-hour tapes containing anywhere from two-thirds to three-quarters of Paul screaming. Just screaming. When he gets to that stage, it means he's had it.

Q: *When he's working really well, he doesn't say much at all?*

PATINKIN: No, he doesn't need to. But he was at Second City for several years after that, hating it more and more.

Then he went into his whole mystical thing and moved back to Chicago to form a commune. I think this was 1966. It never really took shape. That was Game Theatre time. I was so turned off by that Paul that I really didn't get to know him well in that stage. He was coming on like St. Paul and people were following him, worshiping him. . . .

After Paul and Viola were no longer with Second City, they opened Game Theatre fairly nearby. The audience was asked to improvise, to play the games. They discovered very quickly that people usually came only once unless they wanted to play the games. Because the games are not an end unto themselves. They are not a form of entertainment.

Q: *Unless you're involved.*

PATINKIN: But it's not very interesting to watch. So it pretty much turned into a workshop for the people who came regularly.

After that came the Harper Theatre. Paul and I decided we wanted to work on a text and play games with a text. Which doesn't mean what most people think it means. They think that when you improvise or play games on the text that you take the circumstance and improvise dialogue as your character or invent new circumstances for the characters to be in. That's all good stuff, too, but that is not what we did for that year we were in workshop on *The Cherry Orchard*. We played the games using the dialogue written by Chekhov. For instance, we played "Contact," which is one of the best games to play on text. An enormous amount of subtext comes out of trying to figure out another way of touching the other person in a scene. It's very valuable.

Bernie and Paul and I were all involved in the Harper. It was a place where we were going to do plays, and we spent a year training a company. It turned out to be one of the more monumental disasters of the world.

The problem was Paul insisted on fucking *acting!* And he's a terrible actor! He wouldn't come into the group unless he were allowed to act, and he insisted on playing the lead in our opening play, which was a choice Bernie and Paul made against my better judgment. *The Deer Park* by Norman Mailer. At its best, our audience was going to hate it. And it wasn't at its best. It was at its fucking *worst!* Paul wouldn't let me *direct!* He was in a phase of insisting there be no directors, just some peculiar outside eye. I had to sneak direction to the other actors. We destroyed that theater in two months!

Q: *Has he tried acting since?*

PATINKIN: No, the motherfucker took it all out on me! That was in the latter part of '67. It's too bad because it screwed up our friendship for a long while.

Paul is a great director when he's being constructive.

242

The problem with Paul, and you'll hear this from everyone including Paul, is that he destroys something when he sees that it's going to work. I don't want to go into the psychology of why. But as soon as he sees that something will or will not work or what it's going to be when he gets there, he loses interest. So he doesn't finish things. As soon as he sees what the realization could be, he loses interest in doing it. I spent a lot of my time, till when I became a director, finishing off Paul's work. That's how I learned to be a director, finishing off what he didn't feel like going on with.

I didn't know shit most of the time I was at Second City. I ruined a lot of good stuff there. They really threw in an absolute beginner as the director of Second City.

Q: *Who would have been more qualified to take over?*

PATINKIN: No one. I don't feel they made a mistake. It was a big chance and I didn't let them down. I kept the place open and going and as successful as it had been for several years. And most of the shows I did were entertaining, if not anything deep or particularly important.

I'm not much of a satirist, you know. I guess I'm not all that angry. More hurt, or something Jewish like that. The true satiric content of Second City was probably at its lowest when I was the director.

19.

Paul Mazursky

Before going to Broadway, the original Second City troupe played the Ivar Theatre in Los Angeles. When they left the Ivar, a replacement troupe was formed to continue the run in Los Angeles. Paul Mazursky and Larry Tucker were asked to head this new company.

After that engagement ended, Mazursky was associated with Tucker on a number of other improvisational projects, none of which particularly took root. But the improvisational approach affected their subsequent work, which included developing the *The Monkees* (many episodes of which were directed by ex-Premise player James Frawley) and writing for *The Danny Kaye Show* and Jay Ward of "Rocky and Bullwinkle" fame.

They really hit their stride, however, in movies. First came the script for *I Love You, Alice B. Toklas*, then the scripts for *Bob & Carol & Ted & Alice* and *Alex in Wonderland*, both of which Mazursky directed. (The part of Donald Sutherland's mother in *Alex*, incidentally, was played by Viola Spolin.) Since then, Mazursky has gone his own way, writing and directing *Blume in Love* and *Next Stop, Greenwich Village* and co-writing and directing *Harry and Tonto*. His latest film is *An Unmarried Woman*, with Jill Clayburgh, Alan Bates, and Andrew Duncan.

Paul Mazursky

MAZURSKY: I got out of college in 1951. I was studying with Lee Strasberg and Paul Mann and acting on TV, and was in a couple of films. I was in a movie called *The Blackboard Jungle* in 1954, and around that time I was also doing this nightclub act with a fellow named Herb Hartig called Igor and H at places like the Village Vanguard and One Fifth Avenue. So I was into nightclub comedy as an act, but not improvisation. The only improvisation I was into was Method-acting-type improvisation. In the Method, if an actor is working on a scene and gets blocked somehow, in order to get through the block and get to the truth of the scene, sometimes he will resort to improvising the scene in his own words. But that's something other than what you're interested in.

Herb and I did work with Rose and Larry Arrick and a couple of other people whose names I don't remember. The idea was to do a nightclub act, a form of Compass. We did improvisational workshops for a while, trying to come up with material, and then we performed it one night in some club in New York and that was the end of the whole thing. This was probably about 1955 or '56. I think Arrick had already worked with The Compass in Chicago.

After that I started doing my nightclub act as a single. That took me to Chicago, where I worked at a club called the Gate of Horn. Howard Alk and Paul Sills both worked at this club in some technical capacity. I remember around this time they were running some improv sessions with Barbara Harris and Severn Darden and a few other people.

Then I moved to L.A. in 1959. I was doing my comedy act in a place called Cosmo Alley and I got a phone call from either Paul or Howard—I can't remember which—who said they were starting a thing called Second City and they wanted me to join them. I said, "I just moved out here with my wife and my baby and I have no money. How much can you afford to pay?" Well, they had no money, either, and it turned out I couldn't do it.

The next thing I knew this thing was getting tremendous attention and I said to myself, "Maybe I made a terrible mistake. I should have gone. Maybe I would have done what I can do well." At the time I was struggling in L.A. as an actor. The nightclub comedy thing was getting less and less intriguing because when you work clubs as a solo comic, some of the places you're forced to work are just terrible. I finally said, "The hell with that. I'm not going to do that anymore." I was just going to be an actor.

A year or so after that, Second City came to L.A. and ran for several months at the Ivar Theatre. Their plan was to go from there to New York. While the show was running at night they were also holding workshops in the daytime and I and others would get up with them. I think they were probably looking to see who could take over the show in L.A. after they left. You wouldn't call them auditions, but there were a lot of people there just walking up and taking turns and doing this kind of improvisation.

What happened is they asked Larry Tucker and me to take over the new company. We had a very bizarre group, very unlike the people from the original Second City. They had a more intellectual bent. We had more show-businessy people. When we improvised in the latter half of the show, there was very little reference to Tolstoy, Dostoevski and Kierkegaard. It was more Mayor Yorty, the L.A. Rams, and Errol Flynn.

We took over all of the Chicago troupe's set pieces and we did well. We tried to keep their stuff intact. We changed words here and there, but basically we treated it as if it were written material.

After about a month of this, I began to feel very frustrated. So did Larry. So we started coming up with our own set pieces.

The first good sketch that we came up with ourselves was one in which I played a salesman trying to sell a fallout shelter to Larry. We eventually did it on a couple of TV shows and, in my opinion, it was as good as anything Second City ever did.

We did another scene in which I played Abe Tijuana, an agent who goes out looking for a great flamenco dancer. I come into a club. Ed Peck played the owner of the club and Larry Tucker, who is a very heavy man—at the time he weighed over four hundred pounds—played a waiter whose name was Ani Maal. Anyway, someone gets up and does a flamenco act and I say it's terrible. "I want real flamenco," I say. "I want purity, beauty!" And I throw a cigarette over my shoulder, and as it lands on the floor behind me, Larry, who is huge and wearing a red apron, goes like this. (*He gets up and pulverizes an imaginary cigarette with a resounding stomp.*) The audience sees this, but my back is to him as I'm facing the audience. And when I hear that stomp, I do a take which would get a huge laugh. Then I'd turn around and take out my cigarettes and throw them on the floor and he'd start stomping away at them to the music. He becomes a great flamenco star, and the rest of the scene is about his rise and fall. It was really a great sketch. It got enormous laughs.

We came up with about twenty minutes of material that was very good and we were very frustrated because there were no kudos, no attention, no reviews—none of that great thrill of being discovered. It was just fun to do.

Then the show closed and Larry and I decided to open our own show and call it Third City. We got another theater, the LeGrande, which was run by a funny guy here in Hollywood who didn't understand what the hell we were doing. We really should have done it in Westwood near UCLA so that we could have had the kind of thing Second City had with the University of Chicago. It would have been a thrill to play to a college audience. The material would probably have been more satiric. The show we did still included three or four key Second City pieces, but fifty to seventy-five percent of the material was ours. I remember Howard Alk and a couple of the others from Second City came by and saw us, and I think they liked the show.

We did it for several months, and then Gene Norman, who owned a club called the Interlude I had worked in as a stand-up comic, came to Larry and me and said that he wanted to put on a revue there and shake things up. So we worked out a deal and tried to come up with a title. What we ended up with was *Wild, Wicked World*, which has to be the single worst title in the history of theater. It was a compromise between us and Gene's commercial sense of what would go on Sunset Boulevard. I guess we were lucky. It might have ended up being called *Wild, Wicked Tits*.

We put together that show in two weeks. It included my first film, *Last Year at Malibu*, which was a parody of Alain Resnais and the New Wave that I shot in a couple of weekends. Vic Morrow directed. In this revue we had the best of our Third City stuff plus a couple of new sketches Larry and I improvised with Joyce Van Patten, who was in the company and was terrific.

Joyce and I did one called "Divorce" about two people who meet at the zoo. They're both looking at the monkeys and they get to talking to each other, and they find out that they're both divorced. Then, within the six or seven minutes of the sketch, they go through all the emotions of first love, marriage, alienation, hatred, and then they leave each other—all in front of the cage at the zoo. It was really a good sketch. We found its rough shape improvising one afternoon, then we did it for an audience and it just worked. That's the wild thing about improvisation—you can improvise for ten years and come up with almost nothing, or, like that (*snaps his fingers*) your subconscious will start to work and you'll come up with something fabulous that you can then clean up and work on and perfect into a set piece.

Another thing we used to do was, we'd take a suggestion from the audience and improvise a madrigal on it. Say we got "Mayor Yorty" as a suggestion. We'd put scarves around our necks and sing, "Fa-la-la-la-la la-la la-la. I know a girl, she lives in Douerty/Boy, does she like Mayor Yorty/Fa-la-la-la-la. . . ." Unbelievable. Just any kind of nonsense, but the audiences liked it. I'd say that one out of twenty times we came up with a good one. We had a very good piano player named Ellsworth Millburn who contributed a lot of notions and ideas to our work. Later he went on to work with The Committee.

Edie Adams came in and saw us in *Wild, Wicked World*. This was after Ernie Kovacs had died. She was going to open in Vegas but she didn't have an act. So she and her manager got the idea that she would take Larry Tucker, Alan Seuss—who was with us, too—and me with her to Vegas and we would do our material with her playing the parts Joyce Van Patten did. So we put together a deal and it finally came down to doing it one night so that Groucho Marx could see it. That was a big thrill. Groucho loved it. I think he felt akin to our work in a way.

So then we did the act in Vegas. We played the big room at the Riviera, which is thirty million people all eating. It's very difficult to reach those people. You've got to do bangers there like, "The best way not to lose money in Vegas is to step off the plane and into a propeller." But we were doing Second City type of material and we bombed. Only the band laughed. Sweat was pouring out of my body. You know, we knew it was bombing, but we knew it so well that it got to the point we weren't even frightened. After three performances they bought out our contract and said to Edie she'd better do her own act.

Another act we had was called The Munchkins, which Larry and I were going to take on a college tour along with Harvey Korman and Joyce. It was an accumulation of scenes from Third City. We did two college performances and they liked it. But we couldn't get enough money out of it, so we dropped it.

Q: *Your talking about the experience with Edie Adams made me flash on an absurd idea—of Paul Sills doing a Vegas show.*

MAZURSKY: No, but you see, I think he should do it. You have to force yourself to the unique test, and I would love to see Paul exposed to that. Not his making another class from Berkeley laugh, but reaching the mass, to see what would happen to him with his talent and sensibility. Something happens when you have to do what Shakespeare was forced to do.

Q: *You mean make the groundlings happy?*

MAZURSKY: He had to do it for everybody, and the great works come out of that somehow.

Not that all of the Second City stuff was really what you would call deep humor. Some of it was and some wasn't. But some of it was like what Bob Hope would do when he toured for the troops—he'd toss in references to generals and commanders and a couple of Oriental words and the soldiers would scream from the shock of recognition. At Second City, the same thing applied, only the name you would drop would be Kierkegaard. Or you'd say, "As Auden was saying to Upton Sinclair at the stockyard yesterday. . . ." That kind of thing isn't really intellectual humor.

I never got to know Sills very well. I would have liked to have gotten to know him better. He's a remarkable man who's done everything he can to avoid success on a commercial level. He's a very unique and dedicated guy.

Q: *How was it directing Viola in* Alex in Wonderland?

Something Wonderful Right Away

MAZURSKY: Fine. She was a little nervous. She's very talented.

Q: *It must have seemed very strange. Here she was, the queen mother of improvisation and. . . .*

MAZURSKY: I didn't let her improvise, let's put it that way.

Q: *A couple years ago, I met Jules Feiffer, and just having time to say two words, I asked him why he liked working with Second City people so much, and he answered, "Because they're Jewish." Do you think of Second City as being very Jewish in its brand of humor?*

MAZURSKY: There is that to some degree, even though they're not all Jewish. Severn Darden isn't.

Q: *Severn has to be ethnic in some way.*

MAZURSKY: Yes, his religion is New Orleans cape. He was at a New Year's Eve party at my house several years ago and he stood on the lawn and mooed like a cow all night long. That's all he did. People would walk by and he'd just be there and moo.

I think Second City and the whole improvisational thing is a great contribution—and a very American one—to theater, to entertainment, to show biz. But you know, I saw a Second City show in Chicago a couple years ago and it stunned me how out of touch it was. It didn't seem important or dynamic like it used to be. When it first happened, it was spectacular. These people were out there making up material better than most Broadway plays. Only ten-minute-long sketches, mind you, but really interesting, really appealing to people with minds, with social consciousness. Up there on the bare stage with just the chairs. But when I saw this recently, here they were working the same kinds of forms as at the beginning, and, in its own way, it had become slick. It seemed to me a little yesterday. It didn't excite me anymore.

Today you can turn on the TV and on shows like *All in the Family* you can see them making fun of things that only the groups would do six or seven years ago. So if they're doing that on TV, you've got to go deeper and do humor on things TV won't touch. Like the SLA, though I'd be afraid to do that one. What would you deal with today? It's a strange time. The drug time is gone, the Beatles are over, people seem to be walking around with a lack of direction.

250

Paul Mazursky

Most of what's making it commercially seems to be banal reminiscence. There's very little that's now, that's real. I think most of the movies are awful. So there's something to satirize in there about "Who am I, where am I going, what does it all mean?" I think these are things you could get into. But no longer will it work to do the sketch where someone goes to the priest to confess.

I'll give you an idea as to what I'd like to see them do—let's say Redford and Streisand in a porno. That would be a funny Second City–type sketch. John Wayne has got to be in it, too. (*A pretty good Wayne imitation:*) "I'd like ta see y'r ding!" But it's got to be real porno. "Suck it, eat it, and beat it, baby!" The picture will make $50 billion, you understand. The Pope will go to see it. Well, you can't make that movie, but you can satirize the possibility.

Or you could do a thing about what would happen if Solzhenitzyn were in The Second City. What kind of humor would he do? "A funny thing happened to me on the way to the cancer ward." It's not easy to think up this kind of thing.

Q: *Do you think there's something about the discipline of working in a Second City troupe that helps develop an actor's talent?*

MAZURSKY: I don't know if it makes one a good actor. In fact, I think it might sometimes get in the way. A lot of the actors I've seen from there comment on their acting a little bit. They're so intelligent that sometimes that bit of author within them begins to comment, because the best Second City people are authors as well as actors. It's great acting, but it's a little bigger than life.

Certainly most of the funny people working in America today have been working in the improvisational form somewhere along the line. There's got to be something to it.

To me improvisation is like a wonderful tool. I used it as a writer. Larry and I wrote *Bob & Carol & Ted & Alice* and I think we improvised seventy-five percent of it in five days in Palm Springs. We rented a place and went down there and I played one character and he played another and we just put it down on tape. I haven't worked that way since.

Q: *Do you use improvisation when you direct?*

MAZURSKY: Yes, but not as much as some people think.

I'm very disciplined and I try to create a feeling that what you're seeing is happening for the first time, but I'm sure everyone is trying to create that to some degree. I improvise only in the sense that I let the actors change a word or two and make it their own. Or if what they're doing doesn't seem to be working well, I'll fool around with it, but generally, I don't really improvise much. Not in the way we're talking about improvisation. Otherwise why would I have a script? I don't want to hear people who haven't written it make up things. You have to have something to say to be a writer. You don't snap your fingers and come up with "To be or not to be." There's blood in writing. You just don't casually get up on stage and make up the greatest things in the world. I just don't believe it.

Now improvisation can be very good for getting at comedy or satire. My feeling about improvisation like at Second City, though, was that it was very tricky. I had great admiration for them, but I always suspect glibness at a certain level. Also, there was an elitism to it that bothered me.

I think perhaps the most important thing that Paul Sills has done is to create an arena and constant work for a lot of people—work that is obviously gratifying and intelligent. I'm glad I was part of it, but I feel I would like to see some of them drop their pants.

20.

Anthony Holland

Anthony Holland's association with Sills began when both were in their teens in Chicago, continued through the University Theatre, Playwrights Theatre Club, and Second City days, and was most recently resumed for a story-theater interpretation of *The American Revolution* in Washington, D.C., in 1973.

Holland has the reputation for being one of New York's most gifted actors. His stage work includes *The White House Murder Case* (for which he won an "Obie"); the well-received Off-Broadway revival of *Waiting for Godot; Dreyfus in Rehearsal; We Bombed in New Haven; My Mother, My Father, and Me;* and guest appearances with the Yale Repertory Theatre, for which he also directed the premiere production of Terrence McNally's *The Ritz* (then called *The Tubs*). He also taught at Yale. His television credits include appearances on *M*A*S*H, The Mary Tyler Moore Show,* the British *That Was the Week That Was,* and the short-lived but refreshing *ABC Comedy News.* In film he has been seen to advantage in *Popi, Bye Bye Braverman, Klute, Hearts of the West, The Out-of-Towners, Goldstein,* and *Lucky Lady.* He is also a talented playwright.

HOLLAND: I first met Paul Sills when we were both students at a high school in Chicago called Francis W. Parker

253

School. It was a progressive school. I remember it being very Wilsonian-democratic in the sense that it was permeated with the same kind of optimism that had given birth to the League of Nations. There was an Isadora Duncan–like influence there, too. One year all the students wore togas. It was a wonderful school for me because I was always depressed, and Francis Parker gave me a more hopeful attitude.

Paul was very handsome and very well-coordinated. He was also very sensitive and bright, so he had the best of the two worlds. He was popular, athletic, and talented. He was, I think, one of the best-looking boys in the school. He had a nickname—"Apollo" Sills. In a school where togas were sometimes worn, the Greek gods were not very far away from everyone's vocabulary.

I remember that Paul directed me in a play at Francis Parker. *Junior Miss.* I played a Western Union messenger boy.

Q: *Was there any hint of the improvisational techniques he would use later?*

HOLLAND: No, we had a regular script and we just did the play. The one thing we did together that I see as being a forerunner of some of the work we did later was a number he put together for me for a show there. Every year, as at so many schools, there was a night devoted to making fun of the faculty and the school. In a good-humored way. For one of those Paul wrote a little song for me to sing in a German accent. It went over very well.

While I attended Francis Parker, I met two of Paul's family. One was his mother, Viola Spolin, though I didn't know her very well, as she was living in California then; Paul roomed with another Francis Parker student in Chicago. The other was Viola's sister, Beatrice Stronsdorf, who developed and taught a marvelous system of exercises for physical therapy. Later I studied with her, as I was not very well-developed physically. I had the body of a Talmudic scholar. She was an excellent teacher. My impression of that family was that they had a very definite sense of mission. Viola, Beatrice, and Paul were born pedagogues. It was a family characteristic.

After this idyllic time at Francis Parker, I went to the University of Chicago. I was there at about the same time as Philip Roth, right after the Hutchins administration. Robert Hutchins had come and, with Mortimer Adler, had revolutionized the college system. This was the time of the Great Books and OII—Observation, Interpretation, and Integration. It was the sort of school you could get finished with in two years if you could pass the proper tests. Coming from a progressive school, of course, I failed many of the tests on the entrance exam and had to take remedial English and remedial mathematics. (*Laughs.*)

The University of Chicago attracted people from all parts of the United States. Lots of students from New York especially, lots from the Midwest and some from the West. There were also veterans from the Second World War who seemed a lot older than most of the rest of the student body. It was a hothouse mixture. I think it is important to draw attention to the fact that when you talk about Second City and The Compass as being Chicago-style comedy, you're talking about a brand of comedy that was the product not so much of the locale in which it began but of the mix of people from all over who happened to meet in Chicago.

I know it's popular now to characterize the '50s as the period of McCarthy and having the kind of intellect represented in *American Graffiti*, but for me the '50s were a time of tremendous awakening. It was a time for learning. I don't think of it as a silent generation at all. For instance, veterans from the Spanish Civil War came to speak and hold rallies for the Civil War veterans who were starving in France. The '50s may have been a long sleep for the rest of America, but they were not a long sleep for the people at the University of Chicago. I remember that to belong to a fraternity then seemed incredibly stupid. No one bothered with them. No. people bothered about *talking*. You went to the bars or coffee shops and talked about everything that was talkable. I look upon that time as a heroic time.

An important thing to remember about Paul and most of the rest of us who later went on to Second City was that we were very arrogant. None of us had any real interest in what was going on in New York theater. When *New Faces* came to Chicago, we all hated it. We thought we were beyond that kind of thing. Nothing that came to Chicago as a road company ever seemed good enough for us. The things we liked and idolized were always things we had never seen, like the Group Theatre. And we had heard of *The Threepenny Opera* and its impact on Weimar Germany. It seemed that everything we liked was always on an old record. So, in a sense, we lived in fantasy. I know we felt a closeness to European culture as opposed to American. I think this is partially because we had so many refugees as teachers. I recently realized that most of my teachers at Francis Parker were German-Jewish refugees.

But I think that significant groups are formed because of defiance when they're young and striking out into their art. It's a defiance against the status quo, against what is the current fashion. The groups are formed because the people in them are not interested in being imitative of what predominates around them. I am somewhat dismayed when I teach today to see how many of the students are involved in what is happening *now*. I find that not a good idea. It doesn't make for better work for the most part. It makes for imitative work.

In effect, what happened at the University of Chicago is that, after a period of working as "Tonight at 8:30," we took over the University Theatre. Paul was sort of the head of this takeover, and he then directed a production of *The Caucasian Chalk Circle,* which I was in. It was so successful that Paul and David Shepherd opened Playwrights Theatre Club with essentially the same production.

I remember at the time we were opening Playwrights, the Rosenbergs were executed. Chicago had always been, for me, a rather anti-Semitic city. I would hear people talking on the subway or the streetcar, very convinced about the Rosenbergs' guilt and taking pleasure in their execution.

We had to do all the janitorial work ourselves at Playwrights. The only way Bill Alton and I could get through scrubbing a lavatory that had not been cleaned in probably twenty years was to pretend we were two very famous Jewish professors who were forced to do this work by the Nazi regime. Rather grim humor. The only way we could get through this work was to role-play, which I find very interesting because we ended up doing that kind of role-playing in Second City.

I have to say that I was terrible at cleaning. I always

kidded around. There was always music playing, and I would dance and tell jokes. I was so bad at cleaning that the others said, "No, don't bother cleaning. Just entertain us while we clean." And that again was role-playing.

Let's see—I got married in 1952 and it lasted four years. Playwrights began during the first year of my marriage, which would make it 1953. I played with them through the summer of 1953, then I left the company to return to school. I had gotten my bachelor's, now I was going to go back and get my master's. I got a fellowship and was teaching in the adult education department and studying art history with the idea that I was going to become an art historian. I had a whole life mapped out in front of me. And yet, I remember going on an art history convention to the Philadelphia Museum and suddenly getting very bored and realizing that I didn't want an academic life. I came back and could barely write my thesis. And it was then I decided what I really wanted to be was an actor.

So I rejoined Playwrights in their second season. It was a marvelous period of my life when I had a lot of great roles and acted every night with a wonderful company.

After about a year of my second period with Playwrights, I decided to leave for New York to study. While playing all those great roles, I noticed that I would be very good for the first three or four nights, but I didn't have the resources or the skills to sustain the role and make it expand over the remainder of the run. I knew that someone would have to teach me how to do this, so I thought I should follow Zohra, who had already gone to New York, and study with some of the teachers I'd heard about, such as Lee Strasberg and Uta Hagen.

I wasn't around for The Compass. I was busy leading the life of a New York actor: working as a waiter at Howard Johnson's, studying with Lee Strasberg, and doing scenes and being very friendly with the other students in my class.

Q: *Did you keep in touch with what was going on in Chicago?*

HOLLAND: No, not really, and I'll tell you why. I have a tendency to regard what is past as useless. I feel as though the only way I can move ahead is to cut myself off from what has gone before. So I had to get Chicago off my mind. I seldom thought about the people at Playwrights. They dropped out of my life. Oh, I thought it had been a good theater and that the training was good, but, as far as I was concerned, the important thing was pursuing my life in New York. Also, my marriage had not worked out, and I associated that and the fact that I had been so depressed so much of the time with Chicago. So it was a place I wanted to stay away from and not dwell upon.

I realize now that I was lucky to arrive in New York when I did. It was 1955, and Off-Broadway was beginning to break big. There were a lot of Off-Broadway theaters and there was a wonderful feeling that you would find exciting work. So I was happy to be in New York.

Q: *You did, however, return to Chicago during that time, didn't you?*

HOLLAND: Yes, as an actor. I was hired to play in Shaw's *Androcles and the Lion* at the Studebaker, which was directed by Sir Cedric Hardwicke. While I was there, I went to the North Side to the Off-Beat Room to see The Compass, because people who had been my friends were in it. I remember that it was badly lit and the place was physically ugly, and, at least the evening I was there, nothing much was happening onstage. It seemed terribly pedestrian to me. I don't remember anything of what went on on that stage that evening, except that it was an off-night. They were, of course, improvising, but it wasn't interesting to me. What I was really more interested in was seeing my friends again, so it was a social occasion rather than an artistic event. Part of my reaction may have had something to do with the fact that the place where they were playing was not too far from where I had grown up, which I had always thought of as unbelievably dreary. Anyway, it didn't work for me.

After working at the Studebaker, I returned to New York. I was in the first production of Brendan Behan's *The Quare Fellow*, playing a Gaelic-speaking prisoner. It was directed by José Quintero. From that experience I got a job as an assistant to José—running out for coffee, taking notes, and understudying. This was for *The Balcony*. It was very exciting to be a part of this and to watch José direct.

I mention this because Paul had come to New York at this time and I invited him to a dress rehearsal. I think he was very impressed with it, which made me feel good, because I felt it showed him that on my own I had found and become part of a group of people who were as talented and unconventional and defiant of Broadway standards as the people I knew in Chicago. Somehow I think this made Paul and me get along better. I remember at one point, while we were watching this very long dress rehearsal, he mentioned he was going to start Second City. He said, "You'd be wonderful at it because you can do so easily the sort of work we're going to do."

Soon after Second City opened, he asked me to come. I arrived on St. Patrick's Day. It was a very snowy night. I took a taxi straight to Second City and I went in. It was the most enchanting atmosphere I'd ever been in. The theater was beautifully decorated. And I saw their first show, which was the funniest thing I had ever seen. Paul Sand was in it, Mina Kolb, Barbara Harris, and Gene and Andrew and Howard. Roger Bowen had already left and Severn was about to take a leave of absence to be in a production of *Hamlet* with Fritz Weaver. I had come to take Severn's place.

In about one rehearsal I learned everything I was supposed to do. It seemed terribly easy. Paul was indeed right. All the instincts I had at Playwrights Theatre to amuse my fellow actors and be very free seemed to work for me at Second City. One other thing I remember feeling very strongly at rehearsals was that, because I was able to make the other actors laugh in rehearsals, I went out onstage with their support. If the other actors like you and feel you're funny, somehow facing the audience isn't as hard.

I went into the show and did do Severn's parts. A lot of his parts, at least. But I improvised on them, embroidered on them as you might do cadenzas at the end of concertos. I found I was integrated into the show in a week's time. And I loved doing it. It wasn't the period of my best work at Second City, though. It was just an introduction, as I was there only for a few months.

After that I went back to New York and then to Europe, where I stayed and explored for a long time, almost a year. In the spring of 1961, I wrote to Bernie Sahlins to ask for a loan as I had run out of money and he was the only person I knew who had ready cash. He was very

generous and sent me $500, and with the money sent a
message saying, "Can you come back and work in Chicago
by May 16?" Or something like that. Bernie's telegram was
like an omen. It was telling me it was time I came home
and worked. So I saw spring in Greece and took the boat
back.

Zohra was in the company I joined in Chicago. Paul
would literally throw us out onstage to improvise. Every
night Zohra and I would ask the audience for a place and
a time and two characters and improvise an absolutely new
scene. Paul would not allow us to repeat a scene, so we did
eight new scenes a week. The incredible thing was that
most of those scenes worked. It was marvelous training.

Zohra and I did a marvelous scene called "Lilli and
Leon" about two people who meet on a boat. We were
never able to make enough sense of it to put it into the
regular show, but sometimes we did it in the sets afterwards. We both had Viennese accents in it. That was the
scene in which I came up with a character called Dr. Pisk,
whom I used again later. Most of my teachers in high
school had been German-speaking refugees, so I frequently
played a refugee there.

Then Zohra returned to New York to do a Broadway
play called *Look, We've Come Through!* by Hugh Wheeler.
So Paul went to New York just to select a girl to replace
her, and that girl was Joan Rivers.

Suddenly there was this brassy, blond girl who really
wanted to be a stand-up comic. But, on the other hand,
Joan wasn't anything like that. She was an extremely sensitive, intelligent Barnard girl who had a conception of
show business she felt she had to fit into. We got along
very well. I adored Joan and we still have a very strong
friendship.

We did a scene called "Tailor and Model." I saw an ad
in *Vogue* once which showed a very plain tailor fixing the
hem of this beautiful model's skirt. So we reconstructed this
photograph. I was the very plain refugee tailor and she
was the model, and the object of the scene was how could
these two people get together. It was a lovely scene.

I think I was partially responsible for "people" scenes. I
didn't always want to do political scenes. I always seemed
to gravitate to characters who were a little sad. I wanted to

260

take chances and not always work for gags. I wanted to
work for behavior and detail.

One night, we got the suggestion, "Greek vase." Bill
Alton was in the company then. He's a very W.A.S.P.ish,
very proper fellow on the surface. We got together on this
suggestion and decided to use our University of Chicago
experience. I said, "Remember there were people who had
been there for like ten years? Why don't I play a scholar
who's been there all that time, and you play a successful
investment broker, and we used to be friends, and we see
each other for the first time in years, and we'll see what
happens." So there was this scene where he comes up to
my room, and I had just come back from Greece and
brought a rare piece of pottery with designs on it that had
come out of a dig in Greece. A lot of the details in the
scene came out of my own experiences in Greece. The
scene is about how their values have become so different
that they can't really be friends anymore. During the
scene, Bill inadvertently knocks over and breaks the vase.
The scene was called "Lekythos," which was the kind of
vase it was. I remember Tennessee Williams was in town
working on *The Night of the Iguana* before it went to New
York. He came to the theater and saw this scene, and at
the end of it he said, "Bravo! Bravo!" I think he'd had a
little to drink. But he came up to us and said, "That's a
one-act play!" In fact, I have turned it into a one-act play.

Alan Arkin and I did a scene called "Camp Counselor"
in which I played a very repressed child who was painting
very little people, and Alan was the counselor who wanted
me to use fingerpaint to let myself go. Later, the scene was
used as a teaching scene for child psychologists. In fact,
we found out that someone actually came into the club
and secretly taped it.

While I was in New York, I saw Lenny Bruce, and he
had a great effect on me. I knew I could never be like
Lenny Bruce and I was no stand-up comic, but I thought,
"Why not reveal myself a little bit more? What am I hiding?" I always hid myself, I think. I always played kind of
a schmuck or an intellectual. But after seeing Lenny Bruce,
I think more of my psyche came out. I don't know how,
but it did.

Something Wonderful Right Away

Q: *How about your working relationship with Paul at this time?*

HOLLAND: Paul would say, "Oh come on, you've been doing this since high school. Just get up and do it!" Or, "What the fuck are you doing? Get out on that stage!" As simple as that. Sometimes other people would be onstage doing an improv, and they'd be out there for minutes and minutes and the audience would be coughing, and he'd come backstage, take me by the shoulders, and say, "Get the fuck out on the stage," and throw me out there, and I'd say, "Oh hi, I'm from next door and. . . ." Anything that came into my mind to get the scene started again. I'm very pliable and had no temperament. Paul didn't teach me so much as set up situations in which I could learn.

Viola was there then. She ran workshops, which was very good because the company was splitting—not psychologically, but because one group had to go to the Ivar in California. As they were getting ready to leave, more people came in who were going to be replacements, and Viola's work was designed to give these new people a sense of "ensemble."

We worked in the afternoon on Viola's games—handling space objects, doing gibberish and transformations. Something I think was very important and I love and use myself are exercises dealing with changing realities.

Q: *How would that work?*

HOLLAND: You'd start off with two people on the stage who would create their own reality, like working in a bagel shop. Then a third person would enter with a new reality, maybe saying something like, "The Persians have just landed!" and the original two people would have to transform themselves into the new reality. When that was accomplished, the first person would then find an excuse to leave the stage. Say they're talking about getting ready for the Persian invasion, the first one might say, "I'll rouse the people in Corinth!" and go off. The second and third people would continue with the scene, and then a fourth person would come on with a new reality for the scene to be transformed into. An operating room, say.

The point of this exercise was agreement. One of the reasons so many people who try to do improvs go wrong is that they aren't in agreement. They try to be funny and go

262

for a quick laugh. "This coffee tastes good," and the other person says, "What coffee? It's tea." That's how to kill an improv. But this exercise was designed to teach you to accept the other person's reality and then change it in an artful rather than a jokey way.

The new people, among them Avery Schreiber and Dick Schaal, were really trained much more rigorously in Paul and Viola's techniques than I was, and the difference onstage was amazing. I'd be verbally witty and doing "people" scenes, looking for nuances, and they would be handling objects. You see, Paul was going through his object or touching or handling stage . . . I can't tell this in words. What I'm trying to say is that it was a much more nonverbal technique. It was very much like the Strasberg exercises where you're drinking coffee and you want to know how it feels and how hot it is and. . . . Physical reality is the concept. Really experiencing the place. On her way to the icebox, Viola would walk through rehearsals and say, "Remember your 'where,' people!"

Schisms developed. I was aware of them both in Chicago and later in New York. For instance, I always worked on intellectuals or people who had intellectual pretensions. Quite suddenly, in contrast, here were Avery and Jack Burns dealing with the proletariat. Suddenly you had scenes about truck drivers, carpenters, and cabbies. It was a whole different social level. Avery, Jack, and Dick weren't from the University of Chicago. Not everyone could come from the University of Chicago, after all. So, as we from the U. of C., who thought it was amusing to satirize the intellectual pretensions of the U. of C., "graduated" from Second City, we were replaced by another group with non–U. of C. backgrounds. So the verbal wit was being replaced by another kind of humor. Paul was aware of this.

Q: *Was that the way he wanted it to go?*

HOLLAND: I think so. Because I remember once he yelled at Barbara Harris and myself, saying, "I've had enough fucking *wit!* Give me something else!"

So there was the wit group, there was the kind of object-reality group, and then there was the surreal group made up of people like Severn, John Brent, Howard Alk, and Hamilton Camp. I'd say that the surreal group was much more into the emerging drug culture. They would go onstage, you would do a scene with them, and then it would suddenly go into a vision of some sort. They were like the forerunners of another kind of culture. "Lekythos" and "Camp Counselor," scenes about the troubles of professionals, had nothing to do with what they were doing onstage.

Q: *They were into "head" humor.*

HOLLAND: Yes, 'it was "head" humor, which was sometimes marvelous and sometimes far out. I know that we didn't get along with them at all. I don't mean that we had fights. But Andrew and Alan Arkin and I didn't have much to do with that. It really didn't do anything for us. People from different camps didn't do scenes together. If there were six of us in a company and three of us were in "head" humor and two of us in "people" scenes and one kind of neutral, you'd get two people doing "people" scenes and three people doing "head" scenes, and we would work together only on the big group scenes. You and I were talking before taping this about the differences in Christianity—the difference between being a Lutheran or a Calvinist. That's sort of what happened at Second City. It was like we were all members of the same church, but there were sects.

We really found that we were members of the same church when we worked with each other outside Second City. At Second City originally, Avery and I didn't get along at all. But when we found ourselves acting together in a schlocky Hollywood situation comedy pilot, we knew how to work together and our scenes were brilliant.

After a year of working hard in the Chicago company, I went to New York. Second City had opened on Broadway. I wasn't in that company. Nor was Zohra. That was essentially the original Chicago company—Barbara and Mina and Arkin and Sand and Severn . . . those people. But I was in the first Off-Broadway company, which is what I think was the Golden Age of Second City. That was Zohra, Alan, Andrew, Eugene, and myself. This was the company that Paul left for a while, so Larry Arrick took over. We were the people who went on *The David Susskind Show* and did so well that we had full houses for months afterwards.

Anthony Holland

In New York, it was a period when I worked tremendously and became even freer. We did something called "Poetry." The audience would give us lines and each of us would make up one poem. Andrew was always good at that. He'd always play an expatriate poet—Ezra Pound or T. S. Eliot. I would do poems in the manner of e. e. cummings or W. H. Auden. I found in "Poetry" what I had been looking for after seeing Lenny Bruce—a form in which I could express my rage, contempt, or whatever I felt at that moment. It was rather cerebral. Whatever I was reading I would somehow bring into the poem.

I felt so released at this stage that I could handle without inhibition any suggestion thrown out by the audience. One night, when I was working with Barbara, we got "bull dyke" as a suggestion, so Barbara and I went backstage and I said, "Look, *I'll* be the bull dyke and you interview me." I just wore my suit and put on a string of pearls and a crash helmet, and I came on as a tough dyke and it was a good scene. I remember aggressively pointing to an unseen cameraman and demanding, "That cameraman should be a woman and black!" We got the suggestion from Mark Harris, whom we knew from the University of Chicago. Mark was a black novelist, and my saying this was my way of having fun with him for purposely giving us a hard suggestion.

We went into one very marvelous period there I'll never forget. Barbara Harris was going with Arnold Weinstein at the time, and Arnold brought his friends to see us. Larry Rivers, Frank O'Hara, and people like that. Suddenly the people who were important to me came—the New York poets and painters. This was in 1962–63. We had a new audience, to me better than any we'd ever had. The University of Chicago audiences, as much as I loved them, were people who were slightly smug about their education with the kind of attitude that says, "We're part of a great school. We are teachers and we are the elite." But these new people were artists. These were the people the teachers were talking about in their classes. We were getting a new elite, but an elite that wasn't academic. I became friends with Frank O'Hara during that period and was a friend of his till his death.

Paul seemed very unhappy with this shift. Our audience

265

inspired us to become more verbal, but he was no longer interested in verbal flights. He was involved, rather, in the kind of work Avery and Schaal were doing back in Chicago.

Q: *Which I understand laid the foundation for the fight he had with Larry Arrick.*

HOLLAND: Yes, I'm sure that had a lot to do with it.

At this time I also did Dr. Pisk. It was my version of a form Severn had employed since The Compass. Andrew would come out and say, *"Women Have the Right to Know. This is educational television."* And then he would ask for any subject taught in school, and the audience would suggest something (usually psychiatry) and Severn would come out and be an expert on it. I took that over. Andrew would say, "And now we have the world-famous lecturer, Dr. Herman Pisk." (*Pisk*, incidentally, is the Yiddish word for "mouth.") And I'd come on and be interviewed. My character was based on the Viennese refugee I had done in that scene with Zohra. Pisk had known Freud and Mahler and Jung. His function was to shock the audience under the guise of expertise. It gave me free rein to deal with untouchable subjects of the early '60s, like homosexuality and the private lusts of our political leaders.

Also at that time, Alan and I did a scene on the suggestion of "Bleecker Street peddler," because a law had just been passed which would ban peddlers from Bleecker Street. Alan played a little Jewish peddler, and I was a student social worker who interviewed him for a term paper I was writing on "changing neighborhoods." The peddler hinting at the isolation of his life in answer to the prosaic, aimless questions and the student revealing his own mediocrity by the insensitivity of his reactions. The scene took shape the first time we did it and we hardly ever changed it. We later made it into a short film called *The Last Mohican*. That scene came out whole the first time. You know, scenes spring from your psyche. That's all I can say. You don't sit down and write gags. That's why it's different from television. It's so strange to do a TV pilot; you get the script and you read it and the writers come in and change the gags. It's a whole different process.

In this period, one of the good things was that if you really wanted to do a play, Paul would let you leave and then come back if the play closed. During that period, in 1963, I left to do *My Mother, My Father, and Me* by Lillian Hellman. The play was not a success. I left it to come back to Second City, and Bob Dishy, MacIntyre Dixon, and Paul Dooley were there when I came back. That's when Second City did what I thought was its greatest set piece, *Peep Show for Conventioneers,* the first version of which Paul had directed in Chicago.

Peep Show was about two men who come to a whorehouse where they are supposed to realize their dreams, which are really the American Dream. Each time one of the guys is about to get laid, we'd interrupt him by playing out one of his fantasies. It was like *The Balcony* in a way, but different, because it was so thoroughly American. It was Paul's big showpiece and lasted about an hour. It was a "people" scene and a changing-reality scene. It drew on the exercises and had remarkably subtle lighting and music. It was a great piece of theater. Tom O'Horgan created our music.

My feeling was that Paul should have stopped with the exercises he was always involved with and, instead of going into Game Theatre, gone on from *Peep Show* to approach other themes and subjects in the same kind of way. For instance, I wanted to do an hour on the history of the American labor movement. I wanted to do a show about Emma Goldman, the anarchist. I thought Barbara Harris would be good for that. I suppose Barbra Streisand will do it now. I felt we should form a company which would be involved in doing larger works, but Paul couldn't do it. He didn't have the concentration or desire to do it. It wasn't until *Story Theatre* that he got back into it. When we did *The American Revolution* in 1973, I told him this. I said, "We should have been doing this after we did *Peep Show* in 1963. I think we went off the track in some way back then. Now it's ten years later and we've finally gone back to doing a whole evening dealing with a central theme."

Not long after *Peep Show,* I left Second City. I had to. I was exhausted, and I felt I had no psyche left. It was as if someone had bought all my dreams, all my inner life, all my private life, because it was all coming out every night. I couldn't keep up that way. I'd take Dexamyl every night in order to do it, and it would make me slightly manic. Everything I had read, every relationship I had, everything in my life seemed to come up. I'd act it out at night. It would come straight out. It might have been disguised or filtered, but it would come out. So I left. I had used up my psyche. I found I couldn't improvise anymore because there was nothing to improvise. I was used up. I didn't want to go out onstage and make jokes, and I wanted a private life.

I didn't really come back to Second City except to replace Alan in *A View from Under the Bridge,* and I didn't work with Paul again until *The American Revolution.*

Q: *But you were still involved with political satire.*

HOLLAND: Yes. Andrew and I went to England to do *That Was the Week That Was.* We were the first two Americans they used. We did it the third year the show was on the BBC when it wasn't called *TW3* anymore but *The Late Show, or For Those Who Are Too Drunk to Dance.* That's when I started writing. The show would have to be censored, so you'd have to submit a script the Friday before it went out on the air. We had to write out our improvisations. Andrew and I had a room at the BBC office and I would sit at the typewriter while he smoked and read the papers. That's when I realized, "My God, I can write it! I don't always have to do it onstage." We did some outrageous things on that show. We talked about Kennedy's assassination—sacrosanct to the British. The Warren Report came out and I suggested that it would make a marvelous base for a coffee table. People stopped looking at the show and Andrew and I felt we had alienated millions of people in England, which made us very happy. (*Laughs.*)

I hated the BBC. Most of the cast was very insular and cool to us except for Eleanor Bron and John Bird. Jonathan Miller was kind, but he wasn't on the show. He was a friend.

The English satirists also improvised, though they didn't work from Sills and Spolin techniques. That's why you don't see much object-work in them. They relied more on verbal wit. At its best it was the kind of thing Cook and Moore do.

Q: *The satiric movement in England in the '60s mostly sprang out of Oxford and Cambridge.*

HOLLAND: Yes, their equivalent of the University of Chicago. Both the American and British improvisational satiric movements are elitist antiestablishment movements. It's always been my feeling that improvisation comes from political defiance. When you don't have the economic means to have your own theater, your own scripts, and paid actors, what are you going to do? You'll play in a little room and you'll make it up, and it will be very verbal. This happened simultaneously in England and the United States in the late '50s.

Q: *Were you aware of any Sills-like figure in England?*

HOLLAND: John Bird was the head of things at *TW3*, but there were no workshops and the techniques weren't codified. It's not a put-down of Paul, but they worked without any cult figures. They worked without Paul and Viola's exercises. Of course, what they came up with was something very much different. Their end results were different. But their work, like ours, also came from having gone to school together and sharing one political point of view and reading the same books.

Q: *You also did a satiric news show in America on late-night television in 1973.* The ABC Comedy News. *I felt that was very Second City–influenced, what with you and Andrew being regulars and people like Dick Schaal and Joan Rivers doing guest appearances.*

HOLLAND: The people who wrote and conceived it, Bernie Kukoff and Jeff Harris, were very influenced by Paul Sills. Kukoff had gone to Paul's workshops at Second City. They did work from a script, but we were allowed a certain amount of freedom to add and change things.

Q: *It was a wonderful takeoff on the phony* Eyewitness News *camaraderie.*

HOLLAND: The *Eyewitness News* people hated us.

Now it seems like everyone worked at Second City. I know I worked with about twelve people. I don't know where the other sixty came from. You'd go up for a commercial. . . . (This was the sad part of Second City. It was exploited in that suddenly the Second City approach was used to sell aspirin. The agency people would say, "You're a tired suburban husband, an Andrew Duncan type, and this is your wife, a Mina Kolb type, and we need a scene about aspirin." And you'd do, "Honey, I feel so rotten."

"Why?" "Well, that party last night. . . ." You know, improvisation in its most debased form.) They'd say, "Well, how would you like to work with Debbie Schlitz?" You'd say, "Who's Debbie Schlitz?" They'd say, "She knows you. She worked with you in Second City." I mean, I never knew who Debbie Schlitz was.

You would also encounter Madison Avenue types, greedy dopes for the most part, who would tell you to do a scene like Mike and Elaine, as if they'd never heard of you or your work at Second City.

One of the few people I can think of from that world who did see Second City and understood the work, and was and is wonderful, is Howard Zieff. There were a few others who did see Second City and were sensitive in the way they worked with the people. But God, you'd have some of the copywriters who were jerks who'd say, "Now here's the copy. It's very good but can you improve on it?" Naturally, you'd look at this shitty copy and you'd figure out a way to make something funny out of it. They'd tape what you did, say "Thank you very much," and you wouldn't get the job, but they'd use your ideas. Finally there was an AFTRA ruling passed that they had to pay you if they used anything you came up with. It made some difference, but not much.

I was glad I left Second City during the Kennedy administration. When Kennedy was assassinated, I could no longer have done political satire. But then, political satire no longer has the kind of meaning it once held for me. You hardly need Second City to interpret Watergate. The news is so grotesque you don't need to interpret it satirically. Just pick up the paper and read it.

21.

Bill Alton
_____

Bill Alton was another of the early University of Chicago crowd, performing in University Theatre and moving with Sills and company when Playwrights opened. He did not take part in The Compass, being busy working in the East during that period of time. At the time Second City was getting launched, Alton had returned to University Theatre as its faculty head. Then he joined The Second City, where he made a marvelous comic foil as the house "square"—which he is far from being in real life. When he transferred to the New York Second City company, he began to get very involved with television commercials as an actor. Within a short time, he made the switch to directing. He has since built up a reputation as one of the very best directors of commercials, frequently directing his old friends from Second City days.

ALTON: Paul Sills and I met as students. We were all trying to be intellectuals and we would have heavy conversations. I didn't even think of Paul as a theater man at that time. He was more of a thinker and he didn't know what the hell he wanted to do. I was in theater earlier than either he or Mike, and I was sort of an authority at the time. Then Paul got into it and we started to relate on that level.

271

He's a very sweet man, very eccentric and, oddly enough, inarticulate. He's a man with hundreds of thousands of brilliant ideas, but it's very hard for him—and he'd be the first to admit this—to get them across. I think he operates under conflicting influences. On the one hand, he likes very much to talk to the world, and on the other, sometimes he's shy and pulls back because he thinks something is too personal. You can see it in his mannerisms. Sometimes he'll mumble and you can't hear him. Like Brecht, I think of him more as an innovator and a man who's changed theater than specifically as a director. When he works on a play with actors, he has a hell of a time talking to them. Frequently it's because he's trying to get across very complicated and daring ideas. But even beyond that, I think he finds it hard even to relate verbally. He would get angry and pissed off and the actors would get pissed off, and he'd yell, "Get off my stage, God damn it!" He was always fighting a lot of bullshit. It's a tough road with Paul, and it's incredible he gets the results he does get, because he's not that easy, he's not that glib.

Q: *What do you remember of Playwrights Theatre Club?*

ALTON: We really didn't know what the fuck we were doing at Playwrights. We were just doing plays and learning as we went along. The thing I remember in terms of Paul's direction then was a sense of negativism, or so it seemed at the time, though I respected it. Paul was more interested in *not* doing a lot of things than he was in doing them. We didn't do a lot of improvising. In fact, Paul seemed to be avoiding any kind of self-conscious technique. He didn't like to talk about acting. "Just get onstage and do it!"

While we were doing all this, there was a whole other movement in New York at The Actors Studio, which was all very individual, very inner, very introspective, with "private moments" and that kind of thing. We were totally polarized from that. In fact, when people came from New York with that attitude and that technique, we'd laugh them off the stage. Our conceit was that we were working in terms of society rather than the individual, and were working in service of an idea rather than vice versa. We would laugh at the whole idea of torturing yourself to find your own emotion, crying, and all that shit.

Bill Alton

I remember an actor who came to us from New York at the time we were doing Playwrights. He was a good actor, but he'd come from six months at the Studio. To be honest, we were all a little bit in awe, but not that much. After a show one night, we were all having coffee in some greasy spoon and he was going on and on, dropping names left and right. It was Lee Strasberg this and someone else that, with lots of first names. And he said, "Oh, and Gerry is so wonderful!" This was when Geraldine Page was at the height of her stardom, and Mike said, "Gerry who?" And he said, "Geraldine Page!" "Oh," said Mike, "we always called her Gadge."

What we were going for was a very proletarian idea— the de-deification of the artist, the star. Anyone who wanted to be a star in the company was some kind of shit. Our concerns were supposed to be social.

When we did Playwrights, we really didn't know anything. We were like children. We had great arrogance and *chutzpah*. We did *Wozzeck*, Shakespeare, Strindberg. And sometimes it was very effective. I remember a production Elaine directed of *Miss Julie* with Zohra and Ed Asner and Tony that was incredible.

Q: *What was Elaine like then?*

ALTON: Elaine was evolving her own curious techniques of directing. She's tremendously articulate and can go on for hours and hours. The thing about Elaine is that there are no edges; there's no beginning, middle, or end. She writes plays that go on for seven or eight hours. She just doesn't know how to stop them. That was the great thing about Mike and Elaine as a team. She has great ideas and Mike has a great knack for form.

I think the idea of improvisation came about partially because we found that we were not well qualified for what we were doing, so we had to find another means of expression that was ours alone. We started by doing all the great plays at University Theatre and Playwrights— *Oedipus* was the first play I ever directed—but there was something a little thin about our work and it wasn't exactly what we wanted to say. We got closer to it when we started doing Brecht, which was Sills's baby. And Shepherd's concerns were more centered around little theaters like the cabarets in Germany during the '30s. So that was the way we got from Playwrights to Compass.

I wasn't around when they started improvising. I left before Compass started. I taught at HB Studios in New York for a couple of years and headed the drama department at Bennington College. Then I quit because I was offered the job of running University Theatre at the University of Chicago, which seemed to be a good opportunity.

At the same time I was doing that, Second City was getting started, and I reestablished my contact with Paul. After a year of running University Theatre, I was anxious to get out of the academic theater world and back into the other. At about that time, Second City was getting ready to send their original company to New York by way of L.A., so I was hired to be part of the second Chicago company.

Q: *Give me some impressions of some of the people at Second City.*

ALTON: Dick Schaal is a master of physical comedy. Not pratfalls, but real artful stuff. He could create a room with nothing more than his frame. We used to say, "Dick, we want to do a scene about a man fixing his car," and it would be so specific you just *saw* the automobile. Paul would always use Dick as an example of nonverbal communication.

Q: *What about Barbara Harris?*

ALTON: She's a terrific lady. I love her. She hates public attention of any kind. She's a little like Salinger. I mean, if she could perform without anyone watching, I think she'd adore it. She shrivels up when people start talking about public acclaim. She's been shit on a lot by journalists, too. She's had interviews and they tore her apart. She's very fragile.

Severn Darden is a genius, I think, but not a particularly good actor. In the traditional sense of what an actor is supposed to be. When I see him in a movie or a play, I never believe anything he does. But as an improviser for Second City and The Compass, he was the best. Brilliant things, always organic and always Severn. Whenever he does something, he's always halfway acting because he's commenting on what he's doing while he's doing it. This worked wonderfully for The Second City and The Compass because those aren't strictly fourth-wall experiences. It was a great discovery to find out that in doing this kind of work, you *had* to include the audience, that you were playing *to* as well as *in front of.* And the audience could direct•where the show was going sometimes. That's another thing that worried Paul. He wanted the audience involved, but he was also afraid that they would take the show away from us and that we'd pander to them.

But, to get back to Severn, his great genius is in his point of view. So he would be no good, for instance, playing a character in an Arthur Miller play because there you need someone who will surrender his ego to that part. Severn's charm is that he's an oddball. David Steinberg's the same way—he's not an actor and he's not a stand-up comic. He's someone who needs to be in a skit of some kind as himself.

Did you talk to Zohra?

Q: *We set up a couple of appointments which she canceled, until I finally got the word from someone else that she didn't want to talk about it because she doesn't really want to be identified as being part of this community. Either that or she doesn't feel she belongs in this group. It really wasn't made too clear to me.*

ALTON: In a way she's right. She was a part of it all in the sense that she was in University Theatre and she and Paul were very close in terms of ideas. Then we left Playwrights and came to New York and she became very much a part of the New York theater thing. She was taking classes with Uta Hagen and getting cast in Broadway shows and a lot of people knew who she was. And then, it was like she was dropping into Second City. She came by and worked for something like six months in Chicago, and then went back to New York, and when the New York company got started, she replaced Barbara or something. So she was very much a part of Playwrights Theatre—she was a star, really terrific. But she was never a part of The Compass, so I think I know what she means if she says she wasn't a part of it. She wasn't a part like Andrew or Severn or Barbara. Her aims were really individual and personal.

One of my favorite scenes was the dentist scene. One night we got the suggestion "office party." We all went backstage to talk about the suggestions and, I'm not sure who came up with the idea, but Joan Rivers and I went out that night and did this scene. I do know the thrust of the scene came from Joannie. The idea was we were a dentist and his assistant and it's the end of the day. The last patient has left and we're closing up and just about to go home when he says, "Hey, why don't you hang around and have a drink and we'll talk. We haven't had much of a chance to get to know each other." The theme of the scene was that, although both of them were proficient and fairly happy in their work, both of them had some kind of unfulfilled creative bent. He was a painter and she did something artistic, too. She had won the "Draw Me" contest on matchbook covers. So they have a drink and they make a few jokes about Lavoris and that kind of thing, and they both get a little stoned. He shows her an abstract painting he's working on and she says it looks like a tooth. It turns into a little come-on scene where they almost go away with each other. He kisses her, and then they realize that they really aren't going to go anywhere and they say goodnight and go home. It was what we called a "tinkle, tinkle scene," which is to say that it would end with Bill Mathieu playing some wistful music as the lights faded out.

It was a very funny scene and Joannie and I did it for about a year, perfecting it and shaping it. Then Joannie left the company to become Joan Rivers, and Mina Kolb and I started doing it. I also did it with Sally Hart. Then I came to New York and was in a company with Severn and Alan Arkin and Barbara Dana, and I started doing it with Barbara. One day, Alan said, "I love that scene. I've got a couple thousand dollars. I'd like to film it." So we all did it for nothing. The film never made any money. He spent eight or nine thousand dollars and he shot it at his dentist's office and sold it to Columbia Pictures, either at cost or he lost a grand. It's called *T.G.I.F.* It's not bad. It's got kind of a nice feel. The sound is a little funky and it's got rough edges, but it's creditable.

I was also in a company that went to England. It was me, Del Close, Mina, Avery, and Dick Schaal. We played The Establishment. Speaking of history, one night Del and I and David Frost, who was then doing *That Was the*

Week That Was, walked down the street together to listen to Kennedy's Cuban missile speech in a restaurant.
Did you ever hear about the Game? We started this in London and it became a great test of faith. It came out of a kind of negative thing onstage, which is where I stop and confront you and go (*he makes the sound of someone being slapped in the face*) and instead of playing with it you say, "What are you making the sound for?" In other words, you deny the reality I set up.

So the Game was about really accepting the reality. What it was about was that if you were a member of this group that plays the Game, if someone comes up to you and goes "Bang!," shooting you with an imaginary gun, no matter what you are doing, you fall down and do a death scene. Say you're winning a Pulitzer Prize for a novel you've written, and just as they're presenting it to you I go "Bang!," you've got to do a death, and the more convincing and outlandish, the higher your integrity and friendship is. We started doing this in London and it got really crazy with everyone shooting everyone all over the place. We finally had to limit it to one shot a day, and you never knew when it would happen. The Old Vic used to hang out at The Establishment, and they got in on it. There are people all over the world doing it now, and if you see one of them and you shoot them you know they're going to die. I once shot Del on Greek Street in Soho and he died for something like four blocks. Severn came up with a vicious qualification—that if I shot you, you had to die and you were not allowed to get up again until given permission by the shooter.

Q: *Let's talk about Second City and commercials.*

ALTON: As I recall, every once in a while someone would get a commercial in Chicago, but there was never any concerted effort to get Second City people for the creation of copy. But when we came to New York and started working at the Square East, various agency people got the idea that Second City people could improvise within a format, and that's how it got started. Mary Draper from Doyle Dane Bernbach asked me to read for a "Man in a Shoe" commercial. Troobnick and I did it and really got whole new careers going. I remember Arkin did a few and Zohra did some.

277

But in the beginning, I think the most effective use of improvisation was the Excedrin campaign. What they'd do was book five or so hours in a radio studio and bring as many of us in as they needed. They'd have us do very much like what we used to do at Second City—we would play things for as long as they went, then, when we redid them, we'd pare them down and trim them till they were tight. Then they would take all of this tape and very artfully sit down and cut a thirty- or sixty-second spot out of it. Those were the "Excedrin headache" spots.

Andrew and I used to do tons of radio commercials. They wouldn't ask you specifically to come in and create copy for them, but they knew that you had that kind of mind. We'd start with their copy points and horse around, and once we got a sense of advertising, we could come up with spots in no time—twenty-eight seconds on the nose. So the techniques we learned in improvisational theater were directly applied to selling the American public on buying something or other. And then people started saying, "We get a lot of money for residuals, but we should really be getting writers' fees." I think when an actor creates the copy it's proper.

One thing that some people have done that's really larcenous is they may have twenty actors come in to audition, and say Andrew starts horsing around and comes up with something—it may not even be a line—maybe just a look or a gesture or a word. Then he'll leave and someone says, "We don't want to use Andrew, but let's use that thing that he did." My attitude is that you don't do that unless you call him back and give him some money for it, because it's just not fair. The point is all you really have is your head, so if someone else uses it, he should pay for it.

Second City taught me more about this business than anything else I've ever done. I'll never forget that trippy feeling after you get over the initial fright and terror of standing up onstage with nothing but your mind. When you finally get it and you know you're going to think funny and come up with something, it's a very liberating feeling.

22.

Alan Myerson

Alan Myerson directed The Second City both in Chicago and New York. (Prior to that, he had directed Off-Broadway and coached the comedy act Stewed Prunes, all three members of which—Richard Libertini, MacIntyre Dixon, and Lynda Segal—also worked with Second City subsequently.) Myerson left Second City in 1963 with his then-wife, former Second City actress Irene Riordan (today known as Jessica Myerson), and formed a San Francisco–based comedy troupe, The Committee, which played continuously in San Francisco till 1973, was the subject of two films (*A Session with The Committee* and *Funnyman*), released three records, appeared frequently on television, had a run on Broadway, and operated a second facility in Los Angeles on and off for a number of years. Since leaving San Francisco, The Committee has occasionally regrouped to tour clubs and colleges. Quite a few Second City alumni have worked with The Committee, among them Del Close, Dick Schaal, Severn Darden, Bill Mathieu, Murphy Dunne, Larry Hankin, Hamid Hamilton Camp, Roger Bowen, Avery Schreiber, and John Brent.

In addition to producing and directing The Committee, Myerson directed the film *Steelyard Blues* and staged *F.T.A* (which stood for either "Free the Army" or "Fuck the Army," depending on whose interpretation you took), a satiric variety show featuring Jane Fonda, Donald Sutherland, and Peter Boyle which toured Army towns as the counterculture's answer to the USO.

Q: *How did you get involved in theater?*

MYERSON: While I was in college, I had a romance with an actress here in L.A., and through that I did some stage managing and directing on campus and in Hollywood. I dropped out of school—I was a political science major—and I moved to New York. My formal reason was to do some writing, as I had an idea for a play I wanted to write. Actually, it was an excuse to leave L.A. After a year of scuffling in New York, I ended up sharing a house with a guy who was an actor. One day he went to an audition for an Off-Broadway play, and I went with him just to hang out. For a lark I read for a part and was offered either the part or a job as an assistant director. The job as assistant director seemed more interesting, so I took it. Three days later, the director got sick and I became the director, and the show opened to very good notices. This was about 1958 and the play was called *Hope Is a Thing with Feathers.* So now I was a director. I also became an acting teacher and discovered I was inclined to use improvisation as an acting tool.

At that time, improvisation was becoming an "in" tool in relation to acting. The Actors Studio, of which I was a director-member, was flirting with it, but their approach was much different from The Committee's or Second City's. It was much more masturbatory and was what I think of as a bastardization of Stanislavsky's work. The Method seemed to be about drawing images, fantasies, and memories from an actor's mind which might then elicit feelings or emotions which the actor could personally recognize. I didn't see that it had much connection with portraying those emotions or feelings. The substantive difference between our kind of work and that kind of work is that we use it as a performing tool, whereas theirs was an approach to character exploration and freeing the actors from some inhibitions—but they did it very haltingly. The Studio did exercises like the one Strasberg called "The

280

Private Moment," in which you would pretend, in front
of an audience, that no one was watching you and do
something you would do only in private. Another exercise
involved taking a written scene and improvising it without
using the author's words to find the subtext or some kind
of alternate life to the scene. Or you might set up a sort
of ancillary situation. Say a husband and wife might be
having an argument in the script, so you might set up a
scene between the husband and one of their children explaining the argument just to fill in the life of the character
for the actor playing the part. I began working with those
kinds of things and then broadened out as they began to
seem limiting.

There was a long dry period of about a year when I
wasn't working at all and New York seemed to be kind of
a dead end to me. So I started hitchhiking around the country, going to what they now call regional theaters, of which
there were few at the time. One of the places I stopped
was Chicago, at a theater called Playwrights at Second City
which Second City had set up next door to where they
were based. Some friends were working there. This was at
the time Paul Sills took the first company to L.A. in preparation for their opening on Broadway. Paul hadn't been
in Chicago for about three months, and the show they were
doing in the second theater at that time was called *Big
Deal,* which was an adaptation of *The Threepenny Opera.*
It was in shaky shape and the actors asked me to give them
some notes, which I did, and they were enthusiastic about
my assistance.

Shortly after that, Second City opened on Broadway and
Paul decided to stay in New York with the company, so
they needed a director for the Chicago revue company.
Probably because of the recommendations from the actors
in *Big Deal,* he called me while I was in New York, and
we sat and talked, and he hired me. He told someone else
later that he thought I was the most morose person he'd
ever met and anyone like that would be good at directing
comedy.

So I went back to Chicago around 1961 and ran the
company for about six to eight months and then opened

another Second City operation in Cleveland. It wasn't called Second City but was sort of a franchise operation.

Q: *Since this was the first time you were directing improvisation for performance, how did you re-gear yourself?*

MYERSON: Most people do what's necessary to survive or succeed in any given situation. I was merely trying to learn as fast as I could. I was ignorant of the problems and processes of what we were getting into, but I was talented in directing actors, so I used that strength to learn the other. It didn't take long. The company was excellent.

Q: *Whom did you work with in Chicago?*

MYERSON: Bill Alton, Joan Rivers, Del Close, Irene Riordan, Anthony Holland, Hamid Hamilton Camp, Avery Schreiber, Dick Schaal, Mina Kolb, and Bill Mathieu at the piano.

Q: *Did you direct Tony Holland and Bill Alton's scene, "Lekythos"?*

MYERSON: Yes. That was one of the first "people scenes" I was responsible for. When I had been in Chicago before, I had seen it as a scene improvised in a set. It had been dropped as no one had any particular interest in working on it. When I began working at Second City, I insisted that we get into it again and turn it into something good.

Q: *I know from your work at The Committee that you're very involved in politics. Was there much political involvement at The Second City while you were there?*

MYERSON: Basically the people at Second City were curious and intellectually involved in the climate of the country, but we didn't engage in much real political activity, either as individuals or as a group, outside of commenting on events from the stage. I do remember, though, that in 1961 there was a general strike for peace, and I got all the actors together to strike the theater. Not because we had anything against Second City, but in general observance of the strike.

Q: *I heard that all was not smooth between you and some of the actors in Chicago.*

MYERSON: Everything was fine for a while, but after about five months we had a very heavy dispute between Del Close and me. Del was disappointed that I had been hired over him. Another man, Bill Alton, also had wanted

to be director. They decided they didn't want me to direct
them anymore. Del and I got into a very fierce fight, so I
went to Paul and Bernie and told them I needed their support in this argument. Their response was, "It's either you
or Del. You go." I got angry, said it wasn't fair, and
wound up being sent to take care of the New York company, which Paul had left on its own. At that time it involved people like Barbara Harris, Arkin, Tony Holland,
John Brent, Severn, Gene Troobnick, Andy Duncan, Mina
Kolb, and Howard Alk.

I was in New York for about six months, and again I
was caught in the middle of a fierce fight. This one
stemmed from an argument between the companies in New
York and Chicago over autonomy. Paul and Bernie would
come into town once a month and say, "This is no good,"
and we would get upset and a few of us, led by Howard
Alk—who was an equal partner with Paul and Bernie—
would quit and come back and quit and come back and
the whole thing would be a shambles.

The kinds of people attracted to improvisational theater
and the kinds of pressure that are placed on them make
for a lot of turmoil resulting from a number of things, including the neuroses of the people involved as well as a
real affection for one another and the work. There are
strong and fierce fights in this atmosphere, and also very
strong and fierce love affairs. This tends to propel people
forward to different levels of activity. It propelled me to
The Committee and it propelled Arkin and Barbara to
Broadway stardom. A lot of the most involving and in-
tricate pieces of work have come out of the tension and
turmoil, sometimes the tensions being within the people
and sometimes with other members of the company. Del
was responsible—and I'll be frank—he was more responsible than anyone for my being quasi-fired from the
Chicago company, but we're quite good friends and I've
hired him to direct for me. It's like a familial situation
where you have fights, but the family ties remain intact
and are often strengthened by those fights because you feel
yourselves move in other directions and expand.

The arguments in our companies were never made
public. Everybody's first loyalty was to the work. It wasn't
"I don't like you. . . ." Well, the genesis of an argument

may have been "I don't like you," but it always took the guise of "You're not doing the work well." Of course, there's some ego involvement. "I want to be the director and you're the director." But Del truly felt that he could direct better than I could. Whether it was true or not is academic, but that made it all the more intense. In many ways, these fights were like the ideological struggles that people get into in socialist bureaucracies where there is a lot of personal aggrandizement involved—people believing firmly that one way or another was the way things should be done. The work was all-consuming.

I quit Second City in New York as it had become too frustrating for me. Around that time I got married to Irene Riordan. She later changed her name to Jessica. Anyway, she and I thought we'd drive around the country to see if we could find a place where we might start a theater of our own. We first stopped in Phoenix, where her family lived, then went to L.A., where my family lived, and then on to San Francisco, as that was my favorite city next to New York. When we got there, we felt very strongly that this would be a good place to do what we wanted to do. We began talking to people around San Francisco, and inside of ten days, we had started to raise money.

Q: *How did you sell the idea of The Committee?*

MYERSON: We used Second City as an example, as a progenitor of the form. We proposed that it would be similar in form but different in attitude and content. Second City used mostly songs and blackouts, with one or two extended scenes we used to call "people scenes." I felt Second City was more cabaret-ish, and I was more interested in emphasizing the dramatic aspects. I felt that Second City was sketchier—more two-dimensional. I wanted three dimensions.

Q: *Having worked with both The Second City and The Committee, how would you contrast the two groups?*

MYERSON: The people involved in starting Second City had a much more intellectual approach than The Committee. The Second City people were mostly university-oriented, very bright. Of the original company at The Committee, there were only three college graduates. We were all bright and informed, but we did not have the formal educations that the people in Chicago had, and our attitudes were bawdier and more raucous, which was more compatible to San Francisco than to Chicago. They are different kinds of cities and foster different kinds of attitudes.

23.

Joan Rivers

Joan Rivers came into Second City to fill the vacancy left by Barbara Harris. Up until her casting, Second City performers had been enlisted either from the Compass/Playwrights group or from the legitimate stage. Rivers was the first to join the company from a stand-up comic background, and she brought with her a brasher, more joke-oriented approach. But it would be wrong to think of her work there merely as stand-up comedy transplanted. Two of the scenes she helped create, "Model and Tailor" and the dentist scene (which was later made into the short, *T.G.I.F.*) stand among the very best "people" scenes.

Since then, of course, Joan Rivers has become one of the true stars of comedy. She still works improvisationally. To create material, she appears at a small Beverly Hills nightspot, Ye Little Club, where she deals with subjects as they occur to her. These performances are taped, transcribed, and honed into set routines. She also writes for other media. Her book, *Having a Baby Can Be a Scream*, proved to be very popular, and she also has coauthored a Broadway play and written scripts for television. She co-wrote and directed the movie *Rabbit Test*.

Q: *How did you join Second City?*
RIVERS: The first company was coming to New York and

286

they needed new people in Chicago. They auditioned sixty ladies and I was sixty-first. I waited five and a half hours at William Morris, where they were holding the auditions, and when I went in I was angry and aggravated and upset by the whole thing. Paul was there and he said, "Describe what happens in this room," and I said something like, "A lot of fat, middle-aged men won't give people a chance in this room." Crazy stuff. And I got the job right away. Later, when he was directing me, Paul once said, "Where is the fire I saw that day?" That was it. That was the only comment he gave me in a year. That's how I came to Second City. I went to Chicago and later came back to New York to work at the Square East for a little while at the very end.

I tell you, it was a very closed and cliquish group. I think I watched the show three nights before I joined them onstage, and during that time nobody spoke to me because I was the outsider. I remember going to the drugstore for something and realizing it was the first time I'd heard my voice for four days. I thought Tony Holland was the best of that group at that time. I was in awe of him. He was the first one there to do anything for me—he invited me to dinner. I was so thrilled. I thought he was so brilliant and wonderful and clever and evil, and that's everything I like in a friend. When he wanted to be my friend, I was in shock.

Q: *How did you break in after being the outsider?*

RIVERS: Very slowly. Nobody was generous in that company. And I wasn't generous either. No, that's a lie. I was generous at the end to the new girl when I left. But, at the beginning, nobody came to me and said, "Let's do a scene." You had to kind of go out in group scenes and find your own. I can't really explain, but maybe by saying something or pushing in to say something or creating a little something of your own, then they would say, "Oh," and notice you. But it was very hard. I'm not aggressive at all. It's hard to believe because I come on so strong, but I would never, ever be the one to approach any of them to say, "Would you like to do a scene?" I lay back. I guess how I came to feel a part of the group was because of Tony.

The first good scene I improvised I think was "Tailor

and Model" with Tony. Tony saw an ad, in *Vogue* I think, and it showed a lady and a little man sewing her hem. Tony said, "Isn't this great? Let's do something with that." He liked the visual thing of it because he never got off his knees in the entire scene. While we played it, he made a 360-degree turn around me, working on my dress.

Another one Tony and I used to do was called "The Bowling Ball." We played two people who had grown apart and he gives me a big, heavy set of books for our twentieth anniversary, and I give him a bowling bag and ball. And out of that we just see where we've gone wrong. When I gave him the ball, he said to me, "Oh, you can see the glow! I know, you can study the heavens with it!" "No, no," I said, "it's only a bowling ball." Another of his lines was, "Whatever happened to that girl who used to quote Edna St. Vincent Millay, who was so sensitive and carried a rose?" I said, "She's married in Jersey with two kids, but what about me?" I just adored working with him.

After a while, we'd become so close, he would say to me right before we went on, "Tonight I'm going to be Greta, the German lesbian." No one knew this but him and me, and he would play the entire show as this woman. It was not fair, because you're onstage playing with a guy who was playing a lesbian playing a guy. He was evil—sometimes bitchy. But I mean by that he did things that you wanted to do. I remember one time there was this woman in the audience who talked through a whole show. At the end, Tony took these plastic flowers from the back of the stage and went up to her and bowed and gave her these dirty, filthy flowers. He was so special, and Second City was a great showcase for him because you could be special and scenes were kind of worked around your specialty.

Q: *What are your impressions of some of the others you worked with?*

RIVERS: Severn pinched my boobies the first time I met him. It was just madness. I could never relate to Severn. He wore a cape and carried a walking stick. One time he brought me Nivea oil and poured it all over my back. He had a machine that projected the constellations on his ceiling. If you went to his house, you had to lie on your back and look up.

Del Close always made me feel like he was looking down

on me, for the whole time. Hamilton Camp—there was
genius there, but it was so close to insanity that I was
scared at first. Paul Sills never looked me in the eye. There's
nothing to say about Paul except that he hired me and
then I don't think we ever connected.

You forget how good Bill Alton was. When I first met
him, I thought, "There's a man carrying an attaché case.
Why is he here?" He was very businesslike. He was the
interlocutor; he made it look like he was up there so the
audience could relate to him. But you forget he was a brilliant straight man and wonderful actor, and fed you incredibly well.

I did a scene with Bill which was predicated on our
having a husband-wife type of relationship. We'd talk about
mundane things. "Your mother was over and she took your
things to the cleaners." That kind of thing, but funny
within it. And at the end, I went to the clock and I said, "I
better set the alarm. When does your wife get home?" It
was done as a little one-liner at first, but it grew to a
whole scene.

Most scenes came from the improv sets that we did after
the set show, things based on audience suggestions. If you
found something good, you kept doing it over and over
again, and by the time it went in as part of a new set show,
it was very polished, though you changed within it still. We
really honed and pulled and remembered lines and came
in with lines. Tony used to come in with a lot of written
lines because he was naturally a writer. There was nothing
wrong with that because you've still built it from nothing
yourself. You've created it.

Mike Nichols came once and directed us a little. He
didn't do that much, but what he did do was just brilliant.
This was right at the start of his getting into directing.
Don't ask me what he did or how he did it, but he made
you think that you were the best and the funniest and the
most brilliant, and so you gave a little more. He made you
think you were better than the best. He had this way of
drawing it out of you, which is what a good director does.
You'd lift your finger and Mike would fall across the chair
with hysterical laughter. I thought he was the best, even
then. He's never directed me since in anything, but I remember that with such vividness because it was so terrific.

Q: *What about memories of Bernie Sahlins?*

RIVERS: I'm not a fan of his. I don't know if he knew what he had and he thought we didn't know, or he didn't know what he had, but if I heard him say one more time, "If you don't like it, we can replace any one of you with a bartender. . . ." There was no regard or respect for anybody.

Q: *Did he make any creative contributions?*

RIVERS: As far as I was concerned, only the salary check. It was very important in those days. I'd been there about five months when someone told me that Bernie had said that I was the best girl they'd had since Elaine May. But he never said it to me. You know what that does to you?

I remember we were about to move from the little theater to the big theater next door. It was the end of the run of the old show and he said, "Everybody has to take cuts in salary because we aren't doing very well." Tony and I decided we weren't going to take cuts. We said, "We'll take less money, but you'll owe it to us." So we didn't take cuts though a couple of the others did. Then we moved into the new theater, which was twice the capacity, and we became the hit of Chicago again. Then rumor had it that the kids who had taken the salary cuts had come and asked him for more money but he wouldn't restore their salaries. Later, when we were really packing them in and making them a fortune, we all asked for a raise. I think we were getting $150 a week then, and we asked for $160. Bernie said to me, "You're very sick. I won't pay the raise, but I'll treat you to a psychiatrist." So I went all over Chicago looking for a psychiatrist. I was hoping to find one who wouldn't bother to treat me but would bill Bernie for the time and then split the fee with me.

Sometimes we stole from the refrigerator at the club. Tony Holland and I used to take French pastries, orange juice, and half-and-half. It automatically went home with us every weekend.

Let me say also that there was another side to Bernie. For example, there was a time when Tony was sick in Europe and I heard that Bernie sent him some money.

Another thing—we'd done a few local TV shows with Billy Friedkin directing us. So they came up with the idea of us doing a weekly TV show called *The Living News-*

paper. The hitch was that none of us was going to get paid for doing the show. Bill Alton was the businessman of our group and he said, "No," and Tony said, "No way." I went along with them, as they were my friends. We said the only way we'd do the show for no money was if Bernie didn't get any money for it either. That killed it.

Q: *The Billy Friedkin you mentioned, that's the same one who's now the film director?*

RIVERS: Yes. He was very good even then. He was already "taking meetings."

Q: *What do you remember of the workshops?*

RIVERS: There was a children's theater troupe, which you were in if you couldn't make the adults' group. The people in that group were hoping to get into the regular company. Dick Schaal was with them when I was there. They had pantomime once a week, but I never went to any of that. I wasn't going to be told that I had to go to class during the day. I mean, as long as we were working at night and everyone was satisfied with what we were doing, I was not going to be told that Tuesday and Thursday we had to attend these workshops. I couldn't bear passing space objects and have them change. Who *cares?* I used to say, "Come the day I'm in a Broadway show, I won't have to improvise holding a teacup because they'll hand me a real teacup."

I was never truly happy at Second City, but it made my whole career. By working with those people, I learned self-reliance and I found out for the first time in my life that what I thought was funny, other people thought was funny also. I suddenly found out I didn't have to talk down in my humor, that there were a lot of people who could understand what I meant. It was wonderful that I could make a living making bright people laugh. We did a long scene once on *A Nation of Sheep,* and we didn't have to explain anything about the book. Everyone in the audience had read it or knew about it. And we used to do improvs in playwrights' styles. You went into Tennessee Williams or Chekhov and they understood it. That was wonderful and terrific.

Everyone in the company lived close to the theater. I had Barbara Harris's old apartment. I was known at first as "the girl who replaced Barbara." Severn and Avery were in the building, too. Also Dick Schaal and Melinda Dillon, I think. And we had a nice, dumpy landlady who knew everybody, so you felt very safe. Tony was just two blocks down.

Here's some stuff from a journal I kept: "Spent the day writing letters, did a nice show but to a very small audience and a bad improv set filled with jealousies. Del was furious because I used one of his lines." Oh, when a celebrity came! "Anthony Quinn came last night and especially liked the dentist scene. He talked to me and Bill about it later. He was amazed that it was improvised. So all the aggressions and shoving it down everyone's throat to have it accepted is now worthwhile. Alan [Myerson] said last night it would be in the new show." You see, if you had a scene you wanted to go into the new show, you had to push for it. Speaking of celebrities, I remember also one time Mort Sahl came. I had such a crush on him! Did Tony tell you we used to write my name "Joan Sahl" all over backstage? Oh, when a celebrity came, you would fall over dead, you were so thrilled!

Q: *How did people in Chicago regard Second City?*

RIVERS: There was a tremendous sense of community, that you were all a group and if you were from Second City it meant you were very bright. You were invited to Hugh Hefner's parties because you were with Second City. You were invited to lots of things because everyone in Chicago liked Second City at that time. And there was a local radio show hosted by a man named Jack Eigan, and we would be on that all the time. There was a family feeling. Like Thanksgiving, everyone automatically went to Bill Alton's place. In Chicago, we were very close. By the time I joined them in New York, everybody was already a somebody or on the way to being a somebody.

Q: *Whom did you work with in New York?*

RIVERS: Alan Arkin for a while, which was an incredibly rewarding experience, as he was so creative. And Severn was there, and also a girl named Chris Chase. They hired her and me at the same time and they told both of us, "One of you isn't going to make it." This is the kind of thing they used to do. I can't remember if it was Paul or Alan Myerson who said this. "One of you girls isn't going to be here in a couple of weeks. Now, go onstage and be

292

funny." But Chris and I liked each other. She was the one who didn't make it. I still have a warm feeling toward Chris. It was situations like this that caused all the tensions backstage. Situations that were created by the management. If they had left us alone, it would have been a glorious period for all of us.

Q: *This makes me flash on a section in Viola's book where she says that improvisations shouldn't be competitive. That competition kills improvs.*

RIVERS: It certainly does. Don't you think it makes you uptight? You both want the job, you both want to be actresses, you like each other, and you're both blondes? I can't tell you the hysteria.

Paul Sand was in New York, too. I remember he had more sex appeal than anybody I'd worked with up to that time. Ladies just adored him. He'd just go up onstage and look boyish and the audience flipped out. He was very nice and warm and charming, but it was the first time I came close to working with a sex object. I'm not putting down his talent. He had talent plus sex appeal.

He and I had the same character, which led to trouble. We both wanted sympathy. I remember one scene of two shy people on a park bench which got stupid after a while. We sat and kicked at the dirt for a while. He wasn't going to talk to me and I wasn't going to talk to him. Somebody had to be aggressive, but Paul tried to be even softer than I was onstage and more vulnerable, if possible. So you've got two people who are vulnerable on a park bench. It's not much of a scene, is it? I remember it was supposed to be a pickup scene and I finally had to pick him up because he was never going to make a move.

I left Second City in 1962 and I never went back. I remember after I left, I saw the current company on TV doing some of the scenes I helped create. When you see the stuff you wrote being done and you're not the lady doing it nor getting credit for it, it tends to upset you a lot, especially since at the time I was working for Olivetti typewriters and also for a plastic factory.

Q: *Compared with the number of successful men who came out of Second City, there are relatively few women such as yourself who have come out of it and done well. Any idea why?*

RIVERS: Because most ladies don't want to be funny. If you're pretty, you don't have to be funny. If you ever look at comediennes, they're not the most lovely-looking ladies in the world. You have to be not too attractive or else you have to be a little peculiar to want to be funny. It's not a naturally feminine thing.

Q: *Do you still keep in touch with some of the people you worked with there?*

RIVERS: Not really. Tony, of course. Mike—we don't keep in contact, but there's warmth and kisses and hugs when we see each other, which is nice. And Alan Arkin is always very warm—and Andy Duncan. He and Tony did a thing called *ABC Comedy News* and I stopped by to be on it, and it was Thanksgiving and, of course, Andy came to my house for dinner. Listen, we all suffered together and once you've been onstage with someone for months and have learned to read each other's thoughts, there's a bond.

I get very angry with Tony. I keep saying, "Come out here and write." He is a brilliant writer. I'm always telling him, "Write what you can write, and don't be ashamed because it's commercial." The minute something became commercial, it became trash to a lot of them. When we were in Chicago, all of us at Second City were into Truth and Beauty, and they didn't want to take the next step because then it became commercial and anything commercial was not Art. We all believed this to a certain extent.

But then you look at Mike and Elaine. They haven't prostituted themselves at all. You can make the transition without being ashamed of it. When I said I was going to play Vegas the first time, Tony fell apart, dropped the phone, and wanted no part of me. Now sometimes he teases me and wants to know if we can get an act together. But if he were out here now, he'd be writing one movie after another. He'd be Woody Allen. He was the most brilliant of all of them. You think Paul Sills is a genius? I think Tony is the genius of the whole group.

I'd like to see them set up a hall of fame to us and I'd like them to say, "Nobody else can improvise except these people because they were the winner improvisers of all time." A little room with a big plaque and pictures of all of us, how terrific we were, and statues. And I'd like them to throw a dinner for us so I could pick up an award— and my acceptance speech would be: "They were sons of bitches, but we owe it all to them."

24.

Avery Schreiber

Avery Schreiber is the hairy half of Burns and Schreiber, the comedy team known for its classic "Taxi Cab" routine. They met and developed much of their repertoire at The Second City. In addition to their records and frequent TV appearances (they hosted their own series one summer), Schreiber is well known for his crunching of Doritos in TV commercials. He has a number of straight acting credits to his name as well. On Broadway, he starred in *Story Theatre* and *Dreyfus in Rehearsal*. He played the title role in *Volpone* and the First Grave-digger in *Hamlet* at Los Angeles' Center Theater Group. He made his film debut in *The Monitors,* and also appeared as a Polish pirate in *Swashbuckler.*

SCHREIBER: I grew up in Chicago on the West Side . . . got to know a lot of aspects of that city. I knew about everything in Mike Royko's book, *Boss.* I grew up with it around me. I knew "the boys." As a kid I worked for "the boys." I was a money-runner. I knew where their card-houses were. I knew where their hangouts were. I knew about their connections with politicians. If you cared to hear about it, you'd hear more than you wanted, growing up in Chicago. Sometimes you didn't want to hear about it because it got pretty oppressive. But, then again, maybe because of that, people there will spring up and do something about it. Maybe, when you feel that things really can't be changed, that's when you want to try changing them the most. And Chicago seems to harbor that feeling.

That city has always been the place for great modern renaissances. The literary movement in the '20s started there. You had Hemingway and a bunch of other guys hanging around the Pickle Barrel, with *pischers* like Studs Terkel listening, checking out what was happening. And you have some great architecture there—Louis Sullivan to Mies van der Rohe. Some of the modern art renaissance began there. That is a very interesting city.

I grew up there and, as soon as I could, left home. Went into the army. A Jewish boy, how else do you leave home? I came back, thinking I wanted to be a director. So I went to the Goodman Theater of the Art Institute. In order to become a director, I had to study acting. . . . And like finding an O'Neill whore you fall in love with, I've been married to it ever since. I found I had to act in order to get it off. The Goodman trained me in the classic approach to acting. That plus the Method. My first contact with improvisation was the Stanislavsky-based technique. The kind of thing that was pioneered in this country by the Group Theatre.

The Goodman was where I first heard about Paul as a director. Someone on the staff there was talking about him, said, "Oh, that foul-mouthed man!" I decided to check him out. I went to see a production he did of *Measure for Measure* at the University of Chicago. I wet my pants laughing. Everybody was laughing uncontrollably . . . so, I knew I wanted to work with the guy.

I was reading *Variety* and the *Village Voice* to keep up with the new plays that were being done in New York. I read about cabaret theaters starting up there. I was aware of the history of cabaret as part of my studies—Brecht and the other Berliners—and I was very excited and interested in it. So I decided to open my own, which I did. The name of the company was The Trolley Company, and we played in a place called the Blind Pig. There was nothing improvised in the show, but after the show we did some improvs. That was to satisfy the guy who ran the Blind Pig, who wanted us to do it because Second City was doing it.

One day I met Paul in a restaurant and he said, "Why don't you come in and audition for me?" I said, "You want me to do improvs? I don't know that much about the technique." He said I should try, and I said, "OK." I went into this place with black-lacquered walls and little pictures. It was very nicely made up as a coffee shop, and off to the side was a room which was the theater. The coffee shop was bigger than the theater. Little place. I said to Paul, "Who'll I audition with?" He said, "Severn," and I chickened out. I said, "I won't go onstage with that man. I'm *afraid* of that man!" I told Paul, "I can't," and I didn't.

Later, after I had stopped working with the people at the Blind Pig and had done some work around town, I went to Paul and said, "How about now?" and he put me in *Big Deal* as a building inspector. While I was doing that, once in a while I would run next door to where the regular Second City show was playing. I'd bring my guitar and play with Bill Mathieu sometimes. At about this time, Paul went out on the road with the first company, taking them to Broadway, and Mike Nichols came in to help put together one of the shows. He asked me to improvise with the company every night, and I did. I joined the cast and received a hamburger a night for the first couple of months I worked there. Then I received the startling salary of $25 a week. Then I helped organize the company (*laughs*) and made sure that everyone got Equity minimum.

Anyway, I was knocked out because I had wanted to do cabaret theater so much, and, within a year or two of leaving Goodman, there I was, in *the* cabaret theater. It was *the* political satirical company in the world. Terrific! Fantastic!

Paul was the dynamic that made the company spin way up and above, because he refused to let anyone work at less than the peak of their intellectual capabilities. There were no "dumb" characters until years later when we decided the audience had changed so much. . . .

Q: *How did it change?*

SCHREIBER: From being made up of graduates and postgraduates to the great middle class, whose major entertainment was film and theater or TV and radio and masturbation. You could tell the audience had changed from the change in the suggestions. Before, we'd ask for characters and we'd get "Dido and Aeneas." Then it shifted and we would get "Jackie Kennedy at the hairdresser." It was quite a shift. As a matter of fact, the shift came just about the same time Kennedy came in. With Eisenhower we had had a perfect target. It was a classic setup: we were young, he was old. Youth versus age. And Everett Dirksen was *hours* of fun with his poems, his flowers, and his wonderful stentorian voice. We had a terrific time with him.

Kennedy was a different story. He was very close to an age we could communicate with. The only way you could make fun of the man was on the subjects of his accent, his wealth, and his social activities. It wasn't easy. We sided with what the man wanted to do. As opposed to Johnson. I remember the day Johnson became President, I said, "I've got a great anti-Johnson sketch." Everybody said, "No, it's too soon." They were right. However, if we had been The Committee, it would have been up there the night Kennedy died.

There was a time at Second City when, in order to keep up with what was happening so I could go on that stage, I was reading *Time, Newsweek,* the *Wall Street Journal,* the *I. F. Stone Report,* and the Chicago papers. Everything possible. Also the right-wing literature, because you had to know what you were talking about. There were things you had to know about if you were going to go onstage and deal with them. Say you were going to do a scene about a dock worker who wrote a book and became a great philosopher. You'd have to be familiar with Eric Hoffer. And then you'd ask yourself questions. Like how does he relate to his job if his philosophy is, say, nihilism? "The truck got smashed up? Well, that's life, right? So, what else you want to talk about? Oh, your tape recorder's busted? Gee, too bad." That sort of thing. In this kind of atmosphere, your mind not only expanded, it became like a sponge. You picked up on everything so that you might use it onstage.

Q: *Sounds like you put in a lot of work.*

SCHREIBER: I literally broke my back there. I did a show called *My Friend Art Is Dead.* I played an organizer, and at the end of the show I would be hoisted up to Labor Heaven. I weighed 290 pounds then, and one night I felt it go. There was this terrible pain. I said, "Hold it, my back!" and they started to lower me. As they lowered me I started to sing "Joe Hill." We brought the curtain down five minutes early, the ambulance came, and I was hospitalized.

One of the great things happening while I was there was that Viola ran workshops. Viola Spolin is the unsung heroine of Second City. She's the mother of improvisation. Dick Schaal and I worked with her and the games. We got into transformations, and it got to the point where Dick and I could do transformations so fast—shift the reality of a scene and make an agreement so fast—that it became almost like ESP. Doing the transformations helped open me up a lot, helped me present my own personality onstage.

Q: *Do you have any theories as to why so few women shone at improvisation?*

SCHREIBER: I think something happens at the sandlot level. When you're kids. At first the boys and girls play together, but there's a certain point where the girls go off and do girl things, training themselves for the future of being women in the society. At least, this is what I remember happening when I was a kid. Maybe it's different now. But the boys were left alone to compete in team sports. The boys learned about "teamwork." They understood that moment of chaos just before that mystic thing happens and everyone connects into a cohesive whole for a play. Women used to miss out on a lot of that in physical sports, and I really believe that that was one of the major reasons it was so hard to get women into this kind of theater, to be able to improvise as part of a team. They hadn't had enough of those game experiences to trust themselves to be able to do it.

We would be in rehearsal and everything would seem to be falling apart and the women would yell, "Hey, schmucks, what are you doing?" They wouldn't understand that crazy moment that comes before everything clicks together when everything looks like it's about to go to pieces. They would become very frustrated, angry, hysterical, pensive, or closed. Unless they were highly competitive. Sometimes Paul would purposely make them angry so their anger would spark them to compete. Another thing Paul would do: Just as everything looked like it was a total mess, he would walk out. This would usually happen a couple of nights before an opening. He would walk out and we would say, "Hey, we got nobody but ourselves," and then it would snap together. It would start to work, then Paul would come back and throw a little polish on it, and we would go on with a great show. But that moment of chaos, that process, the women then mostly didn't seem to understand, and I think that has something to do with why so few women used to shine in improvisational work. But it's changing. Lately I've seen some great women coming out of improvisational theater. I presume it has something to do with the way society has changed regarding women over the past few years.

All the heavies in Chicago used to come by the club. Sometimes they would get up and futz around onstage with us. Nelson Algren used to come up onstage all the time. He had a great character—Edgar Kennedy, the unknown, bastard Kennedy son who ran the janitorial service for the Merchandise Mart. Harry Bouris and Studs Terkel would show up, too. And Paul Carroll, the poet, who once wrote a seventy-five-page poem to Severn and performed it for us.

Q: *You were in* Peep Show for Conventioneers, *weren't you?*

SCHREIBER: That was a thing to show the rest of the world! It encompassed a multitude of styles. They didn't understand it when it was done in New York, but they got it in Chicago, and the critics got it in London. It was phenomenal! Joan Littlewood saw it and it encouraged her to come out of retirement, and she did *Oh! What a Lovely War!* I wasn't in the New York and London companies. I was in the original one that Paul put together in Chicago.

The subtitle of the show was "Where's the Action?" MacIntyre Dixon and Dick Schaal played two conventioneers who are out on the town, and they tell the cabdriver they want some action, and he takes them to this place. The host comes out and greets them. "What's the action?" the guys ask him, and the host says, "Any action you want." A guy comes out and plays music for them, but no, that's not the action. "How about this? How about that?" the host says. "Women," they say, and there are projections flashed of women out of *National Geographic* with things in their noses. "No," the guys say, "that's not it." And they keep looking for what the action is.

Finally, MacIntyre Dixon is talked into going to Cuba with a pumpkin (shades of Alger Hiss) with an atomic bomb in it to give to Castro as a present. The bomb goes off, kills Castro, and MacIntyre takes over. The CIA gives him a speech to read to the people. There's a projection of a million people, and he's up in front of them reading the speech saying, "You are now free!" and going on until he discovers that the speech they gave him doesn't have an ending. So he has to make the rest of it up himself, and he starts saying, "I will do this, and I will do that!" and the crowd cheers. He is the great dictator! And then the picture fades and he finds that he's standing on top of a table in the middle of this room. The host says, "Did you get your action?" Mac says, "Yeah, it was worth it."

Schaal says, "What do you mean? What are you talking about? That's not the action. What about *the action?*" "What about the Jackie Kennedy Room?" the host says. So they take him to the Jackie Kennedy Room and you see this projection: all you see is bare feet and legs going way the hell up out of sight. They take off their hats as they look up and you get the idea that she's standing there naked. "No," says Schaal, "that's not the action for me."

Finally one of the people at this place says, "I know what you want. Was it a spring day?" Schaal says, "Yes." And you start to hear bird songs and music starts and there's a projection on the back wall of a beautiful knoll, and there's a girl on a swing. "Was it nice? Were there flowers in the air?" "Yes," Dick says, "that's more like it." The girl turns to him and says, "Dick?" He goes over to her on this swing strung with garlands. She says, "Got a cigarette?" and he gives her one, and a giant Salem pack is projected on the background. She says, "You know, we can't keep meeting at the drugstore." He says, "Why not? I'll talk to your father." "No, my father found out." "So what?" he says, getting totally involved in the scene. At which point she says, "I've got to tell you something—I'm pregnant." And Dick stops the scene. "Bullshit! What is this?" he says. "This is ridiculous!"

The whole scene fades away. The host says, "Thank you very much, you've had your action." "No," says Dick, "it was . . . yeah, it was good, but. . . ."

It was at this point in the rehearsal that Paul couldn't

Avery Schreiber

find the ending. And the actors couldn't find the ending. Nobody knew what to do. Paul was walking around, clenching his fists, and his face was red. Then he turned and said, "You know what it's like? The ending's got to be like the ending of that picture, you know, about the balloon." And everyone said, "Of course!" And Paul said, "If they ever make one. . . ." He hadn't seen it! He hadn't seen *The Red Balloon!* He just said this without knowing such a thing existed, but the communication was right.

So Dick demands that they take him back again. The host tells him it can't be done, that you can't go back to a fantasy once it's been realized. But Dick demands it, so they start it up again. The birds start chirping and the girl is on the swing with the garlands and the music is playing and he tries to get into it again. The girl says, "Dick. . . ." He looks at her, the expectation draining from him, then he says, "Yeah, I guess I did have my action." And he leaves. The music starts up again and the slide projects four American flags, and in the center of the screen is a big circle like a doughnut on which is printed, "Whatever you want you can have—for a price." And that was the end of the piece.

If you were to see it today, or were to read it if it were scripted, even in this short time a lot of the references wouldn't be understood. It was tremendously topical. In four hundred years, I really don't believe that an actor would get a laugh about eighteen minutes of tape being erased, even if Neil Simon had framed it as the greatest joke. It's very hard to keep a topical reference fresh.

Q: *How did Jack Burns get into Second City?*

SCHREIBER: He and George Carlin had an act. They split up and Jack joined The Compass in St. Louis at the same time Larry Hankin did. Then they were brought up to Second City, at about the same time Dick Libertini and MacIntyre Dixon joined.

The first few months Jack was in the company, he was really working alone—stand-up style. He had a lot of great characters. Then, in a workshop, he and I did a scene together. I was an old-line liberal father—a worker all of my life. Jack played my kid who didn't want to work. My job was to dig a hole, and the whole scene took place in this hole I'm digging, and I'm trying to get him to dig with

303

me and he won't. Something happened in that sketch—he maintained his character and his reality and I maintained mine, and together we created a third thing. Which is what Viola's work is about, right? Something clicked. We came out of the scene personally moved.

Q: *I'm not familiar with the scene.*

SCHREIBER: It never became a finished scene. We never did it again. It was just an exercise. But it showed us that we had something. So we worked together on and off after that.

I didn't do the first "Taxi" scene with him. He did it with someone else originally. Later, when we were in the New York company, I said, "I've been watching you do that scene a long time, Jack. Let me do it with you." He said, "All right." So we did it and I changed some lines. He said, "Don't change lines." I said, "Why not? Why don't you let me try it? You're forgetting the whole basis of the work." He said, "OK, change it."

And I was able to develop the taxi driver as he is now and I was able to give Jack enough bounce and feedback so he could develop along other lines. I questioned him. I pulled things out of him. He said, "Well, these niggers, you know." I said, "What about the niggers?" to get him to go further with it. He said, "All these black niggers, these upstarts. They're staring all this trouble." I said, "Really?" He said, "Yeah, I'll tell you—they keep that up, they're going to lose my support." And there we had a line, a joke. But I kept pulling at him until it came. I've worked with him enough to know that when I do this, he's going to pull through, I can trust him. He can also throw things at me and know that I will hit him with a reality that's somewhere else.

If you want to look at the taxicab scene the way Jack and I evolved it, it's very similar to the comedy pattern you see between Don Quixote and Sancho Panza. Because you have two separate realities together in the same environment, and every time those realities hit, a tremendous thing happens. Sometimes laughter. Sometimes it's sad as the driver begins to realize that he's a very lonely man. It's a very interesting scene. We've done maybe thirty-seven different versions of it, finding all kinds of things in it.

Q: *I know there's been some controversy over the owner-*

Avery Schreiber

ship of material and whether people should be allowed to use the material outside of Second City. And I know you've had some hassles with this. What's your perspective on this?

SCHREIBER: Someone told me that in Chicago they were mad at Jack and me, saying that we were doing stuff from Second City. We don't do Second City sketches. We've made them our own. What—because Leadbelly wrote some songs, nobody can sing them but Leadbelly? For me improv stuff is like folk stuff. Some of the things we do that began in Chicago, we paid for that. Everything's done business-wise. Years after we left Second City, we agreed to do a show in Paramus, New Jersey, and a show in Toronto in exchange for the use of the material we wanted to use, and *that's* when we started to use the material in our own act. Up until that time, we had no right to it and we didn't use it.

We paid for what we used. John Brent came up with the preacher piece we do. We bought it from him and changed it, made it our own. Later he went to The Committee and he asked us if he could use it there. We said, "Sure!" He used his version, we do ours, and, when Second City does it, they do ours. So there's a give-and-take in all that material. (*Laughs.*) But it's people's theater, really . . . urbane folk theater.

By the way, did you know that John Brent ran for mayor of San Francisco? He ran as an independent. His slogan was, "Whatever You Want!" He had buttons. "Whatever You Want!—Elect John Brent!"

Q: *How long did you stay with Second City?*

SCHREIBER: About five years . . . pure s-and-m. (*Laughs.*) I started out with the Chicago group and went to London with Del, Bill, Dick, and Mina, and later I became part of the New York company. It was fine being a well-known colorful fish in the Chicago pond, but I had to see where it was at in New York. That's the way it still is. You must go to New York no matter what your business is and test yourself in that market.

When I got there, all the scenes I had developed had been done already by other people, had already been seen. What was I going to do . . . redo other people's stuff? No, I wanted to do *my* stuff, so I brought my stuff back into the show, and then came some New York recognition of my work. They said, "Yes, we saw so-and-so do it, but this guy really does it well." We were there for about a year. Jack and I backed an actors' strike because the salaries were being cut down, and finally there were four of us performing for two and a half hours on that stage—Mina, Jack, Severn, and me. We were exhausted, so we asked for more bread. If we didn't get it, we weren't going to go on. The way I understand it, Bernie Sahlins, in response to our demand for a fair shake, closed the theater. And, except for when I occasionally came back and did special things for them, that was the end of my relationship with Second City.

But Second City is only one part of what came out of Viola and Paul's work. There are literally hundreds of groups using improvisation for various things. Not only theater, but education and therapy. Viola was into a heavy number when she put her ideas together, and she knew it. She's pointing the way to the future. Some people don't have anything to do anymore because machines are taking care of them, so the areas of endeavor they're going to get into will have to be creative. And that's where Viola's at. She's leaving signposts. Her book is one. She worked her butt off writing that book, and we all helped her. She was experimenting with us at Second City while she was writing it, and some of what she came across with with us is in there. It's nice to know you were part of that, because that's going to go much further than Second City. I believe what she and Paul have gotten into will last longer than this country. Thousands of years. Their names will be forgotten, as will all of ours, but what they've done has really opened up a new vista for communication.

Q: *Any thoughts on Paul?*

SCHREIBER: Paul took Viola's techniques and carved with them. He's a great technician of the human spirit. He can make things happen. You might not like what comes out. You might not like the hammering that goes into it sometimes, but then . . . he's mellowed out lately.

There was a time when many people could hold Paul up with a sort of reverence. I can't do that anymore. Because he's a conduit. A conduit for creative experience. We can grow and get nourishment by drinking from a cup, but the cup itself, sad to say, can't partake.

Avery Schreiber

Q: *You worked with him last on* Story Theatre. . . .

SCHREIBER: I see in story theater the progression of the work that Viola began, because in that we're really reaching out. The great thing about Paul's work with story theater is that it speaks to a larger community. With Second City you had the university and the city and it had to be commercial. It could act as a political conscience. However, *Gulliver's Travels* did not cause one change, right? Game Theatre had an even smaller community because it was the people in the neighborhood. Though game theater may be another signpost for the future. Maybe someday, instead of going to churches on Sunday, you'll go someplace and have an improvisational-communal experience. A *communion* experience. But, with story theater, you have the opportunity of communicating to a large mass. It can be done in large theaters or on film or tape. It doesn't demand the intimacy of the others and I know it because I did Ovid's *Metamorphoses* in L.A. in a big Hollywood-style production. Tremendous! The costumes were fantastic! The lights were terrific! And the audience went for it.

But I think Paul is being a little safe in the stories he's chosen. I think that he should be bolder in his subject matter. I'd like to see him tackling novels. I'd love to see him do Joseph Wambaugh's *The Onion Field*. Howard Fast wrote a fantastic book that was bastardized in the film version, *Spartacus*. All of the thematic values in that are so cogent today. It would make a *fantastic* stage piece, and he can do it. I think he has to do something that no one expects from him and he has to make people look at it. For God's sake, they did *Ulysses in Nighttown* again on Broadway not long ago. Why didn't Paul do that?

I said to him once, "What you have to do is work with Rod Steiger, Lee Marvin, and people like that. You've got to work with guys of that stature!" I want Paul to work with these people. I'd love to see what would happen if they got involved.

307

25.

Richard Schaal and Valerie Harper

Richard Schaal workshopped with Viola Spolin in Chicago, and then joined the resident company of The Second City, where he proved to be particularly adept at space work. He did what is generally considered to be his finest work there as one of the conventioneers in Paul Sills's landmark piece, *Peep Show for Conventioneers* (described in some detail in Avery Schreiber's chapter). Schaal then transferred to the Square East company where one of the cast introduced him to a dancer-actress named Valerie Harper, whom he married and with whom he subsequently appeared in Second City companies in Toronto and Los Angeles. They also played nightclubs and appeared on television as a comedy team, with Schaal also doing some theater directing and making occasional appearances onstage. They worked with Sills again in *Story Theatre*, first in Los Angeles and then on Broadway.

In the meantime, Harper had begun to attract a following as a regular on *The Mary Tyler Moore Show* (which also featured Playwrights alumnus Ed Asner) and, in 1974, became the star of her own series, *Rhoda*, establishing her as one of the most popular performers on the scene. She made her film debut opposite Alan Arkin in *Freebie and the Bean.* She continues to return to the stage when her schedule permits.

Schaal has also been very active, appearing as guest star on most of the major series, directing an improvisational-based troupe called The Children of Paradise, and appearing as a regular on *Phyllis.*

SCHAAL: I had my own construction company, and I was designing and building buildings outside of Chicago. Then I got divorced, sold the buildings and property and equipment I had, and I did nothing but hang around for a year. Then I met a guy who had gone to Northwestern University with me ten years before. He was now the head of a drama group at Northwestern's downtown campus. He asked me to design and build the set for a show for them, which I did. Then he asked me if I wanted to be in the next show and I said, "I don't care. OK. I have nothing to do." Then someone from some Chicago summer theater saw me and hired me to do summer stock for about forty bucks a week. This was in 1959 or '60. It was a lot of fun and it was very social and, at that point, very good for me.

I went to Second City the second week they were open, and I thought, "Wow, there's something more here than meets the eye." I went to see another revue that had just opened at the Happy Medium, and it was all right, but a little lightweight; it didn't entertain your imagination too much. But then I got an idea and I hired three writers to write a revue and a director and six players. I put myself in it and I sold the package to a guy who owned a restaurant out in Chicago Heights, and I turned his Mardi Gras Room into a cabaret theater. Our show was called *Hit the Heights.* It was not improvisational. It was written and memorized and choreographed except, because I was so busy producing, I never really learned the material but kind of improvised my way through performances. Paul Sills, Bernie Sahlins, and Sheldon Patinkin came to see the show, and I guess they sensed what I was doing because Sills said, "Well, when you close in about three weeks, call me and I might have a job for you." And in three weeks we did close, after having run for twelve, and I joined Playwrights at Second City and was in *Big Deal.*

Q: *When did you realize that you wanted to act?*

SCHAAL: I haven't realized it to this moment. I don't think I'll ever realize that.

Right away I joined Viola's workshop. As a matter of fact, I was in her workshop even while I was still doing my revue. She had three different workshop groups at different stages, and I went to all of them all the time.

The workshop frees the intuitive in order that spontaneous moments are possible. You have to cross that abyss before you can hit the state of improvisation.

Q: *"State of improvisation"?*

SCHAAL: I've almost thrown the verb out—"to improvise." Because I don't think you so much improvise as find yourself in a state in which it is happening. The state of improvisation.

It's only when you don't know, in your head, what to do that this happens. Only at that moment when there is no alternative but to follow your intuitive, and then you just *do.* That's the spontaneous moment.

You can't teach someone how to improvise. There is no "how to." Nothing has ever been *taught,* it's only been *learned.*

Q: *So Viola basically set up the conditions for you to learn.*

SCHAAL: She would say, "Now we are going to play a game. You can't talk unless you make physical contact with another player." The rest is up to you to discover.

Q: *How did you join the regular Second City troupe?*

SCHAAL: Paul was putting together a company to send to Shaker Heights, Ohio, and he felt my work was good enough to put on the stage, so rather than send me there, he sent some other guy and I took his place. I went into the show in two days. I watched the show two nights and was in it the third. That company was Mina Kolb, Bill Alton, Del Close; Avery Schreiber came into it later, also Hamilton Camp and Joan Rivers. There were a lot of girls who drifted in and out very fast because they couldn't cut it. That was pretty much the company that went to London in 1962.

Q: *You told me there was a set there in which you played a doctor. . . .*

SCHAAL: Right. The suggestion was "Doctor" and I

310

played the doctor, and we went into that scene knowing nothing. And I was really able to enter the state of improvisation. The intuitive was absolutely free and therefore everything following was spontaneous. A person in the scene started telling me how he felt, and I started saying words I don't remember ever having heard before. Later, I was at the bar downstairs and a doctor came up to me and asked me if I had ever studied medicine. I told him I hadn't, and he told me that the diagnosis I had made onstage was probably absolutely right and accurate.

Q: *When did you leave the Chicago company?*

SCHAAL: I think it was in '62. I had no plans to leave. What happened was I went down to the bar after the show as usual and ordered a beer—a bottle and glass. Then I found myself pouring an imaginary—no, not an imaginary . . . I was handling the space the beer would occupy if it were really there and was pouring it into the space a glass would occupy if it was really there. And it really wasn't there! And my hand kind of melted into the space and I thought, "I've been at this too long!" (*Laughs.*) So I went to Sills and said, "I'm out. Get yourself another boy. I'm leaving." And I went to Mexico for six weeks. Then, when I went back, I decided to join the New York company.

Q: *Who was in it at the time?*

SCHAAL: Barbara Harris, Bob Dishy, Bernie Kukoff are the people I remember offhand.

Q: *How did you find working with the New York company different from working in Chicago?*

SCHAAL: I find that New Yorkers are . . . I don't know what the right word is. Some are jaded. Some—their brains are beaten out so they become desensitized. Whatever it was, they didn't pick up on subtlety. They couldn't see it or feel it or understand it. It was more an axe in the forehead for New Yorkers. I think they're used to comics or the gross behavior of the Broadway stage.

One scene I did there I liked a lot was called "Truck Drivers." I did it with Bob Dishy and it was just about these two truck drivers. We were going to do it on TV, and the producer of the show wanted to see it written out. So we typed it up for him so he could see what happened in it. He read it and said, "I see only one laugh in here." Now, performing it onstage, it was one solid laugh—hysteria from beginning to end. But the producer couldn't see it from a transcript. It's just that the jokes aren't in the words in this kind of work.

Q: *You worked with other directors at Second City besides Paul.*

SCHAAL: Yes, but the emphasis from the other directors I worked with, like Larry Arrick and David Shepherd, was different. They were shooting for end result, for product. Sills never went for product that we would know of, but the product was always the end result of whatever was on the path. He could have a whole thing in mind, but you'd never know what till you got there.

Q: *What happened between Second City and* Story Theatre?

SCHAAL: A lot of things that New York people go into. I was in Broadway shows: I was the existentialist minister in *Little Murders* and I was in *Kelly.* And I did some Off-Broadway and commercials, and I wrote and directed industrial shows.

When I directed, I used the technique (or whatever you want to call it) I'd picked up from Second City—that way of working. If people had lines, I wouldn't let them say them till they had the thought, because I contend there are no lines in the theater. They don't exist. Only thoughts. So it's going back again, getting away from the printed word to the state of nothing, the state of emptiness. It's very Zen, in a funny way. You have to be very empty in order to be filled with these new experiences. It's like being newborn.

Q: *How did you get involved with* Story Theatre?

SCHAAL: Just my association with Paul over the years. He invited my wife and me and Hamid Camp and Melinda Dillon and her husband, Dick Libertini. . . . Paul would say, "Here's a story we're going to do. I don't know how to cast this, so everybody take a book and start reading it and throw light."

Q: *"Throw light"?*

SCHAAL: It's an exercise. Give-and-take. In other words, I might start out by saying, "A man walked down the road until he met . . ." and then, if it was a girl he met, a girl would come in for that part and carry it on from there and so on. What you have to understand when you do story theater is that, though these words come out of the mouths of different people, the story is one voice. So when you do a story, you don't tell it to an audience, you don't play a character. And the story doesn't just take place on the stage. The feeling is that the story is all the space you can fill, and therefore you share the story among the players on the stage, among the audience, among the musicians, among the lighting man and the lights—among everything. It is one. We all are one story, and the technique or approach to that is that the story leads you. You don't lead the story, it leads you.

So you can't force that work. That work has to be *felt*. So how do you get people in the world who feel that and allow themselves to be moved by that? It takes a training process, a workshop. It takes entering into the art at full commitment. I mean, the reason why the society is so screwed up right now—plumbers, carpenters, for instance —is nobody's an artisan. They are told, "You don't have time to be an artisan." They're told "how to," they're not led into a way of finding out. That's the way life is in this country right now.

They say progress is such a great thing. I say progress is a step backwards. It robs us. We're very careless with each other. I don't mean on a one-to-one basis. But the human animal in regard to the human species is very careless. It lives the life of a mouse—low. It can't see very far, so the thinking doesn't go very far and the feeling stops short. What improvisational theaters and workshops would want to help everybody discover is a deeper intuitive—a wider understanding and more feeling. I've seen stiff spines soften and narrow minds broaden; people just go through incredible metamorphoses in this work.

Q: *I get the feeling you think of the games and improvisation as almost an approach to life—a philosophy.*

SCHAAL: Well, it changed my life, and everyone I've known who's ever really been touched by it has been changed or altered for the better, I think.

Viola and I just finished teaching a course at U.S.C. We had eight psychology professors and put them through theater games.

Q: *What did you hope they would take with them from the experience?*

SCHAAL: To get out of their own ways, to get out of the bureaucratic kind of thinking they're trained to be stuck into. We go to school and we don't get educated. We get trained. My feeling is that it's more important to get educated, and that implies simply getting to the point where you can think and feel and understand. What I wanted from the psychologists was that they find the ability to entertain and stimulate the imaginations of their students to such a point that they—the students—will go out and learn. Teachers aren't there to give you information but to make you want to seek out the information yourself. Information is all computerized anyway. You can go to the library on a university campus and run anything through the machine, right?

Q: *Why psychology professors? Why not economics professors, say?*

SCHAAL: Maybe the psychology professors are a little more sympathetic to the human condition. They know how to recognize when something's wrong. They say, "How do we correct it?" "What do we do to fix it?" This is one possibility, and it worked quite well. In fact, one of them visited me and told me he wants to get out of psychology and get into theater games, maybe as an actor or a workshop director, and go off on his own. The dean of the psychology department, Don Lewis, called me and said it changed his life. He said, "Hey, I'm walking different!"

Q: *You do a lot of work on television. How do you gear yourself for this kind of work?*

SCHAAL: You work another way. You work the way Stanislavsky talked about working. You train yourself to do things on cue so that it comes off *looking like* instead of actually being. Acting is making it look like, right? Improvisation is—it don't look like it, baby, this is *actually it*. It's happening to *you*.

Sometimes I'll be hired because I've been identified as an "improvisational actor." Then I'll come on the set or go to the theater and find that nobody really understands it, including the other players. The word "improvisation" has become lost. They don't know what it means. I'll find that the people who hire me think, "Oh, that means you can do anything . . . that we tell you to do!"

HARPER: I was scuffling around New York, studying acting with Mary Tarcai and doing industrial shows. And schlepping around trying to get commercials, getting called back three times and then losing them. I'd heard about the success Second City was having in New York and Chicago. In fact, I auditioned unsuccessfully for Paul Sills. They were looking for replacements, so I went down and auditioned, they thanked me, but I didn't get it.

My roommate and friend, Arlene Golonka, was in the Second City company, and she insisted I come and meet this "great guy" who was in the show. She'd been telling him about me, too. So I went, and the guy she was talking about was Dick.

He was wonderful. Quite objectively speaking, he's really brilliant at this. He has a phenomenal sense of "space" and using the "where." When you talk about creating something out of nothing . . . I've seen Dick take a bare stage and make it a crowded room, and you'll *see* the clutter. He'll step over the cord of the TV and then not be in that part of the room again for a while, then, in the middle of the scene, he'll walk back that way and step over it and audiences will say, "Oh, it's really there! It's magic!"

The Second City company was in constant transformation, both in the work they were doing and in the makeup of the cast. If someone left for a while, they'd just reorder the show and do different scenes. Say Severn would be gone for three months, they'd bring in Jack Burns to do his scenes with Avery. Dick and I started going together, so I saw many of these people while they were still very involved—Avery, Barbara Harris, Severn, Bob Dishy, Jack Burns, Mina Kolb. And, being with Dick, I began to understand the work. The time I'm speaking of must have been right around 1963.

Dick and Barbara used to do a fabulous scene called "Catholic Dance." It was about two teenagers—about fifteen years old—at a dance. She's the tease and he's totally hot. They're standing out in the courtyard together and Barbara says, "Just look at those stars! Just like God's beady eyes burning down on us." They decide to trade

315

crosses. He has this one he's worn since he was four, and Schaal would have everyone on the floor, because the clasp is welded or something, so it takes him ten minutes to get it up over his chin, and then it gets stuck on his nose. He finally pulls it off, hurting himself, and gives it to her. And then Barbara says, "Now I have to give you mine." So she starts hauling this thing out of the front of her blouse. It's the kind nuns wear—two and a half to three inches long. And Dick takes it, and what he does is put it down his shirt and then into his pants. So the rest of the scene is this young boy, with a hard-on, with this thing clunking into him, and wiggling his leg, and the audience would go up for grabs. It's a very sweet scene. Later, when Dick and I had our own act, we used to do it.

Sometime in mid-'64, some of the Second City people went to San Francisco to be in The Committee. Dick was out there for the fall, and then, around Easter, I joined him and we decided to get married. While he was there, Dick ran a workshop with Howard Hesseman and about forty other people. Viola was running workshops there for a while, too.

That was my first actual workshop experience. I loved Viola instantly, as a person and a teacher. Some of the people in the workshop had a tendency to treat her like a goddess, but she wouldn't have it. She would say, "I'm glad you respect my work, but please don't genuflect, because I'm not like that. I always overcook the ham, my house is in a mess, and I can't even buy a pair of shoelaces properly. So let's get up off our knees and *go to work.*"

Anyway, so Dick and I got married and came back to New York, and he opened a workshop and formed a group. That went on for months and months, but we didn't take the next step, which would have been to form a theater, because the actors kept getting jobs elsewhere. Now he has a troupe.

Q: *How much actual performing did you do with The Second City?*

HARPER: To tell you the truth, I never appeared on the stage at The Second City in Chicago or New York. If I had, I would say it with pride and would love to have it in the book, but it's not true. I was "the wife" at that time and "the workshopee." But I was around so much with Dick

316

and I was in all the workshops, I think that's why some people think I was in the show.

I did do a show in 1965 with Jack Burns, Avery, and Dick. It was an industrial show that we toured all over the country—New York, Minneapolis, Detroit, and some other cities. It had something to do with trying to increase advertising in the Sunday sections of newspapers. We wrote a lot of the show ourselves, using Viola and Paul's techniques, and we did some Second City scenes. I remember that we paid Paul for use of some of the scenes. Dick felt very responsible in that regard. We didn't send the money to Bernie, because Bernie was already getting his cut. I'm sure you've heard a lot about *that.* (*Laughs.*) But we would send Paul a percentage of our salaries, just as a token thing, which he appreciated. Not the money so much as the gesture. We did another industrial show for General Electric. I remember we went to Venice, Italy, with that.

Then, in the winter of 1966–67, I was in an actual Second City company at the Royal Alexandra in Toronto. That was with Dick, Linda Lavin, David Steinberg, and Omar Shapli. Sheldon Patinkin directed the show. He organized it so there was a lot more than usual for the women to do. It had a lot of scenes about romance and female-male relationships. Dick and I did "Catholic Dance," Linda and David did the famous Barbara Harris–Alan Arkin scene, "Museum Piece." And four of us did a take-off on *Who's Afraid of Virginia Woolf?* in which I played Martha. Also Linda and I did a song together that was *so* much fun! We had a ball.

I was also part of Game Theatre in '66–'67 in Chicago. Paul was running it with Viola assisting. That was actually the first time I worked with Sills directly. Game Theatre to me felt somewhere between doing a play and being in a workshop. We did the games we would do in workshop, but people were watching. And the audience participated in the games, too; that was the key thing.

Then Dick and I developed some Second City–type scenes and did an act for a while. We appeared at the Bitter End and the Village Vanguard and Bill Hahn's. Then we were regulars on a TV series in 1968 called *Skitch Henderson's New York,* in which we did improvised blackouts every day with the help of Jeremy Stevens, who is

317

one of the great improvisers. Jeremy also directed a group called The Fourth Wall which Marcia Wallace, who's a regular on *The Bob Newhart Show,* was in.

Dick and I also made a lot of commercials. Something the agencies used to do—they've stopped doing it now—they'd have people audition for commercials by improvising and they'd tape the improvs. The reality was that here were actors writing people's commercials for them, and sometimes they'd write the commercials but they wouldn't get the acting jobs and they wouldn't get paid, and then they'd turn on the TV and see someone else doing what they had improvised at the audition. One day, Dick was at an audition and they were saying, "Dick Schaal: Take five." And then he stopped and said, "Wait a minute. This is a gig. You have to pay me for this." He left and his agent put in a bill for $100. It was token, but the point was made.

I did a second Second City show in Los Angeles at the Lindy Opera House in 1968. That was with Mina, Paul Sand, David Steinberg, Dick, and J. J. Barry. That was really wonderful. I loved working with Mina and Paul. Dick and I came out to L.A. to do that show, and then we stayed because he loved it so much. I hated it. I wanted to go back to New York. But we stayed and Dick got a job writing *Music Scene,* which was a TV show David Steinberg was on. And I sat in Laurel Canyon and got fat. (*Laughs.*)

Q: *Your next improv work was* Story Theatre *in 1970.*

HARPER: Sills just gets more beautiful. Every ten years he creates a new theater form. *Story Theatre* was quite different and distinct from Second City, though a lot of the same elements applied. Paul developed it in Chicago and then formed a company that performed in spring 1970 at the Mark Taper Forum at the Music Center in L.A. Originally it was supposed to be one of the New Theater for Now productions, which are experimental productions which run for five days at the Taper. But then a play that was supposed to be one of the major attractions was postponed practically at the last minute, and they asked us to take its place. It was an incredible success, and later that year we took it to Broadway.

Paul got edgy in the middle of rehearsals in L.A. and came to a standstill in the work. He couldn't break us through that barrier between us and the stories. So he said, "Let's not work for a few days," and he went away, and Viola came in and worked with us, applying some of her games to the stories. When Paul came back, he said, "Now we're getting somewhere!" So there's that combination of having a worshop and doing a show into which what you learn in the workshop can be funneled. This kind of work frees you, and you can apply it to the written word.

Dick told me that when Viola was running workshops in Chicago at Second City was the most nurturing time of his life in the theater. They had workshops during the day in which they worked on projects, and at night they'd go to the theater and perform. Their whole life was theater.

Trust happens in a workshop. All the armor starts to melt. That's the magic of this kind of work. But you've got to lend yourself to it. Viola says that she cannot teach it. She is a guide and leads people to discovery. But she says that one cannot put experience into people's bodies.

Viola's workshops are not set up as approval/disapproval situations. The concept of good or bad is avoided. Emphasis is on playing the games. Sometimes I'll hear an actor talking about this kind of work, saying, "I'm not good. I'm not funny. I'm not clever." And I say, "Clever, good, funny—strike those words from the record! They are absolutely the antithesis of this work."

The thing in these workshops is whether you play the game or not. It's not even did you make a basket, but did you dribble down the court and aim for the little wire ring? There's a security to it because you have the rules of the game to guide you. If you keep the game in mind, there's no bombing because you're actively doing something, so there's always something going on. The games themselves are a theatrical experience. That's what Game Theatre was about.

I've always found improvisation, the way Paul and Viola guided us all in it, to be close to jazz musicians jamming— you're really listening to each other, really hearing. Or like a ball team, playing together. That's when it's at its most beautiful. It's hard to get that kind of a feeling in a company without this kind of work. But I've found that when people have worked this way once, they can go out and work with other actors not trained in this at all and still bring the value of this work into that situation.

Viola really isn't into training actors, but of course she has trained many just by putting her work out. I'm one of them. And she's done this just by doing the work she has done.

She's always said she wanted to work with teachers and get theater games into the schools. Everybody could be in a workshop. Her work is for anybody, for everybody. It's therapeutic, although not therapy. She doesn't want it in any way compared to psychodrama. She will steer people away if she sees that's what they're getting into.

There's another area she tries to avoid. I've heard her call out, "Don't get misty-moisty!"

Q: *"Misty-moisty"?*

HARPER: Floaty, wafting around the room during an exercise in a sort of suspended, dreamlike state, feeling all like, you know, "Oooo, it's magical!" Sometimes people in workshops get into this area, and Viola will say, "No, no, the space is *here,* and it's *real.* It's you and me." It's a cop-out to get ethereal and float away with yourself because that separates you from the other players. The space is our *connection,* so *stay connected.* This takes tremendous concentration and a true willingness to be there with your fellow players. So "misty-moisty" means self-indulgence.

Q: *I understand that you frequently recommend actors with improvisational backgrounds for jobs. For instance, I hear that you recommended Paul Sand for the appearance on* The Mary Tyler Moore Show *that led to his getting his own series.*

HARPER: The thing is I frequently recommend excellent actors and people that I want to work with, and it just so happens that a lot of them do have improvisational backgrounds, though by no means all of them. I'm my own little casting agency. I always have been.

It's not just people with improvisational backgrounds who work improvisationally. Most very good actors work this way, I think—knowing that the moment is improvisational. Oh, you can have lines and all that, but the lines are just a guide. What you do is back up from the script and then reapproach it, finding the impulses behind the lines. Impulses that bring you to the lines with truth. When you find the impulses, you free yourself from the lines so that when you get to any given point in the script, it's like you're there for the first time, as if you're saying the words for the first time. That's where the improvisation happens in acting. That's what Olivier and other great actors do. Maybe they were never in Viola's workshop, but they understand that path. They understand about the moment being improvisational, about letting the moment fill you up.

People used to try to separate improvisation from acting. I remember in the early '60s hearing people say, "Oh, Barbara Harris—she's not really an actress; she does that other thing." Wrong! What was happening, I feel, was that this was a new technique and other actors who were into other approaches did what people naturally do, which is to protect what they know by downgrading what they see as a challenge to their way. So they would say, "Oh no, we can't do the games to get there; we have to do scene study. No, we can't just handle space objects; we have to go through sense-memory exercises." But what they didn't understand is that the games and improvisation don't take away from anything else. You can study classical, Method, or whatever, and Viola's work applied to that can only make it soar.

But now you see its influence on every kind of acting, writing, and directing, whether it's for theater or movies or television shows or commercials.

Q: *Is there much evidence of the effect of improvisation in the TV work you've done?*

HARPER: Oh, yes. During the first year of *Rhoda,* I arranged for Viola to run workshops for the cast and staff of the show. It was absolutely invaluable. But, in TV, improvisation isn't really used fully but sort of grabbed at a little. It isn't used in its full-blown state such as in the theater, where we found that improvisation can be an absolute theater form itself as well as applied to other theater forms.

But on my show the writers don't just sit around making up jokes. When we're working, Jim Brooks and Allan Burns and the other writers are so secure they say, "How does that feel? What's wrong here? Have you got any ideas?" It's funny, Jim and Allan always say, "We're not directors," but the truth is they're *great* directors because they're audience.

And I think that's really true about Sills. When he directs, he makes himself audience and he wants to be delighted and thrilled. I feel truly fortunate to have participated with Paul and Viola. They opened up a lot of space for me to be an actor in, and I acknowledge them for their incredible contribution to the theater and to my life.

26.

Alan Alda

Alan Alda was a member of David Shepherd's Hyannisport
Compass. Later he workshopped extensively with Paul Sills
and performed for a short time with The Second City in
New York. His last work with Sills was as a guest on the
Story Theatre TV series.

Onstage, Alda created major roles in *Purlie Victorious,
The Owl and the Pussycat* (co-starring with Compass and
Premise alumna Diana Sands), and *The Apple Tree* (directed by Mike Nichols, also starring Barbara Harris, and
featuring young Robert Klein in the supporting cast). His
film work includes *Jenny, Gone Are the Days* (the film
version of *Purlie Victorious*), *Paper Lion,* and *The Me-
phisto Waltz.* On television, he was a regular on *That Was
the Week That Was* and continues to maintain his popular-
ity as Hawkeye on TV's *M*A*S*H.* He is also a talented
writer and director; he created the series *We'll Get By,*
and directed and co-starred with Carol Burnett in the TV
production of *6 Rms Riv Vu.*

ALDA: Harvey Epstein, a producer I had worked for for
a couple of years in summer stock, recommended me to
David Shepherd. David was putting together a Compass
company to play Hyannisport for the summer. I think this
was in 1962. It was well after he had had the success with

the first Compass in Chicago, and this was an attempt to use the Compass name to get another troupe going. Anyway, I met him and improvised with him and he asked me to be in the troupe. It was a successful company artistically certainly, and I think we made money. It was a terrific company. Diana Sands was in it. Also Honey Shepherd, who was then David's wife and an extremely good improviser, and Ron Weyand and Reni Santoni, two exceptionally talented men. I think at the same time there was another Compass company that played St. Louis and used some of the material we developed in Hyannis.

Q: *Did David train you with the games?*

ALDA: This was the old school of improvising where you shoved people out onstage and they were on their own. It was quite different from theater games, which I didn't hear about until a year or so later when I first worked with Paul.

Q: *So how did you prepare to perform at Hyannis?*

ALDA: We improvised, toughened up our muscles. We strengthened our nerve is what it really amounted to. And tried to be more open. Also, David tried to work as much as possible from character, which is a good idea. We would try to develop characters and then we'd spend a lot of time sitting around in a circle having bull sessions with each of us speaking as a particular character to try to learn how our characters talked all the time.

The show we did was mostly a satirical revue. We did an interesting satire in which we took "Who's on First?" —the Abbott and Costello routine—and transposed it to a Southeast Asian setting in which you couldn't tell who was in power because the players kept changing.

The favorite thing I did there was an impersonation of President Kennedy, which I did as a press conference. I worked very hard on that. I tried to get a little bit inside his personality instead of doing Caroline jokes. I enjoyed doing that very much. It was interesting to do it at Hyannisport because the people who were asking me the questions in the audience were very often reporters who had asked the real President the same questions earlier in the day at a real press conference. It was very strange because I was getting asked questions that hadn't been in the paper yet and sometimes I didn't know what they were talking about.

Q: *Did you ever compare your remarks with Kennedy's?*

ALDA: Actually, a good deal of the time I would take Kennedy's answers and extend them only a little bit for comic effect. As humanitarian as he was or intended to be, he wasn't enough so for my taste at the time. Of course, this was before he was killed and became a tragic figure. He was just another president then, you know?

After I stopped doing that impersonation, I thought it would be fun to do William Buckley. I would do Buckley at peace rallies and things like that, and I would get asked questions and I would answer them with the same answers I used for Kennedy. The interesting thing was they worked just as well for Buckley.

Not everything we did at Hyannis was satire, though. I remember Ron Weyand and I did a version of the "Vend-a-Buddy" or "Phono Pal" scene in which I played the robot in the subway. Ron came in, and he was a down-and-out musician with dreams of greatness on his last legs, physically and emotionally. He needed me for comfort. I'd tell him to talk to me and I'd get him to pour his heart out, and just as I was about to give him an answer, my machinery would go crazy. I played that the tape in me began to break down and I wouldn't give him answers. I would either slow down or go *fjernikplafoo!* right at the crucial moment, and he would have an emotional breakdown onstage. It was a very moving scene and kind of bizarre.

Q: *How did you begin working with Paul Sills?*

ALDA: David Shepherd recommended me to him. This was about a year after Hyannis and shortly after Viola's book came out. About 1964. I took part in a games workshop Sills ran at Second City in New York. It started out with about twenty or thirty actors. From time to time, all kinds of people would come down. Peter Falk came down one afternoon, but he never really learned the games. Most of the people who came and left within a few weeks never really understood the difference between games and what you could call guts improvising, where you just get out there and brazen your way through, which leads to cleverness and joke-making and self-conscious "playwriting" on your feet. That's not true improvising and it's certainly not games-playing. It's not what Viola invented. Anyway, after about six months, the work was so hard and so demanding that there were only about three or four of us left. The others were Jane Alexander, Olympia Dukakis, and Dana Elcar.

Paul wanted to create a new company which would do theater games. He wanted to make the games a new kind of theater. He wanted to present them as an entertainment. Unfortunately, he took the four of us that were left after six months and put us on at a late show at Second City. It was the wrong audience for this because there's an enormous difference between the kind of work we were doing and the satiric work that Second City audiences expected to get. It didn't work out.

And yet we did a number of lecture-demonstrations at colleges and in church basements when we were trying to pull ourselves together as a company, and those went over really well. They were very exciting. The place would rock with laughter without anything clever being said. It was just the audience responding to the joy of the psychic connection or whatever it was that was happening. But at Second City, the audience's expectation was something quite different. They were drinking a lot of whiskey and beer and a psychic connection of that kind wasn't really possible.

Q: *Maybe it's a difference between audiences interested in a finished result and those interested in and digging the process itself.*

ALDA: I think that would be an intellectual way of saying it. Needless to say, the two kinds of improvising present the audience with two kinds of experiences. If you're in the audience, each kind will involve a different part of your mind. For the satiric thing, you're able to be distant and aloof. In fact, you *must* be distant and aloof. You're experiencing it with your brain. You're getting the jokes—the physical jokes and the word jokes. But in the games you're actually tuned into something that's inside the actor's mind and there's a kind of mental music that's played and that everybody shares. Now this is getting very abstract, but I'm trying to express a basic difference in the experiences. It's not merely two kinds of discrete activity, it's a whole different pot of soup.

I remember Barbara Harris and I improvised a lot in the workshop. We had some really good stuff. We did a scene—I don't know if I did it with Barbara; maybe I did it with Jane Alexander or Olympia—called "Making Out in a Church." It was very rich in Catholic childhood details. A dance at a sodality. The Sodality of Our Lady. A high school dance where we're surrounded by nuns and yet the two of us are off in a corner trying to dance slow. I kept getting up close to the girl but I kept getting stabbed with her crucifix. Finally we slip away from the dance and go into the church. We make small talk about religious things. I pick her a flower from a funeral wreath. I'm trying to make out with her in the church, but as I'm showing her around the place in the process of getting a little closer to her, every time I pass the center aisle I have to genuflect and it kind of cuts into my style. Religion kept impinging on the sex all the time. It was a very funny scene. We found it in a spot improvisation. I think they made that part of the Second City repertoire.

Q: *You were in Second City for a while, weren't you?*

ALDA: I actually worked in the Second City show only for a week. It was while I was in the workshop and Paul asked me to go in and replace some people while they were opening a show in Canada or something.

Q: *What are your impressions of Sills?*

ALDA: The two times when I felt I had very important breakthroughs in my work were the two times I worked with Paul. In some ways, they were very painful experiences. Paul was not an easy person to work with. Everybody gets infuriated with him because he's relentless. He keeps going after what's possible even if the person doesn't seem able to get near it.

One of the most valuable experiences I've ever had theatrically was when I went to Vancouver to do an episode of the television version of *Story Theatre*. The first day I was there, Paul was rough on me and I didn't like it. I told him that it was the first time I had ever been inspired to quit. We hashed it out and developed a working relationship. But he's got that combination of being hard on people and being an extremely valuable influence.

Q: *Paul Sand said all he wants is something wonderful right away.*

ALDA: And always, and from everybody, and it doesn't matter to him that people will go off in tears or fall to pieces.

Anyway, I was in Vancouver for two or three weeks for *Story Theatre,* and I had a really extraordinary time in a fifteen-minute piece called "Lucky John." I think it's a Grimm story. I'm not sure. I found it in a book and asked if we could do it, not knowing how much trouble it was going to be, but I knew there was an opportunity there. It was almost a fifteen-minute monologue with short scenes with other people. It was dying and everybody came down from the control booth and said something different to me. Arnold Weinstein wanted me to get in some social comment and Paul kept saying it wasn't happening. Paul, like Mike Nichols, will not settle for something that "works." They both want to click over into what's exciting, into something that's really fresh ground, unpredictable. Actually, I forget what he said, but I suddenly realized that it simply wasn't funny enough. It wasn't taking place. But what happened was I set myself the task of getting a laugh every ten or fifteen seconds. I didn't know how I would do that. But I gave myself a rule to follow. I would be breaking that rule if I didn't get a laugh every fifteen seconds. What happened was I suddenly came alive. I lit up and the thing worked. It wasn't anything that Paul said that led to that except that he wasn't satisfied with it.

Q: *You said that there were two special experiences out of working with Sills.*

ALDA: That was one, and the other was the improvising for six months in the workshop. That changed me as a person. The games make you more open and more magnetic and more self-confident than anything I've ever come across. Because it's a social experience for one thing. You learn that all there is is the other person. That's a very valuable experience because most people spend their lives learning that they have themselves, period, and that they have to fake their way through and have to disassociate themselves from other people and lie. The games open you up. I think it's the connection with the other people that's what's fun. It's a group experience and it's very pleasurable. We're mainly excommunicated from each other, and to be able to share two or three hours with somebody else painlessly is like dancing.

I think the games can be therapeutic in a very mild way. You have to be very careful how you talk about that, because there are people with very serious problems I don't think would be helped by them. But I suppose a very mild, what you could call normal, neurosis would be helped by games. I played them with friends of mine who are analysts and they loved them and felt very freed by them.

Q: *Have you had much improvisational experience aside from your work with Sills?*

ALDA: Oh, yes. I've taken part in improvising workshops or have run workshops just because I enjoy it and wanted to teach people who wanted to learn. Whenever I was in an acting company where people were interested in it I'd run workshops. I ran one for three or four months during the run of *The Apple Tree*. The chorus took part in it.

Q: *How do you run your workshops?*

ALDA: I do Viola's games. I add an element of my own. I once took part in a workshop in Greenwich Village, and almost all of the people in the group had taught games before, so everybody had his or her own variations. We would improvise until three in the morning, and then we'd stay up talking about it for two or three more hours. It was really an exciting time. We did it for about three months. Experiences like that are so intense that they tend not to last for too much longer than that. Peter Boyle was in that group. He's a terrific improviser. Anyway, the reason I bring this up is I noticed in that group that the people who've taught the games tend to express their own vision of life in the games.

For instance, I'm very interested in parapsychology and I see that in the games. I'm always talking about psychic connections. In the *Apple Tree* workshop, I would start off with a warm-up exercise which was a telepathy experiment. Everybody would have a paper and pencil and would get off by himself or herself in a corner of the room and try to draw a picture everyone else was drawing, but not know what it was going to be. In other words, try to hook into the same picture with everyone else. The interesting thing was that we did it for ten weeks and the first week there were a couple that were the same, and every week after that there were more and more pictures that were identical. Sometimes the shared drawing was an abstract design and sometimes a literal drawing. Nobody knew what it was going to be. In the final week, we had about seven or eight out of ten drawings that came out identical. At the same time, the work in the workshop was getting better and better. The people were getting closer knit.

Q: *You also direct. How has improvisation helped you as a director?*

ALDA: It's been useful in terms of making me open to people and not letting things go by. I find that the best directors are the ones who know what you're thinking when you go through the scene. They know what went wrong, they know what you were going through, they know whether you forgot a line or were taking a wrong choice or whatever. An improviser reads people so well that he can read the actors and know what is wrong and what to go for to improve things. You just relate to people better.

The one time I actually directed something improvisationally was a little play my daughter wrote with a friend when she was ten. I thought it was charming and I asked her if I could direct it. She thought about it for a while and said OK. So we asked her teacher at school if we could do it in class. I worked for only about four or five sessions, for a total of maybe ten hours of rehearsal time, but it was an extraordinary experience. I used a technique that Viola talks about in the book which I hoped would work, namely, that you don't show the actors the script.

And that's what we did with the kids. They were ten- and eleven-year-old kids. We started playing games tossing a ball back and forth, and then we went to a ball made out of space, so they got a sense of sharing an imaginary weight and size. Then we played a game where they impersonated animals and everybody had to guess what animal each person was doing, so they got used to performing for other people without being self-conscious. The reason they weren't self-conscious was it was just a game. It was just, "OK, what am I doing now?"

The play was based on the story of Cinderella. Since they knew the story, I would pick a scene and whisper it to some of the kids and have them play that scene in gibberish. Then the other kids would have to figure out what part of the story it was by how they played it. So the whole thing was a guessing game and the concentration was not on themselves but on a sharing of the experience and communicating it to the audience and to each other. In the process I was finding out who would be best in what part.

Then we edged our way into improvising the scenes in English. They had the impulses that came from their own improvisations, so it was a simple matter of saying to them, "Instead of that line, why don't you say it this way?," and I would get them to do my daughter's lines. Plus they had invented a lot of business of their own improvisationally that was very useful. The play was about twice as long as it had been when it was written, but it was all good stuff.

The interesting thing was that when it was performed, they had enormous energy because all their impulses were genuine. Usually when kids do a play and memorize lines, when they play a scene, they see the script when they're talking. They don't see the other actors. There's a page between them and the others. You always get wooden performances that way. The audience doesn't hear what they're saying because they're busy hiding. They're not interested in being there, because they're not free to be there; they're not there with anything of their own. They're asked always to do somebody else's words and somebody else's feelings, movements. But here, this time they started with each other and everything came out of their relationships with the other people. There was nothing that they had been *told* to do. It came out of their own inspiration. They had nobody else's words between them and the other players.

We did the show for a couple of classes and one class sent back a note saying, "Thanks, it was a wonderful show. (A) We could hear everything, and (B) it was very funny."

I think this method would work with adults, although I've never tried it.

Q: *One of the things I've been struck by in working on this book is that out of these four theaters—The Compass, The Second City, The Premise, and The Committee—have emerged more major theater and film talents than from per-*

haps any other single force, with the possible exception of The Actors Studio.

ALDA: I guess there are two things at work there. One is that wherever something exciting is happening talented people tend to go to become part of it. That happened with the Group Theatre and The Actors Studio, and will perhaps happen with Joseph Papp's Shakespeare Festival.

But there's something else working there, too. I think you'll get a lot more people who become so-called stars coming out of improvisational theater than you would expect to get from any other group by virtue of what improvising gives you as a person.

Now I don't think anybody really knows what makes a star, but one of the things is probably self-confidence. Another is the ability to relax under the most harrowing conditions. Certainly improvising teaches you that. And there's another element which is extremely strong, but very hard to define, and that's magnetism, for want of a better word.

Up to now it has been thought that people are either born with magnetism or they're not. But I think improvising really makes you more magnetic, increases your natural magnetism. As you can guess, my own feeling about magnetism is that it is a telepathic thing—a kind of largely nonverbal bond betwen the performer and the audience. I want to amend that and say that I think it *may* be a telepathic thing. Of course nobody really *knows* what it is. When I say it's a nonverbal bond between the actor and the audience, I mean that there's a middle zone between direct, conscious signaling and telepathy. It's not a broad leap between the two. There's a continuum of communication that we all engage in, and between conscious communication and telepathy there's a middle zone of unconscious communication such as body signals. We process a great deal of information through this middle area of unconscious communication, and sometimes we learn more about another person unconsciously than we do consciously. I think it's this area of unconscious communication that lays the groundwork for telepathy.

Q: *I get a sense of community between all the people who worked in the various improv companies.*

ALDA: That comes partly out of the grueling experience. It's very difficult to do and it's like going through a war together. Anybody who's gone through it has a kinship with anybody else who's gone through it. For instance, I really don't know Burns and Schreiber very well. I've met them on one or two occasions, but I feel that I know them and we sort of feel friendly toward each other.

Q: *Do you bring much of your background to* M*A*S*H? *Is improvisation at all a part of your work on the show?*

ALDA: Very little. There have been times when we've fixed a scene by improvising on the set with Larry Gelbart, who writes and produces for us, around to help shape it. Larry's begun to direct, too, and we look forward to his directing a show in which we'd work from a scenario. I think we'd get a very interesting show out of that. We will probably do it before we're finished.

Viola has made a very important contribution to theater. It's like basic research, you know? She will have changed theater for generations. She already has, to a certain extent. The games are being taught all over the country, in summer camps and high schools. Viola is trying to start a program where it will become part of the regular curriculum in grade school, which I think is where it should be, because it's not just a theatrical experience, it's a human experience. If you teach kids music, you really should teach them theater games. As a result of that, you'll have more and more people coming into the theater who have theater games as part of their background, and their styles of performing and directing will all be affected by that. Acting schools all teach it—some version of it, anyway. Not everybody teaches it with the same point of view from which Viola invented it, but what's good about her invention is that it will withstand a lot of individual changes.

Viola and Paul are both very special people. In some ways you could say they have trouble communicating with others, but they have a lot to contribute. They're in on something very new. I mean, you don't expect Albert Einstein to get off a few good jokes and drink martinis with you. Well, they may not be quite in his category, but they're very close to it in their work.

27.

David Steinberg

David Steinberg first saw The Second City when he was a student at the University of Chicago and, within a few years, was one of the strongest performers on that company's stage. What particularly struck me in listening to tapes of the shows in which he appeared was that, more often than not, he played hostile characters, yet, because of his great charm as a performer, never lost the affection of the audience. No mean trick. It was while at The Second City that he developed his monologues on the Bible which were the basis of his initial success as a stand-up comic.

After leaving the troupe, he went on to become a popular comic, appearing as a guest on virtually all the TV talk and variety shows and frequently acting as host on specials. He also recorded albums, and has appeared as an actor, creating the role of Kenny in the original production of Feiffer's *Little Murders,* starring on Broadway in *Carry Me Back to Morningside Heights,* and performing in the film *The Lost Man.*

STEINBERG: I was at the University of Chicago and I think I wanted to be Dylan Thomas very badly, but all I could really muster up were the ruffled shirts, and I could get drunk pretty good, but I couldn't do the poetry.

David Steinberg

Bill Alton was the head of University Theatre at that time.

Q: *This was at the same time he was with Second City?*

STEINBERG: Yes. Anyway, he sort of discovered me on campus, and he would invite me up to his office to talk. I had no outlet for the comedy in me then, so I was always on with him. He found me unique and started pushing me to be a stand-up comic.

At about that time Second City did a show on campus. The company was Bill and Joan Rivers and Mina Kolb and Tony Holland. I saw them and it was all over with. It was such intelligent comedy. And I said, "I can do that."

Bill did everything he could to get me to be a stand-up comedian before he would take me the Second City route. He insisted I go to the Gate of Horn with him and his wife Delores one night. I thought, "Who wants to go see a comic?" because at the time I thought comics were nowhere.

But sure enough the comic he wanted me to see was Lenny Bruce. I went back to see him every single week for five weeks, to the point where he used to talk to me. I was never funny around him, though. There was only respect. What was interesting is that he never made me laugh, though I thought that everything he did was funny and brilliant. I remember thinking that his material was the best I'd ever seen and yet not laughing at it. I decided then that laughter was never going to be the determining factor of whether or not a piece of material was successful.

You know, though, I think Lenny would be minor if he were alive today. He would have let people put him on TV and done his Dexedrine rap. He wouldn't have taken the next step, the next chance.

Q: *We're talking about a transitional period in comedy —when Bruce was around and Second City was young.*

STEINBERG: Let's talk for a second about what was before. Eisenhower, the '50s, Jayne Mansfield, Doris Day. That's what entertainment was. Sophie Tucker, Georgie Jessel. People were still reeling from being influenced by *The Jolson Story* and all that show-business bullshit. Oh, there were rumblings of a Lord Buckley, but that was elitist and unique. And there was Lenny, but at the time

335

all the people who later kissed his metaphorical ass were putting him down. So that's what was before.

The time was wide open for a break and the first break was in comedy. The reason for the breakthrough was the necessity to break the blandness. But there was no real money outlet for this comic breakthrough, so instead of it happening in comedy, it happened in music with the Beatles. The moment that the Beatles broke, the whole culture moved, and then Second City was seen as just another arm of the entire underground community rather than what they were—the leaders.

Then the Beatles thing died out. I think Woodstock was really the end of it all. And now we're into another era of blandness.

Q: *But you and Robert Klein and a lot of the other "new wave" comics seem to be doing pretty well.*

STEINBERG: That's because the kids who come to see us —Lily Tomlin, Richie Pryor, Klein, and myself—have grown up with that music around them. But you know most of the kids don't know where we come from. They aren't that aware of Shelley Berman or Mort Sahl or Bruce. They come to see us and our kind of comedy for the first time and they're saying, "This is the most brilliant thing I've ever seen." But they don't know there's a tradition of it because they haven't been exposed to the earlier guys.

Q: *To get back to Second City, how did you get in?*

STEINBERG: I had an act with a lawyer named Gene Kadish called Kadish and Steinberg. Del Close and John Brent came by and saw us and thought I should be hired.

I came into a company in which I was promised everything and treated very badly onstage. The Second City notion of there being a team onstage is accurate. The makeup of that team, however, was not necessarily in the giving but in the taking—how you took from each other. People were really more concerned about themselves in the scene than the scene itself.

I remember the first night that I walked onstage. I was standing at the bar with a company that I worshiped— Jack Burns and Avery Schreiber and Dick Schaal and the others. And I went to Jack and said, "Jack, I'm nervous about going onstage." He said, "There's nothing to worry

David Steinberg

about. We get onstage, we all help each other. It'll be easy." I said, "OK."

At the time I was still at the University of Chicago, and the night they introduced me, my professors were in the audience. And the club did a really great announcement about how I was going to be an important new member of the company and that sort of thing.

Anyway, after the set show was over, I was to come onstage and be part of the improvised set. The first thing we were supposed to do was improvise an opera. In order to do that, you had to know something about the different styles of opera and the Grimm fairy tales that they were always based on. That night we were going to do *Rumpelstiltskin*.

So we were supposed to divide up the characters among us. Everyone said, "I'll take this," and "I'll take that." I thought it would be very natural for me to take Rumpelstiltskin by virtue of my size, but Avery took him. And pretty soon everyone but me had a character. They all walked offstage to get their hats and scarves and whatever they were using, and I didn't even have the aplomb to make a joke out of the fact that I didn't have a character. So I walked offstage to watch this opera unfold.

It was incredible. I think Barbara Harris had come back for a week to play with the company, and she was a duality of sexuality and comedy that was amazing to see. She played the princess, and Jack was the prince and came out with a harp and a funny outfit and witty lines, and there was Bill Mathieu improvising this music, and Avery came out as Rumpelstiltskin—and he is one of those people who can't not get a laugh from the audience—and they were just breaking the house down together.

So I was watching all this from the side, very aware that I wasn't up there and that my friends and professors were out front and that they had all come to see me. They were just getting to the point in the story where Rumpelstiltskin is singing. "You have three guesses to guess my name," and it was about to turn into this big trio. And just then, I guess I had no control over my hands or my body or anything. The rage and embarrassment must have taken over, and I took a Leo Gorcey fedora and marked a thing that said "Press" over it and made a quick walk across stage

337

and said, "Hi, Rumpelstiltskin! Haven't seen you since high school!" and walked off. Of course, that was the end of the opera.

But one thing they were always quick to do was acknowledge a good moment, and they gave me the applause. It's a moment I have never forgotten. Jack and I still reminisce about it as it was very special.

He used to get even with me, though. Like when I would be the interpreter in the Khrushchev scene, sometimes Jack would be in the audience without my knowing, and when we asked for questions he would shout up, "Do you like apples?," which is something you can't answer if you want to be political.

Q: *Who directed you there?*

STEINBERG: Sheldon Patinkin and Paul Sills. I worked with Sheldon first. I think he is one of the most underrated directors of Second City. What he tried to do was combine Sills's technique with his own, and he was excellent at it. He was good at duplicating what Paul had done and then taking me into new areas. He is one of the most knowledgeable and well-read people you could ever meet, so he was an immediate challenge. There was no area of topicality that Sheldon didn't know more about than you did. The problem with him was that he had come after someone who was unquestionably a genius.

My feeling about Sills is that he is one of the five people who have been most influential in my life. He told me to go right into my background and not be embarrassed about being a Borscht-circuit comedian. More than that, there was Sills as a man, as a person. I can't ever imagine him being out of touch. He and I liked each other, or at least I liked him. I liked him and I respected him as he had a wonderful sense of humor. Our conversations were very literary. And more than that, he was kind of a scoundrel. And then I saw him change a lot and become Martin Buberish.

Another insight into Sills that is so important is that he is the only person I've ever seen who can break something down theatrically and say, "That's bullshit and this is terrible"—do the negative thing—and then sit down with you and work out the positive alternative; as opposed to most people who gain their reputations by just saying, "That's no good." He works out the alternatives. He was very constructive.

Q: *Any thoughts on Severn Darden?*

STEINBERG: I think he and Jonathan Winters have the most remarkable comic minds I have ever encountered.

I remember he hated working with this one girl at Second City. She wouldn't give anything and she was a pain in the ass. The three of us were doing a scene together once, and when I said, "Where's your wife?" he was supposed to bring her onstage. He said, "I'm sad about my wife." I said, "Is she here with you?" He said, "Yes. There's just some peculiarities about her." I said, "What are they?" I noticed he wasn't bringing her on as planned. And he said, "Some people might not find it peculiar, but my wife is a moose." Never in that scene did he deny that his wife was a moose, and that girl had to come on in her only scene in the show and play a moose to Severn's German professor.

Q: *One of your best scenes at Second City was about the old Jewish grocer and the genie.*

STEINBERG: It came out of a joke of Lenny Bruce's about a guy who tells a genie, "Make me a malted," and the genie says, "Poof! You're a malted!" Alan Arkin's best characters were Puerto Ricans, Jews, and whatnot, so I wanted to try one of those. I was not good at characters, though I didn't know it at the time—I thought I was quite good. Anyway, my father was a rabbi in a grocery store, and I was very influenced by Bernard Malamud at the time, so I tried combinations of all these influences onstage.

The point of the scene was this: My wife had died and I ran the grocery store and I was a misanthrope. I hated the kids that bought candy and I wasn't nice. But more than that, I had no commitment in my life, so I didn't want anything. So this genie comes out of a bottle and offers to give me everything. It's frustrating for him because I don't really want anything. I kind of play with him and say, "If you're so good, take me to Miami," and he snaps his fingers and we're in Miami. But I have my winter coat on and I say, "This is no good. Take me back to my store," and he snaps his fingers and we're back at the store. This kind of thing went on for a while, and nothing he could give me could make me happy.

Then the genie on his own initiative takes me back to Germany in 1943, and he says to me, "You can change history if you want." This coming after being hilariously funny in a Marx Brothers–type scene. I got very angry with him and I made him take me back to the store. I refused to opt for the change, and I put him back in the bottle and sent him on his way.

That scene came from Sheldon allowing me to go that far with it, allowing me to take a scene that was consistently funny and stop it and go to something very serious. What Sheldon and Sills did was help develop me as a writer. They recognized I could write in a way that most people at Second City couldn't. The way we worked on that scene was that we decided what points were in it—what beats—and then I remember writing it in one night and not being able to sleep until I tried it the next morning. That scene packed the houses for four months. Then some reviewers called me Chaplinesque and it almost ruined me. For months all I wanted to do was end a scene with the light going out on my ass as I wandered off. I was finally able to get back to doing what was honest, whatever a scene demanded. If a scene is funny and slapstick, you can't try to turn it into something else, you go with it.

The goal at Second City was to be the smartest and funniest you could be. Comedy up until then had never been like that. Before, the audience went to see the comic and the comic played a schmuck they could feel superior to. There are still comics in Vegas like that, and the audience goes to look at them play fools and laugh at them, even though they know those fools are making millions of dollars. Now I don't look at this as a lesser form of comedy. It's just a different form from what I and a lot of the younger people are into. What Lily and Richie and I are saying is, "Let me tell you what I think is funny." We're assuming that we are part of the same community as the audience and that they know what we know. We don't treat the audience as being above or beneath us. They're our peers.

Q: *Would you say that distinction is the dividing line between the old and so-called new wave of comedy?*

David Steinberg

STEINBERG: I think so.

There was always a challenge at Second City. That challenge was: Are you going to do it again tonight? Is this it or are you going to get better? Are you going to move on or will it level off?

Q: *Generally, I've been talking with people about the way the Second City experience helped them. Can you think of any way in which The Second City hindered people?*

STEINBERG: There were some people who got so they could work only in that game atmosphere and who never got used to reading lines, and that certainly damaged some careers. Also, you would come out of being a big star in Chicago and arrive in New York and have to start from scratch again. The people who started from scratch again would then become successful, but there were those who kept holding onto their Second City identity. Those people sort of disappeared.

Q: *Getting back to your specific work at Second City, I talked to Klein recently, and he said that he thought you were very selfish onstage.*

STEINBERG: He's right. I was. I was selfish onstage, not just with him—with everyone. I was selfish offstage, too. Let me put it this way: I feel that my Second City years were like my asshole years. I think I've changed a lot since then, and I hope the change will continue. But yes, I was selfish.

Let me put this into perspective. When Klein came in, I was one of the "stars." You gained a certain stature there through a combination of longevity and accumulation of material. So when Klein came, I was very well known in Chicago—the sustaining force of the Second City company. I had been there for five years. I was very tuned into the audience. Like I say, I wasn't into the games that Paul and Viola taught. I wasn't good at them. That wasn't my skill. My skill was contact with the audience. From the moment I walked onstage, I looked for any means by which to get my focus. Klein could never take that focus from me. If it had been the other way round, if I had come in after he had been there five years, maybe he would have had the focus and I wouldn't have been able to get it away from him.

341

The downfall of Second City came about as a result of the greed of everyone involved. Once the New York Company became stars—once Arkin opened in *Enter Laughing* and Barbara Harris opened in *Oh Dad, Poor Dad*—everyone wanted to be a star. There was no consideration of that before that happened. So when I say I was selfish onstage, it was within the framework of what was happening in the company. Sills and Patinkin used to say to everyone, "If you think he's being selfish, go get him!" Their only point was that if you were in touch, there was no way the audience wasn't going to find you over someone who wasn't in touch. So they said, "The only way you'll get Steinberg is to beat him at his own game."

Monty Python's Flying Circus is the Second City of today, I think. It's not our style, but they are to the community what we were at our time. They're elitist, irreverent, and, I think, hilarious. The difference between their situation and ours is that if you're intelligent and funny in England, you can be on national TV and command an audience. If you're intelligent and funny in the States, the intelligence is the thing that would stop you from being on TV. But what the networks are finally catching onto is that being dumb or intelligent has nothing to do with whether you work on TV. It's that special unique quality that someone either has or doesn't have that makes him a star on TV. And that quality can come from the highest material as well as the lowest. But the TV people up to now have almost never gone for the smart, assuming that what works is the lowest common denominator.

28.

Robert Klein

Robert Klein was a member of The Second City in Chicago for about a year, and then, after a brief run with the New York Second City, appeared in *The Apple Tree* and *New Faces of 1968*. In films, he played a supporting role in *The Owl and the Pussycat* and starred in *Rivals*.

But it is as a comic that Klein is best known. He is one of the most popular performers on the stand-up circuit, has recorded three well-received records, and is a frequent guest on television.

KLEIN: I left Yale in 1963, after a year of graduate school, and was in summer stock. That fall was pretty tough. That was when Kennedy was murdered by *several* assassins. I did a few Off-Broadway shows that didn't pay anything, and in January '64 I began substitute-teaching, which gave me a little self-respect and some money.

Sometime in the late winter of '64, or maybe it was January '65, a mate of mine from Yale was doing a week-end show in New Haven. Political and cute. He said one of his men was flipping out and could I come up, would I be interested? I said I'd love to. I'd get back into show business a little and it would be fun.

Some weeks after that, an agent named Bernie Sohn from William Morris came to see the show. He had signed many of the Second City people. After the show he said to me, "Second City is coming to town. They're looking for several new people and I think you'd be perfect for it." I said, "Great."

I auditioned for them in March of '65. There was a William Morris audition room with a piano. It seemed like there were sixty people there. Sheldon and Bernie Sahlins were there, and the way they ran the auditions was they'd have you take a suggestion from the other auditionees and do improvs. I wound up doing improvs with Fred Willard and they were great. They were funny and we knew it. Some minutes later, we were ushered upstairs and Bernie said, "Can you be in Chicago on April 1?" or whenever it was. I said, "You bet your ass I can!" I didn't say that actually, but I was very happy. I packed everything I had in my cockroach-ridden little studio apartment and went to Chicago and arrived where The Second City used to be at 1846 North Wells, right across from the Lincoln Hotel. There's a high-rise there now.

So I check into the Lincoln Hotel and I call up the club and say, "Where is it?" They say, "Where are you?" and I tell them I'm in the hotel on the ninth floor, or whatever, and they say, "Look out the window. Look down. You see two balls there?" They had those opera balls out front of the club. They got them from the old opera house when it was torn down.

At the time, the Second City company was on a Theatre Guild tour in large theaters with, I believe, Steinberg, Judy Graubart, Severn, Omar Shapli, and Sally Hart. In the meantime, they'd brought in a show with five English kids called The Oxford-Cambridge Revue to play the club. I came down and watched the show and was shown around the place by Sheldon. And at one point Sheldon told me, "Watch out for Steinberg."

The Theatre Guild tour finished and some of the company came back to work with me and the other new people on putting together a new show while Oxford-Cambridge was still running in the evenings. The group then was Fred Willard, myself, Alex Canaan, Joan Bassie, Judy Graubart, and Steinberg. And when Steinberg and I got to talking, he told me, "Watch out for Sheldon."

Steinberg was the star, that was clear from the start. Not

that it was company policy, but he had been there a year and a half already, he was extremely clever onstage, and now, with all of the other old-timers gone, he really had a chance to be the absolute glowing jewel. This became a source of competition for us.

In all fairness to Steinberg, whom I do not get along with and haven't really seen in years, he just wiped the floor with me. I got on that stage to improvise, and I really was an excellent choice for that company; I was cocky and talented. But he had the technique down and the experience in front of an audience, and he was tough on me. In the end I could say thanks, like in the movies the guy says to the drill sergeant after training is over. But he wasn't kindly. I mean, we would get into a scene and he would maneuver it so that I'd be sitting in a chair as he was pacing back and forth getting the attention. There were little tricks you had to learn and his mind was so quick! Also, he would pick and choose whom he wanted to do improvisations with. He always wanted to dominate the scene. When those little edges of advantage occurred, he always got them. To his own credit. I don't ever, ever put someone down for ambition and for wanting to achieve and get ahead. I just felt that he wasn't as cognizant of other people's feelings and sensitivities as he might have been. David is not a good ensemble player. He has great improvisational talents, but they're peculiar. He needs someone else to work *off*. But that's not the way a true improvisational scene is done.

I don't mean to snipe. This kind of conflict colored and characterized my experience at Second City. There's a history of friction there and it's so understandable. The dressing room was tiny, and you were just on top of one another a lot. Also, most of us were pretty much strangers in town. Steinberg and Judy had roots in Chicago from having lived there six or seven years, but the rest of us didn't have that, so our lives revolved around the club. It was more than just your job. So there was a good deal of friction, though we weren't as bad, I think, as some of the previous companies had been.

Women were always at a disadvantage at Second City. There were fewer of them, though the history is studded with a number of talented women, like Judy Graubart, who has a wonderful quality. She's on *The Electric Company* all the time. But Judy wasn't tough like Zohra Lampert and Barbara Harris were. When I say tough, I don't mean that in any derogatory sense, but that they could stand up and fight for their share of the pie. They could defend themselves.

Q: *But Zohra and Barbara were the exceptions?*

KLEIN: The women were mostly less pushy and aggressive, so they did fewer scenes, so there were fewer women in the companies. It's kind of a mirror of what was happening in society generally.

Q: *This sort of brings me to a question about how you reflected the social and political concerns of the time in your shows.*

KLEIN: We did a good deal of antiwar stuff and some other political stuff, but less than what you'd expect from Second City's reputation. To me, The Second City had always represented politics to a certain extent. One of the reasons I felt proud about being there was it wasn't just a lunatic funny place. It was a place that had a reputation for intellectual humor, political humor. But though a sense of that still pervaded, it very much depended on the company that was operating there, and that company was extraordinarily apolitical. I was very political. I was still in a kind of radical stage at the time. David was political, but he didn't care as much about doing the stuff onstage. He was more content to do good scenes that he could have juicy parts in and all that. But Fred and Joan Bassie and Alex Canaan certainly didn't care much.

The atmosphere at The Second City was really wonderful. Downstairs there was a bar where they showed silent movies continuously—Laurel and Hardy, Chaplin, and Keaton. Also, there was a beer garden outside, and when it was warm they would run the movies out there and serve ice cream. One funny thing about the beer garden— I'm not going to mention names for publication—but there have been some amphetamine freaks in Second City, and they'd step out there during the winter sometimes, so when the snow melted, you'd find all these capsules on the ground.

Incidentally, during the '68 convention and those horrible riots, Paul Sills turned the beer garden into a temporary hospital. I went over there at the time and there were a lot of injured people lying around.

Q: *Any sketch you remember with particular affection?*

KLEIN: The most memorable scene my class, as it were, contributed to Second City literature was "The Amateur Hour." It was so funny that for literally days while we were perfecting it, we were still cracking up and laughing ourselves. It was maniacal. It wasn't particularly disciplined, it was just pure hilarity. It was an amateur hour and Fred was the host, Mr. Mack. He was really the backbone of the whole thing. The first act he introduced was Judy Graubart, who did a quick finger-puppet thing which was very funny, but was just a little taste of what was to come. Then came Alex Canaan, who was a bad impressionist. He did Jimmy Cagney, but with this thick Texas accent. "You dirty rat! I'm a-gonna kill you!" Then I came on with my hair parted in the middle carrying this broom. My name was Herbie Shaloo, and I took on a real heavy Midwestern accent and I was very frightened. My act was I played "I Can't Give You Anything But Love" on the broom. Fred and I never played that part the same way twice, so we were always cracking each other up.

Then Joan Bassie came out. She had on a hat and a little old lady's voice. She was very good at it. She shook just enough. Fred asks, "And what do you do?" "I do impressions of insane people." "Insane people—wonderful! On the Original Amateur Hour! What's your first one going to be, Mrs. Dawson?" "First I'm going to do someone having a catatonic fit." "A catatonic fit on the Original Amateur Hour! All right, Mrs. Dawson, go into your routine!" And she'd hold perfectly still. Then Fred would say, "That's it, a catatonic fit! What's your next impression, Mrs. Dawson? . . . Mrs. Dawson, your next impression? . . . Dear, we're running out of time. Do you have any. . . ." The audience would start to laugh. "Well, Mrs. Dawson, we're going to go on to. . . ." And suddenly he tries to scare her out of it. She doesn't move. She's just standing there facing the audience. "OK," says Fred. "Looks like Mrs. Dawson's become a regular!" Jesus, the night he came up with that!

So then Fred brings Steinberg out. Steinberg was saved till last, naturally. Anyway, he's a ventriloquist. He walks out with a pole with a hat on it—kind of a nothing. It doesn't resemble a dummy, but it's very funny visually. He comes out and sees the old woman and just stands there looking at her and—Steinberg was a *master* at this—he waited to the "nth" degree, and the first thing out of his mouth after as long as a thirty-five-second take of looking: "Looks like a catatonic fit!" And Fred would come in with perfect timing right over his words, "One of the very best we've had on the Original Amateur Hour!" And then Steinberg did a funny bit as the inept ventriloquist and that was it. It was a fabulous sketch in which each person got a chance to work out a little.

Fortunately for me, Steinberg went to London with a company. It allowed me free rein and I learned what to do. I got more and more confidence and really had a chance to bloom. I think that happened for Willard, too.

The interesting thing is that as funny as Fred Willard is, we never felt with each other that kind of negative competition. We enjoyed working with each other and if he got a big laugh—well, I lived with that and was glad for him. I'm serious about this. We worked beautifully together. He has a very peculiar and imaginative mind. His head is what makes Ace Trucking Company go and what started it off, but that's a very commercial outfit and they've had to make tremendous compromises for commercialism—for television and those clubs they play.

Another stroke of luck for me was that Paul Sills, who had been gone from the company several years, came back to direct our next show. So I had the opportunity of working with him for about ten weeks. There are a lot of things that are all legend and are really bullshit at the core, but I would say that the experience with Paul was really something. I wouldn't say it was a happy time because he demanded so much. But he's really brilliant.

The main things that I learned from Paul are certain basic improvisational concepts, like not to "write" onstage and that to talk about what's happened in the past is not interesting. So you don't talk about how your sister-in-law is going to Mexico or had Siamese twins. It's what's *now* that's important. Maybe he didn't articulate it with those very words, but that's the message that came across. When you think about it, it's really simple and you should almost pick it up yourself.

Sills just really ripped me apart in a lot of ways. Later we had a conversation and he admitted that he was tough on me.

I didn't always understand what he meant. Paul Sills is not a great communicator. That was the real crack in the arch of his reputation. Paul knew what to do but couldn't always communicate it.

But the thing with him was really fabulous. The man is unquestionably an enormously important contributor to a lot of people's success and talent. He's that proverbial guy who didn't sell out.

I like to give Sheldon Patinkin a lot of credit for his contribution to the company over the years. Sheldon was very much at a disadvantage because he was coming into the shoes of the great Paul Sills, and that's all he ever heard. It was very unfair, because Sheldon was a very effective director as far as I was concerned. He's not an improvisational genius and he doesn't have the kind of lifelong pursuit of that form of theater and all that Paul and his mother had, but he was absolutely tireless. He would never shirk working. He had a good editing sense and pretty good taste that was most valuable. If you're a director, you can't make up things for the company. They've got to create their own stuff. But you need that observer from the outside.

Another important person around Second City was Fritzie Sahlins. She was the mother of Second City in a way. From time to time over the years, there were certainly a lot of people with emotional problems in the company who needed a mother. I'm not just talking about problems onstage. One girl there was a suicide. Fritzie was involved with the whole experience at Second City. She was always coming to rehearsals and whipping up great meals. They're divorced now, Bernie and Fritzie.

Q: *What are your impressions of Bernie?*

KLEIN: I was the Equity deputy for my company, so I had to face Bernie on certain substantial issues. I would often be treated like his son. He'd get patriarchal suddenly. I don't think he's really a good businessman, but he's kept an essentially excellent product going for—what?—fifteen years. I can't say I ever really felt he had devious intentions. Oh, if it was a question of financing, he would try and fight for his end, but he never became a millionaire from this. He never even really became rich from it. The potential for the thing commercially could have been exploited more—could be to this day—by someone who's a better businessperson.

Q: *What about the whole rights hassle of who owns what material?*

KLEIN: I always compared Second City to a medical school. When you go to medical school, you sign a document that if you ever discover anything in their laboratory —say a little cure for cancer—the school gets a little share. In fact, a big share. It belongs to them basically because it's their lab. Well, Second City has always had this attitude, too. I don't blame them because you didn't create this bit alone. It was created with other people and it belongs in that central file.

I do think that if you had a hand in creating something, though, you have the right to use it elsewhere. Like Steinberg did his Bible routines there and has since done them all over the place, and there's nothing wrong with that. One night when I hosted *The Tonight Show,* I had Fred Willard on just so we could do an old Second City scene we'd done together. It was our scene, so we had the right.

And I think that Avery Schreiber and Jack Burns are completely justified in doing their cabdriver thing wherever, because they created it at Second City. However, they also took a number of valuable pieces from the Second City literature that they didn't create and put them on TV. Like they did "Family Reunion," which was the longest scene ever at Second City—a beautiful classic piece about a homosexual and his parents visiting him. Now, I like Jack and Avery very much. They're funny and they're nice guys, but I personally think that they were wrong in doing that. They had no right to do that on television. They didn't create that piece. They came into it.

Q: *Came into it?*

KLEIN: You see, Second City would always maintain the repertoire of the old classics and the new members would learn them. So maybe they did perform "Family Reunion" at Second City. But they didn't initially improvise it, and I think no one has the right to take a scene and use it outside unless he intially improvised it.

Robert Klein

Q: *To get back to Chicago, Steinberg left for London and you bloomed. . . .*

KLEIN: Right. He was away on the London thing two or three months. It closed early, I think. So he came back and waited around a little while before he joined the company again. I was in Chicago exactly a year, because the following May—1966—we opened in New York at what is now the Bottom Line, which was then Square East.

By that time, Second City had already played Broadway for a limited engagement and there had been, if I'm not mistaken, two pretty successful Off-Broadway engagements at Square East. We were the third, or possibly the fourth. We went in with what they thought would be fairly safe, doing a lot of material from the Arkin-Severn era. It was a mistake, and Sheldon was partly to blame for it. He should have known that the critics, having seen most of that material already, would compare us with the originals. We should have gone with the new.

We were under enormous pressure putting that show together. That last week before we went to New York, I couldn't eat anything that wasn't extremely bland. Tomato juice, ketchup—anything like that would send me into agony. If I drank some milk or had dry bread, I felt fine, but I couldn't eat steak. I couldn't eat anything, really. I had a friend who was a resident physician in the Cook County Hospital, and he told me that those were ulcer symptoms. They disappeared as suddenly as they came some days afterward. But it was a tremendously pressure-laden time.

Steinberg pressured and arranged it so he had the most things to do in the show. Of course, some of the things he created were among the best things in the show anyway, but he also had the juiciest parts in some of the older scenes, like the mad professor that Severn created. Steinberg's done that character a lot on television, too.

Now, the way it was set up was that the show would run four to thirteen weeks, depending on how it was received. So we opened and our reviews were mixed, and it was clear we would not go beyond four or five weeks. We all knew that after the first week. So David was on the phone all the time to Chicago, getting permission to replace such-and-such a scene with this-and-that scene because the agents

351

and producers were coming in and he wanted to show himself off well. By the time we closed, it was ridiculous. It was like a David Steinberg jamboree! Maybe it really wasn't so bad. But there was that dreadful competition felt by us all. This was the big chance in New York for all of us, after all. Anyway, the thing closed and that was it.

Q: *Was that the end of your association with Second City?*

KLEIN: No. In 1968 I was asked to do a kind of Second City alumni show for three weeks at Ravinia, which is in a suburb of Chicago. I was happy to do it. The company consisted of myself, Peter Boyle, Paul Sand, Mina Kolb, and, I believe, Judy Graubart. There may have been someone else, too. Peter had been in the company after me briefly, and we hit it off immediately. We became very good friends. I also enjoyed working with Paul very much. We put together some of the scenes from the past repertoire and it was a nice success.

Also, after leaving I took an active part in recommending new people. For example, that whole crowd that followed my company there within a few months—J. J. Barry, Martin Harvey Friedberg, and Burt Heyman.

Q: *It seems to me that not only has the improv movement produced a number of talented directors and actors, but a lot of comedians.*

KLEIN: Yeah.

Q: *I'd be interested to hear how you feel this background influenced their work.*

KLEIN: Shelley Berman, for example—his style was making a where—a place, you know—and using a phone and creating an acting moment. Most stand-up comedians were doing joke-linked-to-joke-linked-to-joke—not necessarily true or heartfelt but a funny contrivance of several words. Line-laugh, line-laugh, that kind of thing. But Shelley's was an acting thing where he got tears in your eyes and still made it funny. His style was definitely, obviously, influenced by that kind of experience. And, of course, so were Nichols and May.

Steinberg carried away from it his cerebral style. He's clearly an intelligent, articulate, educated person, and is generally characterized in people's minds as an intellectual comic. He does politicize. In his best work it's well thought out. It's good stuff.

With Sandy Baron, the influence is that he never stops doing improvisations. It's a trademark of his—"Let's do an improv." And he does them well. He's a talented guy. The thing is, he's a very good actor.

Q: *OK, now what about yourself?*

KLEIN: Well, in my case, I know the influence is direct. Certainly Second City gave me the technique for writing my material. I really learned my writing procedure there— that is, improvising on my feet and seeing what comes out, tape recording, playing it back and hearing what I did, and then improving on it. That's the best writing machine I have—when I'm free and my mind is clear, let 'er rip and see what happens. I like to devote a lot of my show to either opening up old bits or creating new ones. Of course, it's different from Second City in that there's no other person working with me. But there are things happening in that room at that moment, right? Like I was working at the Main Point in Bryn Mawr a few weeks ago. The local fire department was right across the street and suddenly the siren started to go. I stopped what I was doing and just created a whole thing out of that. "Two by two, women and children first!"

Also, the poise and the general confidence you get from the Second City experience! You're on your feet six days a week in front of a live audience getting paid and getting into shape. Why, that's wonderful! There's nothing better! It's one of the purely positive aspects of my career, and I guess that's why I'll always think fondly of it and almost everything to do with it.

29.

J. J. Barry

Even though all the actors at The Second City get equal billing, inevitably, as Sheldon Patinkin noted, some become the celebrities of their troupes. Stars. J. J. Barry was a Second City star. With his "dese, dem, and doze" diction, he was a far cry from the cultured inflections of Tony Holland and the honed wit of Severn Darden. But he was invigorating. He had an honest vulgar streak which captured aspects of the Chicago spirit which hadn't been seen on that stage before. Finally, there was someone who could portray the crude vitality of the "Hog Butcher of the World." And finally there was someone who could really *do* Mayor Richard J. Daley.

Since leaving The Second City, Barry has become a familiar face via television commercials. On TV he was a regular of *The Corner Bar,* and onstage he was featured in *The White House Murder Case* and *Fun City.*

BARRY: I was a stand-up comic. I *hated* it.

But the thing that used to excite me was, whenever I was in New York, to go to the Improvisation—the club, you know—and get up with some of the other guys that hung around there and play. Do improvs. Marty Friedberg was there, and Richie Pryor and Burt Heyman and David Astor. No technique. I just know Richie used to say, "Come on, let's get up and fool around." What we were going for was what they used to do in the old Sid Caesar days. We'd play samurai warriors and army scenes and anything else that happened. We didn't know what the hell we were doing. We were just making people laugh. Some of the stuff we did there, if anybody had recorded it, would have put *Hellzapoppin'* away. This was 1965, '66 I'm talking about.

Like one night, me, Richie, and I think it was Marty sat onstage and ate a complete meal Budd Friedman, the owner, gave us. It was rice pilaf and chicken, and we just sat onstage under the lights and ate. The audience was out there, watching us, and we just ate. And then Richie went into eating with his hands, and we followed him and started eating like cavemen. Budd kept coming in, saying, "Any more?" And we're licking the dishes. Then I threw a plate and broke it. And then Richie started breaking plates. We saw Budd come running over and we thought he was going to be pissed off, right? He says, "So that's the way you feel about it, hunh?" And he grabs the tablecloth and yanks it, dragging everything onto the floor. All in front of the audience.

At one time, whenever we were in trouble with a scene, Burt used to drop his pants. So one night, Burt has just dropped his pants, and somebody sees through the window (there was a big picture window) Mayor Lindsay coming into the club! You should have seen Burt scramble for his pants! I mean, there the limousine has pulled up, the mayor is getting out, and there's Burt with his pants down to his knees, scrambling under a table.

The thing I loved about it was the freedom of it. In not knowing what we were doing, we were being brilliant. Even if I do say so myself. Just taking that goddamn chance. It was the freedom of ignorance. All we knew was that if you bombed, you bombed. And if you didn't bomb, you were a hit. We never discussed motivation or objectives or any of that actor talk.

Anyway, to make a long story short, we started getting a reputation. People started coming around, saying, "Where are those guys? Are they going to do improvs tonight?" So Sheldon and some people from Second City were coming into town, looking for people in New York for the Chicago company. They had a company in Chicago they weren't happy with, and they were going to replace it. So they came to the Improv and they saw us. I think David Steinberg introduced us. I'm not quite sure, but I think it was David. Well, they thought we were pretty good, and they invited us up to William Morris to audition. They said they were going to put us through exercises. We didn't know what the hell they were talking about. "What are we going to do —pushups?" We didn't know from exercises.

After that, they said, "We'd like to see you again." So they came back to the Improv. I think this second time they brought Alan Arkin along, too, to get his opinion. Which really put everybody uptight. We were pretty funny that night, but we weren't as crazy as we usually were. The reason I think we got the job is because, although there were other people who were better technicians, they thought we had funny bones.

What happened was they only wanted two guys. It was going to be two of the three of us—me, Burt, and Marty. But they wouldn't tell us which two it was going to be. So me and Marty and Burt agreed that if the three of us couldn't go together, we wouldn't go. So we brought a proposal to Sheldon and Bernie. We told them that two of us would take a $50 cut each in salary to help pay for the third guy if he would take the three of us. And, through a series of phone calls—I mean, I can't tell you what we went through—I think it took two weeks, but they agreed. To this day, they've never told us which two of us they were going to take.

We got there in 1967, and the second day we were in Chicago was the great Chicago snowstorm. From that day on, being there was a totally exciting experience. Besides the excitement of Second City and the craziness that went down there, we were there during some very exciting times for the city. We started with the storm, and we were there during the '68 convention and a lot of other fun times.

OK, ready for this? The first show we're going to do is with Paul Sills. He left Second City after directing us, and I can't say I blame him. Here he was faced with these three oafs, and he was going to try to do theater with us, right?

He had a film—see if you can follow me on this—a film of sauce being poured. That was the film. A pan of sauce being poured. He said, "We're going to do something with this." What we were going to do was be ants. We were trying to make a scene that incorporated the film. So we ended up being ants doing a war scene, like we're three soldiers. We didn't know what the hell we were doing. We couldn't follow what he was doing. Nobody could follow Paul. Paul was way ahead of everybody at that time. There wasn't anybody with his kind of head then.

And we were taking workshops from Viola. And all we kept saying was, "Who is this woman telling us to 'walk in space'? I'm thirty-two years old!" We resisted. We made fun of it. I only really got what it was about eight years later.

Paul had us do a thing called *The Trip*. This may sound old and dated now, but you have to realize that this was in 1967. It was a show about a nice Jewish boy who took acid. This was during the early Leary days. And the show was about what happens in his mind. It was supposed to be a series of transformations. It had the beginnings of an interesting show, but he didn't have the company that could go into developing this thing right. Paul is the kind of director, you'd ask him a question and he'd say, "I don't know," and this used to frustrate a lot of people. Because we were taught that when you ask the teacher something, you get an answer. We just didn't understand where he was coming from. I think he could understand where we were coming from, but there was nothing he could do about it.

So, he came up with one act of stuff with us, and then he left. He went out and did Game Theatre. Sheldon came in and tried to put together some kind of show with us so we'd have a full evening. His battle was in turning our heads around. Basically, the three of us thought of ourselves as comics, and what he had to do was turn us around and make us into actors who did comedy. Which I'm very thankful for.

Q: *Did you have a sense of when you switched from being a stand-up comedian to being an actor?*

BARRY: In about the third year I was there. I did a scene with Sandy Holt which was the first time I played someone low-key. What I was always doing was safe—big loud-mouthed characters. Like drill sergeants. And one night,

357

Sandy and I improvised a scene that took place in a doorway. She was the girl, and I played a neurotic guy who was very nervous of chicks. And it felt really good. For me to take down my image of masculinity. It was beautiful. We never did that scene as well as we did it that first night, but Sheldon immediately put it right into the show, word for word. And that's when Sheldon told me, "I think you're making the strides now we were talking about. About becoming an actor." So, toward the end of the time I was there, though I still loved playing the craziness and the wildness, I was trying to get into roles I didn't even identify with myself. That was the turnabout.

Q: *Whenever people talk about you, they talk about your Mayor Daley.*

BARRY: That wasn't really an impression. I mean, I didn't do his voice or anything. I'd just do his attitudes. We'd hold a press conference, somebody would ask a question, and I'd say, "Shut up. I don't wanna answer that. You—you're next. What do you want? No, I don't wanna answer that either." Then I'd mix up the language, which was easy for me to do. And that was my Daley impression. It made me famous in Chicago. I'd put on the Daley hat and walk out onstage and the audience would go berserk. In Chicago they'd go berserk. When I did him in New York, nobody knew what the hell I was doing. I thought, "Why aren't they laughing and clapping?" Of course, they don't see Daley in New York every day, so they don't recognize him like in Chicago. In Chicago, I'd just say, "I'm Mayor Daley," and they would go bananas. I was hoping one day Daley himself would come down and see it. Never did.

Q: *I understand that during the Chicago convention Jerry Rubin wanted you to play Daley in the park?*

BARRY: Yeah, he asked me. He wanted me to do it holding a pig. I said, "Well, gee, I'm for the cause, but I do have a career and they'll disappear me. I mean, I'm going to stand in the park and do Daley and all those cops are going to let me do that? Right. I'm afraid I'm going to have to cop out. My director won't give me permission. And my mother won't let me. And, uh, I don't think my priest would." Sure enough, the day they wanted me to do it was the only time they had trouble during the daytime.

Mostly it was at night when the violence and stuff happened. Usually, in the day it was mostly a carnival atmosphere with vendors, and the cops were taking pictures. It was at night, at midnight, when they asked them to get out of the park that the shit hit the fan.

I remember the first night. We came out of Second City —the new building where they are now—and across the street then there was an empty parking lot, and the cops were using it as barracks with sandbags and automatic weapons. It was so bizarre I can't tell you, man. We came out and got searched.

I remember one night we all came out of the club and decided to take off and go to Rush Street, figuring nobody ever bothers Rush Street. And we were walking down the street, and all of a sudden, we looked down the street as we were heading for the car, and we saw thousands of people running toward us. I said, "Do you see what I see?" We're all sort of calm for a moment, right? "Are those people coming toward us?" And they're getting closer and closer, this horde coming right for us. And we heard pop, pop, pop! Which was the gas going off. We turned around and started running. It was like in Chaplin. In *Modern Times,* I think it was. Remember, he's working in a manhole, and he comes out of it, and he turns around and there's this mob running straight for him. He picks up a flag and tries to wave them off, but they keep coming and he has to run. He has this flag still in his hand and he's running and he's in front, so they think he's the leader. That's what crossed my mind then. We ran around the block, man. I thought we were going to get killed.

We did a show, then, called *A Plague on Both Your Houses.* Fred Kaz had written a song with the same title. A real strong, stirring kind of song. Opening night—wow! It was one of the greatest times in my life. We sang the song and the entire audience got up, tears in their eyes, and the arms went up in peace symbols. It was like a revival, man! Everybody got carried away and started singing with us. We did a couple extra choruses. That was exciting. It was a good show.

Abby Hoffman and Jerry Rubin were staying at the Lincoln Hotel down the street, which is where I lived. And every morning we would meet, and the cops would be sitting in there, too. I think one night Abby took coffee to the cops who were following him. Took it out to their car. It was like a weird joke. Only it wasn't a joke. They played with us a couple of times. I found them delightful guys.

Q: *Were they any good as improvisers?*

BARRY: They were better on the streets. Abby made a remark one time. He said, "What they don't understand is that we're doing street theater. We're doing theater." I don't know whether he meant that symbolically or if that was the trip they were actually on.

Several weeks later, the South Side erupted in riots. There used to be a woman who would run over every day to tell us, "Close Second City. They're coming!" Because where we were was right near the borderline of a big black section—Cabrini Green. She would yell, "They're coming down the street!" Oh, my God, it was like a war zone!

I remember one morning—get this picture. I was sitting having breakfast in the Lincoln coffee shop. It's a beautiful day. I'm having my ham and eggs. The park is across the street and there's a woman walking a baby carriage. Then, I turn around, and over my left shoulder I see smoke billowing. Maybe ten or twelve blocks away, there was a war going on. Ham and eggs, woman walking a baby, and over there, ten blocks away, who knows what's going on? People killing each other. That was Chicago then. Oh, it was an exciting town.

Q: *You say you lived in the Lincoln Hotel.*

BARRY: Two and a half years, man.

Q: *I understand that was quite a place.*

BARRY: Met some interesting guys there. I don't know what the hell they did. They were racetrack guys. Studs Terkel had written about a couple of them. I ain't mentioning no names. But to us they were really sweet guys. They used to be there opening night, and on nights when they didn't have something else going, they'd come by and see us. Bernie used to get very nervous. He'd say, "What is this element doing here?" But the waitresses—they'd never been tipped like that! They threw down ten or twenty for a tip—like that. Very generous. We used to have a great time with them. They used to tell us stories about the old Chicago. They were like hustlers. Older guys. And for

J. J. Barry

some reason they took a liking to us. We used to sit in the Lincoln coffee shop night after night.

There was something fun about the Lincoln coffee shop. You'd always check out who was in there, and there was always someone there and you'd sit down and shoot the breeze for an hour. It was like a little meeting place.

The Greeks who ran the place were a little crazy. Once I went in, ordered scrambled eggs. They came out, hard as rocks. I said, "No, you don't understand. I want them softer." So this time the eggs come out so soft, they aren't even cooked. They're like melted glop. I say, "I don't want that." The guy comes out, says, "What's wrong with these eggs?!" And he puts his hand in them and picks them up, right? Says, "What's wrong with these eggs? Nothing wrong with these eggs. You got to eat them!" I say, "Now for sure I'm not going to eat them. I didn't order hand and eggs." He says, "I'm gonna call the cops!" I say, "Don't call the cops. I just want scrambled eggs." He says, "No, get out!" You know how many times they chased us out?

And the hotel manager—he always suspected us of having orgies in our rooms. If we had done half what he claimed we did, I can tell you we would have been having a really good time. That was the old Lincoln. I love the place, man.

Q: *You stayed with Second City. . . .*

BARRY: Two and a half years, man. Then I was, uh, "discovered." I left to be on *Laugh-In*. I was a disaster on it. They wouldn't let me do any of the characters I could do, just one thing. And they wouldn't let me do *that* one right. I did four shows and then I left and went back to Second City. Then I went with Second City to New York, did a show there, then we broke up. Later I did a special Second City show in L.A.

Q: *Was that with Mina, Dick, and Val?*

BARRY: Yeah, and Steinberg and Paul Sand. Quite a cast. But that show wasn't the best. But that's where I met Val. Very sweet lady. Steinberg directed the show and we did it at the Lindy Opera House. A revue at the Lindy Opera House! Oh my God!

To me, what I found out is that one of the secrets of this kind of thing is a small theater. You've got to be able to see the people's faces.

I don't think Second City was ever the same after they moved into the big theater. I think it lost its charm. The closeness of it. When I first saw the new theater, it was like CinemaScope, whereas the old theater was like the old-fashioned-size movie screen. Also, this stuff is cabaret theater and it's nothing else. People don't like to see this kind of thing on a regular stage. They want to see it in a small club with drinks in their hands.

I went to EST, and it just put Viola and Paul's thing together for me. Now, after eight years or so. I have a new respect for Paul. I really do. Even Viola, man. At the time I really didn't know where they were coming from, because I wasn't there. It's only now that I sort of know what they were attempting to do.

I teach a game workshop now. What I'm trying to teach really is something that can't be taught—freedom. So what I'm trying to create now is a totally safe environment where someone can actually make an asshole out of himself, which I wish the hell people would do. Because if you can't do it in a safe environment, you certainly can't do it in the world of reality out there. Because we know what *that's* all about.

30.

Gilda Radner

Gilda Radner is one of the most recent Second City alumni to reach prominence. Featured on NBC's *Saturday Night Live,* her gallery of cheerfully addled characters has established her reputation as one of television's most gifted comediennes. In addition to The Second City, her credits include the Toronto company of *Godspell* and the *National Lampoon Show.*

RADNER: Kids write me now asking, "How do you get on *Saturday Night?* What do you have to do to become a comedian?" I don't know what the answer is to that exactly, but I do know it was Second City that was like my university for comedy. Certainly for the kind of thing we're doing on *Saturday Night.*

I always knew about Second City. From the time I first became interested in theater or comedy or anything, I just knew about it. I remember I went to camp with kids from Chicago, and they knew about it. And I would drive down from Detroit with friends to see it. And I would see it whenever it came to town. When I was at the University of Michigan, I saw them do a show in Trueblood Auditorium. I must have been nineteen then. After the show, walking out of the theater, I remember somebody saying to me, "That's what you should do."

I should say that when I was in college, some of us started an improvisational group. That kind of thing was always an interest with me—getting up on my feet and, instead of having a script or anything, making it up as I went along.

Well, then I left the University of Michigan and I went to Canada. I was going out with a guy who was Canadian and he wanted to go back and live in Toronto, so I went there. That was in 1969, before it was really difficult to emigrate there. During the first couple years I lived there, I did nothing in theater.

It must have been 1971 or '72, Second City visited Toronto. I still remember everything they did in that show and everyone who was in it. John Belushi, Brian Doyle-Murray, Joe O'Flaherty, Harold Ramis, Judy Morgan, and Eugenie Ross-Leming. It was incredible, and they got wonderful reviews.

I was friends with Valri Bromfield and Dan Aykroyd, who were working around Toronto as a comedy team, and I heard that they met Bernie Sahlins, and he wanted them to be in Second City in Chicago. I was real jealous, but I thought, "That's great for them. That's where they belong." About this same time, I was in the Toronto company of *Godspell*.

Then, all of a sudden, I hear that Second City's decided to open a Toronto company. I couldn't believe it. Suddenly the dream I'd always had was going to be right within my grasp. But, being Jewish, I said, "Well, I'm not going to audition, because if I didn't get in, I couldn't bear it. I'd never be able to live." But Valri and Dan said, "You have to do it. Come to the audition." They told me ahead of time what I'd be asked to do.

So I went. Bernie was there and Joe O'Flaherty and Del. Of course, I didn't know who they were then. They had me get up with this guy I didn't know. What I was supposed to do was come out from behind this curtain four times, each time with a different character, ask him for some information, and leave. I did the typical things— a little girl, an old woman. Real standard things. But I came out real quick, and each time I had a reason for coming out, and I played it and left.

Then we traded places. The guy went behind the curtain,

and I had to be the information desk. Well, he came out, and every time he came out he . . . well, he never did a different character, you know? He was trying to, but he didn't. And the third time he came out, I said, "What, *you* again?" Which was a horrible thing to do to him, but Bernie and Joe and Del really laughed.

So I was called back again, and we did a lot of group improvisations and . . . let me put it this way: They said they'd let us know in a couple weeks, but Bernie kissed me good-bye. (*Laughs.*) Anyway, finally Bernie phoned me. That company was myself, Valri Bromfield, Dan Aykroyd, Gerry Salsberg, Jayne Eastwood, Brian Doyle-Murray, and Joe O'Flaherty. Three girls, four guys.

Q: *That's unusual, to have so many women.*

RADNER: That's why Bernie took so long. He couldn't decide among the girls, so he decided to go with a company with three girls. We were doing the same material that I had seen them do when they visited Toronto before, so what Bernie did was take some of the roles that had been typical male roles and make a couple small changes and let Valri do them.

We opened on a hot summer night, and five months later we went bankrupt and closed. We all knew we had closed, except Gerry Salsberg. He was sick and we forgot to tell him. So he showed up to do the show and found out by seeing this sign on the door: THEATER CLOSED.

Bernie was real upset, because he'd always wanted to start other companies in other places, and because he knew we were a good company. A few months went by and it was real depressing. Then we got this offer to reopen at a place called the Firehall. And we did. Joe, myself, Eugene Levy, John Candy, and Rosemary Radcliffe. (Dan wasn't doing it then.)

Before, we had gotten some complaints that the show wasn't Canadian enough. So, when we reopened, we really kept our nose to the Canadian angle. Of course, Joe and I were Americans, but maybe that helped us in picking up a sense of what was peculiarly Canadian.

At the time, there were many Canadian plays about families fighting with each other by writers like David Freeman. So we did our version of all these plays called "You're Gonna Be All Right, You Creep, Leaving Home and All,

Eh?" Joe played the tyrannical father, I was the retarded daughter, Eugene was the gay son, John Candy was the son who wanted to be a hockey player, and Rosemary was the mother who was always just trying to keep peace.

Also, massage parlors were opening in Toronto at the time, and we did a thing about that as a parody of *Reefer Madness.*

Q: *People flipping out because they've been "massaged"?*

RADNER: Right. We had dancing in that. There's a place called the Yonge Street Mall, so we came up with a dance called the "Yonge Street Maul," and we mauled each other.

We also did Joe's great blackout about the girl who gets hit by a car, and people gather around to try to help her, but they see she's wearing dirty underwear, which disgusts them, so they walk away and leave her.

Eugene and I did a scene in which I was this old woman named Miss Eleanor Teably, and he was interviewing me about how I taught inanimate objects how to speak. I brought along my prize pupil, which was a talking shoe. That's where my character Emily Litella began.

But it was a real strong show, and it satisfied the critics that we were a Canadian show and not just something else from the United States. Second City is now an institution in Toronto. It's as entrenched there as the one in Chicago. It's become culturally a part of Toronto, and reviews can't kill it. I'm really proud to say that I helped make that happen.

One thing about working at Second City—there would be nights when this magical, chemical, extrasensory thing would happen between you and the others, and something incredible would occur onstage. You'd decide quickly backstage, "OK, we'll do a thing about a guy taking his secretary to a hotel room," and you'd go out and do it, and the audience would be truly entertained, and you would have just made it up. And later, you'd be so excited about what had happened, you couldn't sleep all night. You'd be trying to remember exactly what made it click so well and made it come together like a piece of art, with rising action and a climax and an end.

This connection was so strong working with Joe O'Fla-herty that, when he set me up, sometimes I believed he knew what he wanted me to say and that he'd actually put it into my mind. Later he'd tell me he really didn't know what I was going to say, but his belief in his setup would somehow transfer to me. Joe was the type of improviser who made *you* look good onstage. He could set you up better than anybody.

Q: *He didn't just grab the joke for himself. He shared.*

RADNER: You know, Del once told a story about a guy who was a runner training for the Olympics. He clocked ahead of the world record, always. He was tremendous, you know? The actual day of his event, he ran and he exactly equaled the world-record time. His manager and his trainer said, "What did you do? You could have beat it! We saw you beat it every time in training, how could you not do it this time?" And the runner said, "But I've done a greater thing. It's more difficult to equal something than to do better." Del said to us, when you are onstage at Second City, you can always get all the attention, you can always steal the focus and be the funny one. Just stick your finger in your nose and you can get focus. But to equal the other people onstage—to give them their moment and then take yours and go back and forth—that was the much more difficult and greater thing. To really have a game of catch with somebody is the true excitement of improvisation, and it's so much more rewarding.

Another thing about Second City—it was always an out-. let for the emotions and the agonies of that day. You would make comedic choices based on what was happening in your life. Your work would come from your soul. Sometimes there'd be a problem that you couldn't solve in your everyday life, but it would come up in a scene, and acting it out you'd solve it.

One of my favorite Second City games was "Who Am I?" That's where I'd go out of the room and close my ears, and the audience would decide who I was. Then I'd come back in and, by playing with the other person onstage, I would figure out what identity they had come up with for me. What that meant was that when I walked out on that stage, I was unborn. How many chances do you get to do that in life? It's like getting to be a child again for a little while, to be naive, to have empty spaces that can be filled in. What's so sad about so many grown-ups is they

lose those spaces. I mean, it's so nice to be able to clean out
your head and start again, as in a "Who Am I?"

My dad used to say he loved watching children play because they created worlds out of nothing. Like, if you
interrupt a kid who's playing—which is a horrible thing to
do—and you ask him, "What are you doing?" he says, "I'm
in this castle, and these are the stairs coming down and the
queen's up here." That's what we did at Second City. What
did we have? A revolving doorway, two other doors, and
six or seven chairs. And we could make them anything we
wanted.

It's difficult to do that on television. Television is too
literal. Billy Murray, Dan, and Belushi are writers on
Saturday Night, and sometimes they find they can't do a
piece on the show they could have done at Second City because they can't use the audience's imagination properly
on TV.

Q: *You were at Second City when the feminist movement was really gaining momentum. Did you find yourself
doing much feminist-oriented material?*

RADNER: I hate to relate things to feminism or not. When
I get interviewed about feminist stuff . . . I think to take a
hard angle on that is not to be funny. You've got to take
the pickle out of your bum. As a woman in comedy, all
I want is to be comfortable enough to be able to make my
audience laugh at me doing comedy on anything.

Q: *When you can stop asking whether a scene fits in
with feminist ideology, the battle will be won.*

RADNER: Right. Things *are* changing. Women are moving
into more and different areas, so there are more possible
scenes. If I have become popular because I do an imitation
of Barbara Walters, it's because Barbara Walters has become popular. I say thank you to her. She's made somebody
worth parodying. I couldn't get laughs if she hadn't gotten
into the news. So, things are changing. I actually believe
there is going to be a turnover in comedy, that you're
going to see a larger number of women comics. Because
women are where the social action is, and wherever the
social action is is where the comedy is going to be.

Q: *How long were you at Second City?*

RADNER: About a year or a year and a half. I did maybe
three or four shows in all. During this time, I met a lot

368

Gilda Radner

of the other people in the Second City gang. Once the Toronto and Chicago companies switched for two weeks. Then Bernie asked me to come and be in the Chicago company. I thought I would for a change of pace, but then Belushi phoned me and asked me if I wanted to work with the *National Lampoon Show* with Joe, Brian, and Harold Ramis. So I came to New York and did that. And I worked on the *National Lampoon Radio Hour.* And now we're doing *Saturday Night.*

People ask if we improvise on *Saturday Night.* Well, we can't. I mean, you can bite your foot, but if there's no camera on you, then it doesn't do any good. And you can't change lines because they base camera shots on them.

But we sometimes develop material improvisationally. I have certain writers who work with me like that. Like I'll say, "You be the interviewer and I'll be the character," and that way we find stuff. Or if Belushi and I are in a scene, we'll tape it. We'll just start improvising and tape it, because we do better that way than if we try to sit down and write it out. I wish that every writer on our show could spend a couple of months working at Second City and see what it's like. One of the things they'd learn is that people don't talk in paragraphs in normal conversation. Sometimes they just say, "Uh-hunh" and "What?"

I had the best time I'd had in the longest time when Jack Burns came on the show. He's a great improviser. Lorne Michaels, our producer, let us improvise for a while, and he was *so* good! I just did this little stupid scene with him where he came in to ask for a loan, and I felt all that magic return. I find that people who've had Second City training are the easiest people to work with. When you look in their eyes onstage, and you're doing a live television show, there's somebody *home* there, you know? And you know if something goes wrong, they'll be there. They know what it's like to walk out with no words, no music, nothing to fall back on but their own resources.

I think *Saturday Night* is about the closest thing you'll see on TV to Second City because it's live, and it's not being sweetened, and it's always under-rehearsed, and it's always opening night. It's circus. When you watch the guy walk the tightrope, half the thrill is whether he's going to fall. It's like that at Second City and on live TV. The au-

369

dience's energy is working to keep you on the tightrope. On *Saturday Night,* they know if we goof up, we can't say, "Oh, let's stop and go back." So there's an excitement there, and I know it transfers.

It took me a year and a half to get to the point where I could go mad on television. To feel comfortable enough to go insane. Second City afforded that opportunity all the time. The people who were best at it were mad. It's madness to begin with. It's you, writing on your feet, listening to the audience, watching yourself. If you think about it, the concept of creating a reality onstage, and then having to bend that reality to wait for the laugh . . . it's schizophrenic.

I miss Second City so much. Throwing a hat on and being a whole character, or sitting on a chair and pretending it's a car, or bringing on a stick and pretending it's a gun. I miss when you could just pretend anything in the world.

Epilogue

Joan Rivers: "I'd like to see them set up a Hall of Fame to
us and I'd like them to say, 'Nobody else can improvise
except these people because they were the winner improvisers of all time.' A little room with a big plaque and
pictures of all of us, how terrific we were, and statues. And
I'd like them to throw a dinner for us so I could pick up
an award—and my acceptance speech would be: 'They
were sons of bitches, but we owe it all to them.' "
   It didn't happen quite the way she envisioned it, but
close enough. For one weekend, the old guard from The
Compass and The Second City were guests of honor at the
University of Chicago. There were no statues (unless you
count the huge *papier-mâché* elephant Severn had constructed for reasons too involved to explore between paren-
theses), but there was a luncheon at which medals were
handed out.
   The weekend was part of a three-week Festival of Chicago Comedy the university sponsored in October 1976.
Among those who participated in the various concerts,
symposia, broadcasts, and exhibitions were Dick Gregory,
Dave Garroway, Studs Terkel, Will Geer, Steve Allen,
Burr Tillstrom, Fran Allison, and Bill Mauldin. But the
most eagerly anticipated event of the festival was the re-

union of members of the early Compass and Second City troupes.

Sad to say, Joan didn't show up to make her fantasy speech—or any other. Apparently she was otherwise occupied, as were Mike Nichols, Elaine May, and Alan Arkin. (Nichols, May, and Arkin were represented by showings of some of the films they've directed or appeared in.) But though these celebrated alumni were absent, those who did attend formed one of the strongest ensembles in the history of improvisational theater. It consisted of David Shepherd, Paul Sills, Severn Darden, Barbara Harris, Paul Sand, Mark and Bobbi Gordon, Anthony Holland, Eugene Troobnick, Roger and Ann Bowen, John Brent, Del Close, Bill Alton, and Mina Kolb. (In addition, Shelley Berman and David Steinberg gave solo concerts.)

Many of the company had attended (or loitered) at the University of Chicago when younger, so it was as much a homecoming as a reunion. They returned to Jimmy's, where they had spent so many hours drinking draft beer and kibitzing about politics and art. They passed by Rockefeller Chapel, the scene of Severn's legendary encounter with the campus police. They looked up old friends and reminisced about the times they had in the back room of the Compass Bar a few blocks away on 55th Street.

That back room was no longer there. On the site of the Compass Bar was a clean, suburban-looking, red-brick firehouse. But, in honor of the gang's return, the university had constructed in one of the campus galleries a replica of that back room. There again were the louvered panels of which David was so proud, the chairs bunched around café tables, the large picture window with the Compass insignia through which passersby could catch a glimpse of the fun inside. If it wasn't an *exact* duplicate (there were no plans and few photos of the original to go by), it managed to capture something of the spirit of the old place.

The reconstruction was functional, too. During the festival, a student ran films and tapes of early Second City scenes there. David and Del each directed a workshop there. (Viola had been scheduled to hold one, too, but she canceled and didn't attend the festival at all.) Troupes of young improvisers, including a good many performers who had studied with Del at Second City, touched base with their heritage by giving shows on the stage of the reconstructed Compass. And Severn, Mina, Del, Bobbi, and John also took to its boards, re-creating old scenes and improvising new ones for a local television special. (The taping was the occasion of one of my favorite Severnisms. During an improvised lecture, he observed that, since colors tend to fade when exposed to sunlight, it follows logically that the natives of tropical countries are very fair-skinned. After the lecture, he asked if there were any questions. A young black man rose and said, "Professor, I find your theory very interesting. But I was born and raised in a tropical environment and, as you can see, I have a very dark complexion, indeed. How do you account for this?" Severn replied, "You must have led a very sheltered life.")

The two key events of the festival were the Compass reunion performance on the evening of Friday, October 15, and the Second City reunion performance of the following night, both given in Mandel Hall, on the same stage where Sills had directed the University Theatre production of *The Caucasian Chalk Circle* in 1953. Each of the two shows was hastily assembled the afternoon of its performance under the supervision of Sills with the assistance of Ann Bowen. With the exception of one technical snafu which scotched a Barbara-Severn scene midway, the performances went beautifully.

Actually, it would be more faithful to the spirit of those evenings to call them celebrations rather than performances. The participants were there not only to entertain the audiences, but to recapture the joy of sharing with each other. When not actively engaged in a scene, cast members watched from the side, as enthralled by their colleagues' work as anyone sitting in the packed house out front.

There were dozens of wonderful moments: Mina claiming the reason Russians are so tense is that they have only one department store. Severn, as Dr. von der Voegelweide, Chairman of the Department of Interdiscipline, explaining, to a roar of approval from the university community, why sociology is complete and utter nonsense. Paul Sand playing so convincing a dog that, even when he was sitting cross-legged and smoking a cigarette, one never doubted his canineness. Barbara, Severn, and Roger in an inspired bit of spontaneous mime trying to deal with an impossibly huge take-out order in a restaurant where David was a topless dancer. Del, in a segment in which new poems were improvised from the first lines of old, offering, "Under the spreading chestnut tree,/We mute, inglorious Newtons sit,/ Apple-less,/Waiting in vain for inspiration." Followed by Mina's contribution: "Under the spreading chestnut tree,/ I did to him and he did to me./A Hallmark Card." John Brent reviving his quintessentially slimy faith healer, the Reverend "Holy" Moley. Mark and Bobbi miming the dilemma of a pair of horny youngsters trying to overcome the obstacle of the jammed lock of a door behind which lay a waiting bed. Paul Sand and Gene demonstrating again how to win a friend with the aid of a hi-fi. Roger as the head of the AMA (the Anti-Medicare Association), quoting the last words of a three-year-old patient: "Doctor, please tell the American public the truth about socialized medicine!"

For me, the brightest highlight was Tony and Bill's revival of "Lekythos," a scene they hadn't played in over a decade. (They didn't even run it in rehearsal. Their preparation consisted of discussing the key beats and giving the pianist a cue.) The reverberations of their performance of that scene! Here were two University of Chicago graduates portraying two University of Chicago graduates in a University of Chicago hall for a University of Chicago audience. Playing on the same stage where they had played in *Agamemnon* more than twenty-five years before. When they had first come up with this scene back in the early 1960s, they had been young actors at Second City. In the intervening years, not only had they grown into their parts in terms of age, but their lives had described paths not unlike those of the characters they portrayed: Tony, playing the perpetual student, was in reality leading a life largely centered around esthetic and intellectual concerns; Bill, playing the businessman, was in fact prospering as the head of his own production company.

Beyond all this, there was a special relationship between what was happening in the scene and the experience of the audience. The characters onstage were people all too familiar from daily contact. When Tony revealed that after twenty years he was still working on his master's, there was a huge laugh of recognition. In his chapter, Sills expressed the ideal of theater coming out of and speaking to the consciousness of the community. The audience confirmed this ideal was being achieved with "Lekythos." At the end of the scene, the two actors were given a thunderous ovation.

As might be imagined, the reunion held a special significance for me. The bulk of this project was behind me, but, until that weekend, I had never actually seen most of these people perform together in person. (It would have been difficult for me to have seen The Compass. When it opened, I was five years old, and I was going to grade school when most of the alumni with whom I spoke appeared at The Second City.) My familiarity with their work was based on the tapes, records, films, transcripts, and photographs I had unearthed. Valuable as these were, they were no substitute for the experience of a live performance. So, for me, the prospect of a reunion brought to issue whether the energy and time invested in this project had been warranted. When that weekend proved that, yes, these people and their work were and are all they were cracked up to be and more, I felt . . . well, vindicated.

Much has happened since I began working on this book. Watergate has rid us of Richard Nixon, the target of years of satire. Death has removed Hizzonner Richard Daley, profoundly changing the face of Chicago. Large and small events, many of them reflected in the contemporaneous work of The Second City and in the conversations between these covers, have altered the political and social landscape.

And something else has happened. I have had the rare pleasure of the company of an extraordinary group of people. I hope that I have been able to share some of this pleasure through this book.

—Jeffrey Sweet
August 1977

375

Appendix

The following are alphabetical listings of the actors, directors, and musical directors who have been associated with one or more companies of The Compass Players and The Second City. The people named are actors unless otherwise identified. The Second City list does not include members of The Second City's apprentice-level touring companies.

The Compass Players

Alan Alda
Jane Alexander
Alan Arkin
Larry Arrick (director)
Rose Arrick
Lloyd Battista
Walter Beakel (director-actor)
Shelley Berman
Haym Bernson
Roger Bowen
Hildy Brooks
  (a.k.a. Hilda Brawner)
R. Victor Brown
Jack Burns
Mona Burr
Loretta Chiljian

Del Close
Robert Coughlan
Severn Darden
MacIntyre Dixon
Paul Dooley
Andrew Duncan
Tom Erhart
Theodore J. Flicker
Barbara (Bobbi) Gordon
Mark Gordon (actor-director)
Philip Baker Hall
Larry Hankin
Barbara Harris
Jo Henderson
Mo Hirsch
Kenna Hunt

The Second City

Alan Alda
Andrew Alexander (producer)
Howard Alk (actor-producer)
Bill Alton (actor-director)
Bill Applebaum
Alan Arkin (actor-director)
Larry Arrick (director)
Steve Assad
Peter Ayckroyd
Dan Aykroyd
Tom Baker
Sandra Balcovske
Sandy Baron
J.J. Barry
Barbara Barsky
Joan Bassie
Mindy Bell
Jim Belushi
John Belushi
Robert Benedetti
Baldwin Bergerson
 (musical director)
Dick Blasucci
Joel Bloom
David Blum
Eric Boardman
Roger Bowen
Peter Boyle
John Brent
Valri Bromfield
Rob Ronstein
Susan Bugg
Jack Burns
Lucy Butler
Maggie Butterfield
Hamid Hamilton Camp
 (a.k.a. Bobby Camp)
Alex Canaan
John Candy
Sandra Caron
Carol Cassis
 (musical director)
Don Castellaneta
Chris Chase
Del Close (actor-director)

Gabe Cohen
Stephanie Cotsirilos
Suzette Couture
Larry Coven
Dennis Cunningham
Bob Curry
Barbara Dana
Dawn Daniel
Cassandra Danz
Severn Darden
Ian Davidson
Don De Pollo
Rob Derkach
Don Dickinson
Melinda Dillon
Bob Dishy (actor-director)
MacIntyre Dixon
Nancy Dolman
Brenda Donohue
Paul Dooley
Brian Doyle-Murray
Robin Duke
Andrew Duncan
Murphy Dunne
Bekka Eaton
Jayne Eastwood
Steve Ehrlick
Ann Elder
Jeff Ellis
Melissa Ellis
Robert Elman
Patricia Englund
Jane Ericson
Jim Fay
Meagen Fay
Jim Fisher
Miriam Flynn
Josephine Forsberg
 (workshop director)
Martin Harvey Friedberg
Cathy Gallant
Gail Garnett
Susan Gauthier
Michael Gellman
 (actor-director)

Brian George
Piers Gilson
Carey Goldenberg
Arlene Golonka
Ben Gordon
June Graham
Judy Graubart
Ed Greenberg
Joel Greenberg
Mary Gross
Sid Grossfeld
Allan Guttman
 (musical director)
Mike Hagerty
Larry Hankin
Deborah Harmon
Valerie Harper
Barbara Harris
Judy Harris
Melissa (Sally) Hart
John Hemphill
Nate Herman
Burt Heyman
Isabella Hoffman
Pamela Hoffman
Anthony Holland
Sandy Holt
Ken Innes
Tino Insana
Ron James
Bruce Jarchow
Gene Kadish
Steven Kampmann
Irene Kane
Jon Kapelos
Jerrold Karch
Fred Kaz (musical director)
Tim Kazurinsky
Maureen Kelly
Gail Kerbel
Richard Kind
Lance Kinsey
Deborah Kimet
Robert Klein
Keith Knight
Mina Kolb

Bernie Kukoff
Richard Kurtzman
Don Lake
Don Lamont
Zohra Lampert
Kathleen Lasky
Linda Lavin
Eugene Levy
Charles Lewson
Richard Libertini
Ron Liebman
Lynne Lipton
Shelley Long
Roberta Maguire
Andrea Martin
Erin Martin
Sandy Martin
William Mathieu
 (musical director)
Paul Mazursky
Nancy McCabe-Kelly
Robin McCullough
Debra McGrath
Derek McGrath
Jeff Michalski
Ira Miller
Michael Miller (director)
Raul Moncada
 (stage manager)
John Monteith
Judy Morgan
Jane Morris
Harry Murphy
William Murray
Alan Myerson
Audrie Neenan
Nonie Newton-Breen
Joseph O'Flaherty (a.k.a. Joe
 Flaherty; actor-director)
Catherine O'Hara
Tom O'Horgan
 (musical director)
Sheldon Patinkin (director)
David Paulsen
Lawrence Perkins
Denise Pidgeon

Bruce Pirrie
Will Porter
Rosemary Radcliffe
Gilda Radner
Harold Ramis
Suzanne Rand
David Rasche
Fiona Reid
Mert Rich
Maria Ricossa
Rob Riley
Irene Riordan
   (a.k.a. Jessica Myerson)
Joan Rivers
Harv Robbin
Carol Robinson
Tony Rosato
Eric Ross
Eugenie Ross-Leming
Lee Ryan
Ann Ryerson
Bernard Sahlins
   (producer-director)
Janice St. John
Gerry Salsberg
Albert Salzer
Paul Sand
Richard Schaal
Larry Schanker
Harvey Schaps
Avery Schreiber
Jeanette Schwaba
Lynda Segal
John Shank

Omar Shapli
Jim Sherman
Martin Short
Paul Sills (producer-director)
Cyril Simon (director)
Kim Sisson
Joyce Sloane (producer)
John Smet
Viola Spolin
   (workshop director)
Jim Staahl
Doug Steckler
David Stein
David Steinberg
   (actor-director)
Ruby Streak
Maggie Sullivan
Craig Taylor
Paul Taylor
Betty Thomas
Dave Thompson
   (musical director)
Peter Torokvie
Eugene Troobnick
Larry Tucker
Tom Virtue
David Walsh
George Wendt
Penny White
Mary Charlotte Wilcox
Fred Willard
Victor Wong
Paul Zegler
Dan Ziskie

Acknowledgments

During the four years I worked on this project, I was helped by an enormous number of people.

In addition to granting interviews, a great many of the people represented in this book went out of their way to assist me. David Shepherd, Roger Bowen, Andrew Duncan, Mike Nichols, Mark and Bobbi Gordon, Del Close, Theodore J. Flicker, Bernard Sahlins, Sheldon Patinkin, Paul Mazursky, Anthony Holland, Alan Myerson, and Joan Rivers were particularly kind in sharing recordings, photographs, transcripts, documents, and other memorabilia. Virtually every person named in the table of contents has come to my aid beyond the normal bounds of professional courtesy. It would take another book to catalogue their kindnesses.

The Second City community as a whole has been generous and supportive. Joyce Sloane, Carol Rosofsky, and the "first lady," Jane Sahlins, made me feel welcome at the Chicago theater, and Andrew Alexander extended the hospitality of the Toronto base. Many others involved in the past and present of improvisational theater proved themselves friends of the project, among them Adam Arkin, Walter Beakel, Eric Boardman, Peter Bonerz, Ann Bowen,

John Candy, Jim Cranne, Barbara· Dana, Joan Darling, Don De Pollo, MacIntyre Dixon, Carol Duncan, Miriam Flynn, Martin Harvey Friedberg, Michael Gellman, Carl Gottlieb, Allan Guttman, Larry Hankin, Deborah Harmon, Buck Henry, Howard Hesseman, Karen Hirst, Fred Kaz, Richard Libertini, Andrea Martin, John Monteith, Catherine and Mary Margaret O'Hara, Julie Payne, Will Porter, Rob Reiner, Ann Ryerson, Jim Sherman, Carol Sills, Betty Thomas, Dave Thomas, George Wendt, and Mike and Nancy Williams.

A number of others are to be thanked: Jules Feiffer, whose good advice set me off and running. Ray Nordstrand, Lois Baum, Jim Unrath, Norm Pellegrini, Richard Warren, Ron Dorfman, and Don Klimovich of WFMT and *Chicago* magazine, who allowed me access to their extensive collection of rare Second City recordings. Clive Barnes, without whose encouragement and recommendations over the years I'm quite sure I wouldn't have had the opportunity to undertake this book. Kim Carlson, who helped me transcribe a mountain of cassettes. C. Ranlet Lincoln, Marsha Cassidy, and Virginia Wexman, who put together the Festival of Chicago Comedy, from which I learned a good deal.

Also Barbara Baker, Larry Brezner, Beau and Juli Bridges, Norman and Joan Cohen, Tandy Cronyn, Lorna Dallas, Jonathan Dodd, Susan Foster, Henry Gibson, Georgia Griggs, Otis Guernsey, Jr., Sindy Hawke, Don Honig, Sherry Huber, Donna Isaacson, Randy Kirby, John Korty, Stephen Lewellyn, Marilyn Madderom, Melissa Manchester, Elaine Markson, Buddy Morra, Julius Novick, Nancy Nugent, Leonard Probst, Edgar Rosenberg, Arlyne Rothberg, Susan Schulman, Morton Shapiro, Jeff Stein, Linda Strawn, Eric Swenson, Jim Wagner, David Warrack, and Annette Welles. And the University of Chicago, the University of Southern California, the Lincoln Center Library of the Performing Arts in New York, and *Playboy* magazine, whose resources proved to be valuable and whose staffs were sympathetic.

Thanks, too, to Bob Wyatt and Don Chase at Avon for good counsel, Brian and Shan Garfield for helping to sus-

Acknowledgments

tain my sanity in parlous times, and Dan McCarthy, for his continued interest.

And very special thanks to Todd McCarthy, who played host to me in Los Angeles, accompanied me to several of the interviews, and has been a good friend always.

JEFFREY SWEET was born in Boston in 1950, grew up in Chicago, and received a B.F.A. in film from New York University in 1971. His plays include AFTER THE FACT, HOLDING PATTERNS, PARENTAL GUIDANCE, PORCH, ROUTED, STOPS ALONG THE WAY, TIES, 'TIS THE SEASON, and WINGING IT! His work has been presented by the Actors Studio, Actors Theatre of Louisville, Arena Stage, The Body Politic, Earplay, Encompass Theatre, Lincoln Center, Long Wharf, Manhattan Theatre Club, Milwaukee Repertory Theatre, National Radio Theatre of Chicago, North Light Repertory, and the Victory Gardens Theatre. PORCH won the 1978 Society of Midland Authors Award for best drama, was the basis of his 1979 Creative Writing Fellowship Grant from the National Endowment for the Arts, and was published in the 1976 edition of THE BEST SHORT PLAYS. STOPS ALONG THE WAY was published in THE BEST SHORT PLAYS 1981. TIES was produced for television by WTTW, Chicago's P.B.S. affiliate. He has published journalism and fiction in a number of periodicals and languages. Mr. Sweet founded the New York Writers' Bloc, a unit of playwrights, actors, and directors who meet regularly to discuss works-in-progress. He has lectured on and run numerous workshops in playwrighting and improvisation for such organizations as the O'Neill Center, the Goodman Theatre, the State University of New York, the Dramatists Guild, and the Chicago Public Library. He is an active member of the Dramatists Guild and is a regular contributor to *The Dramatists Guild Quarterly*. He is also affiliated with the Ensemble Studio Theatre and the New Drama Forum and writes for a daytime dramatic television series. He is married to Sheridan Sellers, and they live with their son Johnathan Brian Sweet on Manhattan's West Side.